Pioneering Perspectives in

The Literature of
19th Century Criminological Positivism

David M. Horton, Ph.D.
St. Edward's University

COPPERHOUSE PUBLISHING COMPANY
930 Tahoe Blvd. #602
Incline Village, Nevada 89451
(775) 833-3131 · Fax (775) 833-3133
e-mail info@copperhouse.com
www.copperhouse.com

Your Partner in Education
with
"QUALITY BOOKS AT FAIR PRICES"

Pioneering Perspectives in
CRIMINOLOGY

Library of Congress Catalog Number 9968855
ISBN 0-928916-04-X Paper Text Edition

2 3 4 5 6 7 8 9 10

Printed in the United States of America.

He spent hours in the great libraries, those catacombs of departed authors, rummaging among their dusty hoards and long forgotten works in quest of food for his appetite. He was, in a manner of speaking, a literary ghoul, feeding in the charnel-house of lost and decayed literature.

Washington Irving
Tales of a Traveler, 1868

TABLE OF CONTENTS

Introduction .... *xvii*

1. BIOLOGICAL EXPLANATIONS

A. Physiognomy

Musings on Physiognomy. 5

> *Britannia Monthly Magazine*, vol. 2 (March 1836), pp. 227–230.
> A fine historical survey of the belief that character, temperament, and a predisposition to good or evil can be discerned from aspects of facial features, beginning with classical Greek and Roman authors, followed by European writers of the Middle Ages, and culminating with the late eighteenth-century writings of John Caspar Lavater.

A Physiognomic Exemplar. 9

> "The Nose." *American Phrenological Journal and Life Illustrated*, vol. 43, no. 5 (May 1866), p. 138.
> An example of the literature of physiognomy demonstrating the relationship between various types of noses and their attendant behavioral and temperamental characteristics.

Suggestions for Further Reading and Inquiry: Physiognomy 13

B. Phrenology (or Craniology)

Phrenology Epitomized. *17*

> *Continental Repository*, vol. 2 (August 1841), pp. 156–159.
> A synopsis of the propensities, sentiments, and faculties that constitute the system of phrenology advocated by Francis Joseph Gall and refined by John

Gaspar Spurzheim, wherein it is contended that predilections toward crime, vice, and moral degeneracy can be ascertained by a careful observation and study of the shape and protuberances of the skull.

Phrenology in Prison. 25

The Mirror, vol. 12, no. 323 (July 26, 1828), p. 56.
An interesting demonstration of Dr. Gall's reputed ability to discern character and disposition based upon phrenological analyses of convicts in the central prison of Berlin, Germany, in 1805.

A Phrenological Exemplar. 27

"The Correspondence Between the Characters and Heads of Two Murderers Lately Executed at Newgate." James Straton. *Zoist*, vol. 13, no. 57 (July 1856), pp. 202~218.
A very fine example of the two-stage methodology (description of the perpetrator's crime and his background followed by a discussion of the methods employed in ascertaining measurements of the organs of the brain and their subsequent behavioral and temperamental correlations) commonly employed by phrenologists of the mid-nineteenth century in the analysis of the character and disposition of criminals.

Suggestions for Further Reading and Inquiry: Phrenology 41

C. The Italian School of Criminal Anthropology

Criminal Anthropology in Italy. 47

Helen Zimmern. *Popular Science Monthly*, vol. 52 (April 1898), pp. 743-760.
The best-written and most comprehensive article from the nineteenth century periodical literature on the major personalities comprising the Italian school of criminal anthropology and their respective contributions.

Criminal Anthropology:
Its Origin and Application. 65

> Cesare Lombroso. *Forum*, vol. 20 (September
> 1895), pp. 33-49.
> The preeminent, classic piece of criminal anthropo-
> logical literature published in English language peri-
> odicals during the nineteenth century. Written in the
> first person, the article is Lombroso's definitive
> account of the rise and development of the Italian
> school of criminal anthropology.

The Savage Origin of Tattooing. 83

> Cesare Lombroso. *Popular Science Monthly*, vol.
> 48 (April 1896), pp. 793~803.
> Discussion of the origin, characteristics, and atavistic
> significance of tattooing among the criminal class.
> Quintessential Lombroso.

Savages and Criminals. 95

> Guglielmo Ferrero. *The Independent*, vol. 52, no.
> 2710 (November 8, 1900), pp. 2688~2690.
> One of the Holy Three treats upon a cornerstone of
> criminal anthropological thought: the concept of the
> born criminal as a throwback to an earlier phylogenic
> level of development.

Illustrative Studies in
Criminal Anthropology. 101

> Cesare Lombroso. *Monist*, vol. 1, no. 2 (January
> 1891), pp. 186~196.
> Numerous short synopsae of recent and current
> research that clearly and concisely illustrate the
> hallmarks of the Italian school's study of criminology,
> including a focus on the criminal (rather than the
> crime), data collection methodologies, and heavy
> reliance on anthropometric measurement and statis-
> tical analyses.

Suggestions for Further Reading and Inquiry:
Criminal Anthropology 113

D. Hereditary Degeneracy
(Genealogical Researches and Criminal Parentage)

Special Study of Crime and Pauperism
as Presented by the "Juke" Family. 119

> Richard Louis Dugdale. *Annual Report of the
> Prison Association of New York*, (1875), pp.
> 139~187.
> This is a portion of Dugdale's first published report
> of his genealogical research on the hereditary trans-
> mission of criminal predisposition in the Juke family.
> The text of this original report was subsequently
> revised, expanded, and published by G. P. Putnam's
> Sons in 1877 under the title *The Jukes: A Study in
> Crime, Pauperism, Disease and Heredity.* As such,
> this original report represents a seminal contribution
> to the literature of nineteenth century criminological
> positivism.

The Tribe of Ishmael: A Study in
Social Degradation. 145

> Rev. Oscar C. M'Culloch. *Proceedings of the
> National Conference of Charities and Correction*
> (July 1888), pp. 154~159.
> Report of a Juke-like genealogical study of the
> Ishmael family of Indianapolis, Indiana, wherein the
> author argues that one family's descent into vice,
> crime, and pauperism is the product of the heredi-
> tary transmission of degenerative traits from one
> generation to another.

Miscellaneous Notes on
Genealogical Studies. 153

> (1) "Transmission of Criminal Traits." *Green Bag*,
> vol. 3 (June 1891), pp. 215~216.
> A synopsis of Despine's study of the Chretien family
> in France
> (2) "Hereditary Crime." *Popular Science Monthly*,
> vol. 50 (December 1896), p. 285.
> Synopsis of a German genealogical investigation of
> the Jurke *(sic)* family, wherein a progressive, heredi-

tarily induced moral and physical degeneration is
shown occurring from 1740 to1882.

Suggestions for Further Reading and Inquiry:
Hereditary Degeneracy 157

E. Psycho-Physiological Considerations

1. Alcoholic Inebriety

Intoxication a Source of Crime. 161

> *Quarterly Journal of the Statistical Society of
> London*, vol. 1 (June 1838), pp. 124~125.
> An early statistical study documenting the causal
> nexus between alcohol intoxication and a predispo-
> sition to involvement in criminal behavior.

Drink and Crime. 163

> Frederick W. Farrar. *Fortnightly Review*, vol. 59
> (April 1893), pp. 783~796.
> A fascinating article providing a wealth of anecdotal
> evidence (principally quotations from eminent ju-
> rists, philosophers, social critics, and philanthro-
> pists) on the relationship between alcohol and crime.

Suggestions for Further Reading and Inquiry:
Alcohol Inebriety 171

2. Mental and Moral Insanity (Crime as a Disease)

Inebriate Maniacs. 175

> Thomas D. Crothers, M.D. *Popular Science
> Monthly*, vol. 30 (November 1886), pp. 109~114.
> An outstanding article by the period's leading Ameri-
> can authority on alcohol and criminality. The author

treats upon his tripartite typology of criminal alcohol-
ics, arguing that alcoholism is a disease, and that, like
the mentally ill and insane, criminal inebriate maniacs
are deserving of treatment and rehabilitation rather
than punishment.

Developmental Aspects of
Criminal Anthropology............................ 183

Thomas S. Clouston, M.D. *Journal of the Royal
Anthropological Institute of Great Britain and
Ireland*, vol. 23 (August 1894), pp. 215–225.
Psycho-physiological anomalies, manifested especially by arrested development of the brain cortex
and its associated mental and behavioral functions,
distinguish the criminal from the noncriminal, with the
result that criminal behavior is unquestionably allied
with insanity.

The Insanity of the Criminal................. 195

Eugene S. Yonge. *Macmillan's Magazine*, vol. 79,
no. 469 (November 1898), pp. 50–55.
An interesting discussion on the various mental and
physical traits exhibited by both habitual criminals
and the insane.

Suggestions for Further Reading and Inquiry:
Mental and Moral Insanity 205

F.   **Biological Positivism and
     Crime Control Policy**

The Stamping Out of Crime.................... 209

Nathan Oppenheim, M.D. *Popular Science
Monthly*, vol. 48 (February 1896), pp. 527–533.
Relying upon information about the origin of criminal
predispositions developed by both the Italian school
of criminal anthropology and the genealogical researches into hereditary degeneracy, the author
argues that the only logical government policy for

extirpating crime should be one of curtailing the right of criminals to marry and breed.

Asexualization of Criminals
and Degenerates. 217

David Inglis, M.D. *Michigan Law Journal*, vol. 6, no. 1 (December 1897), pp. 298~300.
Again, relying on the results of criminal anthropological researches and genealogical studies suggesting that crime is the end product of degenerative traits hereditarily transmitted, the author takes the last logical step vis-à-vis crime control policy, and argues that degenerative habitual criminals should be castrated.

Suggestions for Further Reading and Inquiry: Biological Positivism and Crime
Control Policy 221

2. SOCIAL AND PHYSICAL ENVIRONMENTAL EXPLANATIONS

A. Arguments Against the Criminal Anthropological and Hereditary Degeneracy Perspectives of Biological Positivism

Criminals Not the Victims of Heredity. 229

William Marshall Fitz Round. *Forum*, vol. 16 (September 1893), pp. 48~59.
A passionate and well-argued case against the hereditary transmission of criminal propensities.

Instinctive Criminality and
Social Conditions.. 241

Ernest Bowen Rowlands, *Law Quarterly Review,*
vol. 13, no. 49 (January 1897), pp. 59~69.
The doctrines of atavism, the born criminal, and the
hereditary transmission of criminal predispositions
are disposed of as absurd and ludicrous explanations for criminal behavior, and instead, the author
argues in favor of criminogenic conditions present in
the social environment.

Suggestions for Further Reading and Inquiry:
Arguments Against the Criminal,
Anthropological and Hereditary Degeneracy
Perspectives of Biological Positivism ... 253

B. The French and Belgian Statistical Schools (of Cartography and Social Ecology)

Guerry on the Statistics of
Crime in France. 257

Westminster Review, vol. 18, no. 36 (April 1833),
pp. 353~366.
The first nineteenth century English language article
treating upon the societal origins of crime from a
purely scientific and statistical perspective. In this
pioneering article the author summarizes Andre
Michel Guerry's findings that both the periodicity and
differentials in the nature and frequency of crime in
France are related to factors such as human aggregation, age, sex, and the cosmicological influence of
the seasons.

Quetelet on the Laws
of the Social System. 271

> *Littell's Living Age,* vol. 21, no. 260 (May 12,
> 1840), pp. 241–244.
> Synopsis of the Belgian statistician Jacques Lambert
> Adolph Quetelet's pioneering work titled *Du Systeme
> Social, et des Lois qui le Regissent,* wherein is set forth
> the idea of subjecting aggregate crime data to
> statistical analysis for the purpose of discovering
> universal laws governing the social phenomenon of
> crime.

Suggestions for Further Reading and Inquiry:
The French and Belgian Schools 277

C. Human Aggregation, Urban Decay, and Moral Degradation (and the Rise of a Criminal, Vicious, or Dangerous Class)

On Crime and Density of Population. ... 281

> Jelinger C. Symons. *Transactions of the National
> Association for the Promotion of Social Science,*
> (1857), pp. 265–271.
> A fine example of the use of official crime statistics to
> support the contention of an urban/rural differential
> in crime rates.

Ishmaelites of Civilization: Or,
the Democracy of Darkness. 289

> Benjamin Orange Flower. *Arena,* vol. 6, no. 31
> (June 1892), pp. 17–39.
> An in-depth discussion of the social and physical
> environmental conditions in large metropolitan cities
> that work in combination to produce inordinately high
> rates of crime, vice, and misery.

Suggestions for Further Reading and Inquiry:
Human Aggregation, Urban Decay,
and Moral Degradation 305

D. Criminal Typology

The Professional, Habitual,
and Casual Thief. 311

Chambers's Edinburgh Journal, vol. 31, no. 265 (January 29, 1859), pp. 84~87.
A discussion about the characteristics that differentiate professional, habitual, and casual thieves.

E. Evil Associates and Learned Criminality

Professional Thieves. 321

Cornhill Magazine, vol. 6, no. 35 (November 1862), pp. 640~653.
A truly seminal article in the literature of nineteenth-century positivistic criminology. The unknown author gathered data on the criminal class infesting large metropolitan cities by actually living among them and observing first-hand their habits, associations, language, and subcultural idiosyncrasies, and concludes that criminal behavior is learned. The participant observation methodology is eerily reminiscent of two twentieth century criminological classics, William Foote White's 1943 work titled *Street Corner Society*, and David Mauer's 1964 work titled *Whiz Mob*, and the observations on the dynamics of learned criminality are startlingly similar to Edwin Harcourt Sutherland's theory of differential association.

F. Poverty, Destitution, and Economic Perturbations

The Relation of Economic Conditions
to the Causes of Crime. 341

Carroll D. Wright. *Annals of the American Academy of Political and Social Science*, vol. 3 (March 1893), pp. 764-784.
An interesting discussion of the criminogenic aspects of a variety of historical as well as modern economic systems.

Relation of Crime to Economics. 359

Samuel G. Smith. _Lend A Hand,_ vol. 17 (November 1896), pp. 408-419.
Text of a paper read before the National Prison Congress at Milwaukee, Wisconsin, in September 1896, wherein the author argues that "the economic relations of crime are the most pressing for study, the most vital in importance, and the most promising in their practical application" for preventing the development of criminal behavior.

Suggestions for Further Reading and Inquiry: Poverty, Destitution and Economic Perturbations 369

G.   Ignorance and Illiteracy

The Relation Between Ignorance and Crime: Or, Statistics Showing the Reign of Ignorance Among the Criminals of the World. 373

Western Journal and Civilian, vol. 8, no. 5 (August 1852), pp. 297-308.
The unknown author statistically demonstrates the connection between ignorance and crime, and the efficacy of education to restrain men from transgressing the criminal laws of society.

Suggestions for Further Reading and Inquiry: Ignorance and Illiteracy 387

3. COSMICOLOGICAL INFLUENCES (TEMPERATURE, HUMIDITY, AND BAROMETRIC PRESSURE)

Crime and the Weather. 393

> *Public Opinion*, vol. 22, no. 16 (April 22, 1897), p. 494.
> Synopsis of the investigations of the English statistician Troup on the effect weather has on the nature and frequency of criminal offenses.

Influence of Weather Upon Crime. 395

> Edwin Grant Dexter. *Popular Science Monthly*, vol. 55 (September 1899), pp. 653~660.
> A statistical study correlating the prevalence of crime with meteorological conditions in Denver, Colorado, during the 14-year period ending 1897.

Mental Effects of the Weather. 405

> Edwin Grant Dexter. *Science*, vol. 10, no. 241 (August 11, 1899), pp. 176-180.
> Dexter's second famous study on the relationship between meteorological conditions and the prevalence of misdemeanor crime in New York City. The results corroborate the findings of his earlier study in Denver, Colorado.

Suggestions for Further Reading and Inquiry: Cosmicological Influences 413

INTRODUCTION

Prior to the nineteenth century, the prevailing approach to crime causation was dominated by the classic school of thought, founded in 1764, by the Italian Cesare Bonesana, the Marquis de Beccaria when he published anonymously his great essay titled *Trattato Dei Delitti e Delle Pene* (Essay on Crimes and Punishments). Beccaria's ideas concerning crime and punishment were later elaborated upon and refined by the English philosopher Jeremy Bentham in his 1789 work titled Introduction to the Principles of Morals and Legislation. Together, Beccaria and Bentham's classical, or utilitarian, approach to criminological etiology held that people possessed free will and exercised choice in their decision making, and that criminal behavior was therefore purposeful activity resulting from rational decision making in which the benefits and consequences of criminal actions were weighed before making the decision whether or not to engage in them. If the potential unpleasantness associated with criminal behavior outweighed the anticipated illegal gain, it was argued, then people would desist from committing criminal acts. Punishment was therefore justified on the grounds of its presumed social utility in deterring potential as well as actual lawbreakers. Hence, the notion of swift and certain punishment, coupled with just the right amount of severity (albeit humane) to offset the hedonistic benefits associated with criminal behavior and tilt the equation in favor of law-abiding behavior (a concept Bentham referred to as "moral calculus") became the predominant government crime control policy in Europe and the United States. This policy subsequently gave rise to the birth of the first great penitentiaries, such as Pentonville and Millbank in England, and the Eastern State Penitentiary in Pennsylvania.

In the early decades of the nineteenth century, a major revolution in the perspective of crime causation began to occur, slowly at first, and by the dawn of the twentieth century the classicism of the Enlightenment Era was in full decline, eclipsed by the positivistic approach to criminological etiology. The positivistic approach to crime causation views criminal behavior, like any other naturally occurring phenomenon, as a product of prior antecedent causes over which the criminal has little or no control. The criminal now came to be viewed as fundamentally different from the noncriminal, and the Holy Grail of positivistic criminology has remained, even to this day, one of identifying those factors and conditions which are predisposing to the commission of socially unacceptable behaviors.

This sea-change in perspective resulted in four momentous readjustments in the direction of criminological thought and practice which, for the most part, remain today as the bedrock foundation of modern positivistic criminological inquiry. First, criminal behavior came to be viewed as the result of either internal biological or psychological deficiencies, conditions in the social and physical environment, or the consequence of cosmological conditions such as temperature, humidity, and barometric pressure. Because of this hard deterministic stance, the nineteenth-century criminological positivists rejected the classical view that individuals exercise free will and were capable of rational decision making. Second, with criminological inquiry now brought to bear upon the biological and psychological character as well as the social and physical environmental background of the individual offender, the focus of criminology shifted from an emphasis on the crime to an emphasis on the criminal. Third, government crime-control policy was dramatically affected by the new perspective, as is evidenced by the rise of the reformatory and industrial school ethic first in the United States and later in Europe, with the result that words such as treatment, correction, and reformation entered the vocabulary of criminology. And finally, the search for determinant factors resulted in the first applications of scientific methodologies to empirically study not only the causes of crime, but also the characteristics of criminals and the relationship between law and human behavior. The criminological positivists of the nineteenth century pioneered the use of scientific and statistical data acquisition and analysis, participant-observation studies, and typological methods to classify and study criminals, and they laid the foundations for a great many of the most intriguing and thought-provoking deterministic explanations for crime causation, some of which remain current even to this day. Indeed, so sweeping were the changes wrought by the positivistic perspective that by the beginning of the twentieth century, criminology had already matured into an accepted scientific discipline, complete with university courses in both the United States and Europe. Because of this rich legacy passed down to us, the nineteenth century may very well be styled as the golden age of positivistic criminology.

However, the student and scholar interested in the rich heritage of positivistic criminological thought and practice during the nineteenth century have rather good reason to be frustrated about the lack of primary, or period, literary sources from this era to draw upon. Usually lacking both a multilingual proficiency and a working knowledge of archival bibliographic methodology, those interested in the historical aspects of the discipline are often wont to rely on secondary and tertiary sources of criminological literature to sustain their curiosity and researches, sources which will always be found to be inferior to, and not to be preferred over, period originals. As a consequence, criminologists whose interest runs to matters historical have, for the most part, been limited to relying principally on the obvious and easily secured nineteenth century "classic" books (and only those few that have been translated into English), and on such commonplace secondary and tertiary materials as are easily accessible or lay directly in their paths. The process of identifying those few works which have, for almost a century now, been taken for granted as comprising the body of classic literature in nineteenth century criminological positivism [such as Havelock Ellis's *The Criminal* (1890), Arthur MacDonald's *Criminology* (1893), Cesare Lombroso and Guglielmo Ferrero's *The Female Offender* (1895), and Enrico Ferri's *Criminal Sociology* (1896)], has been the result of a sort of hearsay, in that an unofficial "handlist" of classic books has, in a manner, been passed down, without question, and by word of mouth, from one generation of criminologists to another. As such, the really rather paltry number of criminological classics from the nineteenth century which today form the staple of our literary heritage may best characterized as the product not only of an unquestioning and blind repetition of what other unattributed sources in the past have said, but also the result of a literature survey conducted through lenses that have revealed, for the most part, only mountain peaks. It is difficult to believe that the literary topography of nineteenth-century positivistic criminology consists of only a few glittering landmarks, or, for that matter, that the landmarks can be accurately ascertained without a full knowledge of the literary terrain of which they form a part. It seems fairly clear that sooner or later criminologists interested in the historical foundations of positivistic criminology will have to quit the easy practice of depending on the little bits of obvious material readily at hand and undertake the task of bringing the antiquarian literature dating from the nineteenth century into focus. This, of course, involves something more than an steadfast reliance upon, and mere passing acquaintance with, what may best be characterized as the belletristic monuments of our nineteenth century criminological literature.

Furthermore, contemporary textbooks on criminology, regardless of whether they are written for either an undergraduate or graduate level audience, will be found to be of little value to the student and scholar interested in the historical development of positivistic criminological etiology. Textbooks have traditionally devoted little attention to the historical development of positivistic criminology. This observation is not meant to disparage the fine work of past or present authors of criminology texts. Criminology textbooks are, in the main, designed to survey and communicate current, cutting-edge theoretical perspectives and report the findings of the most recent research, and they do this admirably, but with the result that they tend to touch only briefly the historical development of positivistic criminological thought and practice during the nineteenth century. Additionally, the bibliographic citations to the historical material contained in textbooks are very rarely to period, or primary-source literature. Not surprisingly, the authors of textbooks have traditionally relied on the few commonplace classics and on secondary and tertiary bibliographic sources to sustain their short historical discussions, and these bibliographic citations constitute an additional source of frustration to the student and scholar of historical positivistic criminology.

Of the extant English language primary-source material on the literary heritage of positivistic criminological etiology, no portion, for either general interest or importance, can compare with that appearing in the periodical (or serial) literature of the English-speaking peoples during the nineteenth century. The medium of periodical literature (i.e., publications released serially on a weekly, fortnightly, monthly, quarterly, semiannual, or annual basis) uniformly takes the complexion of its time by chronicling the thoughts and practices of the age, and by commemorating in its pages such events as excite public curiosity and attention, and this is as equally true for the periodical press of the nineteenth century as it is today. As such, the articles in the periodical press of any age represent a valuable cultural and intellectual repository of the history of ideas. During the nineteenth century, magazines, more than any other popular media for disseminating information (including books, pamphlets, and lectures), served a practical cultural function that helped shape the attitudes of the general public as well as government crime control policy makers on matters relating to crime, the administration of justice, and punishment.

Bound books, on the other hand, which were relatively expensive compared to the cost of a magazine subscription, were circulated much less widely and reached a smaller, often exclusive, audience. The sum and substance of books were frequently distilled down in magazine articles which presented their ideas in a cohesive, unified form for the general reading public, and capitalized on comparative brevity, timeliness, and a limited aspect of topic, and presented the information in a readable style. Indeed, the international fame and reputation enjoyed by criminologists, such as Andre Michel Guerry, Jacques Lambert Adolph Quetelet, Cesare Lombroso, and Guglielmo Ferrero, rested not upon the general public's information gained from their published books (most of which were never released in English language editions), but rather upon articles written in their native tongue, translated into English, and published in English language periodicals.

The periodicals of the nineteenth century provided provocative and informational articles that gave a large reading audience an awareness of the tremendous diversity of opinions and attitudes about crime, criminals, and criminological etiology. The great diversity of positivistic criminological perspectives found in the periodical literature of the nineteenth century is a product of the varied disciplinary backgrounds and interests of the contributors who weighed in with their comments, observations, suggestions, and criticisms. Statisticians, physicians, attorneys, theologians, university educators, penologists, economists, sociologists, and social reformers all contributed articles to the periodical press on a great many ideas relating to crime causation, and they championed their theoretical perspectives with the same strength of conviction that is today a hallmark of the ongoing international and multi-disciplinary debates in criminological etiology. Within the periodical publications of the nineteenth century are found the reports of a vast number of varied criminological researches, the substantive eddies and currents of the great criminological debates which were international in scope, and critical commentary by a wide range of authors, whose articles far surpass in clarity of exposition those later writers whose works now constitute the much relied upon secondary and tertiary source literature in the field of historical criminology.

To date, however, nineteenth-century English language periodical literature treating on the heritage of positivistic criminological thought and practice has been totally overlooked as a quarry of primary source material. Indeed, so vast is both the sheer volume and diversity of positivistic criminological thought contained in the articles published in the periodicals of the nineteenth century that the curious student and scholar in search of our literary criminological heritage will not be disappointed. What they will find is nothing less than an embarrassment of riches. Notwithstanding the great value of these articles for the information they afford on the early development of positivistic criminological etiology and their concomitant suggestions for government crime control policies, they remain, for all extent and purposes, lost, and among the articles are a great many truly classic pieces of forgotten criminological literature which lie presently like so much uncoined bullion in the dusty recesses of library archives.

No anthology has ever been published which is devoted solely to exhibiting the rich literary heritage of positivistic criminology contained in the English language periodical publications of the nineteenth century. It is the purpose of this *sui generis* anthology to furnish the student and scholar interested in the historical aspects of positivistic criminological etiology with a small but representative sample of the diverse primary source literature from this medium. All of the articles in the anthology, none of which has ever been reprinted, are specimens of pioneering perspectives in positivistic criminological theory that students as well as scholars will find interesting, instructive, and entertaining. Furthermore, the text of each article has been accurately transcribed to preserve the author's original paragraph formatting, subheadings, use of italics for emphasis, grammar, syntax, and orthography. As such, professors of criminology should find the anthology an especially useful pedagogical tool to supplement the traditional criminology textbooks used in their undergraduate or graduate level courses because it will serve to provide the historical perspective, detail, and illustrative exemplars on the development of nineteenth-century positivistic criminological etiology which is lacking in contemporary textbooks.

The anthology is organized according to three broad positivistic criminological perspectives which emerged during the nineteenth century: biological explanations, social and physical environmental considerations, and cosmological explanations. The biological explanations include articles on the physiognomy of John Caspar Lavater and the system of phrenology developed by Franz Joseph Gall, Johann Gaspar Spurzheim, and George Combe. Also exhibited in the section on biological explanations is a sequence of truly classic articles on the rise of criminal anthropology, including an outstanding overview of the state of criminal anthropological thought and practice at the close of the nineteenth century; three articles by Cesare Lombroso; and one article by his student and collaborator, Guglielmo Ferrero. This is followed by literary specimens discussing hereditary degeneracy, including the original periodical publication by Richard Louis Dugdale reporting the initial findings of his genealogical research on the Juke family; articles on Juke-like studies; and exemplars of psycho-physiological explanations involving alcoholic inebriety and crime as a disease. The section concludes with two interesting articles which address, from the perspective of biological positivism, how best to extirpate crime.

The second section of the anthology exhibits the broad range of perspectives dealing with the roles that social and physical environmental factors play in crime causation. This section begins with two literary exemplars that succinctly set forth the body of argumentation in opposition to the biological positivistic perspective. This is followed with articles by and about the great French and Belgian cartographic statisticians Andre Michel Guerry and Jacques Lambert Adolph Quetelet. The remainder of this section is devoted to articles which champion a diverse range of social and physical environmental explanations, including human aggregation, urban decay, moral degradation, poverty, destitution, economic perturbations, ignorance and illiteracy, evil associates, learned criminality, and criminal typology.

The third and final section of the anthology contains cosmological explanations, including the influence of temperature, humidity, and barometric pressure in producing criminal behavior.

After each of the subtopics is a "Suggestions for Further Reading and Inquiry" section which contains fully annotated citations to similar articles in the English language periodical literature of the nineteenth century that will enable interested students and scholars to easily secure copies of them through the use of their campus library's interlibrary loan service.

If some of these specimens of primary source literature contain more shocking language and observations on crime causation and government crime control policy than what we are accustomed to encountering in the criminological literature of today, they may nonetheless prove to be valuable and interesting for the pleasing picture they offer of an unfolding and evolving theoretical perspective, and of the sober habits of research and literary industry exhibited by the staunchest adherents to the positivistic approach to criminological etiology. The English-language periodical literature on criminological positivism dating from the nineteenth century has filled libraries with such a vast collection of primary source material that the term of human life is too short for the critical study or even the casual perusal of it all. So much exists, yet this rich body of literature is little known, and even less relied upon, as a primary source of information to sustain the historical interests and researches of students and scholars. The labor of this anthology will not be lost if the reader is left with a just appreciation of the content of these extraordinary writings that have for too long been neglected as a primary source of the rich literary heritage of nineteenth century criminological positivism.

David M. Horton, Ph.D.
St. Edward's University
Austin, Texas

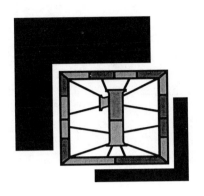

BIOLOGICAL
EXPLANATIONS

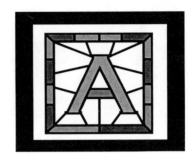

PHYSIOGNOMY

MUSINGS ON PHYSIOGNOMY

Britannia Monthly Magazine
Vol. 2 (March 1836), pp. 227–230

Physiognomy is the ancient art of determining the mental character of an individual by the examination of facial countenance manifested in its outward appearance. The notions, still current in the popular imagination, of the indications of good and evil character afforded by different kinds of facial features are of great antiquity.

References to physiognomy are to be found in many of the Greek classics. Indeed, the name originated with the Greeks. Homer is said to have been a close observer of facial appearance as correlated with character, this being shown in his description of Thersites, and elsewhere in his writings. Hippocrates, writing about 450 BC, refers to this subject, but not in any great depth, while Galen speaks of it in great detail. We learn from both Iamblichus and Porphyry that Phythagoras was in the habit of diagnosing both character and aptitude from the facial features of candidates for pupilage before admitting them. However, he seems to have discredited the current mania of the times for physiognomy, as he rejected Cylo the Croatian from his disciple-ship on account of his professing these doctrines, and was thereby brought into considerable trouble. Plato also tells us that Socrates predicted the promotion of Alcibiades from his visage, and Apuleius speaks of Socrates recognizing the abilities of Plato upon first casting eyes upon his face. On the other hand, it has been recorded by Cicero that a certain physiognomist, Zopyrus, who professed to know the habits, inclinations, and manners of men from their eyes and forehead, characterized Plato as stupid, sensual, and dull. Alexander Aprodisiensis adds, however, that when his disciples laughed at the judgment, Socrates said it was true, for such had been Plato's nature before the study of philosophy had modified it.

The first systematic physiognomic treatise which has come down to us is that attributed to Aristotle, in which he devotes six chapters to the consideration of the method of physiognomic study, the general signs of character found in the face, the particular appearances characteristic of the dispositions, of strength and weaknesses, of genius and stupidity, of timidity, cupidity, imprudence, intemperance, violence, anger, and their opposites. While discussing noses, he says that those with thick bulbous ends belong to persons who are insensitive, swinish, and prone to acts of theft, fraud, and intemperance; sharp-tipped noses belong to the irascible, those easily provoked and liable to assaultive behavior and ruffianism; rounded, large obtuse noses are characteristic of the magnanimous; slender, eagle-like hooked noses belong to the noble; round-tipped noses to the hedonistic; noses with a very slight notch at the root belong to the impudent; open nostrils are a sign of passionate appetites, and in both men and women are frequently found in the sexually promiscuous. Apion speaks of the metoposcopists who judge character and temperamental inclination by the appearance of the face, and Cleanthes the Stoic says it is possible to tell a proclivity for refined or vicious habits from the aspect of the face. Polemon (c. 150 AD) has left a treatise on the subject, similar in character to that of Aristotle, but he excels in graphic descriptions of different dispositions based upon the peculiarities of facial qualities. A more important late Greek contribution to the literature of physiognomy was added by a converted Jew, Adamantius, about 425 AD. This work, mostly Aristotelian in nature, is in two volumes, the first on the expression of the eye, the second on the nose, ears, and forehead.

The Latin Classics occasionally refer to physiognomy, but not to any great depth. Juvenal speaks of the examination of forehead and face to discern character. Seutonius, Pliny, Clement of Alexandria, and Origen all refer to physiognomy in varying degrees of detail and substance.

The extant writings from the early through the late Middle Age evince a continuing interest in physiognomy. The Arabian Ali Ragel and Rhazes (1040) both took up the study of physiognomy, and the latter devoted several chapters of his medical work to it. The Iberian Averroes (1165) made many references to it in his *De Sanitate*. Avicenna also makes some acute physiognomic remarks in his *De Animalibus*, which was translated by Michael Scott, the famous sage of Balwearie, about 1270. Scott wrote his own treatise *De Hominis Phisionomia* about 1272, but it was not printed until 1477, and the edition was not illustrated. The physiognomic treatise forms the third part of his work *De Secretis Naturae*. Albertus Magnus (born 1205) devotes much of the second tract of his _De Animalibus_ to the consideration of physiognomy. In 1335 Petrus de Abano of Padua delivered in Paris the first formal course of lectures on the subject (afterwards edited by Blondus, 1544), a few years before he was burned for heresy.

The 16th century was particularly rich in publications on physiognomy. Not only were the classical works printed, but additions were made to the literature, the greatest of all by Giambattista della Porta. Several works also appeared in England, one of the earliest being the anonymous _A Pleasant Introduction to the Art of Physiognomie_, published in 1558. The first English work with the author's name is that of Dr. Thomas Hill (1571), _The Contemplation of Mankynde, Contayning a Singular Discourse After the Art of Physiognomie_. Occasioned by a hard eye being cast by the Crown upon those who professed either a knowledge or practice of physiognomy, it was held in no small ill repute in England for many years. Act 39 Elizabeth, c.4, declared "all persons fayning to have knowledge of Phisiognomie or like Fantasticall Ymaginacions" are liable to "be stripped naked from the middle upwards and openly whipped until his body be bloudye." This was reinforced by the Act of Parliament 17 George II c.5 which declared that all persons pretending to have skill in physiognomy were deemed rogues and vagabonds and were liable to be publicly whipped or sent to the gaol until the following quarter sessions.

The rise of the study of anatomy in the late 17th and early 18th centuries altered greatly the purely speculative, and for the most part, descriptive basis upon which the Classical and Middle Age writers based their observations and philosophies. It was during this period that the notion became popular in some learned and scientific circles that the circumstance on which the chief and surest indications of character and temperamental predispositions are afforded by the countenance depend, is that when certain feelings and habits are much indulged in, the positions of the features which are associated with them are apt to become permanent, either by the formation of wrinkles or other marks in the skin, or by the enlargement and disproportionate strength of the muscles chiefly exerted. Thus, a person in the frequent habit of sneering contemptuously acquires at last a slight curve in his upper lip by the disproportionate size and power of its elevator muscle; he who is often meditating has the wrinkles of the slight frown and the contraction of the brows which are commonly associated with deep thought, permanently fixed.

Despite the views of the anatomical physiognomists, interest in physiognomy flagged among learned men in the late 18th century, and remains popular today chiefly with the low born, those given to belief in old saws, supersitions, and the marvelous, and as a parlour game among adolescents and courting couples. Indeed, the only name worthy of note is that of Lavater. The popular style of his *Physiognomic Fragments* (1775), its good illustrations, and the pious spirit pervading the work, have given to both him and physiognomy a recent following little deserved, as there is really no system in his treatise, which largely consists of rhapsodical comments upon the several portraits. Having a happy knack of estimating character, especially when acquainted with the histories of the persons in question, the good pastor contrived to write a graphic and readable book, not with a view to benefiting of men of science, but as an illustrated manual for the gullible public, with the result that it is much inferior to Porta's or Aristotle's as a systematic philosophical treatise. Alas, with him the descriptive school of physiognomy may be said to have ended. The few straggling works which continue to intermittently appear today, each succeeding one more ludicrous than the previous, are scarcely deserving of notice, the rising attraction of phrenology, especially as professed by Gall, Spurzheim, and Combe, having given to pure descriptive physiognomy the *coup de grace* by taking into itself whatever was likely to live of the older, and now generally discredited system.

A PHYSIOGNOMIC EXEMPLAR

THE NOSE

BY J. W. M.

AMERICAN PHRENOLOGICAL JOURNAL AND LIFE ILLUSTRATED

VOL. 43, NO. 5 (MAY 1866), P. 138

Noses, like faces, have quite a variety of forms, but they may be reduced to two kinds, namely, the snub nose and the Roman nose—the nose that is chiefly developed on the bridge, and the nose that is chiefly developed at the end. And there is no use of undertaking to make the insignificant markings of the nose intelligible as indexes of character until the radical distinctions of character belonging to these two opposite forms is understood; especially so when we consider that the principles involved in these two grand distinctions are equally applicable to all the minor details.

Noses, then, may be divided into first, the concave, physical, or snub nose; secondly, the convex, mental, or Roman nose. These two divisions, simple as they are, comprise all the noses of the entire human race. I have here applied three different epithets to each of these two kinds of nose. One of these epithets to each of these kinds will likely be new to the reader, namely, "physical" to the first, and "mental" to the second kind. My reasons for the employment of these terms will appear hereafter. The other terms are sufficiently plain. I will first give some attention to the snub nose, or, more properly, the concave nose; for snub is a term more especially applicable to a particular kind of concave nose. "Concave" is the more comprehensive term. The general physiognomic law of concavity of the nose may be thus stated: In proportion as the nose is concave, the mind is passive to the external, to the *non ego*; and as a second law subsidiary to the above, I will give the following: In proportion as the nose is concave, the inclination is to be related to the external as the opposite.

We now have before us the two great physiognomic laws of relation between the character of the mind and the concavity of the nose. The first, however, is that with which we have principally to do, the second being only the means by which the evils of the first are corrected. It is the natural compensation of the first. The snub-nosed man is not so much anything of himself, as he is a constituent part of a complicated machine. He does not so much act as he is acted upon. He is an instrument in the hands of superiors. Coarse and ignoble in his nature, he has a vigorous body, and a cast of mind that finds its chief gratification in taking care of and making a display of that body. I have found the snub nose and its concomitant temperament, when manifested in its most extreme, to be a readily recognizable characteristic of not only the dangerous classes which inhabit our larger towns and virtually every city, but of convict populations as well. The snub nose, when inclined to vicious tendencies, is most often found acting in the capacity of a lackey for a more astute and mentally well developed malefactor. Hence the phrenologist will find in his head the following organs large: in the back-head, *Approbativeness*, *Combativeness*, *Adhesiveness*, and *Secretiveness*, the first being the largest of all. These organs which have no independence of activity (except *Secretiveness* to a slight degree), but merely put us in relation to others, and to a greater or less extent subject us to the control of other persons and things. The stimuli are exterior to self. Predominant *Approbativeness* and *Combativeness* are the two horns to which the goads are applied and the brass buttons by the "big gineral" when he steers his livestock to the field of carnage! But they make not the individual *independent*, defeating or defeated. These organs are huge in the Irish. Is Ireland free? [She will be one of these days – so the Fenians assure us].

In the front head we find large Acquisitiveness, Constructiveness, Calculation, and Causality, but with respect to the functions of this last organ, I may have a word to say at another time, and will therefore, not give it much attention now. All these organs, it may be perceived, concern themselves with the external as their direct stimuli, and with the material rather than the spiritual. And though they are chiefly selfish in the *ends* which they serve, they are entirely subservient to persons and things which are beyond the control of the individual. They put us in intelligent relation to the material universe about us. They are the intellectual complements of the occipital organs named. To illustrate: the organ of Approbativeness gives the mechanic or laborer the desire to please his employer; the organ of Constructiveness enables him to employ successfully the means of doing it; but they are all faculties of a low order. They only perceive the *external* properties of material things, and take no notice of spiritual existence.

But I called the concave nose the "physical" nose. It is a nose that marks a defect of character, but this defectiveness does not so much appertain to the body as to the mind itself. I call it physical, because all the *positive* qualities which it indicates are qualities of body and not of mind. It has a hearty relish for the various pleasures and performances which require physical *sensibility* and physical force; but it is blunt in its perceptions of the higher nature of man, and even to its perceptions of the finer and more delicate qualities of material things, as their color and smell.

The concave nose is not a nose of great moral courage, though it has physical courage in a high degree. Under the first, or great law of concavity of the nose, we have an Approbativeness and activity of passion generally in the individual, that make him subservient to the purposes (including those of evil design) of others. But under the second, or subsidiary law we have Combativeness, to correct in a measure his otherwise directly passive character. But we must not lose sight of the important fact, that Combativeness is itself a passion by which we are subjected to the external, only in such a manner as to operate conservatively as to the individual. And we must not mistake Combativeness for anything that leads *directly* to *independence*. Combativeness is a passion finding its stimulus in the *non ego*, and as such it exposes to the direct control of the external, and all independence originates from within.

I will now make a few remarks upon the convex or Roman nose. You remember that to the concave nose belongs the faculty of *will* – of motion from self. In the one case the individual is acted upon, in the other he *acts*. The concave nose is preserved from being merged in the external by acting in an antagonistic relation thereto. The convex nose is preserved from the control of the external by means altogether different, namely, by exclusion or ostracism therefrom. What the snub nose is offended by, he fights; what the Roman nose hates, he shuns or destroys. The great physiognomical law of the Roman nose is *independence* of action. The Roman nose has a few objects of affection which he loves as himself, and which he loves as individuals and for what they are.

The snub nose has *many* objects of affection to which he is attached as a *class*, and for their accidental relations to him or to some particular class *in which he ranks himself*. The legendary general affection and tolerance for which thieves exhibiting the snub nose regard one another, even though they be total strangers, upon hearing tell of or actually meeting for the first time, is exemplary of the notion previously alluded to. The Roman loves the individual; the pug nose is attracted to the *class* of individuals. It may now be asked, is the Roman nose, then, an indication of the greater excellence? This will depend upon our notions of what is excellent. But since the Roman nose indicates a predominance of the causative forces of the *mind*, we may answer in the affirmative. But since the concave nose indicates the presence of an extensive apparatus acting as modifying conditions of body, it is also indicative of its own peculiar excellence. The *character* of the Roman nose we *esteem*; the *performances* of the concave nose *excite* our more base instincts and desires. The Roman-nosed George Washington fought for a *cause*, *i.e.*, the defense of principle, and commands the *esteem* of mankind. The concave-nosed Napoleon Bonaparte fought because he was skilled in the *art* of war, and to gratify his *passions*—and *excite* our primitive lust of savagery and blood.

SUGGESTIONS FOR FURTHER READING AND INQUIRY: PHYSIOGNOMY

"Physiognomy." Elizabeth Eastlake. *Quarterly Review*, vol. 90 (1851), pp. 62–91.
A very detailed discussion of "nasology," or the classification of noses according to temperamental disposition.

"Physiognomy of the Human Form." James Paget. *Quarterly Review*, vol. 99 (1856), pp. 452–491.
A very detailed and lengthy discussion of the evidence in support of physiognomy as a valid doctrine.

"Physiognomy." *Ballou's Dollar Monthly Magazine*, vol. 14 (1861), p. 171.
An interesting account of an experiment set up for Lavater, the champion of eighteenth-century physiognomy, in which he was shown two portraits, one of a highwayman (subsequently broken on the wheel), and the other of the philosopher Kant. Asked to discern from the facial features the philosopher, Lavater selected the criminal!

"On Physiognomy." E. S. Dallas. *Cornhill Magazine*, vol. 4 (1861), pp. 472–481.
A very fine article that explores the historical development of physiognomy as well as the leading principles on which Lavater based his system, and concludes that the system is without scientific merit.

"The First Principle of Physiognomy." E. S. Dallas. *Cornhill Magazine*, vol. 4 (1861), pp. 569–581.
A second, and more in-depth article that challenges the physiognomic premise that character and temperament may be accurately discerned from distinguishing facial features.

"The Eyebrows Physiognomically Considered."
American Phrenological Journal and Life Illustrated, vol. 44 (1866), p. 109.
A fine illustration of the physiognomic approach to the analysis of character and disposition based upon the eyebrows.

"Practical Physiognomy." *American Phrenological Journal and Life Illustrated*, vol. 44 (1866), p. 174.
A fine review of the leading nineteenth century book on physiognomy, which provides a very useful overview of the foundations upon which the theory and practice of judging character and mental qualities through an analysis of facial features is predicated.

"Physiognomy of the Nose." *Frank Leslie's Popular Monthly*, vol. 6 (1878), p. 105.
Another exemplar of the practical application of physiognomic principles to the analysis of character and disposition.

"Something About Noses." *National Repository*, vol. 3 (1878), pp. 88–89.
A short but interesting commentary on the nature of temperamental deduction based upon the physiognomy of the nose.

"The Hair as an Index to Temperament." *Tit~Bits*, vol. 2 (1882), p. 407.
An illustration of the absurd lengths which physiognomists were compelled to go in order to recapture the attention of the general public for a system in which they no longer believed.

"Character in the Mouth." *Frank Leslie's Popular Monthly*, vol. 21 (1886), p. 671.
An interesting account of the belief current in sixteenth-century Europe regarding the shape of the mouth and a propensity toward villainy and evil.

"Fate in the Face." Louis Robinson. *Blackwood's Edinburgh Magazine*, vol. 159 (1896), pp. 680–689.
An historical overview of physiognomy, and arguments tending to disprove its tenets.

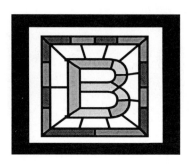

PHRENOLOGY

(OR CRANIOLOGY)

PHRENOLOGY EPITOMIZED

CONTINENTAL REPOSITORY

VOL. 2 (AUGUST 1841), PP. 156-159

The name *Phrenology* was given by Forster in 1815 to the empirical system formulated by Gall and developed by his followers, especially by Spurzheim and Combe. At first, it was named "cranioscopy," "craniology," or "zoonomy," but Forster's name was early adopted by Spurzheim, and became that whereby the system is now known.

Today phrenology answers as a reliable guide for reading character by means of a careful examination of the exterior surface of the skull. The fundamental principles upon which it is based are four: (1) the brain is the organ of the mind; (2) the mental powers of man can be analyzed into a definite number of independent faculties; (3) these faculties are innate, and each has its seat in a definite region of the brain; and (4) the size of each of these regions is the measure of the power manifesting the faculty associated with it. Phrenology, viewed in its entirety as a philosophical system, advocates that the manifestation of each of the several faculties of the mind depends upon a particular part of the brain, and that the degree or strength in which each faculty is manifested in each individual, depends on the size of its appropriated portion of the brain or (as it is properly termed) its organ.

The Fundamental Hypothesis.—The principle which underlies phrenology is that mental phenomena are resolvable into the manifestations of a group of separate faculties. Combe says a faculty is "a convenient expression for the particular states into which the mind enters when influenced by particular organs, and is used to denote a particular power of feeling, thinking, perceiving, connected with a particular part of the brain." Each organ is considered as engaged, either independently in bringing forth its own product, or collectively with others in elaborating compound mental states, according to their several degrees of development and activity which are considered capable of perceiving, conceiving, recollecting, judging, or imagining each its own subject.

The Faculties and Their Location.—Gall enumerated nearly twenty-six mental faculties, which are admitted, with more or less modification, by all phrenologists of the present day (and their number has been augmented by Spurzheim to thirty-five). Having selected the place of a faculty, Gall examined the heads of his friends and casts of persons with that peculiarity in common, and in them he sought for the distinctive feature of their characteristic trait. Some of his earlier studies were made among low associates, in gaols, prisons, and in lunatic asylums, and some of the qualities located by him were such as tend to become perverted to crime. These he named after their excessive manifestations, mapping out organs of murder, theft, and vice (but as this cast some discredit on the system the names were later changed by Spurzheim). Gall marked out on his model of the head the places of twenty-six organs as round enclosures with vacant interspaces. Spurzheim and Combe divided the whole scalp into thirty-five oblong and conterminous patches.

The following epitome of phrenological faculties, propensities, and sentiments (illustrated by corresponding number in the accompanying figures) is that of Spurzheim, who, to his credit, greatly refined and revised the system first developed by Gall, and whose arrangement is here adopted as being received by the great majority of phrenologists. Spurzheim separated the component faculties of the human mind into two great groups and subdivided these as follows:

I. Feelings, divided into (1) propensities, internal impulses inviting only to certain actions, and (2) sentiments, impulses which prompt to emotion as well as to action.

II. Intellectual Faculties, divided into (1) perceptive, and (2) reflective.

Propensities

(1) *Amativeness* (the mental faculty which produces the propensity to physical love).

(2) *Philoprogenitiveness* (origin of the feeling of love towards offspring; said by Gall to be exceptionally well developed in females).

(3) *Concentrativeness* (the seat of the power of concentration).

(4) *Adhesiveness* (the propensity to attachment or friendship, by which individuals of the same kind are induced to associate together).

(5) *Combativeness* (discovered by Gall, who is said to have been in the habit of calling together street urchins and paying them in an endeavor to make them fight. There were of course some who were fond of it, and others who were peaceable and timid. In the former this part of the head was prominent, it the latter it was flattened or depressed. In the low, gross, and uneducated, this faculty is manifested in brawling and a general tendency to street ruffianism).

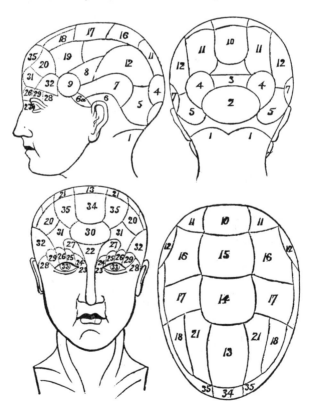

(6) *Destructiveness* (or the propensity to destroy, is the feeling which is gratified by any kind or mode of destruction. First found by Gall in the head of a student so fond of torturing animals that he became a surgeon, and later by Spurzheim in the head of an apothecary who became an executioner. In the perverted condition, the propensity is regarded as the source of the irresistible desire for the destruction of life, and is prominent in murderers. "In the beginning of the last century," Dr. Spurzheim says, "several murders were committed in Holland, on the frontiers of the province of Cleves. For a long time the murderer escaped detection, but at last suspicion fell on an old man, who gained his livelihood by playing on the violin at country weddings, in consequence of some expression of his children. When led before the justice, he confessed to thirty-four murders, and said that he had committed them without any cause of enmity, and without any intention of robbing, but only because he was extremely delighted with bloodshed. At Strasburg, two keepers of the cathedral having been assassinated, all efforts to discover the murderer for a long time were ineffectual. At last a postillion was shot by a clergyman named Frick. This monster had hired a post-chaise for the express purpose of satisfying his horrible propensity to destroy. Arrested, he confessed himself the murderer of both the keepers of the cathedral. This wretch was rich, and had never stolen. For his crimes he was condemned to die at Strasburg. Upon an examination of their skulls, I found them both to exhibit abnormally large cerebral development in the region of destructiveness.").

(6a)*Alimentiveness* (love of food and drink, particularly well pronounced in gourmands, and in its perverted form, found in gluttons and drunkards).

(7) *Secretiveness* (the propensity to act in a clandestine manner, and to conceal emotion, and to be secret in words, things, deeds, and projects).

(8) *Acquisitiveness* (the propensity to acquire, especially by illegal acquisition. Its organ being found by Drs. Gall and Spurzheim to be very large and prominent in notorious thieves, pick-pockets, those of a kelptomaniacal disposition, as well as authors of false fiduciary instruments. M. Kneisler, govern of the prison of Prague, spoke to Drs. Gall and Spurzheim about the wife of a rich merchant, who stole continually from her husband in the most adroit manner, and who was at last shut up in a prison, which she had scarcely left, when she stole again, and was again confined. She was condemned to a third and longer imprisonment, and again commenced her operations in the gaol itself. At Copenhagen, Drs. Gall and Spurzheim saw an incorrigible thief who, not requiring the ill-gotten lucre, many times distributed the produce of his larcenies to the poor; and in another place, a robber, who was in confinement for the seventh time, assured them, with sorrow, that he felt himself unable to act otherwise).

(9) *Constructiveness* (detected by its prominence on the head of persons of mechanical genius and those particularly adept at various manual operations. First found by Gall on a skull reputed to be that of Raphael. In its perverted form, Gall found it prominently developed among those engaged in making counterfeit money, false keys, and other dishonest contrivances).

Sentiments

(10) *Self-esteem* (the sentiment which gives an individual a high opinion of himself, found by Gall in a beggar who excused his poverty on account of his pride).

(11) *Love of Approbation* (the sentiment which makes us regard the opinion entertained of us by others. Discovered by Gall when he saw a protuberance on the head of a lunatic who fancied herself queen of France).

(12) *Cautiousness* (the disposition of the mind which lead a man to take precautions in whatever he has to do).

(13) *Benevolence* (the disposition of the mind from which result compassion, kindness, philanthropy, mildness, charity, and various other amiable social virtues).

(14) *Veneration* (called by Gall the organ of religion, he first noticed that it was prominent in those who prayed with the greatest fervor in church).

(15) *Conscientiousness* (the fundamental and innate sentiment which disposes mankind to look and to wish for justice).

(16) *Firmness* (the faculty which gives constancy and perseverance to the other faculties. Lavater first pointed out that persons of determination had lofty heads).

(17) *Hope* (the sentiment which induces man to believe in the possibility of whatever their other faculties desire).

(18) *Marvelousness*, or *Wonder* (the sentiment which is principally manifested by a belief in miraculous and supernatural circumstances, and said to be large in vision-seers and many psychic researchers, and well developed in those who have a belief in ghosts).

(19) *Ideality* (Gall regarded the organ of this faculty as the organ of poetry, finding it much developed in the busts all the great poets of ancient times).

(20) *Mirthfulness*, or *Wit* (the sentiment which disposes men to view everything in a gay or joyful manner; the organ of the sense of the ludicrous, prominent in Rabelais and Swift).

(21) *Imitation* (Those who have this faculty highly developed are fond of acting, and of imitating acts, gestures, voices, and manners of men and animals).

Perceptive Faculties

(22) *Individuality* (the capacity of recognizing and respecting external objects and individual beings, and forming ideas therefrom; said to have been large in Michelangelo, and small in the Scots).

(23) *Configuration*, or *Form* (the capacity of recognizing faces, forms, and figures; found by Gall in a squinting girl with a good memory for faces).

(24) *Size* (the capacity of estimating space and distance).

(25) *Weight* (a region determinative of intellectual capacity).

(26) *Colour* (The faculty for the full appreciation of the relation of colour, particularly well developed in artists regarded as good colourists).

(27) *Locality* (the faculty by which we appreciate and remember the places occupied by objects around us).

(28) *Calculation*, or *Number* (the faculty of arithmetic; Gall first found it to be large in a calculating boy in Vienna).

(29) *Order* (the faculty which gives a disposition to arrange and put things in order as well as a tendency to cleanliness; first noted by Spurzheim in an orderly idiot).

(30) *Eventuality* (the seat of the memory of events; individuals who have this organ large are attentive to all that happens around them, to phenomena, to events, to facts; they are fond of history and of anecdotes; are inquisitive and desire information).

(31) *Time* (the faculty which conceives the duration of phenomena, their simultaneousness or succession).

(32) *Melody*, or *Tune* (bears the same relation to the ears as that of colour does to the eyes; found by Gall when he noticed a bulge on the head of a musical prodigy of five).

(33) *Language* (This was the first organ noticed by Gall, as a clever schoolfellow. Gall observed that while he had great difficulty in committing his lessons to memory, there were many boys who could easily learn by heart. He noticed that all these boys were "bull-eyed," that is had a peculiar prominence of the eye-ball, which seemed to project from its socket).

Reflective Faculties

(34) *Comparison* (the faculty which induces men to argue from analogy, to draw illustrations of their subjects from things well known, to speak by parables, and explain by examples and similes. Located at the top of the bare region of the forehead, where a savant friend of Gall's, fond of analogies, had a prominent boss, and later found by him to be frequent in professors of philosophy and practitioners of law).

(35) *Causality* (noticed first by Gall on the head of Fichte and on a bust of Kant, the seat of the faculty of correlating causes and effects).

You now have before you, learned and gentle reader, a general view of the principles of phrenology, as stated in the writings of Drs. Gall and Spurzheim, and adopted by most of the present advocates of the system.

PHRENOLOGY IN PRISON

THE MIRROR

VOL. 12, NO. 323 (26 JULY 1828), P. 56

In 1805, Dr. Gall, the celebrated phrenologist, accompanied by his devoted student and collaborator, Johann Gaspar Spurzheim, visited the prison of Berlin in the course of their experimental travels to establish Gall's theories. On April 17, in the presence of many witnesses, Gall was shown upwards of two hundred culprits, of whom he had never heard until that moment, and to whose crimes and dispositions he was a total stranger. Dr. Gall immediately pointed out, as a general feature in one of the wards, an extraordinary development in the region of the head where the organ of theft is situated, and in fact every prisoner there was a thief. Some children, also detained for theft, were then shown to him; and in them, too, the same organ was very prominent. In two of them particularly it was excessively large; and the prison-registers confirmed his opinion that these two were most incorrigible. In another room, where the women were kept apart, he distinguished one dressed exactly like the others, occupied like them, and differing in no one thing but in the form of her head. "For what reason is this woman here," asked Gall, "for her head announces no propensity to theft?" The answer was, "She is the inspectress of this room."

One prisoner had the organs of benevolence and of religion as strongly developed as those of theft and cunning; and his boast was, that he never had committed an act of violence, and that it was repugnant to his feelings to rob a church. Gall was, from his first meeting, suspicious of the man's declared innocence. The disposition of the man's charges of theft later proved Gall's suspicions well founded. The man was convicted of theft.

In a man named Fritze, detained for the murder of his wife, though his crime was not proved, the organs of cunning and firmness were fully developed; and it was by these means that he had eluded conviction. In another convict, named Maschke, he found the organ of the mechanical arts, together with a head very well organized in many respects; and his crime was coining. In the convict Troppe he saw the same organ. This man was a shoemaker, who, without instruction, made clocks and watches, to gain a livelihood in his confinement. On a nearer inspection, the organ of imitation was found to be large. "If this man had ever been near a theatre," said Gall, "he would in all probability have turned actor." Troppe, astonished at the accuracy of this sentence, confessed that he had joined a company of strolling players for six months. His crime, too, was having personated a police officer, to extort money. In another convict, Heisig, who, in a drunken fit had stabbed his best friend to death, the organs of circumspection, prudence, and foresight were sadly deficient. In some prisoners he found the organ of language, in others of colour, in others of mathematics; and his opinion in no single instance failed to be confirmed by the known talents and dispositions of the individuals.

A PHRENOLOGICAL EXEMPLAR

THE CORRESPONDENCE BETWEEN THE CHARACTERS AND HEADS OF TWO MURDERERS LATELY EXECUTED AT NEWGATE

BY

JAMES STRATON

ZOIST

VOL. 13, NO. 57 (JULY 1856), PP. 202~218

"Those who have a large head, are sagacious—are like dogs; those who have a small head, are stupid—are like asses; those who have a conical head, have no shame—are like birds with curved claws. The sites, the basest scoundrel who went against Troy, had a conical head."

Homer, *The Illiad*

It is sometimes alleged that we know nothing of the true moral character of persons and that intellectual faculties may exist in strength which has never shown itself. Frequently, however, there can be no doubt of either moral character or intellectual powers. The positive conduct may render the moral character indisputable; and the positive exhibition of an intellectual power proves its existence. Can any one doubt the moral character or intellect of Mr. Haydon the artist; the moral character of Rush, of the two Mannings, or the others whose heads have been displayed in previous numbers of *Zoist*? We take the positive history of these individuals as it is furnished to all the world; and we take the developments of their heads as presented by genuine casts taken immediately after death and in almost every instance without any interference on our part. In every case our readers perceive the correspondence between the two, the proofs of the truth of Dr. Gall's science, and the nothingness of the arguments brought against it by ignorance, short-sightedness, false views, and misrepresentation.

The following accounts of the Frenchman named Emmanuel Barthelemy, and of the Italian named Luigi Buranelli, and their respective phrenological analyses, serve as further demonstrable and irrefutable evidence of the reliability of Dr. Gall's science, and the exactness to which modern methods have taken his original thesis. The casts were taken by order of the Sheriffs by B. Casci, of No. 3, Harford Place, Drury Lane, in the presence of many persons; and any number of these casts may be purchased of Mr. Casci, whom I am happy to recommend for taking casts from the living and the dead, for purposes phrenological or otherwise.

I. Barthelemy's Crimes and Further Particulars of Him

Emmanuel Barthelemy, a Frenchman, aged 32, a turner in metal, and calling himself an engineer, knocked and rang at the door of Mr. Moore, soda-water maker, No. 73, Warren Street, Fitzroy Square, in company with a woman with a veil over her face, on the evening of December 8, 1854. He had been there several times before to repair an engine. They were shown into the back parlour where Mr. Moore was. In ten minutes, the noise of violent scuffling was heard in the room, and all three were seen coming out of it – the woman first, Barthelemy next, with a pistol in his hand near Mr. Moore's head, at which he fired it with the effect of instantly killing Mr. Moore, who seemed to be either pushing him or holding him back. Two or three persons, and among them Mr. Collard, a green-grocer, attracted by the quarrelling, collected round the door, which the maid-servant had opened, dropping her candle; and Barthelemy, observing them, shut and fastened the door, and ran through the house to an opposite door which led into the New Road. Mr. Collard ran round to this door and was shot in the abdomen by Barthelemy while endeavouring to prevent his escape. In Barthelemy's pocket were found a dagger in a sheath sewn into his body coat, twenty-four ball cartridges which fitted the pistols he had used, and two door keys. A cane was taken from him with a piece of string at one end, and a heavy piece of lead, to which seemed to have been attached a handle, but broken off, was found in the room. A strong mahogany chair was lying broken in the room, and there were several marks of blood upon the wall at about the height of the head of a person sitting in a chair, as well as on different parts of the floor and in the passage. Mr. Moore's head was found lying in a pool of blood, with three lacerated wounds at the top, and a smaller wound on the back, such as the piece of lead might have made; there was also above the right eye a pistol-ball wound from which blood and brains were flowing. Mr. Collard died in University College Hospital of his wound the same night.

Barthelemy was tried on January 4th for the murder of Mr. Collard alone. The trial lasted nearly eight hours, and during the whole of that period the prisoner, who was a most ferocious, repulsive-looking man, stood firm and erect in the front of the bar and did not betray the least emotion. The jury found him guilty, and he exhibited the same callous indifference while the sentence of death was being passed. While lodged in prison awaiting his execution he declared that he had no intention to murder Mr. Moore and he went to that person's house, had found the cane loaded with lead in the room, and that it was a thing used in Moore's business; that he accompanied the woman for the purpose of inducing Moore to pay her an allowance which she received from Moore, who was a friend of her father—a Roman Catholic priest, and, Moore not paying her the money, a quarrel ensued. He also declared that the pistol which shot Collard went off accidentally.

On the day after the sentence was passed, the Rev. J. E. Davis, the ordinary of Newgate, visited Barthelemy in his cell for the purpose of offering his services. On some allusion being made to spiritual matters, he said, "I am visited by a catholic priest, but he has the good sense not to speak to me on matter of religion." Rev. Davis took much interest in the prisoner's case, and devoted much of his time to him, and attempted on many occasions to draw his mind to a consideration of religion, but his efforts were unsuccessful, for the prisoner gave utterance to infidel sentiments of the boldest character. He denied again and again the existence of a First Cause. Being pressed upon this point by Rev. Davis, he exclaimed, "Well, well, if there is a God, I hope he speaks French." He added that he should soon know the great secret if there were one, but he did not believe in anything of the sort. Being urged to penitence and prayer, he said, "If I pray, it will not open the prison-door, or break the rope."

Adverting to his trial and sentence, the prisoner expressed his opinion that Lord Campbell was guilty of a greater crime in sentencing him to death than he had been in committing the crime for which that sentence was passed. He did not appear to think that he had committed any crime. He asserted that there was a vast number of men as bad as he, and their crimes went unpunished. He particularly mentioned the Emperor Napoleon, who, he said, had committed more daring and more violent acts than he, and that while the Emperor was now receiving the acclamations of Europe, he was sentenced to death on the gallows.

It is usual for prisoners under sentence of death to attend the services in the prison chapel on the Sunday previous to their execution, but of this privilege Barthelemy declined to avail himself. At ten o'clock that evening he retired to rest, and slept soundly until four o'clock in the morning, at which time he dressed himself and partook of some refreshment. Shortly before eight o'clock Monday morning he was visited in his cell by the Rev. Davis and a number of other prison officials who would be superintending his execution later that morning. Calcraft, the executioner, was introduced, but his appearance in no respect shook the remarkable coolness and self-possession of the prisoner, who said, while his arms were being pinioned, "I hope I shall be a good example." Rev. Davis, who was deeply affected, said, "I hope, Barthelemy, you have made your peace with God," to which the condemned replied, "I have no faith in God."

St. Sepulchre's bell tolled, and the funeral procession was formed. Barthelemy strode up to the scaffold with an unflinching tread, and met his doom with the coolness which was so eminently characteristic of his life. Ten thousand witnesses had assembled to witness the execution; but the sight of this vast multitude failed, as everything else had failed, to move him. At the given signal the bolt was drawn, Barthelemy fell, and died without a struggle. At nine o'clock the body was cut down, placed in a coffin, and removed to the College of Surgeons for dissection.

It is said that in the former revolution he shot a man in cool blood, and was sent to the galleys, but afterwards was liberated on the ground that the affair had been entirely political. I learned from one who employed him as a workman that his countenance was very forbidding, his temper very violent, and his nature very revengeful; that he cruelly cheated a poor fellow-workman, and declared that he would kill the present Emperor of the French; yet that his speech was ordinarily subdued and gentle. An eminent musical composer who was present at his examination before Mr. Hardwicke, the magistrate, tells me that it was absolutely melodious. I hear on good authority that, feeling himself insulted by a French refugee, who was an excellent swordsman, he went to France and practiced sword exercise for a year, and on his return spat in the other's face the first time he met the man in the street, and caused the man to send him a challenge; the other, thinking him no swordsman, offered to fight him with pistols, the offer was accepted, and Barthelemy, as is well known, shot his man dead. It is reported that he was a red republican, and that on the very morning of the day of the murder in Warren Street he had planned to set off for Paris with the intention of shooting the French Emperor, but was too late for the train. The dagger sewn in his coat, and the pistols and four and twenty balls found upon him after the murders later that day, he no doubt started with in the morning, and did not have an opportunity to relieve himself of them before joining the woman in her visit to Mr. Moore. It is no improbable that he had no murderous intention when he went to Mr. Moore's, but that, taking up the woman's quarrel, he became violent, struck Mr. Moore with the leaded cane which he found in the room and fired, and afterwards fired at Collard in order to escape. The woman has not been heard of since the murders, and his story respecting her is not improbable.

II. Buranelli: His History, Crimes, and Insanity

Luigi Buranelli, an Italian, aged 31, who had formerly been an upper servant in a gentleman's family and latterly resided at Penhurst as a tailor, came to London and formed an acquaintance with a Mr. Latham, who went by the name of Lambert, was separated by agreement from his wife, and lived at No. 5, Foley Place with another woman, both assuming the name of Lambert. Buranelli had first known Mr. Latham by lodging in the same house in Newman Street. After a short acquaintance, they all three removed to Foley Place, together with a woman named Mrs. Williamson, who, along with Buranelli, Mrs. Latham set up together as milliners. Mrs. Williamson became in the family way by Buranelli, and requested Mr. Latham to order Buranelli to take his leave. Subsequently, he was compelled by Mr. Latham, with the threats of blows, to leave the house on the twenty-eighth of December. They feared his continued residence there would injure the millinery business.

Buranelli afterwards wrote to the Williamson woman, but received no answer, became desperate, and deliberately resolved to murder her and Mr. Lambert–so called. On the seventh of

January, about 9 o'clock in the morning, Buranelli rang the bell at No. 5, Foley Place, and, betraying nothing particular by his voice or manner, gave his greatcoat and a parcel to the woman who opened the door, and asked where Mr. and Mrs. Lambert and Mrs. Williamson were. He entered Mr. Latham's room at the back on the ground floor with a pistol in his hand, and, seeing the latter asleep with his back to the edge of the bed, fired the pistol at the back of his head and instantly killed him by dividing the spinal cord. Mrs. Lambert jumped out of bed, and Buranelli exchanged a second pistol from his left to his right hand, and, firing at her, wounded her in the arm and neck. He then proceeded upstairs to Mrs. Williamson's room, entered in agitation, told her that he had murdered Mrs. Lambert, went into another room, fastened the door, fired a pistol in his own face, and, when the police arrived shortly thereafter, exclaimed to them that he should die and that he was an assassin and murderer.

He had a little daughter in the country, but ceased to enquire about her after his connexion with Mrs. Williamson. He once lived in Italy with a member of a Scotch family, who afterwards allowed him 20 pounds sterling a year. He afterwards lived for months as a butler with a gentleman in Grafton and Bond Streets, having been highly recommended. His conduct was good, and he was a universal favourite. After losing his wife – an Italian – he became inconsolable, constantly wept, declared he could not bear his trouble, and should destroy himself, and said that his sufferings were greatest on Fridays. When a tailor at Penhurst, he was considered a quite inoffensive man, married a native of the place, lost her suddenly in childbirth, was distracted and continually talked about dying. He had a trifling fistula, which was cut, and he seemed to suffer mentally from it, and fearing he should die, refused at first an operation, but after it was performed, he became very violent, almost unmanageable, and tearing off the bandages, wept much, and said, "Poor Louis, poor Louis, many troubles, many troubles." Who exactly was Louis? The nature of his troubles were, despite repeated questioning, never ascertained. After the operation his mental condition deteriorated further; he would not be left alone, talked of throwing himself into the river, and asked an acquaintance to shoot him; he thought his medical attendant tried to poison him, had awful dreams, believed he should come to an unhappy end; begged for laudanum to poison himself; was affected by wet weather, had a constant pain in his side, congestion of the liver, and was believed by his medical attendant to labour under, not melancholy, which is merely lowness of spirits, but *melancholia*, which is a disease – a form of insanity, for he had many delusions.

He came up to London, and entered the Middlesex Hospital, where he was desponding, cried for hours together, and often insisted that his bed was flooded with water. Just before the crime, he would talk to himself and gesticulate when alone, and complained of pain in his head and heart. He exhibited no signs of insanity either during his trial or when in Newgate awaiting his execution. I have not the least doubt that he had previously been insane at different times, and was insane at the time of the murder, although as soon as he had committed the heinous deed he was himself again. To declare him not mad previously, because no sign of insanity was detected afterwards is ridiculous, I contend, despite a *post-mortem* examination of the body made by the medical superintendent of St. Luke's hospital, where it was found that the brain and its membranes were perfectly healthy, thus confirming the opinion of the jury as to the sanity of the man, and his consequent responsibility for the crimes into which his vicious nature had impelled him.

He was tried by an English jury, and during the entire course of the proceedings suffered from the wounds inflicted by his own hand at the time of the dreadful occurrence, a ball having passed through his neck into his face, where it still remained embedded behind and up his nose, and in consequence of this, he held a handkerchief to his face during the trial. When sentence of death was passed upon him he nearly fainted, and was assisted from the dock. While awaiting execution in Newgate his behaviour was excellent, and he never once evinced the slightest indication of insanity; but, on the contrary, he appeared to be a very shrewd and clever man, and the letters he wrote during this time to his mother and to some other persons exhibit proofs that he was possessed of considerable education and good feeling. While in Newgate he still appeared to suffer a good deal from the injury he had inflicted upon himself, and an attempt was made to extract it, but as he complained of the pain that was occasioned to him, the attempt was abandoned. During the whole of the medical procedure the culprit exhibited considerable composure, but it was evident that it was only by a great effort that he succeeded in controlling his feelings, and that nature would not have sustained him much longer.

Before leaving his cell to proceed to the place of execution, Buranelli earnestly thanked the sheriffs and Mr. Cope, the governor of Newgate, for the kindness he had received from them, and he also expressed his deep gratitude to Father Gavazzi, a Roman Catholic priest who was summoned to attend to his spiritual needs. A few words passed between the wretched man and the reverend gentleman, and then the melancholy procession was formed and proceeded to the scaffold. Buranelli walked with a firm step, and appeared to pay deep attention to the exhortations of his spiritual adviser. At the foot of the steps leading to the scaffold he appeared to falter, and Father Gavazzi assisted him to ascend. He was then placed under the beam, and surveyed the crowd with a calm and composed aspect, and very shortly thereafter the drop fell. He appeared to struggle convulsively for two or three minutes, and then all was over. It would seem that death was not so instantaneous as usual on account of the culprit being a man of very light weight, but from the placid appearance of the face after he was cut down, and which more resembled that of a man in a calm and sound sleep than of one who had just suffered a sudden and violent death, it appeared pretty clear that he could not have suffered much physical pain. The crowd, however, appeared to think that the executioner had not performed his duty adroitly, for, upon Calcraft making his appearance to cut the body down at nine o'clock, he was greeted with a tremendous yell, to which, when he had concluded the operation, he responded by making a bow, which was the signal for an additional shout of execration.

III. A Phrenological Account of the Heads

Both casts seem to represent their respective head with a fair degree of accuracy.

Absolute size of the casts, heads, and brains. —The part of each cast above the eyes and external openings of the ears, representing, of course, the brain with its coverings,—skull, skin, and muscles, measures 170 cubic inches. The *shape* of the heads is so different that most observers who estimate by the eye will consider the one decidedly larger than the other; but this is incorrect. The difference between them is so trifling as not to be perceptible in measurement.

As the stucco generally expands a little in working, the casts are larger than the heads they represent. I therefore deduct a tenth of an inch from each of the three dimensions, – length, breadth, and height, as the least probable correction necessary for this source of error. This correction made, we obtain 160 cubic inches as the size of each head when alive.

The cast of _Barthelemy_ seems to indicate a rough texture of bone and skin, both being beyond the average thickness; at least half a tenth of an inch will require on this account to be deducted, which will leave 155 cubic inches as the nearest approximation to the size, with cranium and skin of average thickness, which it is possible to make from the cast.

The cast of _Buranelli_ seems to indicate a finer texture of bone, skin, and muscle than usual, and they were probably thinner than the average; but, as this is uncertain from the cast, I leave the size as stated above, _viz._, 160 inches.

The age of _Barthelemy_ is said to have been 32 years at death; and, from the appearance of the cast of _Buranelli_, he seems to have been a little younger. But, as a year or two make little difference in the size of the head at that age, we may for our present purpose call the age of both 30 years at the time they were executed.

The average size of the male head at 30 years of age, in this country, is 145 cubic inches; and the largest, excepting a few individuals, is 205; and the smallest, excluding idiots, 106 cubic inches. The absolute and relative or comparative size of the two heads will now be obvious, _viz._, – _Barthelemy_, 155; _Buranelli_, 160. The average male at 30 years of age has a head measuring 145: largest, 205, and smallest, 106. The former is therefore ten, and the latter fifteen cubic inches above the average, and both are far below the largest of their age and sex. Fully 10 per cent of male heads at 30 years are equal to, and nearly 30 per cent are larger in size than _Barthelemy_, whilst there are about 7 per cent equal to, and about 12 per cent larger than _Buranelli_.

The following table shows the absolute and relative development of each of the cerebral organs of the two heads, and, to show how far each resembles and differs from the mass of the community of males at age 30, the general average of all classes is given in column 3, the average of the superior class in column 4, and of the inferior class in column 5. All these averages are deduced from a great number of individual cases.

A short explanation of the numbers used to indicate the development of the organs will make the whole plain, especially to our new readers who may not be yet apprised of the exactitude with which we now commonly treat the principles of our science. When the numbers 120, 130, 140, &c., are used in reference to heads, crania, and brain, they show *size*, or *extent of development* of the propensities, faculties, and sentiments referred to. When the numbers are used in reference to the separate parts or organs, they indicate *extent of development* also, but not inches. Thus, *"Wit 125,"* means that *"Wit"* is just equal in development to the organ of *Wit* in the average male heads of 12 years of age. Again, *"Hope 135,"* shows that the organ is just equal to *Hope* in the average male head of 18 years. The development is ascertained by precise and careful measurement exclusively, and each number has its definite, invariable meaning, and indicates one degree of absolute *development*, whether applied to large organs, such as *"Cautiousness"* and *"Amativeness,"* or to small organs, such as *"Form,"* *"Weight,"* or *"Colour."*

Having obtained the absolute or positive degree of development of each of the organs, we thus obtain the natural power also, showing the capability, whilst the *relative* developments, that is, the differences between the positive degrees of development, shows not only the direction of the tendency, but the force or power of that tendency. If in a head of 140 cubic inches all the organs were in equal development, that number (140) would be used after the name of each organ to indicate its development and power or capability, which would be that of the average man of 21 years; and, the organs being equally developed, there would be no natural tendency in any direction. However, such a head is seldom, perhaps never, to be met with. As a general rule, the difference between the development of the least and the greatest organs in the same brain ranges from 5 to 15, and this difference gives but a very feeble tendency in any direction.

It will be observed that in *Barthelemy's* development the difference between the least and the greatest organs is 40, 45, and 50—a degree of difference which is fortunately not often to be met with. In some particulars (*Self-esteem, Firmness, Destructiveness,* and *Secretiveness*) he is a *very giant*, in others (*Wonder, Ideality, Wit,* &c.) he is a *tiny dwarf*. If we suppose for a moment that he was equal to the average mature man in the largest organs, then he would only equal the average boy of four, five, or six years in the least developed parts. The influence of this variety of development of the organs in the same brain must have been obvious to intelligent observers at all times, *stubborn, overbear-*

NAMES OF THE ORGANS	Barth-elemy	Bura-nelli	Males at 30 Years		
			Average	Superior	Inferior
1. Amativeness	155	140	155	145	170
2. Philoprogenitiveness	130	140	150	155	140
3. Concentrativeness	140	140	150	155	135
4. Adhesiveness	140	130	145	150	140
5. Combativeness	165	170	150	150	160
6. Destructiveness	175	165	150	150	160
7. Secretiveness	175	160	150	150	160
8. Acquisitiveness	170	155	150	155	160
9. Constructiveness	140	155	150	150	140
10. Self-esteem	180	180	155	155	145
11. Love of Approbation	150	140	145	145	135
12. Cautiousness	150	140	150	155	150
13. Benevolence	145	140	140	170	130
14. Veneration	160	140	145	170	135
15. Firmness	185	140	155	170	145
16. Conscientiousness	150	145	150	170	135
17. Hope	140	145	150	150	130
18. Wonder	135	145	150	160	130
19. Ideality	130	145	150	160	130
20. Wit	125	140	145	160	125
21. Imitation	130	145	150	160	130
22. Individuality	175	165	150	165	140
23. Form	175	165	150	160	140
24. Size	175	155	150	165	140
25. Weight	175	165	150	165	140
26. Colour	175	160	150	160	140
27. Locality	175	160	150	155	140
28. Number	175	160	150	155	140
29. Order	175	160	150	155	140
30. Eventuality	160	145	150	155	135
31. Time	160	150	150	155	130
32. Tune	165	150	150	155	130
33. Language	160	160	150	160	140
34. Comparison	140	160	145	170	130
35. Causality	140	155	145	170	130

ing, conceit, and *dogmatism, cunning, cruelty,* and *unreflecting coarseness,* would be constant traits of character. As a consistent character in his own way, *Barthelemy* would form quite a contrast to *Buranelli.* The training and circumstances in which he is placed exert an influence over every human being, but the power of such influences is very far from being equal on different organization. On such as *Barthelemy* the circumstances external to the man has the least, and on such as *Buranelli* nearly the greatest influence. The former would, as I have just stated, be proud and stubborn, cruel, cunning, coarse, and unreflective, *under every condition* calculated in any degree to bring out the features. *Buranelli* would, on the other hand, be proud or humble, constant or vacillating, kind or cruel, haughty or courteous, reverent or profane, *according to the circumstances of time and place* with which he was surrounded.

As may readily be observed from an inspection of the casts of the heads, the shape of *Barthelemy's* is that of a well-known type of idiot, ranging from a third to about half (50 to 80 cubic inches) the size of that of *Barthelemy.* There are two casts copied from Dr. Gall's collection in most of our museums, and living cases are to be seen in almost every hospital for the reception of idiots. *Buranelli* approaches very much more nearly the common type of European head, and many individuals of even inferior shape, when surrounded with favourable circumstances, pass through life in a creditable manner.

The list of organs adverted to in the preceding table differ slightly from both the number and type first described by Dr. Gall and later modified and expanded by Drs. Spurzheim and Combe. While I do not believe all the organs appearing in the chart have been established to any great degree of satisfaction (I think at least twenty have been conclusively established), I think it is well as a general rule to put down the size of each, in order to furnish facts for an ultimate judgment respecting all.

Barthelemy was unmarried. His organ of *Amativeness* was average; his love of offspring (*Philoprogenitiveness*) 20 *below* the average. *Buranelli* had been twice married and had lived with a third woman; his organ of *Amativeness* was 25 *above* the average.

Barthelemy showed enormous resolution. His organ of *Firmness* was 30 *above* the average. *Buranelli* showed very little; his organ of *Firmness* was 15 *below* the average.

Barthelemy's organ of *Self-Esteem* was 25 *above* the average; and that of *Vanity or Love of Approbation* rather above it; *Buranelli's* organ of *Self-Esteem* was 5 *below* it, and so was his organ of *Vanity*.

Barthelemy's organs of *Combativeness* and of *Destructiveness* were both much above average—15 and 15 *above* it; and so were those of *Buranelli*—20 and 15 *above* the average.

In *Barthelemy* the organ of *Cunning* or *Secretiveness* was very large—25 *above* the average; in Buranelli large—10 *above* it.

In *Barthelemy* the organ of *Acquisitiveness* was 20 *above* the average; in *Buranelli* only 5 *above* it.

In each culprit the organ of *Benevolence* was only *about the average*; in *Barthelemy* only 5 above it, and in *Buranelli* it was average.

In *Barthelemy* the organ of *Ideality*, that which gives taste and refinement, was 15 *below* the average; in *Buranelli* it was of *average* size.

In *Barthelemy* the organ giving rise to a love of justice was of but *average* size—not at all a match for his enormous *Destructiveness, Acquisitiveness, Cunning, Pride, Firmness*, &c.; and in *Buranelli* it was rather *below* average.

The *lower intellectual organs*, for observation, were large in *Barthelemy*; that of *Individuality*, 25, and of *Eventuality*, 10, both *above* the average; and in *Buranelli*, that of *Individuality* 15 *above* the average, though that of *Eventuality* was a little below average.

But in *Barthelemy* the higher organs of *Comparison* and *Causality* were each 5 *below* the average; in *Buranelli* the organ of *Causality* was good—10 *above* the average, and *Comparison* was a little—5, *above* the average.

The organ called *Wit*, whatever be its function, probably intellectual, was in *Barthelemy* 20 *below* the average; in *Buranelli* 5 *below* it.

In regard to what is called the organ of *Veneration*, it was 15 *above* the average in *Barthelemy*, and 5 *below* it in *Buranelli*. If it gives the sentiment of respect and veneration it does not direct this to any particular object— not more to God than to man. Many professed atheists have it large, as well as the higher intellectual faculties; and many of the most devout and most superstitious persons have it small. Dr. Gall was accused of atheism, and therefore dwelt much upon the direction of the action of this organ to the Deity.

Let every really *good* man learn humility from these casts, and be thankful that his head and brain are not such as were the heads and brains of *Barthelemy* and *Buranelli*.

SUGGESTIONS FOR FURTHER READING AND INQUIRY: PHRENOLOGY

"Origin of Craniology." *Mirror,* vol. 8 (1826), pp. 198–199.
A fine historical overview of the rise of phrenology in late eighteenth–century Europe.

"Attacks on Phrenology." *Mirror,* vol. 18 (1831), pp. 392–293.
Commentary on the various criticisms leveled against the claims of phrenologists.

"Phrenology: Detection of Character From the Skull." *Mirror,* vol. 23 (1834), pp. 20–31.
A fine synopsis of the *modus operandi* of phrenological examination.

"Phrenology: Combativeness." *Mirror,* vol. 28 (1836), p. 127.
A concise overview of one of the propensities Gall believed to be instrumental in predisposing one to acts of criminal violence.

"Phrenology: Its Place and Relations." G. D. Campbell. *North British Review,* vol. 17 (1852), pp. 41–70.
A very detailed overview of George Combe's classic phrenological treatise titled *The Constitution of Man in Relation to External Objects.*

"Phrenology in France." G. H. Lewes. *Blackwood's Edinburgh Magazine,* vol. 82 (1857), pp. 665–674.
An overview of the state of phrenological thought and practice in France at mid–century.

"Mr. George Combe and His Phrenology." Richard Simpson. *Rambler*, vol. 10 (1858), pp. 373-377.

An examination of the phrenological system of Scotsman George Combe.

"Phrenological Examinations by Professor Bumps, B.D." *Harper's New Monthly Magazine*, vol. 21 (1860), p. 141.

A series of humorous drawings that illustrate the nonsense of the doctrine of phrenology and its practitioners.

"Phrenological Anecdotes." *Harper's New Monthly Magazine*, vol. 25 (1862), p. 860.

A series of humorous short notes which illustrate the absurdity of judging character based upon phrenological considerations.

"Phrenology." *Duffy's Hibernian Magazine*, vol. 3 (1863), pp. 100-106.

A scathing indictment of phrenology as a means of discerning character, temperament, and behavioral predispositions.

"George Combe." *American Phrenological Journal and Life Illustrated*, vol. 41 (1865), p. 175.

A third biographical sketch of the Scottish phrenologist Combe who, along with Gall and Spurzheim, constitute the triumvirate of phrenology.

"Francis Joseph Gall." *American Phrenological Journal and Life Illustrated*, vol. 42 (1865), p. 171.

A short biographical sketch of the founder of phrenology.

"Henry Wirz, the Andersonville Fiend." *American Phrenological Journal and Life Illustrated*, vol. 43 (1865), pp. 120-121.

A fine exemplar of the application of phrenological principles to the analysis of the character and behavioral predilections of the notorious commandant of the Confederate prison at Andersonville, Georgia.

"John Gaspar Spurzheim." *American Phrenological Journal and Life Illustrated,* vol. 44 (1866), p. 9.

A short biographical sketch of Gall's colleague, the second of the three great names associated with the theory and practice of phrenology.

"Antoine Probst: Murderer of the Deering Family." *American Phrenological Journal and Life Illustrated,* vol. 44 (1866), p. 13.

An illustrative study in the application of phrenological principles to the analysis of the character and disposition of a mass murderer.

"Phrenology." *Round Table,* vol. 5 (1867), pp. 294–297.

Another fine overview of the tenets of phrenology.

"Phrenology: Its Principles and Proofs." *American Phrenological Journal and Life Illustrated,* vol. 55 (1872), pp. 18–19.

A synopsis of the updated revisions made to the phrenological system of Gall and Spuzheim, wherein seven basic principles and three temperaments are recognized.

"A Handsome Murderer." *American Phrenological Journal and Life Illustrated,* vol. 58 (1874), pp. 398–399.

Another interesting exemplar of the application of phrenological principles to the analysis of a murderer.

"Signs of Character: Our New Dictionary of Phrenology and Physiognomy." *American Phrenological Journal and Life Illustrated.*

In 19 parts. Vol. 41 (February 1865), pp. 44–46; vol. 41 (March 1865), pp. 76–77; vol. 41 (April 1865), pp. 108–110; vol. 41 (May 1865), pp. 140–142; vol. 41 (June 1865), pp. 173–175; vol. 42 (July 1865), pp. 20–21; vol. 42 (August 1865), pp. 40–41; vol. 42 (September, 1865), pp. 72–74; vol. 42 (October, 1865), pp. 104–105; vol. 42 (November 1865), pp. 136–137; vol. 42 (December 1865), pp.

172-173; vol. 43 (January 1866), pp. 9-11; vol. 43 (February 1866), pp. 44-45; vol. 43 (March 1866), pp. 79-81; vol. 43 (April 1866), pp. 109-110; vol. 43 (May1866), pp. 141-142; vol. 43 (June 1866), pp. 172-173; vol. 44 (July 1866), pp. 8-10; and vol. 44 (August 1866), pp. 40-42. An outstanding collection of articles arranged in alphabetical order treating upon the many and varied aspects relating to the philosophies of phrenology and physiognomy. The collection of articles constituting the dictionary is richly supplemented with numerous fine illustrations.

THE ITALIAN SCHOOL OF
CRIMINAL
ANTHROPOLOGY

CRIMINAL ANTHROPOLOGY IN ITALY

BY

HELEN ZIMMERN

POPULAR SCIENCE MONTHLY

VOL. 52 (APRIL 1898), PP. 743-760

"Enemy" ye shall say, but not "wicked one," "diseased one" ye shall say, but not "wretch," "fool" ye
shall say, but not "sinner."

F. Nietzsche

If we were asked to name in what particular Italy stands
to-day quite head and shoulders above her fellows, we
should unhesitatingly say in the science of criminal
anthropology. This is an essentially Italian study, whose origin we
discover as early as 1320, when the King of the Two Sicilies
decreed that no one should be permitted to practice medicine who
had not studied anatomy for at least one year. After this, in the
fourteenth century, we find men who devoted themselves to the
study of skulls, thus laying the basis of the science of craniology.
It was Italians, therefore, who initiated this science, and to Italy
has been reserved the proud place of bringing it to its high
development in the nineteenth century, even though the discov-
eries of Darwin, which gave it a fresh impetus, date from England.
Beyond question the peninsula is at the head and front of all studies
connected with criminal anthropology, and not of criminal
anthropology only, but of all cognate sciences connected with
crime and the criminal.

To the Italians belongs the merit of reviving the study of a
question with which philosophy, law, and medicine have always
been occupied. It has been well remarked that whenever philosophical studies have free expansion, that whenever the desire to
safeguard society, the spirit of toleration, the methods of amelio-
rating the fate of the guilty, have been studied by thinkers, their
conceptions have eventually conquered public opinion. It is to the
glory of Italy, the land where Roman law, the foundation of
modern law, was born, that it has again put into the crucible this
problem of criminality, and that it has proceeded to the study of

this problem by the only truly scientific method—namely, that of studying the psychology of criminals and their pathological abnormalities. It will be its distinction to have declared against illusory enthusiasms, and to have founded a science which will contribute to the more efficacious protection of society. The recognized chief of this Italian School is Prof. Cesare Lombroso, of Turin, who has illustrated his theories by a number of remarkably able and interesting books. Until quite recently, to the world at large, the criminal figured is of the Bill Sykes type—and who, reading *Oliver Twist*, has not shrunk with horror on perusing the intimate drama of the ruffian's mind after the brutal murder of the faithful Nancy? These things move us as the highest efforts of Dicken's imagination. Bill Sykes was written in prescientific days. It is instructive to turn from him, and the class of melodramatic ruffians of whom he is but an example, to the criminals dispassionately laid bare in mental, moral, and physical dissection by Lombroso and his fellow-workers. Certainly no such type as Bill Sykes, a projected image of the novelist's brain, coinciding with a highly strung nervous system, is to be found in the gallery of habitual malefactors presented to us in the *Uomo Delinquente* and other books. Habitual malefactors, according to Italian students, are a class apart from other men, a distinct species of "genus *Homo sapiens*," must be judged by special standards, and must by no means be informed with the feelings of normal men. Herein consists the fundamental basis of the new science of criminal anthropology—a science which bids fair, in spite of conservative and clerical opposition and even of ignorant ridicule, to modify profoundly our present manner of considering and treating these enemies and pests of society.

"Criminal anthropology," says Signor Sergi, one of the ablest exponents of the new system, "studies the delinquent in his natural place—that is to say, in the field of biology and pathology. But it does not, for that reason, put him outside the society in which his criminal manifestations occur, for it considers human society as a natural biological fact, outside of which man does not and can not live. As normal anthropology, like other biological sciences, studies and observes the individual in his natural *milieu*, and finds that this *milieu* is double, physical and organic, and under this double aspect sees him develop and act, so criminal anthropology does the same with the very limited and specialized aim of discovering the nature and origin of the phenomenon of crime.

Every phenomenon, however, remains inexplicable if it be examined alone; the explanation is easier if it be studied in the complex of phenomena developed in the double physical and social _milieu_ of which we have spoken."

Words such as these, where we find embryology, physiology, anatomy, chemistry, and statistics, invoked as aids to the origin of crime, place us at the antipodes of ancient philosophies; yet Lombroso and his school are in reality acting on the old-world notion embodied by Horace in his _"mens sana in corpore sano."_ The delinquent, they argue, acts abnormally. Acts being the visible results of functions performed by the brain and reflective nervous system, it follows that these functions are abnormal. The functions being abnormal, the organs which perform them must be either abnormal or troubled in their action by the habitual or accidental interference of disturbing causes, for no normal organ acting under normal conditions can perform abnormal functions. The founders of this new school, therefore, dedicate themselves first of all to the study of the skull, brain, and nervous system of the criminals; then make careful observations not only on other parts of the skeleton but on the living body; the height, length, and proportion of the members, the total or partial development of each part; the weight of the body, its muscular development, the deeper-seated organs, such as the heart, liver, kidneys, intestines; the various functions which may directly or indirectly affect those of the brain, such as the circulation of the blood, digestion, and the disturbances which show themselves there, and in consequence of the general state of the organism as regards the balance of the vital functions, sleep, sexual manifestations, normal or abnormal muscular force, and other factors besides. Everything, indeed which concerns the morphology of the criminal is passed through the sieve of the severest scrutiny. This scrutiny reveals, as might be expected, various irregularities. The skull, for instance, presents anomalies of shape and size, being in a large percentage of cases abnormally small; anomalies indicative of regression and of arrested development; anomalies in the position, shape, and closing of the sutures, "the doorways of the head" being invariably closed too early. Morphological irregularities are also found in the bones of the face, notably in those of the nose and lower jaw. The brain itself, say the investigators, shows unmistakable signs of degraded form, in the number and distribution of the cerebral convolutions, in the entire atrophy of some parts, in the extraordinary development of others. The shape and structure of the skull and brain, says Lombroso, connect criminals very closely with primitive man, and even with his animal ancestors. Criminals must be regarded either as forms belated in the race of development, or as physical and therefore also moral degradations—unavoidable, regrettable products of our civilization. In either case they form a distinct species, in need of scientific investigation.

The action of the brain is, however, not only modified by its form and development, but also, in a very large number of cases, by pathological occurrences. Traces of old wounds, "some head-blow not heeded in his youth," said Sir Kay of King Arthur's self-hemorrhages, affections of the investing membrane and of the blood-vessels are seldom wanting. In other words, the organ that controls and originates actions is in a morbid state. Further, the slight irregularities constantly verified in the branching of the blood-vessels in the heart, liver, and other viscera can not but conspire, by the abnormal functionings they occasion, toward the production of physiologically irregular organisms.

Intimately connected with the physical conditions of the criminal are his psychic peculiarities. These consist chiefly in great instability of character, coupled with overwhelming development of some passion and the atrophy of some others. The criminal acts from impulse, although he often displays, as madmen do, a low cunning in finding means to carry out his impulse. He is intensely vain, priding himself on the number of crimes he has committed. He is further devoid of all remorse, fond of boasting of his evil deeds and of describing them in detail. Thus Lombroso gives the reproduction of a photograph, in which three murderers who had assassinated one of their number caused themselves to be represented in the very act of committing their deadly deed, a photograph taken for the benefit of their less fortunate associates.

This inordinate vanity is often in itself the primary cause of terrible crimes, especially in young men who have just attained puberty, an age observed to be especially fruitful in crimes of violence. The critical character of this period, even in well-balanced minds, is abundantly known; little wonder, then, if it prove fatal to those whose constitutions urge them to extremes. It is noticed also that the criminal needs to lead a life full of noise. The necessity of orgies entailed by the irregularities of his feelings is often the moving cause of some act of violence, such as robbery and assassination, calculated to procure the means of indulgence.

His affections, too, are abnormal: he will assassinate father and mother, and yet be capable of making sacrifices for some companion in time of illness. This trait, however, occurs more often among women than men. We used to believe there was a species of honor among thieves, but Lombroso asserts that it is rare to find any consistent attempt to shield each other; on the contrary, the almost physical need they feel of talking incessantly renders them specially inclined to mutual betrayal. The criminal is fond of tattooing himself, and so distinctive a mark of criminal tendencies is this held in Italy that tattooed recruits are looked on as likely to make bad soldiers; and a private once spoke to Lombroso of tattooing as "convict habits." He presents, too, an extraordinary insensibility to pain, tattooing himself in places which even the Indians spare, and receiving or inflicting on himself the most terrible wounds without murmur.

He has a language of his own, employed even in cases where he would run no risk from using ordinary speech, and this still further isolates him from the rest of mankind. He has a writing of his own, too, made up of hieroglyphics and rough pictures.

Such briefly is the Frankenstein, which the modern science of criminal anthropology evokes; an unbalanced being, a pathological subject, whose illness takes a form which, hurtful to society, is defined as crime. For the facts collected by Lombroso place beyond all doubt the intimate connection between crime and mental derangements which has so long been suspected to exist. Madmen and criminals belong to the same family; not in the sense of the vulgar and unthinking expression that all criminals are mad, though everyday experience in the police courts puts it beyond doubt that many are actually deranged, but in the sense that both classes are in a similar pathological state, which manifests itself on the one hand in lunacy, on the other in crime. This position is rendered still stronger by the revelations of genealogical statistics, which reveal the heredity through long generations of criminal tendencies, as they do of insanity, and alternations of criminals and madmen, in the same or successive generations.

Lombroso divides criminals into two great classes, the original or born delinquent, and the fortuitous offender, a man who becomes criminal through outward influences.

The first, the synthesis of every degeneration, the outcome of all biological deterioration, commits crimes against society by virtue of a morbid process passing from one generation to another, derived from cerebral and other physiological conditions. In him the impulse of passion is not sullen or isolated, but associates itself almost always with reflection. The second, on the contrary, the criminal of passion and impetus, acts at a given moment in consequence of an overwhelming stimulus, say a sudden access of jealousy. The two classes frequently merge into each other, for the mere fact that a man, suddenly, without reflection, by a reflex act, as it were, stabs his offender or his unfaithful wife, proves that he is not normal. The want of reflection constitutes an extenuating circumstance before judge or jury, but before pathological psychology, says Signor Sergi, "it constitutes an accusation."

The importance of the distinction is seen in the views taken on criminal jurisprudence by Lombroso and his school. It is generally said that to act logically in face of these views we should have to make extensive use of capital punishment. The most hasty perusal of Lombroso's book will show that this is not his view of the case. He lays immense stress on prevention, for even the morbid process may, he asserts, be modified in the very young, just as a disease, taken in time, may be cured, but, when neglected, becomes chronic.

He examines carefully the means adopted in various countries for refining the minds of children, and speaks warmly of English ragged schools. Juvenile refinement, strict but judicious control, education in the highest sense of the word – these must be, he argues, the primary object of every nation which aims at decreasing its criminality. He also advocates an association between various nations for the hunting of criminals, and for making such observations on their lives and habits as shall lead to their easier classification. In reformatories he has small belief; statistics shout that they in no way decrease the percentage of recidivists; the fact of recidivism shows the habitual criminal, and here no punishment will suffice. The man must be treated as though afflicted with a serious illness and removed from society, for which, however, he may and should be made to work. He insists that these questions are of vital importance to every nation, and asserts repeatedly that teachers in ragged schools and founders of polytechnics are patriots and philanthropists in the highest sense of the words, because they are helping to stamp out crime more than all the long-term sentences in the world. Crime is at once a biological and social phenomenon. The criminal is a microbe which only flourishes on suitable soil. Without doubt it is the environment which makes the criminal, but, like the cultivation medium, without the microbe it is powerless to germinate the crime. To use Professor Ferri's expression, up to recent times the criminal has been regarded as a sort of algebraic formula; the punishment has been proportioned not to the criminal but to the crime. Anthropologists are teaching us to strive after scientific justice. Time and events have brought into clear relief the inadequacy of legal maxims, founded on antiquated and unscientific conceptions, and thus modern Italians show us that not the nature of the crime but the dangerousness of the offender constitutes the only reasonable legal criterion to guide the inevitable social reaction against the criminal. This position is the legitimate outcome of the scientific study of the criminal. And where the man of science has led the way the man of law must follow.

Such, in brief and somewhat in the rough, are the conclusions of Italian criminal anthropology, which we have given at some length, as the subject is too vast as well as too new to be clearly comprehensible in a few words. In the autumn of 1896 an International Congress of Criminal Anthropologists was held at Geneva, and on this occasion the Italian school triumphed as never before over all adversaries and schismatics, and especially over their French colleagues, who have carried their antagonism to Italy and things Italian even to the serene fields of science. The French objections were beaten down by a very hailstorm of facts, so carefully collated, so industriously collected, that opposition was perforce silenced. In the front ranks of the combatants, indeed, leading the attack, was that eminent criminal sociologist, Enrico Ferri, whose legal vocations have not hindered him from continuing his favorite studies, though he is no less valiant as a lawyer than as a scientist. Indeed, he holds that the two studies ought to go hand in hand. All lawyers, he affirms, should dedicate themselves to the study of criminal anthropology if they would go to the fountain-head of human responsibility; all judges should be inspired by this doctrine, ere blindly punishing a culprit on the faith of a code not always founded on direct observation of the environment or of the individual. "It is not true that with Lombroso's theories all prison doors would be broken down and respectable humanity given over to the mercy of delinquents, as our opponents say. And were the first part of this strange paradox to be verified – _i.e._, that which demands that in order to be logical all prison doors be opened — there would open also those of the lunatic asylums in order to permit the entry of the men ejected from the prisons, individuals whose mental and physical constitutions pushed them into crime." It was just this theory of the *born* criminal, which Lombroso was the first irrefutably to prove, and whose effects must shortly be felt in criminal legislation, that carried off the most clamorous victory at Geneva.

Cesare Lombroso, who is a Hebrew by birth, was born at Turin in 1836. As a mere lad he loved to write, and composed, with the same facility and rapidity that distinguishes him to this day, novels, poems, tragedies, treatises on archaeological, physiological, and already on sociological subjects, those dating from his student days being actually published, so much talent did they show. Medicine was the study to which he devoted himself, and his first independent researches were directed to examining into the causes that produce the idiotism and the pellagra that exist, unfortunately, so largely in Lombardy and Liguria. His treatise on this theme attracted the attention of no less person than Professor Virchow. After fighting for the independence of Italy in 1859, he was appointed professor of psychiatry at Pavia, where he founded a psychiatric museum. From Pavia he passed to Pesaro, as director of the Government madhouse, and thence to Turin as professor of forensic medicine, a position he still retains. It was in his native Turin that he began those original studies destined to make his name famous over all the globe. Endowed by nature with a strong intelligence, a robust will, and a keen intellectual curiosity, he was indifferent to the incredulous smile, the sarcasms, that greeted his first efforts at solving problems hitherto held insoluble. Very bitter, very hard were his struggles – how hard only those can appreciate who have talked with Lombroso in intimacy and have noted the pained scorn with which he speaks of his adversaries – adversaries some of whom are not silenced to this hour. But his science, his studies conquered, which if not always complete yet are always serious, wherefore criminal anthropology, a mere infant some thirty years ago, may be to-day be said to be adult; a raw empire but a while ago, to-day a science, young if you will, but vital and destined to overturn the facile, fantastic monuments erected by so many penalists. The work with which Lombroso will go down to posterity is a huge book, huge in every sense of the word, in which criminal man is studied on a scientific basis. We refer to the *Uomo Delinquente*, of which its author has published most recently a new, revised, and enlarged edition, wrestling with new facts, new observations, and new deductions. This edition is limited to one hundred copies, perhaps to allow its prolific author soon to issue another, enriched with yet more facts, yet more acute deductions.

It is dedicated to Max Nordau, the author of the noted book, _Degeneration_, who had in his turn dedicated his work to his master, Cesare Lombroso. The dedication reads thus: "To you I have wished to dedicate this volume with which I close my studies on human degeneration, as the most sincere friend I have found in the sad course of my scientific life, and as to the one who has wrested fecund fruits from the new doctrines I have attempted to introduce into the scientific world." Needless to say that Lombroso is the very first person to admit that in the almost virgin field of criminal anthropology there is still much to do, and that Science has not yet spoken her last word; but it is his magic wand that has indicated the horizon and has swept over vast new areas, often with lightening rapidity and intuition. Thus the base of the new edifice was laid, and the rest of the new monument rose up rapidly around it, notwithstanding its occasional faultiness, pointed out eagerly by adverse scientists, criticisms that could not shake down the edifice, for its base was too solid and strong. Gradually a few apostles of the new science gathered around Lombroso, and although Morselli, one of the most acute and cultured observers, after a time severed himself from the group and joined the French schismatics, nevertheless the little compact mass moved from success to success, from triumph to triumph, up to the late ultimate triumph at Geneva.

Another of Lombroso's books which aroused much discussion and which may almost be said to have founded yet another school, if we may designate the group devoted to the study of another branch of anthropology, was _Genio o Follia_, which largely helped to make its author's name known even outside of strictly scientific circles. This work enchanted all thinkers, psychiatrists, doctors, indeed, all men who dedicate themselves to the search for signs of madness in the lives and works of eminent authors and artists. For Lombroso had striven in this book to prove scientifically how closely genius and madness are allied. As was the case with Criminal Man, so here too the master's disciples strayed from the paths laid down by the pioneer, exaggerated his conclusions and carried them to absurd excesses. Lombroso had at last to raise his voice against the extravagances into which he was dragged. Besides various absurdities, there were published some careful serious studies having for their themes the lives of Napoleon I, Leopardi, Ugo Foscolo, and Byron, in which it was made to appear that these men were all victims of heredity, and neither their virtues nor their vices were their own – studies of interest, academically considered, but of no tangible utility, and which did not add or detract one iota from the merits or demerits of their subjects. Against this method of dealing with men of genius as pathological subjects Mantegazza recently very rightly upraised his voice in the name of art, tradition, and history.

Space does not permit of our naming Lombroso's varied and voluminous writings, whose enumeration any biographical dictionary can supply. *La Donna Delinquente* (The Criminal Woman), written in collaboration with G. Ferrero, one of the most promising of the younger criminal anthropologists, of which an incomplete and inadequate translation appeared in England, aroused a storm of discussion on its publication four years ago, and was especially attacked by the adherents of the old methods. He has since published The Anarchists, in which he also takes unusual views with regard to these latter-day society pests – pests for whom society itself, as nowadays conditioned, he holds as alone responsible – and Crime as a Society Function, which has aroused the fury of the clerical and moderate factions in Italy. Chips from the workshop of his extraordinarily prolific brain, ever evolving new ideas, new points of view, he scatters in the many articles he loves to write for English and American periodicals; but his most important scientific communications he reserves for the *Archivio di Psichiatria*, which he edits together with Ferri and Garofolo. His work is by no means perfect: he is apt to jump too rapidly at conclusions, to accept data too lightly; thus he was led at the beginning to overestimate the atavistic element in the criminal, and at a later date he has pressed too strongly the epileptic affinities of crime. Still, when all is said and done, his work is undoubtedly epoch-making, and has opened up valuable new lines of investigation and suggested others.

We said that Lombroso's first studies were directed to the pellagra, that strange and terrible disease which annually mows down such a vast number of victims in the fair land of northern Italy, and which is a luminous proof of the grave financial conditions of the laborers in some of the most beautiful and richest regions of the world. Concerning this terrible illness, which densely populates Italian madhouses, all students of natural science have long been gravely occupied. For the terrible increase in lunacy noted by Italian statistics in the last five years the pellagra is largely responsible. Psychiatry, which has abandoned the old methods in Italy, is no longer a jailer employing the methods of an inquisitor, but science that seeks for ultimate causes and remedies, and, conjoined to economic and political science, endeavors to restore to society a large contingent of forces which would otherwise be destroyed by disease. Especially active in this department is Enrico Morselli, at present director of the hospital attached to the Genoa University. Morselli is in the flower of his life, and much may be still hoped from him. Like Lombroso, he is small of stature and square built; like Lombroso, he has piercing eyes that shine forth acutely from behind glasses that he always wears. Psychologist, anthropologist, psychiatrist, philosopher, and literary man, Morselli has right to all these titles, and in each branch he is noteworthy. He was born in Modena in 1832, and studied at his native university, carrying off high honors. As a mere student he attracted attention by disputing the conclusions of a noted celebrity on some anthropological points, proving himself right. For a while he was the assistant of Mantegazza in arranging his Anthropological Museum, one of the finest as well as one of the most important in Europe. When only twenty-eight he was called to preside over the Turin lunatic asylum, and soon distinguished himself by his profound knowledge of everything connected with the study and treatment of the demented. Besides attending to his profession he found time to write a number of works dealing with normal and abnormal mental maladies, whose mere enumeration would fill pages, some of which, like his work on Suicide, have been translated into English. Morselli's latest work was a reply to Brunetiere's assertions regarding "the bankruptcy of science," demonstrating that here was a case in which the wish was father to the thought, and for which no real foundation existed.

Paolo Mantegazza has been dealt with at length in these pages, and we need not go over the ground again. What is needful to say is, however, that he has been left behind in the rapid onward tramp of his younger colleagues. Mantegazza is perhaps entitled to lay claim to the name he loves to sport, that of the father of Italian anthropology; but according to the more precise views of our day, he can hardly be regarded as a real scientist. As is often the case, the sons have outstripped the father, who now combats the views of his legitimate offspring. A reproach cast at Mantegazza, it would seem not without reason, is that he too closely follows Moliere's precept, "*Je prends mon bien ou je le trouve*," and that he has passed off as his own the conclusions and the work of German scientific men. Another reproach that is certainly well founded is his manifest delight in handling obscene themes, and handling them not in the calm, scientific spirit that removes from them a real obscene character, but treating the details with a gusto that reveals how these prurient matters rather delight than disgust him, and what is worse, these works are written in popular language, frankly appealing to a popular rather than a scientific audience. To this class belong all his works on Love, on Women, on the Art of taking a Wife, of Being a Husband, etc. It may safely be asserted that his fame is steadily declining, and that his want of perseverance and observation is itself to blame for this. By nature Mantegazza was endowed with a fine and versatile intelligence, but he has lowered it in the search after cash and easy success. This handsome old man, with the face and smile of a satyr, is a familiar figure on the streets of Florence.

The number of men who are strict anthropologists without being sociologists is extraordinarily great in contemporary Italy, and there is none of them who has not done good and original work. Limits of space oblige us perforce to pass them by, in order to speak of yet others of the new school created by Lombroso's theories, and who take rank in the files of criminal anthropology, a science far more interesting to the general reader than that which deals with biology pure and simple. To this section in the first rank belong the alienists, besides a large number of lawyers, judges, and journalists. The highest position among them belongs indubitably to Enrico Ferri. His verdict, like that of Cesare Lombroso, is constantly appealed to in complicated criminal cases where the sanity or the natural proclivity to crime of the person is in question. A man of really unusual physical beauty is Enrico Ferri, as well as of charm of manner and of eloquence which, when stirred to a theme dear to his heart, carries all before it. Enrico Ferri was born in 1856, in the neighborhood of Mantua, a city whose very name in Austrian days was synonymous with cruel despotism, for this and Spielburg were the favorite fortresses of the German persecutors. At a tender age he lost his father, and his mother, left in straitened circumstances, had a hard struggle to give her only child an adequate education. Already at the university Ferri distinguished himself, publishing a thesis which dealt with criminal law. When Lombroso published his great work on Criminal Man, Ferri was at once attracted by its scientific nature and sought to become acquainted with its author. Since then they have been fast friends as well as co-workers. In 1881 he was called to fill the chair of penal law at the University of Bologna. His opening discourse dealt with the theme which was to prove the first draft of his great work, _Criminal Sociology_, a work which has been translated into many European tongues. The lecture was entitled "New Horizons in Penal Law." He says: "It was in this inaugural discourse that I affirmed the existence of the positivist school of criminal law and assigned to it these two fundamental rules: 1. While the classical schools of criminal law have always studied the crime and neglected the criminal, the object of the positivist school was, in the first place, to study the criminal, so that, instead of the crime being regarded merely as a juridical fact, it must be studied with the aid of biology, of psychology, and of criminal statistics as a natural and social fact, transforming the old criminal law into a criminal sociology. 2. While the classical schools, since Beccaria and Howard, have fulfilled the historic mission of decreasing the punishments, as the reaction from the severity of the mediaeval laws, the object of the positivist school is to decrease the offenses by investigating their natural and social causes in order to apply social remedies more efficacious and more humane than the penal counteraction, always slow in its effects, especially in its cellular system, which I have called one of the aberrations of the nineteenth century."

Ferri has occupied himself less with the instinctive than with the occasional criminal, and his clear and philosophic spirit has placed him at the head of criminal sociologists. Elected to Parliament even before the age of thirty, previous to which he could not take his place, according to Italian law, he began an avowed liberal, but soon passed over to the ranks of scientific socialists, whose acknowledged leader he has since become. He also holds the post of professor of penal law at the Roman University. But his home is on the vine and olive-clad shores of Etruscan Fiesole, within a short walk of Florence. Of his great work on Homicide we have treated at length in these pages. Though in some points he has grown to differ from him, Ferri continues to venerate his master Lombroso, and with rare eloquence defends his theories from attacks at moments when the less eloquent scientist seems silenced by the arguments of his adversaries. It was due to his energy, conjoined to the initiative of Lombroso, that the first International Congress of Criminal Anthropologists was held in Rome in 1885, which constituted the installation of international criminal anthropology in sight of the European public. The second was held at Paris in 1889. It was there that the scientific misunderstanding arose, which was still more openly affirmed at the third congress held at Brussels in 1892, but was finally and conclusively beaten down at Geneva at the fourth congress in 1896; a result in a large measure due to Ferri's fascinating, all-persuading eloquence. In a letter written to me he has stated the whole matter so clearly that I can not do better than reproduce the same: "As you know, the positive school of criminal studies was consolidated in Italy by the contemporaneous publication in 1878 of the second volume of the *Uomo Delinquente*, of my volume on the imputableness and Negation of Free Will, and of the pamphlet of Garofolo on the Positive Criterion of Penalty. In these first affirmations there naturally preponderated the conclusions of Lombroso, which gave and left on the public the impression that the new school only studied the criminal from his organic side as a biological monstrosity. Yet, in 1880, I had published my studies on Criminals in France from 1826 to 1878, in which I expounded the natural factors of the three orders of crime – anthropological, physical, and social – laying stress on the social causes that conduce to crime. As a reaction from the aforementioned impression in Italy, Turati, Colajannie, and Battaglia published in 1882 to 1884 pamphlets and volumes maintaining that crime is an exclusively social phenomenon. I replied to Turati—Crime and the Social Question—with the volumes on Socialism and Criminality (1883), now out of print, where I combated: 1. Aristocratic and romantic socialism while recognizing the fundamental truths of scientific socialism. 2. The unilateral theory that crime is the product *only* of social factors, and that, therefore, with time it must certainly disappear. Continuing to maintain these two propositions, even after my avowed adhesion to scientific socialism, it has come about that in Italy this unilateral thesis has gradually become abandoned even by socialists. On the other hand, this thesis was taken up again in 1885 at the congress in Rome, and above all in 1889 at Paris, and in 1892 at Brussels by the French anthropological criminal socialists—Lacassagne, Tarde, Topinard, Coree, etc.—who succeeded in spreading the belief that there exists a French criminal anthropological school founded on the theory that the criminal is an exclusively social phenomenon – a thesis that had, for a matter of fact, already been sustained in Italy by the socialists. It is thus that was circulated among the international public, who can not read Italian publications unless they are translated, the impression that opposing the Italian school there was a French school; the former maintaining the exclusively biological origin of the criminal, while the latter regarded his genesis as exclusively social. The congress at Geneva has cleared up this misunderstanding, which has lasted too long. Crime is a phenomenon whose origin is both biological and social. This is the final conclusion which the Italian school has proclaimed since the beginning of its existence."

It is noteworthy and also significant that almost all thoughtful Italians who have dedicated themselves to the studies of anthropology in general and criminal anthropology in particular are socialists in politics. Assiduous, dispassionate observation of mankind would seem to have brought them to this conclusion. A leader in the Italian Parliament in this sense, as well as a gifted criminal anthropologist, is Napoleone Colajanni, by original profession a doctor, but now too absorbed in his political duties to practice. Colajanni is by birth a Sicilian, and has much of the quick, fiery temperament of these islanders, in whose veins the blood courses hotly. A facile orator, his speeches always command attention in Parliament, while his rigid, incorruptible honesty makes him esteemed in a _milieu_ of unscrupulous politicians and wire-pullers. As both a philanthropist and as a politician, he was early attracted to study the problems of misery and crime, whence resulted his great work on Criminal Sociology. Like Ferri and all the other thoughtful students of the criminal, he has seen the direct bearing on criminality of what he himself well calls "social hygiene." He points out how we may neglect the problems of social organization, but must do so at our peril. In many respects he is opposed to Lombroso. He holds, for example, that Lombroso has too much accentuated the atavistic element in the criminal He agrees with those who deem that of a great number of modern habitual criminals it may be said that they have the misfortune to live in an age when their merits are not appreciated. Had they lived in the world a sufficient number of generations ago, the strongest of them might have been chiefs of a tribe. As Colajanni has said: "How many of Homer's heroes would to-day be in convict prisons or at all events despised as unjust and violent!" He has strenuously combated Lombroso's indiscriminate method of collecting facts, and compares it to Charles IX's famous order on St. Bartholomew's Eve: "Kill them all! God will know his own."

And now it is time we should speak of Garofolo, the Neapolitan lawyer who, accepting generally the conclusions reached by Lombroso and Ferri, has become the most distinguished jurist of the moment, the pioneer of the reform of law through the method of natural science. His *Criminology* is marked by luminous suggestions of wise reform. Like Morselli, Garofolo does not blindly follow where his compeers lead. His latest volume, entitled Socialistic Superstitions, has excited much wrath and astonishment in socialistic and anthropological camps, and was severely combated, especially by Ferri, who wrote a pamphlet on purpose to confute the publication. R. Garofolo was born in Naples, in 1852, of an old patrician family, hence perhaps by atavism he is debarred from being a socialist. He holds the position of professor of law and penal procedure in his native city, and was intrusted by the Government in 1892 to draw up a scheme for the revision of the penal code. Garofolo has occupied himself chiefly, nay, entirely with the legal side of criminal anthropology, and his great work *Criminology* deals with the means of repressing crime quite as much as with its nature and causes. He also studied the question of what reparation is due victims of crime. His only flight into sociology has concerned his attack on socialism, in whose curative Utopia he does not believe.

Among the latest contributors to this fascinating science the highest places belong to three young men: Scipio Sighele, Guglielmo Ferrero, and A.G. Bianchi. All three are journalists, all three distinguished by the same qualities of keen observation, of more than ordinary cultivation, with sometimes a tendency to write a little hastily and to jump to conclusions too rapidly. This reproof especially concerns Sighele, who has allowed himself to judge and write of matters English and American of which he has but the most superficial and second-hand knowledge. Here the newspaper writer has done wrong to the scientist. Sighele made his name with an admirable book entitled *The Criminal Crowd,* which a French writer has thought to fit to appropriate in outline and almost entirely in substance, obtaining for it the honor of translation into English, while the real author has been left out in the cold. Able, too, is _The Criminal Couple_. A paradoxical pamphlet directed against parliamentary government, and revealing the failure of a system on which the hopes of Europe were once based as the sheet anchor of liberty, excited some attention on its appearance in 1895, and was dealt with at length in _Blackwood's Magazine_. His last work, on _Individual Morality as Opposed to Public Morality_, inspired by the doubtful morality of Signor Crispi's government, also aroused discussion, especially among Crispi's adherents, who looked on the book as a bit of special pleading in favor of their master's dubious political proceedings.

Guglielmo Ferrero is a Piedmontese, and belongs to an old aristocratic family of Turin. Although his name is already well known in scientific circles, he is still little more than a youth. Together with Lombroso, he wrote the _Criminal Woman,_ spoken of at length in these pages, and which at once brought him to the front, as all the world knew that it was he who collated and collected the facts therein contained. His first independent work was the most remarkable one dealing with Symbols, of which we have also spoken before. His latest publication deals with Crispi, whose personality he subjected to a scientific analysis qualifying him as a born madman. Ferrero, too, is a convinced socialist, and on this account was arrested during the reign of terror that prevailed in the course of the last months of Crispi's dictatorship. He was ordered to leave Italy, and profiting by this enforced exile, he visited Germany and learned the language and the condition of anthropological studies in that land. He has but recently returned. His magazine articles are always able, and marked by a high and independent tone.

A.G. Bianchi, a Milanese by birth, is also young. Not rich, like Ferrero, he had to make his own way, and entered into journalism as a means to obtain daily bread. He began life as a railway official, writing at the same time reviews of new books, Italian and foreign. Together with a colleague he founded a paper called _La Cronica Rossa_, and it was in these pages that he began to occupy himself with scientific literature, and to prove himself an enthusiastic follower of Lombroso. He entered the best Italian newspaper, _Corriere della Sera_, as its legal editor, and thus became even more enamored of criminal anthropology. Intelligent, industrious, studious, he dedicated himself to the new science with ardor, and in a short time became allied to Lombroso and

Morselli, who both applauded his zeal and his methods of working. Together with Sighele he issued a publication on Criminal Anthropology, richly illustrated with pictures, diagrams, and statistics, which met with favor even outside of strictly scientific circles. A remarkable book published by him is the *Romance of a Born Criminal*, the autobiography of a convict, founded on authentic papers committed to his hands by the eminent psychiatrist Silvio Venturi, director of the lunatic asylum at Catanzaro, a book which was translated immediately on its appearance into German, but which no English publisher has had the courage to issue, though it states at once in its preface that its scope is purely scientific, and that the word "Romance" is employed in a subjective sense. This piece of pathological literature throws a lurid light upon the inner nature of the criminal. Bianchi has written a long and careful preface, in which he points out just how and why this human document has scientific value. As yet, Bianchi has not had time to write many books, but his careful, studious articles are all of value and denote his knowledge, intuition, and observation.

Limits of space, which we have already exceeded, oblige us to leave unmentioned yet other valiant followers of criminal anthropology in Italy, but we hope we have said enough to prove that this science has in the peninsula both numerous and able adherents, and that Italy is justified in considering herself at the head and front of studies of this nature—a position which, indeed, few dispute to her. Seeing how useful is this science as an auxiliary to the right study of history, literature, and political economy, it would be well if its propagation were more encouraged at universities, in place of philosophy and metaphysics, which, when untouched by this new breath, have become fossilized and are as arid as they are sterile.

CRIMINAL ANTHROPOLOGY: ITS ORIGIN AND APPLICATION

BY

CESARE LOMBROSO

FORUM

VOL. 20 (SEPTEMBER 1895), PP. 33-49

One thing strikes you when you enter one of our courts —the sight of the judges, state employees like others, who think that they cannot fulfil their functions unless they are masked in a costume of the Middle Ages. The same spirit pervades their judgments. These are often evoked from remote ages. Antiquity is more honored than the truth. The lawyer who can cite in behalf of his client a law of the twelve tables has a better chance to gain his case. Worse yet, the courts are often led astray by formulas that had some sense at the time of their origin, but have none now and simply turn justice from the true path. In Italy, for example, sentences are often annulled because the clerk had forgotten to preface them with the formula, "In the name of His Majesty, by the grace of God and the will of people, King of Italy." The law prescribes times for the accomplishment of certain formalities. Now justice is often denied to poor wretches who are quite in the right, because they come a half an hour too late, or because they have made a mistake of a few moments in the execution of these formalities.

What is the reason for all this? It is because of the tendency of the human mind to reduce to a minimum the number of mental associations required in a given task. The literal interpretation prevails in practice over all considerations of justice. Legal provisions can be the only rude and imperfect indication of the legislative will, useful only as a guide to the magistrate in attaining justice by a personal mental effort. But they have taken the place of justice and right, and the magistrate has to apply them literally. To judge right he ought, in each case, to have resort to his own consciousness, to give free course to those associations of ideas and emotions of which the complexity is so great. He ought to compare the answer of his own consciousness with the customary interpretation of the law. If they do not agree he should examine the differences, analyze the provisions of the law, and, comparing the ideas of the more frequent cases for which the law was made with the idea involved in the specific case, modify the application as justice requires.

But this is a long, complex, difficult task. If the comparison be not obvious enough, the judge becomes lost in doubt, and every new case requires a renewed effort. How much simpler it is to apply general provisions of law, drawing from their logical inferences, not bothering with all the concomitant associations of ideas and emotions, but merely following a longer or shorter chain of reasoning. Once this habit of idio-emotional, or let us call it professional, judgment is formed and the mind continues to consider only the logical relations of the general principle to the specific case. It excludes all collateral associations of ideas and feelings, numerous and varied as they are, which lead to a just solution to the actual question. The lofty and complex sentiment of justice is reduced to a sentiment of satisfaction in the logical application of the general principle. All notion of the wrong done to the victim, and the causes of that wrong, is excluded. In brief, the idio-emotional judgment results in the substitution of pure logic for observation and investigation of facts, a characteristic of the primitive periods of science and of periods of scientific degeneracy and decadence.

The consequences of this heedlessness are enormous. The judges pronounce judgment as if the crime formed the simplest incident in the life of the criminal. The criminal, on the other hand, does all that he can to prove the contrary by the rarity of his repentance and his continual relapses, which often reach 80 per cent, with enormous peril and expense to society, and discredit to justice—which is often only a futile fencing with the criminal for the sole benefit of some rhetorician. The trouble is still greater when the same penalty is administered to a man who kills and steals from cupidity, and to one who has been impelled to crime by a great and noble passion—patriotism, for instance, or love. It is a long time—thirty years—since I began to think that to avoid these pitfalls the criminals and not the crime must be studied. How did I reach this conclusion? How did I succeed in establishing it?

I. History of the Discovery—Atavism of the Criminal

I arrived in Paris in 1861, a very young clinical professor of mental disease, a boy, with my head full of philology and comparative physiology. I soon saw that the most serious lack in this science was that of anatomical and anthropological knowledge. They were studying insanity in general without studying individual lunatics. I set to work. I insisted that we should study lunatics as we would a special variety of the human race, noting the skin, the form, the skull, and particularly the functions, sensibility, etc. My colleagues laughed at me and called me the "Doctor of the steelyard." Little by little the idea prevailed, and now they seem almost to have forgotten who it was that introduced the new somatic school. I had a strong desire to study the morally insane who have since been shown to be the born criminals. It was a principle of mine to deny everything which I did not see, and as there were none of these in our clinic I was inclined to deny their existence. Nevertheless, to make sure of the facts, I commenced to occupy myself with criminals, to frequent prisons, and carefully to gather skulls and brains of prisoners. One evening there died in one of the prisons of the city a celebrated brigand, robber, and incendiary who had often escaped by means of his great agility. Upon the death of this man, who was a true type of the born criminal and morally insane, I examined his skull. It presented an enormous median occipital fossa in place of the occipital median spine which occurs in the interior of the skull. This is a characteristic wanting in the superior apes and existing in all other vertebrates. I made the autopsy in the yard of the prison in the early hours of the morning. The day was very foggy, in the winter of 1864. The weather and the place did not permit me to make a thorough autopsy, but I recollect how, at that moment, the whole idea of my future work rose before me like a picture.

I instantly perceived that the criminal must be a survival of the primitive man and the carnivorous animals. The idea, though yet embryonic, was perfected a few days later, when I was called as an expert by the tribunal of Bergamo in the case of a sort of Jack the Ripper—one Verzeni. This young peasant, with crossed eyes and enormous jaws, was possessed with a desire to disembowel, chew, and eat morsels of women, young and old, who happened to cross his path. He afterward confided to me in secret the great erotic pleasure which he experienced in this.

Then I went furiously to work in the examination of facts, in museums, in prisons, especially in Pesaro (when I was director of an insane asylum), near a great cellular prison where, with a corps of aides, I could go whenever I wished. Some of these took weights, others measured the figures or sketched the faces of the criminals. As for myself, I noted the more important characteristics, questioned the prisoners, treating them to cigars and wine, and applied to them all the modern methods. While the criminal had his hand in the plethysmograph, which gave me in graphic lines all the psychic impressions and reactions of the brain, I showed him things likely to interest him strongly—a woman, a purse, a glass of wine, cigars—and noted the effect of these impressions and especially the effect of electric currents. The result indicated a curious insensibility. To complete my studies I finally shut myself up for three years in the great cellular prison of Turin as a physician, until my health was undermined.

It was there that I perceived that my earlier ideas fell short of the truth. I saw that the criminal was worse than the savage, worse sometimes than the true carnivora, especially as regards analgesia. On one occasion I saw one of these criminals, who was working upon a roof several yards in height, fall to the ground and immediately return to his work as if nothing had happened. On another occasion a woman refused, for many days, to allow herself to be cared for, until the odor warned us of the presence of gangrene. It had, in effect, eaten away four fingers from one hand, where she had been cut by her lover. The total of these facts thus gathered was enormous, so that the image of the criminal arose from them in perfect clearness. The anatomy of criminals showed a great number of completely atavistic changes: surcillary arch and frontal sinus enormous; median occipital fossa; suture of the atlas; virile aspect of the skull in women; double articular face of the occipital condyle; flattening of the palate; large oblique orbits varying from 2 per cent to 58 per cent. These traits are often grouped in the same individuals, producing a *type*, in the proportion of 43 per cent. The convolutions of the brain present frequent atavistic anomalies, such as the separation of the calcareous fissure from the occipital, the formation of an operculum of the occipital lobe, and absolutely atypical variations, such as the transverse furrows of the frontal lobe.

The study of 25,000 living beings confirmed, though less constantly, the frequency of the anomalies revealed by the anatomical table. It showed analogies between savages and delinquents in the proportion of 35 to 36 per cent. Among these anomalies were prognathism: the hair black and crisp; the beard thin; oxicephaly; oblique eyes; small skull; the jaw and the zygomes developed; the forehead retreating obliquely from the eyes; the ears large; analogy between the two sexes; a greater extension of all new characteristics added to the neeroscopic characteristics which assimilate the European criminal to the Mongolian and Australian type.

A photographic study of 5,000 criminals furnished a means of verifying and fixing the frequency of the criminal physiognomic type in the proportion of 25 per cent, with the maximum of 56 per cent for assassins, and a minimum of 6 to 8 per cent for bankrupts, swindlers, and bigamists. Photography showed how often the ethnic type is effaced among criminals, while they have with each other a veritable resemblance. It shows the frequency of feminine aspect among certain thieves and pederasts, and virility among many female criminals, especially murderesses. A study of 800 free men showed that there may often be found among these the characteristics of degenerate physiognomy, but very rarely, almost never, combined in the same person, and frequently justified by latent criminality. It often happens that greater shrewdness, wealth, or political influence avert the action of the law and hide the criminal in men of great power—Crispi, for example, or, in New York, the leaders of the Tammany ring.

The anomalies appeared still stranger on studying the psychology and the biology of these unfortunates. Here the analogy with savages was more striking, especially as to tattooing, which in certain criminals prevails to the extent of 25 per cent, among thieves 16 per cent, among minor criminals 34 per cent, and which often serves, as among the savages, to indicate a sect or to boast of a crime. Tattooing is something composed of true pictographic characters, as in the writing of the Indians reported in the publications of the Smithsonian Institution. Thus one man was tattooed with the figure of a woman, winged and crowned. "I cause her to take flight," he said, "for she fled with me, and by me she lost her virgin's crown." She had in her hands two bleeding hearts, denoting the parents who mourned her. Like savages, criminals display great insensibility to pain, which explains their longevity, their ability to bear wounds, their frequent suicide. As with savages also, their passions are swift but violent, vengeance is considered as a duty, and they have a strong love for gambling, alcohol, and complete idleness. Thus the New Caledonians were accustomed to repeat, without knowing it, the remark of the murderer Lemair, "Better to die than work." In connection with this, I remember reading one day in a scientific review that among the Australian savages there were found more left-handed persons than among Europeans. I immediately made observations upon 600 criminals in Turin, and found the proportion of left-handed ones double that in the same number of journeyman printers. Again, having read that savages have greater visual acuteness, I set to work with the oculists and found indeed that the acuteness of their vision was far greater than the normal, contrasting with their dullness of touch, hearing, and sense of color. At another time I read concerning a tribe of American Indians that their plays were like combats. Then I studied the games and amusements of young criminals in the reformatories, and I found that almost always these amusements involved wounds, even more often than among the savages. Thus, in one game, the object of a player was to save the head and hands from the wounds of two knives used by the others.

However, these observations were not so original as I at first thought they were. The knowledge of a criminal physiognomic type, which at first appeared most novel, and was most generally denied by the savants, is often instinctive among the common people. There are often persons, especially among women, who are far from suspecting even the existence of criminal anthropology, and who yet, at the sight of those who bear criminal characteristics, instantly experience a lively repulsion and know that they are in the presence of a malefactor. I was acquainted with one lady whose life was quite withdrawn from society, who on two occasions discovered the criminal character of certain young people, not before suspected, but afterward detected by the police. How often we read in the reports of trials, of perfectly honest people, unfamiliar with the slightest anthropological observations, who escape certain death from being warned in time by the sinister glance of the assassin, in which they read his criminal intention. It was in this way that the first letter-carrier who was to have been the victim of the murderer Francesconi had time to flee, haunted by that glance. At my request schoolmasters have shown to forty young girls twenty portraits of thieves and twenty of great men. Four-fifths of these children recognized the first as wretched creatures or as scoundrels, and the second as honest men. The universal although involuntary consciousness of the existence of a physiognomy peculiar to criminals has given birth to the epithets "a thief's face," " the look of an assassin," etc. The only way to explain the opposition to the fact is the reluctance of men to draw a general conclusion from individual observations. But how is this universal consciousness itself to be explained? In young girls there is certainly no knowledge acquired by experience. Then what is there? An intuitive sense, is it said? That is a vulgar explanation with which the public is contented because it has no meaning.

I suspect that the phenomenon is heredity. The impression left us by our fathers and transmitted to our children has become unconscious knowledge, like that of the little birds born and reared in our houses, who strike their wings and beaks in fright against their cages when they see pass above them birds of prey only known to their ancestors. Every day teaches us the importance of the unconscious part in human actions, and what a role is played by atavism and heredity. Who of us can realize, when he bends the knees and joins the hands in prayer, that he is making an hereditary movement transmitted from those epochs of barbarism when war was the normal state?

II. Epilepsy of Born Criminals

My work was only at its beginning. In the earlier years, possessed by the idea of the skull with its occipital fossa, I believed that the criminal was solely and simply an atavistic phenomenon. I was soon compelled to admit that there are born in criminals, not in others, still stranger anomalies than are presented by savages, and with which atavism has nothing to do. There are: precocious wrinkles, irregular teeth, strabismus, synostosis, osteoma, hernia; meningitic, hepatic, and cardiac lesions. These show the criminal to be abnormal before birth, through the disease of various organs, especially the nervous centres. This again is confirmed by histologic observations, dilation of the cerebral lymphatic vessels, pigmentation of the nerve and connective cells, and obtuseness of the senses.

I must confess that in my studies I have never reached the solution of my problems suddenly. Thus, in the study of the nature of the *pellagra*, or Italian leprosy, I reached a solution only by successive stages and by accidents occurring in the path of my studies. This time, also, I was aided by an accident after much time lost in investigation. A soldier at Naples, one Misdea, assassinated without any plausible motive three or four of his companions. It was not noticed in any way, on this occasion, that he had an attack of epilepsy. He showed great coolness in his murder and remembered it sufficiently well, though not quite correctly. The entire life of this man, who was descended from a line of degenerates, murderers, and epileptics, was a mass of crimes and diseases. One day he set out to kill his *fiancée*, fell fainting in a church, and lay there all night, foaming at the mouth. He remembered nothing of it. He was a barber by trade. In his regiment he had been relieved of this duty on account of his disease. He was straightaway seized with a boundless rage, tore his razors into bits with his teeth, and spit them out before his superior officers. In studying this curious criminal I divined instantly that the disease which was confused with and obscured by the atavism of the crime, was epilepsy.

In effect, in epilepsy there is found the same absence of moral sense, the same dullness of the physical senses, the same impulsiveness as among criminals. This discovery, strange enough in appearance, is very simple in reality. We often hear the spontaneous remark that certain attacks of criminal rage are marked by "epileptic fury." The discovery was rejected with great unanimity, even by those who, like Tamburini and Morselli, had seen cases of psychic epilepsy without convulsion and without amnesia as is often seen in the case of criminals. As for me, I am used to this reception from savants and demi-savants. Indeed, I see in it the sign that I have struck a new and fruitful vein. For thirty years my colleagues ridiculed me for maintaining that *pellagra* is a poisoning by spoiled maize; and during all those years I was known in Italy as the "pellagroseine crank." But there is one thing more trustworthy than academicians—Time. After some years the proofs in this direction became very numerous. Left-handedness was found to be very frequent among epileptics, as well as insensibility to wounds. Dr. Ottolenghi discovered a characteristic peculiar to epileptics and born criminals alone, the interruption and contraction with scotoma of the periphery of the visual field. Rossi demonstrated that the proportion of epileptics among criminals was 40 per cent. Even the official statistics of the criminals showed the proportion to be six times more than normal. Krafft-Ebing, and Panata of Verona, found epilepsy in the case of many sexual psychopaths, which explains almost all the more curious crimes due to luxury. Literature, both the ancient and the most modern, agrees with these views. Shakespeare surmised epilepsy in the mind of Macbeth, who suffered from hallucinations. Goncourt saw epilepsy in the murderer of the girl Eliza. Dostoievski described all his criminals as epileptic in his *Crime et Chatiment.* Zola, without knowing it, gave us a complete type of psychic epilepsy in the murderer of *La Bete Humaine.* I was able to found the first editions of my *Delinquent Man* on living documents, taking as a basis atavism and epilepsy.

III. New Studies: Ferri, Garofalo, Marro

By a strange coincidence, which may be called the maturing of an idea, a young man of Bologna, Ferri, about this time wrote a book in which he demonstrated that if there is no free will all the laws should be changed, for punishment has no influence upon the criminal. He continues in this direction, entered completely into my ideas, and showed that I had not taken sufficient account of the occasional criminal and the habitual criminal. Finally he applied himself to the study of *Fifty Years of Criminality in France,* supplying for me another of my defects—that of statistics, which has never been my forte. Later he gave his *Criminal Sociology* all the sociological bases of our school. At the same time a young magistrate of Naples, Garofalo, who acknowledged no standard of punishment but the defense of society, summed up his studies in the sentence, "The more a man is to be feared, the more he should be confined." Shortly after, Marro, a laborious and learned alienist of minute exactness, contributed powerful support to my theories by studying with the patience of a Benedictine all the moral, physical, and psychical characteristics of five hundred criminals, divided, according to the crime, into thieves, swindlers, etc., and compared them with two hundred normal persons of the same country and age. As a climax of exactness he prepared in twelve personal tables all the observations that he had made and provided for the verification of his conclusions. It will be seen that the little edifice, which was quite rudimental when I began to work alone, was beginning to be completed. Thanks to these critics I was able to add to the criminal born the insane criminal (who is quite as formidable, and resembles him closely), the mattoid (also known as the "crank"), and the criminaloid (a semi-criminal born, who requires a great occasion to violate the laws), and the occasional criminal (who violates them when forced by circumstances). But the gap was not yet entirely filled. One last and almost tragic accident revealed to me the criminal through passion. I was one day in a printing-office, correcting the proofs of my *Delinquent Man* with the chief reader. I came to a page which spoke of a young man in the diplomatic service who, impelled by jealousy only too well justified (his *fiancée* had almost shown him the price of her prostitution), had stabbed her with a knife, and afterward stabbed himself. Sentenced to a light punishment, he had disappeared. The proof-reader was this man. Suddenly he threw himself at my feet, declaring he would commit suicide if I published this story with his name. His face, before very gentle, was completely altered and almost terrifying, and I was really afraid that he would kill himself or me upon the spot. I tore up the proofs and for several editions omitted his story; but I had discovered the criminal through passion. There is a class of men, young, honest, of gentle appearance, whose beauty of soul corresponds to their beauty of body, in no wise apathetic like born criminals, but of an exaggerated affectionateness. One of these young men, being in love and unable to talk with his lady-love, put his ear to a wall, transported with delight to hear her step. My proof-reader declared that he wished to burn his ears with red-hot iron when he heard his *fiancée* uttering unclean things. All these men are capable of remorse and repentance, and are impelled to crime by a strong and often just cause. They commit the crime in broad daylight, with whatever weapon is at hand, and never seek to prove an alibi. It is my opinion that many political criminals belong in this category—Orsini, for example, and Sand, and Charlotte Corday.

After this the work arose, it may be said, if not complete, certainly vital and fecund. A large number of monographs appeared upon special crimes, which would not have been published before. Balestrini made a wonderful study of infanticide and abortion, and demonstrated that these crimes might almost be stricken from the code—on the one hand because criminals through passion are incapable of relapse, and on the other hand because, in the case of abortion especially, what is killed is not a man, but a being inferior in the zoological world. Margri at Pisa undertook a study of theft. Florian took up another on defamation, showing that what resembles defamation and is severely punished by the Italian law—which always goes contrary to right—is a necessity of moral and political liberty; that the liberty of criticism, even when it is offensive, should not be restricted, but favored in every possible way. Sighele studied collective crime. He showed, more amply than I had been able to do, that aggressions of human beings have a character quite opposed to that of the units of which they are made up. Though the majority of the crowd may be good, the crowd itself can be converted into a cruel beast. The passions of each, when shared by a great number of individuals at once, become doubly intense, because the emotion of each is communicated from one to another, and the latent criminality of every individual breaks out through the certainty of impunity or through the influence of someone not so honest. This is the basis of his *Foule Criminelle*. In another work, *Le Crime a Deux*, he demonstrated that persons associated with evil are far more feared than any single criminal. Occasional criminals, or criminals through passion, never have accomplices. I, myself, with Laschi, constructed a complete penal system for political crimes, starting from misoneism. In nature the law of inertia prevails, and still more in the human race, which has a horror of the new. Every precipitate change which is not extorted by necessity is painful to it, and in politics is punished, for it goes against the opinions and sentiments of the majority. If organic and moral progress does not take place slowly, through powerful attrition, provoked by exterior and interior circumstances, and if man and society are distinctly conservative, it must be concluded that those efforts in favor of progress which adopt means too abrupt and too violent are not physiological. They may sometimes be a necessity for an oppressed minority, but in the eyes of the law they are anti-social and therefore a crime. Often it is a useless crime, for it awakens reaction in the misoneistic direction, which, since it is solidly based on human nature, has great force. All progress, to be accepted, must be slow, otherwise it is futile and mischievous. Those who wish to impose a political innovation upon society, without tradition, without necessity, offend misoneism and arouse that reaction in the public mind which comes from a dread of the new, and invite the application of the penal laws. Here appears the distinction between revolutions and revolts or seditions. The former are slow, long-prepared, necessary, or at the most hastened a little by some neurotic or passionate spirit. The latter may be an artificial and precipitate incubation, at an exaggerated temperature, of embryos doomed to certain death. These latter are for the most part the work of mattoids (semi-lunatics), lunatics, and born criminals who have a strong tendency to innovation. The former prevail more among the Germanic and Anglo-Saxon races in cold or temperate climates (Luther, Cromwell); the latter are more often found in Latin, Catholic, and warm countries.

Mr. Henry Ferri made a brilliant beginning with the biological, psychical, psycho-pathological study of homicide in his *Criminels, avec Atlas*. Under natural conditions of primitive humanity homicide bore, in many respects, a great part, and Mr. Ferri notes with great perspicacity a double process of evolution, toward diminishing ferocity and moral sentiment, and toward judicial institutions. Homicide, therefore, in the form of sanguinary vengeance, is the embryo of all social rights of repression. He infers that murder is not the product of an abstract voluntary fiat, but that it has its roots deep in the animal organism; that it is the natural effect of physio-pathological, physical, and social causes. He gives us the evidence in insensibility, which is the key of innate criminality; in the indifference, and sometimes the pleasure, taken in the sufferings of others; the cool ferocity of crime; the apathetic impassability as to the crime itself and its penalties—evident proof that this psychic analgesia is founded upon physical anesthesia. He shows the futility of motive, the disdain of human life which is a characteristic of savages, and finally the behavior of born homicides, cynical and vain during their trial, and very different afterward. Ferri reports numerous original observations which show that, contrary to the general belief, many homicides confess their crimes, and do so much more frequently than thieves or pickpockets. Quite novel, and capable of a still greater development, is his study upon moral daltonism, by which, in certain criminals, there exists a strong aversion for certain crimes and for the causes and reasons for committing them. Moreover, despite these abnormal conditions of their general senses, criminals also possess sentiments common to other men, but differently developed, lacking the guide and check of the moral sense. For instance, the religious sentiment, which is very frequent among homicides, has nothing to do with the genesis of the crime, because it represents rather a moral sanction than a true and proper moral sense. The most extraordinary part of this work is the atlas. The figures of arid criminal anthropology are handled with striking certainty. Accounts are given of 695 investigations of greater variety and interest. It is the geography not only of homicide, but of all crimes in all the countries in Europe.

Madame Tarnowski, in her studies of the *filles de joie*, thieves, and village women, demonstrated that the cranial capacity of prostitutes is inferior to that of the female thieves and the villagers, and still more to that of women of good society. *Vice versa* the zygomatic process and the mandibles were more developed among the former, who also showed a greater number of anomalies—87 per cent; while the thieves had 79 per cent, and the villagers only 12 per cent. According to the author, what distinguishes the thieves from the prostitutes is their utter repugnance to giving any information as to their sexual relations, and the silence that falls upon them when the question is raised as to the causes of their confinement. They deny their offense and will not yield even to proof. The hereditary defects of thieves are less marked than those of prostitutes. The latter have, for example, among their ancestry, 82 per cent of inebriate relatives and 44 per cent of consumptives, while the thieves have only 49 per cent and 19 per cent respectively. Thus the thieves possess fewer signs of physical degeneration. Moreover the number of births among them exceeds that of the other class, 256 to 64, a circumstance approaching the normal.

Kurella and Fraenkel in Germany, Havelock Ellis and Morrison in England, extended the horizons of these studies by their own works and by translations from the Italian. A large number of reviews, entirely special, appeared on every side. *L'Archivio di Anthropologia Criminale* is already in its eighteenth year. Kowalewski and Mucewski have two in Russia, Lacassagne one in France, and Kurella one in Germany. There sprang also into existence a publishing house devoted exclusively to books on criminal anthropology in Italy, which has already issued more than sixty works in three series. A similar one was established in Germany, under the direction of Kurella, and another by Morrison in England, which unfortunately commenced with the poorest of my works, making it still poorer by the cruelest mutilations.

IV. Practical Applications

It is easy enough to see the application of these theories. The criminal code has been conceived through the study of crime as an abstraction. It must be modified by knowledge of the criminal. There should be in it no dream of theological expiations, which man has no right to impose, but it should aim solely at the defense of society. The greatest criminal anomaly—even insanity —should not be considered as an extenuating circumstance. Even lunatics should be arrested in order to protect society, especially the morally insane, who are a great peril, and the masked epileptics. In the punishment of crime the tendency of its authors should be considered. If the author is a born criminal, he must be confined for life, even though the crime itself is not great. On the other hand, a crime committed by an honest man impelled by some strong motive should be punished with much indulgence, especially political and religious crimes, which often only anticipate by some centuries the thought of the people. In our time, when hours are years and years are centuries, a political idea which appears to be dangerous, and even criminal through its excessive novelty, after some time may appear practical and just. Such, for instance, were the ideas of Christ and Luther, and at the present time the ideas of the equality of all classes and of the participation of workmen in profits. There was a time when it would have been a crime to maintain these ideas. Now they pertain to a possible reform. Then it must be understood that for these crimes there should be no irrevocable penalty, like death. The penalty should be revocable when the novelty has passed away and the idea is no longer criminal.

Vice versa, the hand of the law must fall heavily upon the recidivists, putting aside all sentimentality, especially if they have accomplices. And the complicity must not be judged arithmetically, for whether there are four or ten they are equally dangerous. It is merely preferring formulas to facts to exempt an association with less than six members, as is done in Italy, and to ignore the perils of any criminal association. A man who is not contented to steal himself, but enlists others, is more dangerous, and must be treated without pity. Justice cannot be an emanation from the Eternal Father repressing sin and disregarding interests. It especially should undertake to compensate the victims of crime at the expense of the criminal, making him work in order to pay the indemnity if he is not rich. It is a blunder also, when society has lost through the crime, to compel it to lose still more for the support of the criminal.

All efforts at reform should be concentrated upon occasional criminals. They are the only ones for whom much can be done.

They should be removed from all opportunity by procuring them employment and protecting them from the mischievous influence of alcohol, not only by prohibitory laws and fines, which are generally a dead letter, but by giving them mental amusement, which will satisfy that cerebral excitement that is gratified by alcohol. Above all, the tendency to crime which appears in infancy must not be allowed to continue in youth and become habitual. All this has received no application in Italy. I was fairly startled when *The Forum* requested from me an account of the applications made in Italy of my ideas. What can one expect from a race of advocates and rhetoricians? When there is a great evil to correct we are contented to make laws, and speeches which have quite as much force. The speeches vanish, and the laws with them, producing no effect. But people get along contentedly because their apathetic quiet is not disturbed. In their hatred of the new they prefer suffering to change. It is true that a new criminal code has been made in our country since my school sprang up, but it is wholly opposed to my ideas. The penalties in the case of relapses have been almost suppressed with great applause in the Senate and Chamber of Deputies. These great legislators take no account of the foes of free will or of classic law. Nevertheless the *manicome* (guardian of the insane) is necessary for criminals despite the law, and three establishments have been founded in Italy. The penalty of death, which is a sovereign remedy for us, has been abolished, though murderers continue and even multiply their offences.

No provision for judicial anthropometry has been established. An Italian, one of my dearest disciples, Anfasso, has invented an instrument, the tachianthropometer, which rapidly and automatically takes all the measures of the body (I call it, half in jest, the "anthropometric guillotine"), but after much negotiation the government did not accept it. The only countries where anything has really been done in the direction of my school are North America, England, and Switzerland. We must admit there is a tendency to crime at a very early age. Children are liars, thieves, etc. This tendency in well-born children disappears with a good education, when they are removed from bad examples and evil incitements, but in the criminal born it is continued in spite of everything. Every effort that we can suggest to combat crime should be concentrated, not upon the criminal born, but upon the occasional criminal, to prevent him from wandering from the right path. This class forms about 75 per cent according to our calculations. Now, almost unconsciously, by that intuition which comes from practical vice joined to religious fanaticism unspoiled by formulas and by the bonds of Catholicism, London and Geneva have found the means to prevent the child not criminal born from being driven to evil through the abandonment of his parents or the want of work or of nourishment, so that he does not become an occasional criminal and afterward an habitual one. In this work the ragged schools, etc., Dr. Barnardo's missions, and enterprises of the Salvation Army are engaged. While in England millions of rescued children are reported, in Italy there are only 12,000; and these are not really rescued, for the house of correction and reformatories are in reality universities of crime. In the United States, especially Boston and New York, great efforts have been made in this direction. In all these countries—in America, England, Norway, and Switzerland—an effort has been made to restrict alcoholic poison, which may transform the honest adult into a criminal. Unfortunately, in some countries, continual immigration composed always of adventurous men, together with the mixture of blood, black and yellow, having no common moral sense, and the evil influence of professional politicians, prevent results as important as at London and Geneva. But the United States alone can boast of having conscientiously applied scientific knowledge of criminal anthropology to criminal therapeutics, for at Washington there has been founded the first bureau for degenerates and abnormal people. The worthy founder of the Elmira Reformatory, with the frankness which is no longer found among our old races, has declared that his whole system of education is based on the knowledge given by our school as to the criminal, and especially to his psychology. To give new strength to good tendencies; to make of mischievous tendencies—vanity for instance—the stimulus toward the right way; to engraft the taste for work; to avail one's self of the natural desire of the prisoner to shorten his penalty; to remove from all adult occasional criminals the opportunity for relapse,—that is, according to our school, the greatest possible effort for the cure of the crime: and I believe that these efforts would be crowned with still greater success if masses of individuals had not been brought together in the same place, and if the adults had not been employed to take care of the young; if, following the example of Barnardo, instead of making the prisoners servants or workmen, they had been made good farmers. Nevertheless, when I compare these establishments with those which I see in Italy and in France, where there is only the appearance of work, with a varnish of bigotry, I am happy and proud. If the new ideas sprung from our old European soil must perish there for want of people who understand them, they will find in the new world fervent supporters, able to perpetuate and apply them. As the inspiring fruit of the vine, which was the first joy and the first sin of the ancient world, is now commencing to be returned to us from the new world modified and improved, so the true political liberty, a Utopian dream in our ancient continent, has already taken deep and sure root in North America, whence the great thinkers of Europe may draw new force for work, and whither they may direct their last glance, finding consolation for a life misunderstood and disdained.

THE SAVAGE ORIGIN OF TATTOOING

BY

CESARE LOMBROSO

POPULAR SCIENCE MONTHLY

VOL. 48 (APRIL 1896), PP. 793-803

I have been told that the fashion of tattooing the arm exists among women of prominence in London society. The taste for this style is not a good indication of the refinement and delicacy of the English ladies; first, it indicates an inferior sensitiveness, for one has to be obtuse to pain to submit to this wholly savage operation without any other object than the gratification of vanity; and it is contrary to progress, for all exaggerations of dress are atavistic. Simplicity in ornamentation and clothing and uniformity are an advance gained during these last centuries by the virile sex, by man, and constitute a superiority in him over woman, who has to spend for dress an enormous amount of time and money, without gaining any real advantage, even to her beauty. But it is not desirable that so inordinate an accession to ornamentation as tattooing should be adopted, for an observation I have made on more that 5,000 criminals has demonstrated to me that this custom is held in too great honor among them. Thus, while out of 2,739 soldiers I have found tattoo marks only among 12 per cent, always limited to the arms and the breast; among 5,348 criminals, 667 were tattooed, or ten per cent of the adults and 3.9 per cent of the minors. Baer recently observed tattooing among two per cent of German criminals and 9.5 per cent of soldiers (*Der Verbrecher*, 1893).

CHARACTERISTICS OF CRIMINAL TATTOOING: VENGENCE.—The minute study of the various signs adopted by malefactors shows us not only that they sometimes have a strange frequency, but often also a special stamp. A criminal whom I studied had on his breast between two poniards the fierce threat *Je jure de me venger* (I swear to avenge myself). He was an old Piedmontese sailor, who had killed and stolen for vengeance. A recidivistic thief wore on his breast the inscription *Malheur a moi! Quelle sera ma fin*? (Woe to me! What will be my end?)—lugubrious words, reminding us of those which Filippe, the strangler of public women, had traced on his right arm, long before his condemnation, *Ne sous une mauvaise etoile* (Born under an evil star).

Malassen, a ferocious assassin, who became in New Caledonia an executioner of convicts (Meyer, *Souvenirs d'un Deporte*), was covered from his head to his feet with grotesque and frightful tattoo marks. On his breast he had drawn a red and black guillotine, with the words in red letters: *J'ai mal commence, je finirai mal. C'est la fin qui m'attend* (I have begun evil, I shall end evil. That is the end that awaits me). His right arm, which had inflicted death upon so many human beings, bore the terrible device, very appropriate to his hand, *Mort a la chiourme* (Death to the convict).

The famous Neapolitan camorrist [i.e., member of an Italian secret society that became notorious for extortion and violence] Salsano had himself represented in an attitude of bravado. He held a stick in his hand, and was defying a police guard. Under the figure was his sobriquet, *Eventre tout le monde* (Disembowel everybody); then came two hearts and keys connected with chains, in allusion to the secrecy of the camorrists.

We see, then, by these few examples, that there is a kind of hieroglyphic writing among criminals, that it is not regulated or fixed, but is determined from daily events, and from *argot*, very much as would take place among primitive men. Very often, in fact, the key in the design signifies the silence of secrecy, and the death's head vengeance. Sometimes the figures are replaced by points, as when a judicial arrest is marked on the arm with seventeen points, which means, according to the criminal, that he intends to strike his enemy that number of times when he falls into his hands.

Another characteristic of criminals, which is also common to them with soldiers and savages, is to trace the designs not only on the arms and the breast (the most frequent usage), but on nearly all parts of the body. I have remarked one hundred tattooed on the arms, breast, and abdomen, five on the hands, three on the fingers, and three on the thigh.

A certain T—, thirty-four years of age, who had passed many years in prison, had not, except on his cheeks and loins, a surface the size of an English pound coin that was not tattooed. On his forehead could be read *Martyr de la Liberte* (Martyr of Liberty); the words being surmounted by a snake eleven centimetres long.

On his nose he had a cross, which he had tried to efface with acetic acid.

A Venetian thief, who had served in the Austrian army, had on his right arm a double-headed eagle, and near it the names of his mother and his mistress Louise, with the strange epigraph for a thief: *Louise, chere amante, mon unique consolation* (Louise, dear loved one, my only consolation). Another thief wore on his right arm a bird holding a heart, stars, and an anchor. On the left arm of a prisoner Lacassagne found the words, *Quand la neige tombera noire, B— sortira de ma memoire* (When the snow falls black, B— will pass out of my memory).

The multiplicity of marks results from the strange liking these curious heroes have of spreading on their body, just after the fashion of the American Indians, the adventures of their lives. For example, M— C—, twenty-seven years old (Fig. 1), who had been condemned at least fifty times for rebellion and assaults on men and horses, who had traveled, or rather wandered, a vagabond, in Spain and Africa with women whom he left suddenly, wore his whole history written on his skin. One design referred to the ship L'Esperance (No. 1), which was wrecked on the coast of Ireland, and on which he had gone as a sailor. A horse's head (No. 2) represented an animal which he had killed with a knife, from simple caprice, when twelve years old. A helmet (No. 7) indicated a policeman he had tried to kill. A headless woman with a heart on her neck indicated his mistress, who was frivolous (No. 8). The portrait of a brigand referred to a robber chief whom he took for his model (No. 9). A lute (No. 3) recalled a friend, a skillful player of the guitar, with whom he traveled over half of Europe. The star, the evil influence under which he was born (No. 4). The royal crown, "a political souvenir," he said, but rather, we say, his new trade of a spy – that is, the destruction of the kingdom (No. 5).

A French deserter who desired to avenge himself against his chief drew a poniard on his breast (Fig. 2, No. 1), to signify vengeance, and also a serpent. He further drew the ship on which he wished to escape, the epaulets which had been taken away from him, a dancing girl who had been his mistress, and then the sad inscriptions which were truly appropriate to his unhappy life.

Dr. Spoto sent me a study of the tattooing of a criminal who had been under his care. He wore all his sad adventures painted on his arm (see *Archivio di Psichiatria*, June 1889). He had one hundred and five signs on his body, ten of which represented

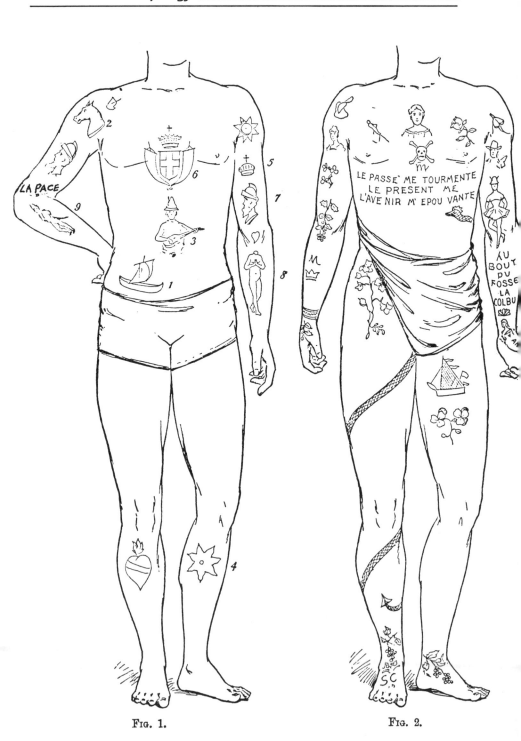

FIG. 1.   FIG. 2.

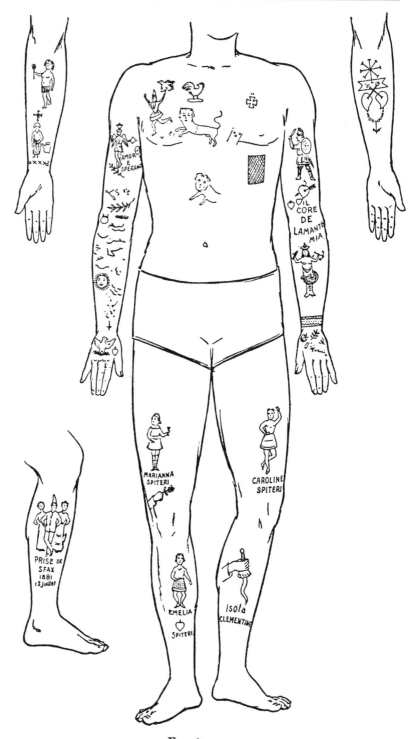

FIG. 3.

mistresses, nine hearts, eight flowers or leaves, five animals, twenty-eight names, surnames, or descriptions, and thirty-one poniards or warriors (Fig. 3). On his arm he had a figure of a lady winged and crowned; winged, he said, "because I made her take flight" (he had run away with her); crowned, because she had substituted for the crown of virginity the royal crown of becoming his mistress. She held in her hand a heart and an arrow, signifying her parents, to whom her flight had caused great grief. Beneath her were two branches, which signified that she kept herself always fresh. Two other of his loves explained their sad adventures by holding crumpled roses in their hands. In his hand he had an eagle, representing the ship on which he sailed, and beneath it a heart with three points, referring to the sufferings of Christ, whose birthplace he had visited in Bethlehem. A heart on his arm represented a mistress with whom he lived several years. It was pierced with an arrow, because he had abandoned the woman with two little children, who were represented by two bleeding hearts. Two hearts pierced with swords, on his forearm, represented two mistresses who would not yield to his desires except when threatened with death. They were connected by a chain with an anchor hanging from it, which signified that the woman belonged to a sailor family, and a Greek cross above them indicated that they were Greek. On his breast was a dancing girl carrying a bird, because she bounded like a bird. On his sides were a cock and a lion, the cock corresponding to women who wished to be paid: "When the cock sings, Spiritelli will pay." The lion meant that he felt as strong as a lion. A smaller lion a few centimetres from this meant that even as among lions the stronger gains the victory over the weaker, so he, the stronger, had overcome those who would play the camorrist with him.

Never, I believe, have we had a more striking proof that tattooing contains real ideographic hieroglyphs which take the place of writing. They might be compared to the inscriptions of the ancient Mexicans and Indians, which, like the tattooings we have described, are the more animated history of individuals. Certainly these tattooings declare more than any official brief to reveal to us the fierce and obscene hearts of these unfortunates.

This multiplicity of figures proves also that criminals, like savages, are very little sensitive to pain. Another fact that characterizes tattooing is precocity. According to Tardieu and Berson, tattooing is never remarked in France before the age of sixteen years (excepting, of course, the cases of ship-boys who have borrowed the custom from sailors); yet we have found, even among the general public, four cases in children of from seven to nine years of age; and of eighty-nine adult criminals, sixty-six displayed tattooings which were made between nine and sixteen years.

Some tattoo marks are used by societies as signals of recognition. In Bavaria and the south of Germany the highway robbers, who are united into a real association, recognize one another by the epigraphic tattoo marks *T. und L.*, meaning *Thal und Land* (valley and country), words which they exchange with one another, each uttering half the phrase, when they meet. Without that they would betray themselves to the police.

What is the origin of this usage? Religion, which has so much power over peoples and which proves so obstinate in preserving ancient customs, has certainly contributed to maintain it among the more barbarous part of our populations; we see a quasi-official proof of it at Lorette. Those who cultivate a devotion for a saint believe that by engraving his image on their flesh will give him a proof, a clear testimony, of their love. We know that the Phoenicians marked the sign of their divinity on their foreheads (Ewald, *Judaischen Alterthum*, iii); in the Marshall Islands they have to ask the permission of the gods to tattoo themselves; and the priests alone in New Zealand perform the office of tattooing (Scherzer). Lubbock adds to this that a woman who does not wear a tattoo mark can not enjoy eternal felicity. The women of Britain tattooed themselves in obedience to religion (Pliny, 33).

The second cause is the spirit of imitation. A Lombard soldier answered me laughingly one day when I rallied him on his having spent a small sum to spoil his arm: "See, monsieur, we are like sheep; and when one of us does anything we all imitate him at once, even if we risk doing ourselves harm."

Love of distinction also has its influence. A thief of the most incorrigible sort, who had six brothers tattooed like himself, implored me, although he was half covered with the oddest tattoo marks, to find him a professional tattooer to complete what might well be styled the embroidery of his skin. "When the tattooing is very curious and spread all over the body," he told me, "it is to us other thieves like the black coat of society with decorations; the more we are tattooed, the more we esteem one another; the more a person is tattooed, the more influence he has over his criminal companions, either in or out of prison. On the contrary, one who is not tattooed has no influence; he is regarded simply as a good fellow, and is not esteemed by the company."

There are also tattooings inspired by vengeance. Bastrenga, the cruel assassin of T—, had various tattoo marks on his arm (a horse, an anchor, etc.). On the advice of his father, who remonstrated with him that they would make him more easily recognizable, he effaced them. But in 1868 he was arrested anew by the police agents, and when he resisted actively one of them struck him so violently on the head that his eye was permanently hurt. Then, forgetting all prudence, he tattooed himself anew on the right arm; engraved there the fatal date of 1868, and a helmet on the arm that was to strike. "I shall keep this mark many years," he said, "till the time comes when I can satisfy my vengeance." This fact is curious, and illustrates one of the causes that induce savages to tattoo themselves – for registration. It shows, too, that with the born criminals the spirit of revenge prevails over the most ordinary prudence, even when they have been put on their guard. Indolence also counts for something. It explains the number of cases of tattooing which we meet among deserters, prisoners, shepherds, and sailors. Among eighty-nine tattooed persons, I saw seventy-one who had been tattooed in prison. Inaction is even harder to endure than pain. The influence of vanity is still greater. Those even who have not studied the insane know how powerful this passion is, which is found in all grades of the social scale, and perhaps even in animals, and can lead to the strangest and most foolish actions, from the chevalier who dotes on a little bit of ribbon to the idiot who struts with a straw behind his ear. For this, savages who go entirely naked wear figures on their breasts; for this, our contemporaries who are clothed tattoo that part of the body which is most exposed to sight, especially the forearm, and more frequently the right than the left. An old soldier told me that in 1820 there was not a man in the army, especially not a subordinate officer, who had not been tattooed to exhibit his courage in supporting pain. The figures of the tattooing vary in New Zealand as do the fashion styles with us.

The spirit of the organization and the spirit of sect contribute to it. I have been led to this conclusion by the examination of some initials which I studied upon incendiaries at Milan, and of certain signs found on young police prisoners at Turin and Naples. Figures of tarantulas and of frogs appear often. I suspect that some groups of camorrists have adopted this new kind of primitive ornamentation to distinguish their sect, as they formerly adopted rings, pins, chains, and different cuts of the beard.

Lastly, the stimulus of the noblest human passions has had its part. It is very natural that the rites of the village, the image of his patron, the recollections of infancy and of the heart's friend should return to the mind of the poor soldier, and be rendered more lively by the tattooed design, when he is struggling against danger, suffering, and privations.

But the primary, chief cause that has spread this custom among us is in my opinion atavism, or that other kind of historical atavism that is called tradition. Tattooing is, in fact, one of the essential characteristics of primitive man, and of men who still live in the savage state.

Some of those pointed bones which are used by modern savages in tattooing themselves have been found in the prehistoric grottoes of Avignac, and in the tombs of ancient Egypt. The Assyrians, according to Lucian, and the Dacians, according to Pliny, covered their whole bodies with figures. The Phoenicians and the Jews traced lines which they called "signs of God" on their foreheads and their hands (Ewald, *Judaischen Alterthum*, ii, p. 7). This usage was so widespread among the Britons that their name (from Brith, painting), like that of Pict and Pictons, seems to have been derived from it. See Caesar. "These peoples," he says, "trace, with iron, designs on the skin of the youngest children, and color their warriors with *Isatis tinctoria* (woad) to render them more terrible on the field of battle."

I do not believe there is a single savage people that does not tattoo more or less. The Payaguns painted their faces in blue on feast days. The various negro tribes distinguished themselves from one another, especially the tribes of Bambaras, by horizontal or vertical lines traced on the face, the chest, and arms. Kafir warriors have the privilege of decorating their legs with a long azure line, which they are able to make indelible. In Tahiti the women tattoo only the feet and hands or the ear, tracing collars or bracelets; the men, the whole body, on the hairy skin, on the nose, and the gums; and they often produce inflammations and gangrene, especially on the fingers and the gums. On the Marquesas Islands tattooing is a custom as well as a sacrament. Beginning at the age of fifteen or sixteen years, they put a girdle upon the young people and tattoo their fingers and legs, but always in a sacred place. Women, even princesses, have no right to tattoo anything but their hands and feet; grand personages cover their whole body; and while the designs on the lower part are delicate, those on the face lend it a grotesque and horrible aspect, so that enemies may be struck with fear. At Nukahiva, noble ladies are permitted to wear more numerous tattoo marks than the women of the people. In Samoa, widows, it seems, tattoo the tongue; men paint the body from the girdle to the knees. The bald heads of old men in the Marquesas Islands may be seen covered with tattoo marks. The fashionable ladies of Bagdad stained their temples and lips with azure, drew circles and rays of the same color on their legs, painted a blue girdle round their waists, and surrounded each of their breasts with a crown of blue flowers. Tattooing is practiced in Polynesia at the age of from eleven to thirteen years; and is to these natives what the *toga pretexta* was to young Romans. In the Marquesas Islands it serves as a kind of clothing to the men; they might be mistakenly supposed to be covered with armor. Their face is hidden under the marks. The women here are generally but little tattooed, but coquettes wear the marks on their feet, hands, arms, legs, and forearms – designs so delicate that they might be taken for stockings and gloves in the daytime.

In order to please the women and to be able to find a wife, writes Delisle, the Laotian should be tattooed from the navel to below the calf, all round the thigh; while among the Dyacks the women submit to the operation in order to get husbands. Laotian tattooing is very animated, and represents fantastic animals, like those on the Buddhist monuments. Among the aborigines of the Marquesas Islands the tattooing exhibits, on the women, designs of every sort: boots, gloves, suns, and lines drawn with remarkable fineness and perfection; on the men, animals – sharks, crabs, lizards, snakes – or plants, or geometrical figures. Here tattooing constitutes real works of art.

Sometimes tattooing and mutilation are combined, as in the famous chiefs' heads of New Zealand, which are overloaded with curved lines, with deep incisions showing as hollows, and with dark colors, with the intervals colored with dotted tattooing that gives the skin a bluish tinge. These curved lines spare no part of the face, and are closer and more numerous, according to the fame of the bearer of them as a warrior, or the antiquity of the origin of his chiefly dignity. The tattooing of the New Zealanders has found an unanticipated use in their relations with Europeans. Thus, the missionaries having bought a tract of land, the facial tattoo patterns of the vendor were drawn at the bottom of the deed, to serve as his signature.

The skins of all the grand chiefs of Guinea are in effect damascened. In New Zealand tattooing forms a sort of coat of arms. The common people are not allowed to practice it; and the chiefs are not permitted to decorate themselves with certain marks till they have accomplished some great enterprise. Toupes, an intelligent New Zealander, who was brought to London a few years ago, insisted upon a photographer taking pains to bring out his tattoo marks well. "Europeans," he said, "write their names with a pen; Toupes writes his this way. No matter," he said also to Dumont d'Urville, "if the Chonqui are more powerful than I, they can not wear the lines on their foreheads, for my family is more illustrious than theirs." The ancient Thracians and the Picts distinguished their chiefs by their special tattooing. The Pagas of Sumatra add a new color every time they have killed an enemy.

Tattooing is the true writing of the savages, their first registry of civil condition. Some tattoo marks indicate the obligation of the debtor to serve his creditor for a certain time. The number and nature of objects received are likewise indicated (Krausen, *Ueber die Tatouiren*, 1873).

Nothing is more natural than to see a usage so widespread among savages and prehistoric peoples reappear in classes which, as the deep-sea bottoms retain the same temperature, have preserved the customs and superstitions, even to the hymns, of the primitive peoples, and who have, like them, violent passions, a blunted sensibility, a puerile vanity, long-standing habits of inaction, and very often nudity. There, indeed, among savages, are the principle models of this curious custom of tattooing.

A last proof of our position is given by the hieroglyphics which we have found to be so frequent among the tattoo marks of criminals, and upon which certain inscriptions which undoubtedly go back to an ancient age. A very interesting specimen of this kind is found in a study of tattooing in Portugal by Dr. Peixotto (*Tatouage en Portugal*, 1893), which I reproduce here:

Sator .... SATOR
Arepo .... AREPO
Tenet .... TENET
Opera .... OPERA
Rotas .... ROTAS

As the reader will see, it is the formula of a square, which reproduces the words, "Sator," "Tenet," "Opera," and "Rotas," on whichever of the four sides we read it, and in whichever vertical or horizontal direction – one of those magical formulas which, according to Kohler (*Anthropological Society of Berlin*, 1891), were used to drive away fevers from the age of the Romans, as far back probably, at least, as Cato's time.

The influences of atavism and tradition seem to me to be confirmed by the fact that we find the custom of tattooing diffused among classes so tenacious of old traditions as shepherds and peasants.

After this study, it appears to me to be proved that this custom of tattooing is a completely savage one, which is found only rarely among some persons who have fallen from our honest classes, and which does not prevail extensively except among criminals, with whom it has had a truly strange, almost professional, diffusion; and, as they sometimes say, it performs the service among them of uniforms among our soldiers. To us they serve a psychological purpose, in enabling us to discern the obscurer sides of the criminal's soul, his remarkable vanity, his thirst for vengeance, and his atavistic character, even in his writing.

Hence, when the attempt is made to introduce it into the respectable world, we feel a genuine disgust, if not for those who practice it, for those who suggest it, and who must have something atavistic and savage in their hearts. It is very much, in its way, like returning to the trials of God of the middle ages, to juridical duels – atavistic returns which we can not contemplate without horror.

O Fashion! You are very frivolous; you have caused many complaints against the most beautiful half of the human race! But you have not come to this, and I believe you will not be permitted to come to it.

SAVAGES AND CRIMINALS

BY

GUGLIELMO FERRERO

THE INDEPENDENT

VOL. 52, NO. 2710 (NOVEMBER 8, 1900), PP. 2688-2690.

O ne of the ideas of the Italian school of criminology which has given rise to the most lively discussions is that of the atavism of crime. Lombroso has affirmed that the actions we call crimes, and especially the more serious offenses, such as murder and theft, are normal and regular actions among savage nations, by whom they are by no means looked upon as worthy of censure or punishment. In a state of civilization, therefore, crime would be atavistic resurrection of a condition of things that is the normal one during the first barbaric periods of the history of mankind.

This theory has been answered by many with a weighty objection – *viz.*, that there are savage nations in existence, without the least trace of civilization, among whom crimes, and especially theft and murder, are very rare; that crimes are found to abound rather among those barbaric nations who have begun to adopt some of the principles of civilization rather than among entirely savage nations; for which reason crime should be considered the first poisonous fruit of the tree of civilization, rather that the normal and spontaneous growth of that which Rousseau would have called the state of nature.

Anyone who is thoroughly acquainted with the documents we possess concerning savage nations and races will find that the second assertion is nearer the truth than Lombroso's. Hence the theory of the atavism of crime might seem erroneous and one to be discarded. However, I think the theory of atavism is correct, and that it gives the very best possible explanation of the essence of the crime in civilization, provided the idea of atavism can be transferred from the crime to the criminal, from the action called crime to certain moral characteristics which are met with among the majority of criminals and are the principal incentives to the crime. Among those who have been guilty of the most serious offenses certain moral characteristics are met with, that seem to be peculiar to the psychology of the savage and barbarian, and render him a being in whom atavism reproduces certain characteristics which evolution has by now caused to disappear from the mind of civilized man. These atavistic characteristics of the criminal are, in my opinion, incapacity for work and impulsiveness.

Savage and barbaric nations, whether their natural disposition be good or bad, are all at the same time impulsive and slothful; that is to say, they cannot resist the stimulus of their sensations and feelings, and immediately decide upon action; any kind of activity, muscular or intellectual, that is continuous, methodical and regular is repugnant to them. It would seem as if that annihilation of consciousness, that Nirvana which is the ideal of life for the wise, according to Schopenhauer, were also the ideal of savages. Those seek it in an inert condition of the muscles and of the mind, as they usually live in a kind of continual torpor, out of which they awake, however, from time to time, upon the slightest provocation, when they are assailed by tremendous attacks of fury or by an irresistible need of violent exaltation. They then either commit excesses and acts of violence of every description, or they enter upon tumultuous, unbridled dancing, violent bodily exercise, licentious singing or orgies, till they sink back again into their habitual torpor.

According to an old missionary, Father Venegas, the characteristics of the natives of California were "stupidity and obtuseness, inconstancy, impetuosity and the blindness of their desires; and an extreme indolence which made them hate work." Among the indigenous tribes of America, the Dacotahs were described as usually quiet and impassive, but subject to frightful attacks of fury; the Serpente Indians as children, irritated and amused by trifles. We are told that the Tupis (South America), if they happened to tread on a stone, became so furious that they would begin to bite the latter like dogs. Speaking of the natives of North and South America in general, an old observer, De La Condamine, says that they are "enemies of all work, without anxiety for the future, incapable of foresight and reflection; ready to give way to puerile joy which they show by immoderate laughing and jumping; they pass their lives without thinking, they grow old without ever leaving childhood behind them, the defects of which they still retain." How it affirms that the feelings of the Australians are intense, but very transient; they are aroused and quenched in an instant. At the same time Peron, speaking of their indolence, says, "They see the earth cleared, they are offered implements and seeds, but neither example nor the hope of bettering their condition will induce them to work."

In Africa we find a proverbial giddiness and levity among the Hottentots. They are so little given to labor that they almost all live by begging and are reduced to a state of extreme muscular debility. Baines observed that it required four Hottentots to lift a sack of flour which a European sailor carried himself. Also, the negro tribes of Africa, when observed in their native country, before having been put to the test of slavery, proved essentially lazy and impulsive. The negro, said Winwood Reade, passes his days in indolence, and according to Pruner Bey, the most important characteristic of the African negro is the ease with which he passes from one extreme to the other, and the sudden violence and brevity of his fits of rage.

The same remarks apply to nations which afterward became civilized when they were barbaric. The Teutonic race is nowadays universally reputed calm and tenaciously laborious, yet eighteen centuries ago Tacitus describes it as extremely impulsive and choleric, desirous of prolonged leisure and indolent. Writes Tacitus in his book on Germany: "Rarely do they scourge and chain their slaves. More frequently they kill them, not from a premeditated severity of correction, but on the impulse of passion." And elsewhere: "When not engaged in war... they do nothing but sleep and eat. The strongest and most warlike live in idleness, leaving to the women, the old men and the weak, the care of the houses and fields and becoming stupefied in their sloth."

This is why unbridled, violent dancing and games of chance were so much liked by savage and barbarous nations. The habitual torpor in which they usually live is succeeded from time to time by restlessness and a need of exaltation and excitement, which vents itself in frenzied movement or the anxieties of gambling.

Now these same characteristics are met with among criminals who have been guilty of serious offenses, especially among those whom Lombroso has called *born criminals*. The latter are principally lazy and impulsive, like savages. Lombroso has studied a great number of murderers and thieves whose perversity was such as to point to their having been born criminals, and has found that the majority were eccentric men of an extraordinary irritability, which a trifle sufficed to change into impulsive actions; that they were men of the most capricious temper, irritated against themselves and others, by turns gay and depressed without any reason, and ready to pass without any cause from one state to another.

At the same time, impulsiveness in criminals is accompanied by laziness, which is perhaps their chief characteristic. In some recent statistics made in Germany, Sichart found that among 3,181 prisoners almost half the number—*viz.*, 1,347—had a horror of work, and 962 of these were thieves. This confirms Vidocq's words: "The thieves are incapable of anything which calls for energy or assidiuty; they cannot do anything except steal." For America, the researches made by Wines prove that among 6,958 murderers who were convicted in 1890, 5,175 were without any trade or profession, and Wright has calculated that in Massachusetts 2,991 of the 4,340 criminals condemned for various offenses had no profession, and that in Pennsylvania the convicts without any calling were found in the proportion of 88 per cent. The general superintendent of the Elmira Reformatory, Z. R. Brockway, affirms that in the case of 34 per cent of the inmates no moral suggestion is able to induce them to work or arouse their attention.

Does not Brockway thus almost unconsciously affirm that this minority of refractory criminals is composed of beings resembling the primitive savage, who cannot be induced to work except when reduced to a state of slavery and forced physical violence? That they are, in other words, savages lost in modern life, because they cannot bring themselves to work. Therefore, it is not the propensity to commit some crime or other which is atavistic in the criminal, but inability for methodical work added to impulsiveness.

The mind of the criminal has not properly developed, through some congenital or acquired deficiency; its development has stopped at an inferior stage, which resembles in many respects that of the minds of savages and barbarians; it is therefore naturally incapable, or has become artificially, of acquiring that self control and taste for methodical work which are peculiar to civilized man. Not that the criminal is absolutely and always inactive; he is at times capable of displaying intense activity; for certain crimes, such as theft and swindling, very often call for a great amount of labor, because they must be prepared for a long time beforehand, and many difficulties must be overcome in their execution. But it is regular and methodical work that is repugnant to the criminal; work that is prolonged for many hours and unvaried day by day, the modern work of the workshop or the office; hence, even if he is capable of making a great effort sometimes, in order to commit a crime, he will never submit to any occupation which takes him back daily at the same hour to the same desk, to the same instrument, in order to perform the same task for the same number of hours.

Hence the criminal is a man whose inability to submit to regular work recalls in the midst of civilization the inferior types of the human race. This inability is innate and incurable in the small group of criminals that Lombroso has called born criminals; but it is acquired and remediable in the class of the incidental criminals. The habit of methodical work which disciplines all the violent passions of man may easily be acquired by men who are normal or even a little degenerate, if education is begun early; above all, especially in the youth who has the example of work constantly before his eyes. It is difficult on the other hand, when, on account of unfortunate circumstances, the youth grows up in idleness, because the farther advanced a man is in years the harder it becomes to train him to work. This is, therefore, the principal form of social influence on crime, because our state of society has unfortunately not yet succeeded in providing every one, as it ought, with an efficacious training to work; it abandons many young men in idleness, thus reducing them artificially to the state of savages and barbarians, exposing them to the risk of becoming criminals in one way or another. This proves how good an idea it was which directed the organization of the State Reformatory at Elmira, where the young criminals are carefully trained to work; to transform the semi-barbarians, idle and impulsive, into self controlled, hard working men, with definite moral ideas. And it proves how mistaken and absurd a system that of cellular confinement is, which is prevalent in Europe, by means of which criminals whose worst moral defect is laziness are supposed to be reformed by condemning them to inactivity for years within a narrow cell, and to the compulsory torpor of long days passed in a small room, either thinking of nothing at all or thinking of new crimes to be committed as soon as their term of imprisonment shall expire.

ILLUSTRATIVE STUDIES IN CRIMINAL ANTHROPOLOGY

BY

CESARE LOMBROSO

MONIST

VOL. 1 (1890), PP. 186-196

It is my desire to provide the learned reading audience of this august publication with some knowledge concerning the researches which have lately been undertaken by myself and others in support of criminal anthropology and psychiatry.

Secretions.—Dr. Ottolenghi has made in the laboratory a number of important observations with 15 born criminals and 3 occasional criminals, for the purpose of ascertaining the proportional quantities of urea, chlorides, and phosphates eliminated under the same alimentary conditions. Here are the average results as they were given in *The Journal of the Medical Academy of Turin*, 1888, in the *Archivio di Psichiatria, vol. 9, 1888*, and in *Scienze Penali et Antropologia Criminale*, Turin, 1888:

Urea per 100 Grammes of the Weight of the Body

Born Criminals	0.39
Occasional Criminals	8.53

Phosphates per 100 Grammes of the Weight of the Body

Born Criminals	0.024
Occasional Criminals	0.019

Chlorides per 100 Grammes of the Weight of the Body

Born Criminals	0.28
Occasional Criminals	0.29

There is therefore amongst the born criminals a diminuation in the elimination of urea; and an augmentation in that of phosphates, while the elimination of chlorides does not vary. He has obtained the same results in the case of psychical epilepsy, while the occasional criminal offers no anomaly in this respect. In connection with this it may be stated, that, on the other hand, Mr. Rivano found amongst epileptics on the days of paroxysm a greater quantity of urea and less phosphates (*Archivio di Freniatria*, 1889).

Power of Smell.—Dr. Ottolenghi has also studied the power of smell amongst criminals. He has contrived with this object in view an osmometer, containing 12 aqueous solutions of the essence of cloves varying from 1 part in 50,000 to 1 part in 100. He made his observations in several series, one each day only; the conditions of ventilation being the same, and the solutions being renewed for each observation, to avoid errors caused by evaporation. He looked first for the lowest degree at which olfactory perception began. In former experiments he proceeded differently. He disarranged the different bottles, and requested the subject to replace the same in the order of the intensity of their odor. He has divided the errors of disposition which resulted into serious and less serious errors, according as, in the order of the solutions, there occurred a distance of several or only one degree. He examined 80 criminals (50 men, 30 women) and 50 normal persons (30 men, mostly chosen amongst the prison warders, and 20 respectable women). Here are the results:

While amongst the normal males the average power of smell varied between the third and fourth degree of the osmometer, amongst the criminals it varied from the fifth to the sixth degree; 44 individuals had no power of smell at all. While the honest men made an average of three errors in the disposition of the bottles, the criminals made five, of which three were so-called serious ones.

The normal women touched the fourth degree of the osmometer, the criminal women the sixth degree; with two the power of smell was wanting entirely. While the normal women made an average of four faults in the disposition, the criminal women made five.

In eight cases of anosmia (loss of the sense of smell), presented in a certain set of criminals, two cases were due to nasal deformities; the others were a kind of smell-blindness; the subjects were susceptible to odoriferous excitations, but were unable to specify them and still less to classify them.

To verify what was really true in the assertion, that criminal offenders against morality and customs have a highly developed power of smell, he examined this power in 30 ravishers and 40 prostitutes (see Krafft-Ebing, *Psychopatia Sexualis*, 4th edition, Stuttgart, 1889, and *Archivio di Psichiatria*, vol. 10, 1889). In the former he found olfactory blindness in the ratio of 33 to 100; the remainder possessed an average power corresponding to the fifth degree of the osmometer. Arranging, then, the different solutions according to their intensity, he observed three so-called serious errors. In 19 per cent of the girls examined, he found olfactory blindness; and for the others an average acuteness corresponding to the fifth degree of the osmometer. Comparing these results with those obtained for the normal subjects and for regular criminals, the power of smell appears much less developed in the class just considered.

Taste—Dr. Ottolenghi has also examined the sense of taste of 100 criminals (60 born criminals, 20 occasional criminals, and 20 criminal women). He compared them with 20 men taken from the lower classes, 20 professors and students, 20 respectable women, and 40 prostitutes. These series of experiments were made with 11 solutions of strychnine (graduated 1 part in 80,000 to 1 part in 50,000) and of saccharine (from 1 part in 100,000 to 1 part in 10,000), and 10 of chloride of sodium (1 part in 500 to 3 parts in 100). The criminals showed remarkable obtuseness. The lowest degree of acuteness was found in the proportion of 38 to 100 in born criminals, 30 to 100 in occasional criminals, 20 to 100 in criminal women; while he found it in 14 per cent of the professors and the students, in 25 per cent of the men from the lower classes, in 30 per cent of the prostitutes, and finally in 10 percent of the respectable women.

Walk.—A study which I have made with Perachi (see our *Sur la Marche Suivant la Methode de Gilles de la Tourette*, 1889), shows us that, contrary to the case of normal men, the step of the left foot of criminals is generally longer than that of the right; besides they turn off from the line of the axis more to the right than to the left; their left foot, on being placed on the ground, forms with this line an angle of deviation more pronounced than the angle formed by their right foot. All these characteristics very often are found among epileptics.

Gestures.—It is an ancient habit among criminals to communicate their thoughts by gestures. Ave-Lallemant describes a set of gestures used among German thieves—a real language executed solely with the fingers, like the language of the deaf. Vidocq, the great Parisian detective of police, says that pickpockets, when they are watching a victim, give each other the signal of Saint John, which consists in putting their hand to their cravat or even in taking off their hat. But Pitre especially has published the most important information on this point. In his *"Usi e Costumi della Sicilia"* (Usages and Customs of Sicily), he describes 48 special kinds of gestures employed by delinquents. This phenomenon is explained by the exaggerated mobility with which born criminals are endowed, as is the case with children.

Morphological Anomalies

The Skeleton. —Mr. Tenchini, having made studies upon 63 skeletons of criminals, has found in the proportion of 6 out of 100 cases, the perforation of the olecranon (the bony prominence at the back of the elbow) which one observes in 36 out of 100 Europeans, and in 34 out of 100 Polynesians. He likewise observed additional ribs and vertebrae in 10 cases out of 100 of the criminals, and also too few, in the same proportion, the results of which remind us of the great variableness of these bones observed in the lower vertebrates. Lately he has even found in a criminal four sacral vertebrae too few, made up by four supplementary cervical vertebrae.

Madame Tarnorosky in her study of prostitutes, female thieves, and peasant women has demonstrated that the cranial capacity of prostitutes is inferior to that of female thieves and peasant women, and particularly inferior to that of women of good society. *Vice versa*, the zygomas (bones of the upper jaw) and the mandibles (lower jaw) were more developed among the prostitutes, who also exhibited a greater number of general atavistic anomalies, in the proportion of 87 to 100, while the proportion of the female thieves showing such anomalies was 79 to 100, and the proportion of peasant women was 12 to 100. (_Archivio di Psichiatria_, vol. 9, page 196, 1888).

Measurements

	Prostitutes 50	Prostitutes 100	Female Thieves 100	Peasant Women (No) 50	Peasant Women (So) 50	Ladies of Society 50
Anteposterior Diameter 17.7	17.8	17.9	18.3	18.0	18.3
Maximum Trans. Diameter 13.9	14.4	14.9	14.5	14.5	14.5
Maximum Circumference 52.9	53.3	53.5	52.7	53.6	58.8
Zygomatic Distance 11.4	11.3	11.2	10.9	11.4	11.3
Mandible Bi-angle Distance 10.1	10.8	09.1	09.1	09.9	09.8

In addition, it should also be noted that the prostitutes studied by Madame Tarnorosky had 33 in 100 of their parents addicted to drink, while the female thieves had 41 in 100 and the peasant women 16 in 100. Mr. De Albertis has found tattooing among 300 prostitutes of Genoa in the enormous proportion of 70 in 100 (_Archivio di Psichiatria_, vol. 10, 1889). He has also found the tactile sensibility of the debauched women very much diminished: 3.6 millimetres to the right and 4 millimetres to the left.

Among criminal women, Saloalto has made studies altogether new and exciting. He has recognized among 130 female thieves the degenerative character, anomalies of the skull and of the physiognomy, in a less degree than among the men thieves; he has found brachycephaly in 7, oxycephaly in 29, platycephaly in 7, the retreating forehead in 7, strabismus in 11, protruding ears in 6, the sense of touch was normal in only 2 out of 100, the reflexions of the tendons decreasing in 4 out of 100, and exaggerated in 12 out of 100.

Marro and Marselli have explained by sexual selection this enormous difference, which one also finds among epileptics and particularly in insane people. The men in fact do not choose ugly women with degenerative characteristics, while the women have no choice, and very often an ugly man, criminal, but vigorous, for this reason triumphs over all obstacles, and sometimes he is even preferred! (Flaubert, *Correspondence*, 1889). Let us add that the care of maternity softens the character of women, and augments in them the sentiment of pity.

Dr. Ottolenghi has studied in my criminal anthropological laboratory the wrinkles of 200 criminals and 200 normal persons (workingmen and peasants), and he has found that they occur earlier and much more frequently among the criminals. In fact, two to five times more so than among normal persons, with predominance of the zygomatic wrinkle (situated in the middle of each cheek), which wrinkle may well be called the wrinkle of vice, and is the characteristic wrinkle of criminals.

	Under 25 Years of Age		Between 25 and 50 Years	
Location	Normal Per 100	Criminal Per 100	Normal Per 100	Criminal Per 100
Wrinkles of the Forehead	07.1	34	62	86
Nasolabial Wrinkles	22.0	69	62	78
Zygomataic Wrinkles	0.00	16	18	33

In criminal women (80) also, wrinkles have been found more frequent than in normal women, although here the difference is not so marked. One calls to mind at once the wrinkle of the sorcerers. It is enough to look at the bust of the celebrated Sicilian woman poisoner, preserved in the National Museum of Palermo, whose face is one huge heap of unsightly wrinkles.

Dr. Ottolenghi, studying with me the frequency of canities (turning grey) and baldness in people, has demonstrated either absence or lateness of the same among criminals, as also among epileptics and certain cretins (*Archivio di Psichiatria*, vol. 10, 1889). Among the first, swindlers only tend to approach more the normal type. On the other hand, among 280 criminal women canities was found more frequently, and baldness less frequently, than in the case of 200 honest workingmen.

Classes	With Canities Per 100	With Baldness Per 100
400 Normal People	62.5	19.0
80 Epileptics	31.5	12.7
40 Cretins	11.7	13.5
490 Criminals	25.9	48.0
Thieves	24.4	02.6
Swindlers	47.0	13.1
Maimers	23.7	05.3
80 Criminal Women	45.0	09.7
200 Honest Women	60	13.0

We shall not terminate this part of our discussion without making mention of the beautiful discovery that we owe —it pleases us to state—to a lawyer, Mr. Anfosso. The tachyanthropometer which he has constructed is a real automatic measurer (*Archivio di Psichiatria*, vol. 11, page 173, 1890). We might name it—if the word did not possess a little to much local color—an anthropometric guillotine; so quickly and with the precision of a machine, does it give the most important measurements of the body, which makes the research of criminal anthropometry very easy, even for people who are entire strangers to the science, and it facilitates, moreover, the examination of the description of individual criminals, the perfection of which will always remain one of the most glorious distinctions of M. Alphonse Bertillon. And at the same time that this instrument renders services to the administration of justice, it permits on a grand scale observations which hitherto were only obtainable by the learned.

Experiments were made a short time ago by Mr. Rossi, who studied the result of these measurements in 100 criminals (nearly all thieves). He found the breadth of the span of the arms to be greater than the height of the body in 88, and in 11 to be less. In 30 he found the right foot larger, and in 58 he found the left foot larger. In only 12 were both feet found to be of equal dimension. The right arms of 43 per cent were longer than the left, and the left in 54 per cent were longer than the right. The valuable research of Mr. Rossi only serves to confirm to a most marvelous degree the *gaucherie*, mancinism, or structural misproportion, that had before been indicated by dynamometry and the study of the walk and gait of criminals (*Archivio di Psichiatria*, vol. 10, page 191, 1889). The very frequent recurrence of anatomical misproportion and *gaucherie* could not be better confirmed, and there are in this atavistic symptoms, for Rollet has observed in 42 anthropoid apes the left humerus to be longer than the right, in the proportion of 60 to 100, while among men the proportion is only 7 out of 100 (*Revue Scientifique*, 1889).

This anatomical misproportion I have recently verified with Mr. Ottolenghi by measurements of the two hands, the middle fingers, and the feet, right and left, in 90 normal persons and in 100 born criminals, the results of which appear in *Archivio di Psichiatria*, vol. 10, page 8, 1889. For your convenience, I provide below for your inspection a summary of my findings:

Types	Hand Longer Right Left Per Centum		Middle Finger Right Left Per Centum		Foot Right Left Per Centum	
Normal Persons	14.4	11.0	16.6	15.5	38.5	15.6
Criminals	05.0	25.0	10.0	27.0	27.0	35.0
Swindlers	04.3	13.0	13.0	21.7	21.7	26.0
Ravishers	07.0	14.2	14.2	28.4	35.7	35.7
Maimers	15.0	25.0	05.0	25.0	20.0	55.0
Thieves	00.0	34.8	13.0	30.4	26.0	26.6
Pickpockets	00.0	35.0	05.0	30.0	35.0	25.0

Tattooing— I was under the belief that in this respect nothing more was to be said after the beautiful studies of Messrs. Lacassagne and Marro, and after, of course, my own, which have appeared in *Nouvelle Revue* (for 1888), and also in my latest, 4th edition of *Uomo Delinquente*, (Turin, 1889). However, the researches made by Messrs. Severi, Lucchini, and Boselli on 4,000 new criminals have given results of a high importance and first of all a proportion of eight fold greater than that of the alienists of the same district (Florence and Lucca). The prevalency of this practice is enormous. It amounts to 40 in 100 among military criminals and to 33 in 100 among criminals under age. The women give a proportion of only 1.6 in 100, but this would be increased to 2 in 100 if we included certain kinds of fly-tattooing (*tatouages mouches*) resembling beauty spots, which are found even in high life prostitution.

What chiefly astonishes us in these researches, next to the frequency of the phenomenon, is the specific character of the tattooings: their obscenity, the vaunting of crime, and the strange contrast of evil passions and the highest sentiments.

M. C., aged 27 years, convicted at least fifty times for affrays, and the assaulting and wounding of men and horses, has the history of his crimes literally written on his skin; and in this respect, let us note that the infamous De Rosny, who only lately committed suicide in Lyons, had her body covered with tattooings in the form of erotic figures. One could read there the list of her lovers and the dates at which she left them.

F. L., a carrier, aged 26 years, several times convicted, bears on his breast a heart pierced by a poniard (the sign of vengeance), and on his right hand a female singer of a *café chantant*, of whom he was enamoured. By the side of these tattooings, and others which propriety forbids us to cite (but which you may consult at your leisure in *Atlas de L'Homme Criminel*, Paris, 1888), one sees with surprise the picture of a tomb with the epitaph: "To my beloved father." Strange contradictions of the human mind!

A certain B, a deserter, has on his chest a St. George and the cross of the Legion of Honor, and on the right arm a woman, very little dressed, who drinks with the inscription: "Let us wet the interior a little."

Q. A., a laborer, convicted many times for theft, expelled from France and Switzerland, has on his chest two Swiss gendarmes with the word "Long live the Republic!" On his right arm he has a heart pierced through, and at the side the head of a fish—a mackerel, to signify that he will poniard a bully, his rival.

We have seen on the left arm of another thief, a pot with a lemon tree, and the initials "V. G." (*vengeance*), which in the strange language of the criminals means treason, and afterwards, revenge. He did not conceal from us the fact that his constant thought was to revenge himself on the woman who loved him and then abandoned him. His desire was to cut off her nose. His brother offered to perform the operation for him, but this he refused, reserving for himself the pleasure of executing his purpose when he should ultimately be liberated.

One sees, therefore, from these few examples, that there is among criminals a kind of hieroglyphical writing, but which is not regulated or fixed. The system is founded on daily happenings and slang, as would be the case among primitive mankind. Very often, in fact, a key signifies among thieves the silence of secrecy; and a death's-head (the bare skull), revenge. Sometimes points are used instead of figures. In this way one criminal marked himself with 17 points, which means, to his mind, that he proposes to inflict injury on his enemy seventeen times, whenever he meets with him.

The criminal tattooers of Naples have the habit of making long inscriptions on their bodies, but initials are used instead of words. Many Camorrists of Naples carrying a tattooing which represents iron bars, behind which there is a prisoner and underneath the initials "Q. F. Q. P. M.," which means "*Quando finiranno queste pene? Mai!*" (When will these pains end? Never!). Others bear the epigraph C. G. P. V., etc., which means "*Courage, galeriens, pour voler et piler; nous devons tout mettre a sang et a feu!*" (Courage, convicts, to steal and to rob; we must put all to the sword and fire!). We see here at once that certain forms of tattooing are employed by criminal federations, and serve as a sort of rallying-call. In Bavaria and in the South of Germany, the pickpockets, who are united together in real alliances, recognize each other by the epigraphic tattooing "T und L," which means *Thal und Land* (valley and country), words which they must exchange in a low voice when they meet each other, in order not to be denounced to the police. A thief, R, who has on his right arm a design representing two hands crossed, and the word *union* (unity) surrounded by a garland of flowers, told us that this tattooing is extensively adopted by malefactors in the South of France (Draguignan). According to the revelations made to us by emerited Camorrists, a lizard or a serpent denotes the first grade of this dangerous association.

I pass over in silence, and for good reasons, the tattooings spread over all the remaining parts of the body.

In the *Rivista de Antropologia Criminal*, a new periodical publication which has just appeared in Madrid, Spain, Mr. Sallilas has published an excellent study relative to the tattooing of Spanish criminals. According to him, this is a frequent custom among murderers. The predominance of the religious character is there noticeable, but always with the seal of lewd obscenity, universally observed. I have lately had occasion to verify that the impulsion which leads criminals to inflict on themselves this strange operation is atavistic. One of the most incorrigible thieves I have met, who has six brothers tattooed like himself, begged of me, notwithstanding he was half covered with the most obscene tattooings, to find him a professional tattooer who should complete what might well be called the carpeting on his skin. "When the tattooing is very odd and grotesque, and spreads over the whole body," he said, "it is for us thieves what the black dress coat and the decorated vest is to society. The more we are tattooed the greater is our esteem for one another; the more an individual is tattooed, the more authority has he over his companions. On the other hand, he who is not much tattooed enjoys no influence whatsoever with us; he is not considered a thorough scoundrel, and has not the estimation of his fellows." "Very often," another told me, "when we visited prostitutes, and they saw us covered all over with tattooings, they overwhelmed us with presents, and gave us money instead of demanding it." If all that is not atavism, atavism does not exist in science.

Of this characteristic, of course, as of all the other characteristics of criminals, one may say that it is to be met with among normal people. But the chief thing here is its proportion, its commonness, and the exaggerated extent to which it is practiced. Amongst honest, respectable people its peculiar complexion, its local and obscene coloring, and the useless, vain, and imprudent display of crime are wanting.

Again, it will probably be objected that this is not criminal anthropology, and that only through the latter science can we trace out the picture of the criminal. I could well answer here, that these tattooings are really psychological phenomena which are an adjunct to criminal anthropology. And I may add that Mr. Ferri, in the introductory part of his work on Homicides, (*L'Omicidio*, Turin, 1890) has given us in addition to a real statistical psychology, an analysis of all criminal propensities and of their extent before and after the crime. Among born criminals, for example, 42 in 100 always deny the crime with which they are charged, while among occasional criminals, and in particular among maimers, only 21 in 100 deny all; of the first 1 in 100, and of the second 2 in 100 confess their crime with tears.

SUGGESTIONS FOR FURTHER READING AND INQUIRY:

CRIMINAL ANTHROPOLOGY

"Hereditary Nature of Crime." Hugh Barclay. *Journal of Jurisprudence and Scottish Law Magazine*, vol. 14 (1870), pp. 251-260.

An interesting account of J. Bruce Thompson's theory that criminals are a quite distinct variety of *homo sapiens* who differ from modern or civilized man in their low physique and other degenerate characteristics. Thompson, like Lombroso, was trained in medicine and served for many years as the Chief Surgeon to the Perth Prison in Australia. His theory of the criminal as a hereditary throwback is significant because it pre-dates Lombroso by almost a decade.

"The Criminal Type." William Noyes. *Journal of Social Science*, vol. 24 (1888), pp. 31-42.

A fine overview of the principles advocated by the Italian school of criminal anthropology, followed by the results of criminal anthropometric studies made in houses of correction and grammar schools in the United States to ascertain whether juvenile criminals exhibit the same physical anomalies found by Cesare Lombroso in adult criminals.

"Professor Lombroso's New Theory of Political Crime." Helen Zimmern. *Blackwood's Edinburgh Magazine*, vol. 149 (1891), pp. 202-211.

A very detailed discussion of the ideas expressed in Cesare Lombroso's book titled *Il Delitto Politico e la Rivoluzione*. Zimmern was the longtime editor of the *Florence Gazette*.

"The Child and the Savage: A Study in Primitive Man." Louis Robinson. *Blackwood's Edinburgh Magazine*, vol. 151 (1892), pp. 568-572.
A comparison, from the criminal anthropological perspective of atavism, of psychological and temperamental characteristics shared by adult savages and normally developed European children.

"Reformatory Prisons and Lombroso's Theories." Helen Zimmern. *Popular Science Monthly*, vol. 43 (1893), pp. 598-609.
A valuable and excellent discussion of the nature of prison and reformatory discipline that is logically suggested from the results of Cesare Lombroso's criminal anthropological researches, theories, and philosophies.

"The Increase of Crime, and Positivistic Criminology." Henry Charles Lea. *Forum*, vol. 17 (1894), pp. 666-675.
An interesting article with the thesis that the increase in the nature and frequency of crime during the nineteenth century is due, in great part, to the humanitarian influences which have steadily been interjected into criminal jurisprudence since the inception of the free-will movement during the Age of Enlightenment. Mitigation of punishment (including lax sentencing and the abandonment of capital punishment), legislation that coddles criminals, increased use of trial by jury, and relaxed prison discipline are all seen as facts contributing to an increasingly crime ridden society. The article contains a very fine outline of the leading tenets of the Italian school of criminal anthropology, with the conclusion that the government crime control policies suggested by the Italian school (i.e., the elimination of criminals by either perpetual confinement or death) would best serve to protect society.

"Criminal Women." Helen Zimmern. *Popular Science Monthly*, vol. 44 (1894), pp. 218-223.
A very detailed discussion of the book by Cesare Lombroso and Guglielmo Ferrero titled *La Donna Deliquente*.

"The Stuff That Anarchy Is Made Of." *Public Opinion*, vol. 16 (1894), p. 551.

Criminals are physical and mental degenerates and savages, who, as a consequence of their inferior evolutionary development, are unable to keep pace with and adapt to modern civilization.

"The Criminal: Is He Produced by Environment or Atavism?" Isabel Foard. *Westminster Review*, vol. 150 (1898), pp. 90–103.

A very fine overview of numerous criminal anthropological researches that bolster the notion that the criminal is produced from a heredity of physical, mental, and moral degeneracy aggravated by vice, alcohol, and poverty. The article concludes with two observations: first, the recidivist (or habitual criminal) is in a state of atavism and degeneracy from birth, and because he is cranially and morally deficient, he is a hopeless case for reform and should be perpetually confined; second, the occasional criminal is on a slightly higher evolutionary plane, and it is to his rehabilitation through a reformatory regimen that philanthropists should turn their attention.

"Criminal Anthropology and its Relation to Criminal Jurisprudence." Frances Alice Kellor. *American Journal of Sociology*, vol. 4 (1899), pp. 515–527, 630–648.

An outstanding article, written by the first great American female sociologist (University of Chicago), which treats upon, in very great depth, the entire range of reforms that ought to be made in the administration of criminal justice in order to capitalize on the body of knowledge about crime and criminals developed by both the Italian and American schools of criminal anthropology.

"The Power of Heredity." Isabel Foard. *Westminster Review*, vol. 151 (1899), pp. 538–553.

A comprehensive overview of the research that serves to suggest that physical as well as mental characteristics are the product of hereditary transmission.

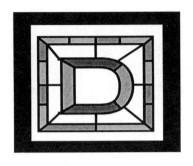

HEREDITARY DEGENERACY

(GENEALOGICAL RESEARCHES AND CRIMINAL PARENTAGE)

SPECIAL STUDY OF CRIME AND PAUPERISM AS PRESENTED BY THE "JUKE" FAMILY

BY

RICHARD LOUIS DUGDALE

THIRTEENTH ANNUAL REPORT OF THE PRISON ASSOCIATION OF NEW YORK (1875), PP. 139-187

In July of 1874, I was deputed by the New York Prison Association to visit thirteen of the county jails of this state and report thereupon, and subsequently I made a tour of inspection in pursuance of that appointment. No specially striking cases of criminal careers traceable through several generations presented themselves until Ulster County was reached. Here, however, I found six persons, under four family names, who, on inquiry, turned out to be blood relations, belonging to a long lineage, reaching back to some of the early colonists, and who had intermarried so slightly with the emigrant population of the old world that they may be called a strictly American family. They had lived in the same locality for generations, and were so despised by the reputable community that their actual family name had come to be used generally as a term of reproach. The name I employ to designate this family, "Juke," is not the real name of any family, but a pseudonym I have chosen so as to protect from aspersion worthy members of this large family of degenerates. The word "juke" is a colloquialism of upstate New York, and it means "to roost." It refers to the habit of fowls that have gone wild, and have no home, no nest, and no coop, preferring, instead, to fly into the trees and roost away from the places where they belong. It is also used in this area of the state as a pejorative term used to describe people who are indolent, lazy, and generally worthless as contributing members of the community.

Of these six persons, the oldest, a man of fifty-five, was waiting trial for receiving stolen goods. His daughter, aged eighteen, was being held as a material witness against him. Her uncle, aged forty-two, was waiting trial for burglary in the first-degree. The illegitimate daughter of the latter's wife, aged twelve years, upon which child the latter had attempted rape, was being held until such time she could be sent to the reformatory for vagrancy. Two brothers from another branch of the family, aged respectively nineteen and fourteen, were being held upon an accusation of assault with intent to kill, they having maliciously pushed a child over a high cliff and nearly killed him. Upon trial the oldest man was acquitted. Although the goods stolen were found in his house, the guilt belonged to his brother-in-law, the man aged forty-two, above mentioned, who was living in the house. This brother-in-law is an illegitimate child, an habitual criminal, and the son of an unpunished and cautious thief. He had two brothers and one sister, all of whom are thieves, the sister being the contriver of crime, they its executors. The daughter of this woman, the girl aged eighteen above mentioned, testified at the trial which resulted in convicting her uncle and procuring his sentence for twenty years to the state prison, that she was forced to join him in his last foray; that he had loaded her with the booty, and beat her on the journey home, over two miles, because she lagged under the load. When this girl was released, her family in jail and thus left without a home, she was forced to make her lodging in a brothel on the outskirts of the city. Next morning she applied to the judge to be recommitted to the county jail "for protection" against specified carnal outrages required of her and submitted to. She has since been sent to the house of refuge. Of the two boys, one was discharged by the grand jury, and the other was tried, convicted, and received five years' imprisonment in Sing Sing.

With comparatively little inquiry, it was found that out of 29 adult males in ages ranging from 15 to 75, the immediate blood relations of these six persons, 17 of them were criminals, or 58 per cent; while 15 were convicted of some degree of offense, and received 71 years of imprisonment. Fuller details are shown in Table I below, the name "Juke" standing for the blood relations of those found in the jail, the capital X for relations by marriage.

The crimes and misdemeanors they committed were assault and battery, assault with intent to kill, murder, attempt at rape, petit larceny, grand larceny, burglary, forgery, and cruelty to animals. With these facts in hand, it was thought wise to extend the investigation to other branches of the family, and for this purpose measures were taken to search more thoroughly.

TABLE I.

Showing Crime in the Illegitimate Branch of Ada Juke.

	Total number of adults.	Adult males.	Adult females.	Number of male criminals.	Number of convicted male criminals.	Years of sentence.
Juke blood............	49	29	20	17	15	71
X blood	32	16	16	5	5	8¼
Total....	81	45	36	22	20	79¼

The sheriff communicated the names of two physicians, both life-long residents of the county—one of them 84 years old, who had been for many years the town physician. These gentlemen gave me the genealogies of most of the branches of this family, furnishing many particulars of the individuals composing them. This opened up a large field of study, so large indeed, that at the time, I had no idea of its extent and still less of the variety of information which an analysis would yield.

Having brought back to New York City a very incomplete genealogical tree, including nearly 100 persons, it was thought wise to push the inquiry further. For that purpose a return to Ulster County was decided upon, and a further search instituted. By a modification of my original genealogical schedule—a modification not of the original matter, but one affecting the form and adding the element of time—it was easily adapted to the objective point of the present inquiry, _viz._, the study of the sequence of phenomena as set forth in criminal careers, to discover if there is a law in the evolution of crime, knowing which, it becomes easy to institute measures adequate and appropriate to the extinguishment of such derelictions. The authorities for the facts collected, therefore, became: for genealogies, intemperance, and social habits, the testimony of old residents who have known the older branches, of relatives, of employers, and of county and city officials. For diseases: physicians and their medical records. For pauperism: the poor-house records; for out-door relief, the books of the town poor-masters. And for crimes, the records of the county clerk's office and the county sheriff's books. No other testimony has been accepted for crime and pauperism except that of official records, and as many of the books could not be obtained, the tables in these respects are incomplete.

Experience showed that any given series of social conditions —such as honest childhood, criminal maturity, and pauper old age which might occur in the life of a single individual – might also be stretched over several generations, each step being removed from the other by a generation, and possibly, in some cases, by two. With this illustration, it will be seen that the nature of the investigation necessitated the study of families through successive generations, because only in that way was it possible to reach the entire facts embraced in the two main branches of inquiry into which the subject necessarily divides itself: the heredity that fixes the organic characteristics of the individual, and the environment which affects modifications in that organic heredity. It reduces the method of study then, to one of historico-biographic analysis, and enables us to judge of the cumulative effects of any condition which has operated through successive generations: heredity giving us those elements of character which are derived from the parent as a birth-right, and environment giving us all the events occurring after birth which have had an influence in the shaping of the individual character.

Heredity and environment, then, are the two parallels between which the whole question of crime and its treatment stretches, and the objective point is to determine how much of crime is due to heredity, and how much to environment. The answer to this will determine the limits of possibility in the work of amending vicious lives, and further, will indicate some of the automatic methods which the organization of society sets in motion, which, without this special design in view, nevertheless have the effect of changing criminal careers into useful one. The study of such spontaneous social activity will probably repay study as models to be followed in dealing with the criminal and dependent classes.

Now, heredity takes two leading forms that need to be contrasted: first, consanguinity, and second, the crossing of stocks, each presenting diverse results. The environment may judiciously be divided into two main branches: the surroundings which throw families into criminal careers and keep them in that groove, and the surroundings which take them out of criminal careers and keep them out of it. These two natural divisions, with their subdivisions, form the key-note to the present inquiry. A reference to the various tables which accompany this report will show how the events in the life of one parent may influence the career of the children, and likewise enable a strict comparison to be made between the life of any individual and that of his ancestry or his posterity, so that any characteristic which is hereditary will thus be revealed. On the other hand, the environment of each generation can be studied, the changes in that environment can be noted, and the results of the same can be ascertained. We can then know just what is the warp and woof out of which the life of any given individual is woven, and, given our cloth, we know what cloak we can cut out of it.

For the purpose of convenient illustration, the treatment of the facts gathered may be arranged according to the following diagram, which, however, is not intended to present a generalization of the facts themselves. Taking a general survey of the leading characteristics of the particular family under consideration, the arrangement is as follows:

CONSANGUINITY.

	Crime.		Fornication.		Pauperism.
	Prostitution.			Illegitimacy.	
	Exhaustion.			Intemperance.	
	Disease.			Extinction.	

NOT CONSANGUINEOUS.

In other words, we find that fornication, either consanguinous or not, is the backbone of their career, flanked on one side by pauperism, and on the other by crime. That the secondary features are prostitution, with its complement of bastardy, and its resultant neglected and miseducated childhood; exhaustion, with its complement intemperance and its resultant unbalanced minds; and disease, with its complement extinction.

The Habitat of the "Jukes."—The ancestral breeding-spot of this family nestles along the forest-covered margin of five lakes, so rocky as to be at some parts inaccessible. It may be called one of the crime cradles of the State of New York. Most of the Juke ancestors were squatters upon the soil, and in some instances have become owners by tax-title or by occupancy. They lived in log or stone houses similar to slave-hovels, all ages, sexes, relations, and strangers "bunking" indiscriminately. One form of this bunking has been described to me. During the winter the inmates lie on the floor strewn with straw or rushes like so many radii to the hearth, the embers of the fire forming a centre towards which their feet focus for warmth. This proximity, where not producing illicit relations, must often have evolved an atmosphere of suggestiveness fatal to habits of chastity. To this day some of the Jukes occupy the self-same shanties built nearly a century ago. The essential features of the habitat have remained stationary, and the social habits seem to survive in conformity to the persistence of the domiciliary environment. I have seen rude shelters made of boughs covered with sod, or the refuse slabs of saw mills set slanting against ledges of rock and used in the summer as abodes, the occupants bivouacking much as gypsies. Others of the habitations have two rooms, but so firmly has the habit established modes of living, that, nevertheless, they often use but one congregate dormitory. Sometimes I found an overcrowding so close it suggested that these dwellings were the country equivalents of city tenement houses. Domesticity is impossible. The older girls, finding no privacy within a home overrun with younger brothers and sisters, purchase privacy at the risk of prudence, and the night rambles through woods and tangles end, too often, in illegitimate offspring.

The Origin of the Stock of the "Jukes."—As the point of departure, and forming the first generation of the family who was found in the Ulster County Jail, was a man, who shall be called Max, born between 1720 and 1740 of the stock of early Dutch settlers. He is described as a hunter and fisher, and a hard drinker, jolly and companionable, averse to steady toil, working hard by spurts and idling by turns, who lived much as the backwoodsmen upon our frontiers now do. He became blind in his old age, entailing blindness upon his children and grandchildren. He had a numerous progeny, some of them almost certainly illegitimate. Two of his sons married two out of six sisters. These six sisters were born between the years 1740 and 1770, from what parents and under what circumstances it has been impossible to learn. Of one of them no reliable account was obtained, but the progeny of the remaining five sisters has been traced with more or less exactitude through five generations, thus making the total heredity which has been enrolled to stretch over seven generations, if we count Max as the first. The number of descendants registered includes 540 who are directly related by blood, and 169 related by marriage or cohabitation; in all 709 persons of all ages alive and dead. The total number of this lineage reaches to probably 1,200 persons, but the dispersions that have occurred at different times have prevented me from following up and enumerating many of the lateral branches. To distinguish those who are directly descended from these five sisters, they will be spoken of as belonging to the "Juke" blood. As the heredity of those who enter the family by marriage is in most instances not well traced, those persons will be spoken of generically as "the blood of X."

Consanguinity.—In order to trace the relationships more easily, I assigned each of the five sisters a name (assumed) beginning with the first five letters of the alphabet, which letter, in the tables appended, will be used in some instances instead of the full name "Ada," "Bell," "Clara," "Delia," and "Effie," and individuals outside the line will be marked by an X. A glance at Table II shows: (1) that the lines of intermarriage of the Juke blood show a minimum of crime; (2) that, in the main, crime begins in the progeny where the Juke blood has married into X; (3) that the illegitimate branches have chiefly married into X; (4) that the illegitimate branches produced a preponderance of crime; (5) that the intermarried branches show a preponderance of pauperism; (6) that the intermarried branches show a preponderance of girls; and (7) that the illegitimate branches produced a preponderance of males.

Harlotry.—The distinctive tendency of the Juke family is fully displayed by the statistical exhibit herein presented, for the most notable figures are those that relate to harlotry and bastardy. In Table III it will be noted that all girls of 14 are included among the marriageable women, because there are at least two mothers under 15 years of age. Under the heading of harlots are all women who have made lapses, however seldom. The term is not used synonymously with prostitute.

TABLE II.

Second generation.	Third generation.	Fourth generation.	Fifth generation.	REMARKS.
Ada, harlot before marriage.	A. × B., no crime *.	A. B. × X., crime	A. B. X., crime.......	Preponderance of males } Bastard line.
	A. × C., no crime....	A. B. × D. × X., reputable	A. B. D. X., reputable...	Semi-successful........ }
	A. × D., no cr:me....	A. C. × B., × X., no crime..	A. C. B. C., no crime....	Legitimate. Preponderance of girls.
	A. × X., no crime....	A. D. × X., no crime....	No crime	Legitimate. Distinct vely pauper line.
		A. X. × E. X., pauper....	A. X. E. X., pauper.....	
Bell, harlot before marriage.	B. × X., no crime....	B. X. × X., reputable....	Honest.......	Successful branch } Bastard line.
	B. × C., no crime....	B. X. × X., crime.......	B. X. X., crime	Criminal branch }
Clara, of good repute	C. × X., not traced	B. C. × X., no crime....		Legitimate.
	See A. × C. and B. × C.			Legitimate. Not traced.
Delia, harlot before marriage	D. × X., no crime	D. X. × X., crime.......	D. X. X., crime.......	Legitimate.
	E. = X*.	D. X. × B. C., no crime	D. X. B. C., no crime....	Legitimate.
Effie, reputation unknown.	E. × X., no crime	E. X. × X., crime.......	Not traced.......	Bastard line.
				Bastard line and barren.
				Legitimate.

* Explanation.   × Married.   = Cohabiting with.

The variations in the above percentages are accounted for by the fact that all the sources of information have not yet been exhausted. A full account would no doubt bring them more nearly approximate, and also increase the percentage of harlotry. How enormous is this percentage, amounting to a distinctive social feature, is demonstrated on comparison with the average prostitution in the community, which has been estimated by good authorities as only 1.66 per cent. These figures are probably too low, and supposing them to be 1.80 per cent, we find harlotry over twenty-nine times more frequent with the Juke women than in the average of the community.

Making a comparison between the women of the Juke and the X blood, we find, first, among the Jukes: marriageable women, 162; harlots, 84; percentage, 52.40, and second, among the X blood: marriageable women, 67, harlots, 28; percentage, 41.76. Having the figures that establish the sexual habits of the women of the Juke family and their accompanying tendency, we take up the question in its details. In the study of licentiousness, the lives of the women have, by preference, been chosen, because the maternity is more easily established by testimony, is much more significant of the social condition of the whole class, and more profoundly affects the next generation.

TABLE III.

Harlotry in the " Juke " blood.

	Gen. 2.	Gen. 3.	Gen. 4.	Gen. 5.	Gen. 6.	Totals.
Number of marriageable women..	5	16	39	90	12	162
Aggregate of harlotry	3	6	27	44	4	84
Percentage of harlotry..........	60	37.24	69.23	48.88	38.33	52.40

In Table IV the marriageable female children of Clara, who was chaste, are compared to the marriageable female children of Ada, a harlot, and are divided respectively as to the legitimate and illegitimate branches. In this table the children of Clara are divided into two classes—the first column being those who married into X, and the second, the total number of her children, including those who intermarried with the children of Ada and Bell. It will be seen by this, that the percentage shows a progressive increase as you pass from left to right, the first column showing a lower percentage than that of the average Juke blood, the other increasing as you proceed to consanguinous marriages with the children of Ada and Bell, to the illegitimate children of Ada. From this point of view it would seem that chastity is a hereditary characteristic possible of entailment, and *vice versa*.

TABLE IV.

Showing percentages of harlotry.

	Clara's, who have married outside the Ada and Bell lines.	Clara's, total number who have married into A and B.	Ada's legitimate.	Ada's illegitimate.	Average of "Juke" women, as by Table III.
Number of marriageable women......	18	64	36	20	
Unascertained	2	6	6	2	
Reputable	8	19	6	4	
Harlots before marriage.............	3	5	5	8	
Harlots after marriage	2	10	4	1	
Prostitutes	3	24	15	5	
Total harlotry......................	8	39	24	14	
Percentage of harlotry to total women.	44·44	60·93	66·66	70	52·40

This table, however, illustrates how the statistical method may lead an investigator into the error of supposing that a coincidence is a correlation, for, reasoning from the figures, we see plainly that it demonstrates the force of heredity, the chaste mother bearing a progeny more chaste than the unchaste mother, and the legitimate branch of the unchaste mother being more chaste than the illegitimate branch. From a consideration of special cases, which space does not permit me to present in detail here, but which will be reported in full in a later publication, we now come to formulating a few preliminary inductions on the subject: (1) harlotry may become a hereditary characteristic, and be perpetuated without any specially favoring environment to call it into activity; (2) in most cases the heredity is also accompanied by an environment which runs parallel to it, the two conditions giving cumulative force to a career of debauch; (3) where there is chastity in the heredity, the same also is accompanied by an environment favorable to such habits; (4) where the heredity and the environment are in the direction of harlotry, if the environment be changed at a sufficiently early period, the career of prostitution may be arrested and the sexual habits amended; (5) that early marriage tends to extinguish harlotry; and (6) that prostitution in the woman is the analogue of crime and pauperism in the man.

Illegitimacy.—In examining the question of harlotry it was found that out of 535 children born 335 were legitimate, 106 were illegitimate, and 84 were unknown. Discarding from the computation the 84 who are not ascertained, we get 23.50 per cent as the proportion of illegitimacy.

TABLE V.

Illegitimacy.

	Boys.	Girls.
Total number of children	224	251
Of legitimate birth	155	190
Of illegitimate birth	49	33
Per cent of bastards to total number, by sex	21.42	13.22
" " " " legitimates, by sex	33.61	17.36
" " " " total number, both sexes		23.50

From this it appears that there is an excess of girls over boys among the legitimate, while there is an excess of boys over girls among the illegitimate, and when we compare them by percentages the illegitimate boys are twice as numerous as the girls. If the object of our inquiry rested here, and a generalization upon the above figures contained in Table V were made, based on the conventional and generally accepted effects of illegitimacy on the question of crime and pauperism, the conclusion would be inevitable that the above figures explain the cause of pauperism and crime. The facts being at hand, it is perhaps safer to enter into a more minute inquiry. Passing from the consideration of aggregate numbers, we can now contemplate the analysis of particular cases revealed by my investigations. Of the five Juke sisters three are known to have had illegitimate children, Ada, Bell, and Delia. The two bastards of Delia were lazy neer-do-wells, who never married, and are not known to have had children, but little has been gathered respecting them. Of her legitimate children one, a girl, was the mother of criminals, and is the only line in the legitimate branches in which crime is found. Of the children of Ada the oldest was the father of the distinctively criminal branch of the family. Two of his sons, though never sent to prison, were notorious petty thieves and the fathers of convicted criminals, while two of their daughters were the mothers of criminals. None of the legitimate children or grandchildren of Ada are known to have been criminals. But while the children and grandchildren of Ada's oldest were criminals, the majority of them were legitimate. Thus we find 10 legitimate and 5 illegitimates among the descendants.

Of the children of Bell, the first four were illegitimate, three of them half-breed mulattoes. The three boys were, on the whole, more successful in life than the average of the Juke family. They all three acquired property, the youngest being the father of one child who was successful in life, also accumulating property. Of the oldest, a gentleman who knew all the earlier members of the Juke family, says: "He was the best of his generation, being honest, sober, and in every way manly." On the other hand, one branch of the posterity of Effie, almost all of whom are legitimate, exhibits a widespread and almost unbroken record of pauperism.

From these considerations and others from my investigations into particular cases, it follows that illegitimacy is not necessarily the cause of crime and pauperism, and the following preliminary inductions may be made: (1) among the first-born children of marriages, the female sex preponderates; (2) among the first born bastard children, the males preponderate; (3) it is not illegitimacy, *per se*, which is dangerous, but the environment of neglect which attends it, that is mischievous; and (4) illegitimates who are placed in a favorable environment may succeed in life better than legitimate children in the same environment.

Disease and Pauperism.—Running alongside of licentiousness, and as inseparable from it as is illegitimacy, are the diseases which are distinctive of it and which produce social phenomena closely connected with the present investigation. In the wake of disease follows pauperism, so in studying the one, we must necessarily discuss the other. But disease treats of physiological states, it is a biological question; therefore, the social questions included in the consideration of pauperism rest, in large measure, upon the data furnished by the study of vital force. Before taking up the statistics of disease, I give those of pauperism to show the general tendency of the Juke family to pauperism so that we may study the causes that produce that condition.

Comparing the alms-house relief of the state at large with the Jukes, according to the sexes, we find from an examination of the data displayed in Table VI that there is seven and a half times more pauperism among the Juke women than among the average of women for the state, the Juke men are over nine times more numerous, while the average for both sexes of the Juke and X blood mixed gives six and three-quarter times more paupers than the average of the state. According to the records of poor-houses and city alms-houses, the men found as inmates are in excess of the women, the ratio for 1871 being as 100 women to every 110 men; of the Jukes the ratio is 100 to 123, but when we look at the alms-house relief of the X blood the ratios are inverted, the women being to the men as 100 is to 79. Why this is, the present inquiry does not show, and has been revealed only during the preparation of this report; but that it is not an accident proved by the fact that the out-door relief shows the same relationship, though in a less degree, the ratio being 85 women to every 100 men.

We now take up the question of diseases, malformations, and injuries, in their relations to pauperism, first presenting the general statistics in Table VII. In this table the children who have died of diseases inherited from their parents and who were buried by the town are not included.

So we find that, while the percentage of pauperism for the whole family is only 22.22 per cent, the percentage of pauperism among the sick and disabled in 56.47 per cent. In one case, the hereditary blindness of one man cost the town 23 years of out-door relief for two people and a town burial. Another case of hereditary blindness cost eight years of out-door relief and three years of poor-house relief, with a town burial.

But the disease which Table VII shows as the most common, as it is by all odds the most destructive, and the most subtle and impossible to eradicate, is syphilis. Here, again, we test the value of aggregate statistics as an index of a social tendency. In this exhibit are enumerated only the cases properly vouched for by competent physicians, or so notorious as to have been widely known, or directly drawn from the records of the poor-house. Of these latter not more than six have been accepted. Here we find the proportion of those blighted by its reaches 10.86 per cent, but this percentage does not include half of the victims of this class of disorders. On the authority of physicians who know, from 25 to 30 per cent of the family are tainted with this disease.

In summing up this branch of the inquiry, the following preliminary inductions may be stated as the laws of pauperism

TABLE VI.

Of Pauperism, showing Out-door * and Alms-house Relief.

	Number of persons receiving out-door relief.	Number of years.	Estimated cost at $15 a year.	Number of persons receiving alms-house relief.	Number of years.	Estimated cost at $100 a year.	Total number of persons.	Percentage receiving out-door relief.	Percentage receiving alms-house relief.	Percentage of alms-house pauperism, male, female, and total for New York State in 1871.	Ratio between pauperism of State at large and the Juke family.
Women of the Juke blood....	45	242	$3,630	24	35	$3,500	251	13.94	9.56	1.26	As 1 to 7.590
Men of the Juke blood.......	50	270	4,050	29	46	4,600	224	20.09	12.94	1.39	As 1 to 9.309
Women of the X blood.......	20	125	1,875	5	7	700	67	29.85	7.44	1.26	As 1 to 5.900
Men of the X blood.........	27	97	1,455	6	8	800	102	26.56	5.83	1.39	As 1 to 4.239
Total number of Juke blood..	95	512	$7,680	53	81	$8,100	540	17.59	9.80	1.33	As 1 to 7.368
Total number of X blood.....	47	222	3,330	11	15	1,500	169	27.81	6.51	1.53	As 1 to 4.893
Grand total..............	142	734	$14,080	64	96	$9,600	709	20.02	9.02	1.33	As 1 to 6.767

* The out-door relief is dispensed by eight poor-masters, who live in four different towns, each town keeping a separate record of names and amounts of help. These records, since the beginning of this century, amount to an aggregate of 225 years, of which only sixty-four years could be consulted, the records of the 191 missing years being in many cases destroyed.
This table exhibits only the amount of relief which this family has obtained as shown by the records.

TABLE VII.

Diseases, Malformations and Injuries.

	Blind.	Deaf and Dumb.	Insane.	Idiotic.	Tubercular consumption.	Syphilis.	Constitutional syphilis.	Epilepsy.	Deformed.	Total number injured, deformed and diseased.	Number diseased persons receiving relief.	Percentage.
Juke blood..	10	......	1	1	1	29	22	......	1	65	33	50.77
X blood	1	1	......	......	1	13	3	1	......	20	15	75.00
Total.....	11	1	1	1	2	42	25	1	1	85	48	56.47

which are applicable to the case in hand, and may, upon a broader basis of facts, prove to be general laws applicable to pauperism in general; (1) pauperism is an indication of weakness at some essential point, either youth, disease, old age, injury, or for women, childbirth; (2) it rests chiefly upon disease in some form, tends to terminate in extinction, and may be called the sociological aspect of physical degeneration; (3) the diseases and debility which enter most largely in the production of pauperism are the result of sexual licentiousness; (4) the different degrees of adult pauperism, in the main, are indications of gradations of waning vitality. In this light the whole question is opened up, where indolence, which the dogmatic aphorism says "is the root of all evil," is not, after all, a mark of undervitalization, and an effect which acts only as a secondary cause; (5) pauperism in adult age, especially in the meridian of life, indicates an hereditary tendency which may or may not be modified by the environment; (6) pauperism follows men more frequently than women, indicating a decided tendency to hereditary pauperism; (7) the pauperism of childhood is an accident of life rather than a hereditary characteristic; (8) the youngest child has a tendency to become the pauper of the family; (9) that the youngest children are more likely to become the inmates of the poor-house through the misconduct or misfortune of parents than are the older ones; (10) that such younger children, who remain inmates of the alms-house long enough to form associations that live in the memory and habits that continue in the conduct, have a greater tendency to spontaneously revert to that condition whenever any emergency of life overtakes them, and domesticate there more readily than older children whose greater strength has kept them out; (11) that children old enough to provide for themselves are forced by necessity to rely upon themselves, and in consequence are less liable to become paupers in old age. (In consideration of the last two propositions, which practically treat on the question of environment, and show how great an influence it has on determining the career, I add a twelfth proposition, which is dogmatically put forth, although not fully sustained by the forces enumerated by the facts enumerated in the present study); (12) that pauperism which depends on social and educational disabilities, and not upon deep-seated constitutional disease, can and must be prevented by sound and felicitous measures of administration that will conform to the measures spontaneously set in motion by society, and for that reason generally acceptable as they will be efficacious.

Intemperance.—It may well be asked of me at this point, "You have treated of crime and pauperism and you have said nothing whatever about the one great and conspicuous cause of both, intemperance." The answer to this is that the importance of intemperance as a factor in crime and pauperism is not denied, and that in the investigation it received a place in the inquiries which were to be made about the careers of each individual. But there were certain considerations which made me hesitate to accept the current opinions as to the part which ardent spirits play in the carnival of crime. The temperance agitation has for many years taken a partisan character and become an "element of politics," with this inevitable result, that the discussion of the subject has been shifted from the domain of dispassionate observation into that of sentimentalist agitation, the conclusion arrived at being of the nature of hasty deductions from cherished opinions, or equally hasty and equally erroneous inductions from irrelevant facts. In visiting the jails it was not infrequent for a criminal to call me into a corner, and, in a semi-confidential tone, ask whether I wished to know what was the cause of his duress. As this was a main subject for my making visits to the jails, I always gave an affirmative answer, after which, with great gravity, the axiom was propounded that "It wasn't me, it was the rum." In other words, gin was the responsible Blue Beard who held the key to the secret cabinet of assassination.

Thus it happened that while the current opinions could not be accepted because they gave not adequate reason for the phenomena, and because they neglected to give many phenomena that might be fatal to the theory of the agency of rum in the drama, other explanations presented themselves as indicating a more correct conception. It must be remembered that the value of the present inquiry rests on the method of viewing the career of individuals and of recording the facts of each life such as is ascertainable in chronological order. Applying this to the solution of the intemperance question, I present the aggregate figures in Table VIII.

TABLE VIII.

Comparing temperance and intemperance.

	Healthy.	Diseased.	Licentious.	Chaste.	Licentious previous to intemperate.	Diseased previous to.	Total.
Temperate.......	13	1	7	....	....	....	26
Intemperate	3	10	29	....		3	45

In this table most of those who are marked healthy are not licentious. The table is not full because the information which has been furnished on the subject of intemperance has been much less full than on other points, and the order of time in which licentiousness and disease have taken place as related to drunkenness has not been given. Nonetheless, the law shadowed forth by this scanty evidence is that licentiousness has preceded the use of ardent spirits and caused a physical exhaustion that made stimulants grateful. In other words, that intemperance itself is only a secondary cause. It is more probable that a fuller investigation will show that certain diseases and mental disorders preceded the appetite for stimulants, and that the true cause of their use is the antecedent physical exhaustion. The remedy: healthy, well-balanced constitutions.

If this view should prove correct, one of the great points in the training of pauper and criminal children will be to pay special attention to sexual training, and to prevent and cure constitutional diseases which may have come to them as a heritage. Then the question of intemperance will be a long way toward its solution, the gin palace will cease to be a temptation, and prohibitory legislation will be superceded by hygienic training. Of course what is here presented is very inadequate to the subject, but careful reticence is better than brilliant error.

The points that need special observation seem to be; at what age has delirium tremens shown itself first; at what age habitual intemperance became confirmed; at what age drinking first began; what were the sexual habits at various periods, especially in youth; whether any deep-seated disease has preceded the intemperate habits; whether excessive study or labor has exhausted the vitality; whether there is a hereditary predisposition to dipsomania; whether the trade or occupation is detrimental to health; whether the locality of the habitation produces disease, and if so, of what kind; and, what is the temperament of the slave of the bottle? All these questions must be answered by ascertained facts before I can give an intelligent answer to the question "Is intemperance the cause of crime and pauperism?" or only a secondary cause that must be reached by well-ordered sanitary and hygienic measures.

Crime.—In Table IX, as only official records of crimes are entered, two principal causes for the smallness of the numbers of offenses need explaining. As respects crimes, the records of only one county (Ulster) were examined and this reaches back only to 1830, the earlier records, I have been told, are down in the cellar of the county clerk's office under the coal. To get a full record of the crimes of the Juke family the criminal records of three other counties need to be examined. As respects misdemeanors, these are to be found in the books of justices of the peace and the books of the sheriffs, both of which are almost all destroyed or laid away in private hands, packed in barrels, or stowed in garrets, and are presently inaccessible to me.

By reference to the table it will be found that crime runs chiefly in the illegitimate branches, and that crime chiefly appears after a marriage of the Juke blood into X. From this and other individual case data to voluminous to report in the space allotted for this report, I have reached the following preliminary conclusions respecting crime: (1) that the burden of crime is found in the illegitimate lines; (2) that the legitimate lines marry into crime; (3) that those streaks of crime found in the legitimate lines are found chiefly where there have been crosses into X; (4) that the eldest child has a tendency to be the criminal in the family; (5) that crime

TABLE IX.

CRIMES AGAINST PROPERTY.

		NUMBER OF OFFENSES.												
		2d Gen.		3d Gen.		4th Gen.		5th Gen.		6th Gen.		Total.		Total.
		M.	F.	M.	F.	M.	F.	M.	F.	M.	F.	M.	F.	
Misdemeanor	Juke	..	..	1	..	7	6	14	14	1	2	24	22	..
	X	..	..	1	..	1	1	8	1	..	..	9	3	..
Petit larceny	Juke	..	..	..	..	1	..	6	..	..	..	7	..	..
	X	..	..	.	..	3	..	2	..	..	..	5	.	..
Grand larceny	Juke	..	..	..	..	..	..	..	..	..	..	..	..	..
	X	..	..	..	..	1	..	2	..	..	..	3	..	..
Burglary	Juke	..	..	..	..	2	..	11	..	..	..	..	..	..
	X	..	..	..	..	2	1	..	..	..	..	..	..	..
Forgery	Juke	..	..	..	..	..	..	..	..	..	..	..	..	..
	X	..	..	..	..	1	..	..	..	..	..	1	..	.
False pretenses	Juke	..	..	..	..	..	..	..	..	..	..	..	..	..
	X	..	..	1	..	..	..	..	..	..	..	1	..	..
Robbery	Juke	..	..	..	..	..	..	1	..	..	..	1	..	..
	X	..	..	..	..	..	..	..	..	..	..	..	..	..
Total	Juke	..	..	1	..	10	6	32	14	1	2	44	22	66
	X	..	..	2	..	8	2	12	1	.	..	22	3	25
Grand total, offenses		..	..	3	..	13	8	44	15	1	2	66	25	91
Number of offenders	Juke	..	..	1	..	8	4	12	9	1	2	22	15	37
	X	2	..	2	..	6	2	8	1	..	..	16	3	19
Total		2	..	3	..	14	6	20	10	1	2	38	13	56

CRIMES AGAINST THE PERSON.

		M.	F.	M.	F.	M.	F.	M.	F.	M.	F.	M.	F.	Total
Assault and battery	Juke	..	..	..	..	3	..	3	..	..	..	6	..	..
	X	.	..	..	..	1	..	3	..	..	..	4	..	..
Assault, intent to kill	Juke	..	..	..	..	1	1	..	..	1	..	2	1	..
	X	..	..	..	..	..	..	..	..	..	..	..	..	..
Murder	Juke	..	..	..	..	1	..	1	..	..	..	2	..	..
	X	1	..	..	..	2	..	1	..	..	..	4	..	..
Rape, and attempt at rape	Juke	..	..	..	..	..	..	5	..	..	..	5	..	..
	X	..	..	..	..	..	..	..	..	..	..	..	..	..
Total offenses	Juke	..	..	..	..	5	1	9	..	1	..	15	1	16
	X	1	..	..	..	3	..	4	..	..	..	8	..	8
Grand total, offenses		1	..	..	..	8	1	13	..	1	..	23	1	24
Number of offenders	Juke	..	..	..	..	4	1	6	..	1	..	11	1	12
	X	1	..	..	..	4	..	4	..	..	..	9	..	9
Total number of offenders		1	..	..	..	8	1	10	..	1	..	20	1	21

chiefly follows the male lines; (6) that the longest lines of crime are along the line of the eldest son; (7) that crime as compared to pauperism is an indication of vigor; (8) that for this reason there is greater chance for reform in the criminal than there is in the pauper, whose condition is an indication of under-vitalization, and consequent untrainableness. This last proposition brings me now to a comparison of crime and pauperism.

The ideal pauper is the idiotic adult who never could and never will be able to help himself, and may be justly called a living embodiment of death. The ideal criminal is a courageous man in the prime of life who so skillfully contrives crime on a large scale, that he escapes detection and succeeds in making the community believe him to be as honest as he is generous. Between these two extremes there are endless gradations which gradually approach each other, until at last you reach a class who are too weak to be dangerous criminals, and too strong to be alms-house paupers. These men prefer the risks and excitements of criminality and the confinement of a prison where they meet congenial company, to the security against want and the stagnant life of the alms-house.

To more fully illustrate this I give Table X, in which is made a comparison of the distinctive criminal branch of Ada, with the distinctively pauper branch of Effie, so that the difference can be contrasted. It will be seen that while the criminal branch shows 35 per cent of out-door relief and 21 per cent of alms-house paupers, with 60 per cent of crime, the pauper branch shows 61 per cent of out-door relief, 38 per cent of alms-house pauperism, and 53 per cent of crime. But when we come to study the intensity of crime, we find that while nine offenders of the line of Ada have been sent to state prison for 60 years, only one has been sent for five years of the line of Effie. Again contrasting the crimes against property, against person, and vagrancy, the percentages show great fluctuations. While Ada's offspring perpetrate 54 per cent of crimes against property, including burglary, grand larceny, and highway robbery, Effie's only show 30 per cent, the highest crime being petit larceny, which is the lowest crime of the other branch. Of the crimes against the person, the children of Effie show a preponderance, 30 per cent, compared to 28 per cent, while the offenses compare on the other hand as to intensity; murder, one, attempt at rape, three; on the other, attempt to kill, one. When we come to vagrancy and breach of peace, the percentage stand between Ada's and Effie's children as 16 per cent to 46 per cent, and for vagrancy as 2 per cent to 38 per cent.

TABLE X.

Showing the Contrast between the Distinctively Pauper and the Distinctively Criminal Branches.

	Total number of males.	OUT-DOOR RELIEF. No. receiving it.	Per cent.	No. of years.	No. of years for each person.	Age of youngest adult receiving.	No. under 20 years who receive it.	No. under 25 years and over 20.	No. over 35 and under 40 who first received.	No. over 45 who first receive it.	ALMS-HOUSE RELIEF. No. receiving it.	Per cent.	No. of years.	No. of years to each person.	Children under 15 receiving it.	Age of youngest adult receiving it.	No. of adults under 30 receiving it.	No. of adults over 35 receiving it.	No. of adults over 50 receiving it.
Juke males (1) A. x B. branch	28	10	35.71	48	4.80	19	1	4	.	.	6	21.42	17	2.853	.	17	1	.	.
Juke males E. x X. branch	13	8	61.54	52	6.50	*19	1	.	2	3	4	38.86	5	1.000	5	23	1	.	1
Criminal males (1) A x B.	17	6	35.30	38	6.333	17	3	4	.	.	5	23.53	9	2.250	3	17	1	2	.
Criminal males E. x X.	7	7	100.00	44	6.285	17	1	.	4	2	4	57.14	4	1.000	.	23	1	.	1

* Town burial.

TABLE X.—(Continued).

	No. of criminals.	Per cent to total males.	No. of offenses.	No. of offenses to each criminal.	Offenses agt. property.	Per ct to total offenses.	Offenses against the person.	Per ct to total offenses.	Vagrancy, breach of peace.	Percentage to total offenses.	Years of prison or penitentiary.	Average No. of years to each person.	Years of county jail.	AGAINST PROPERTY. Highest crime.	Lowest crime.	AGAINST PERSON. Highest crime.	Lowest crime.	Longest sentence, years.
Juke males (1) A. x B. branch..	17	60.71	42	2.470	23	54.70	12	28.57	7	16.08	70¾	1.133	1¾	Burglary, 1st. H. robbery..	Petit larceny.	Murder. Rape....	Assault and battery.	20
Juke males E. x branch	7	53.84	13	1.857	4	30.77	4	30.77	8	46.15	5	.7143	¾	Petit larceny.	......	Attempt to kill.	Assault and battery.	5

Comparing the criminals of each branch to each other, we find while all of Effie's are pauperized, only 35 per cent of Ada's have received out-door relief, while the alms-house pauperism compare as 23 per cent of Ada, to 57 per cent of Effie. Looking still closer and comparing ages at which relief was received, we find only one of Ada, to five of Effie, received out-door relief under 25 years of age, while two of Ada's resisted application until after 35, and one after 45, while every one of Effie's seven criminals was a pauper before 35, in point of fact at 30. The contrast as to the alms-house pauperism appears much less than it really is, for, while Ada's account has three children in the poor-house whose ages range from four to ten, Effie's are all adults, ranging from 23 to 56 years of age.

From this comparison, it would seem that the distinctively pauper stock is less aggressive than the criminal, the crimes of contrivance are characteristic of the criminal branch, while petty misdemeanors are the characteristic of the pauper criminal.

Preliminary inductions on the relations of crime and pauperism: (1) where a person oscillates between the poor-house and the jail, it raises a presumption that there is either constitutional disease or an entailment of weakness inherited from the parents; (2) that with true criminals pauperism either occurs in old age or in childhood, and is not synchronous with the term of the criminal career; (3) that the misfortune of one generation which throws the children into an alms-house may lay the foundation for a criminal career for that generation if the children are of an enterprising temperament, but paupers if of low vitality and early licentious habits; (4) that the crime of one generation may lay the foundation for the pauperism of the next, especially if the children thrown into the alms-house are girls, and remain inmates long enough to become mothers; (5) that pauperism is more likely to become hereditary than crime, because it rests upon organic disabilities of mind or body, such as insanity, consumption, or syphilis; (6) that criminal careers are more easily modified by environment, because crime, more especially contrived crime, is an index of capacity, and wherever there is capacity, there the environment is most effective; and (7) that rape, especially of little girls, is a crime of weakness, and when occurring after the meridian of life has passed (from 35 to 45), marks the decadence of vitality and the consequent weakening of the will-power over the passions.

Relations of Honesty, Crime, and Pauperism. – It has already been noticed that the illegitimate children of Bell were industrious and honest, and that the eldest, a half-breed mulatto, was "the best of his generation," but the fourth child was the father of criminals. On following down to the next generation of this fourth child, I found the two oldest children honest, the first one acquiring property, the fourth one a criminal contriving crime, and the two next children the parents of criminals, and that the youngest child is a pauper. The order then seems to be that in the most vigorous branches honesty and industry are the first in order, crime is second, and pauperism third.

Now this line of facts points to two main lessons. First, the value of labor as an element of reform, especially when we consider that the majority of the individuals of the Juke blood are given to intermittent industries, which can be dropped at any moment the desire comes to go and fish, or gun, or take a spree. The element of continuity is lacking in their character, and enforced labor seems to have the effect of supplying this deficiency. The second fact which needs also to be observed, and which is quite as important but which is less obvious, is that crime and honesty run in the lines of greatest vitality, and that the qualities which make contrivers of crime are substantially the same as will make men successful in honest pursuits. In all the individual cases I was fortunate to acquire criminal histories on, I found burglary to be the preponderating crime. This crime requires a strong physique, a cool head, a good judgement, and dexterity backed by pluck. All these are qualities essential to any successful career, and, therefore, the solution of the problem of reform appears bound up in the question of how a new direction may be given to the activity of the faculties which are employed in a bad direction. Indeed, so true do I believe this view to be, that it is safe to venture the position that all criminals of sound mind and body who commit crimes of contrivance, and who have not passed the meridian of life, can be reformed if only judicious training is applied in time, and they are, after leaving the reformatory, surrounded by social influences which will make them strive for the good opinion of reputable people. It rests on the same human nature. Where there is vitality, there morality can be organized and made a constituent part of character.

With the criminal class gambling is widely prevalent. The risk run, the expectation of winning the stakes, the excitement of uncertainty, are features which are attractive to them, and these are the characteristic amusements which might be expected of the temperaments and habits of a man who chooses, by preference, to engage in intermittent industry. But the excitement of gaming is exhausting and draws off the vitality in a direction which is of no benefit to the community, add to this the licentiousness of the class and we have a large share of wasted energy. Any method of dealing with criminals, then, which would direct this wasted power into other directions would produce an amended career. The whole problem stated amounts to this: given a certain amount of vitality how shall it be expended so that the community shall not suffer injury? If, by training, such modes should be closed up, not only could the energy of the criminal be used for other purposes, but it would be so used, for life is activity of some sort, and will assert itself by effort of some kind.

This for crime: but what for the pauper? With him there is less hope, because of less vitality, and he is, therefore, much less impressible to praise or blame, to example or ambition. But with the pauper is almost invariably found licentious indulgence in some form. Here we have a key to solving the difficulties of his case. Now, virility is a mark of vitality, and sexual licentiousness an index that there is yet vital strength, while reticence is a mark of power, for it indicates the subjection of the passions to the dominion of the will, storing up the vital forces, so to speak, for expenditure in other directions. Hard, continuous labor checks the erotic passion, prevents waste of vitality in that direction, tends to decrease its intensity by substituting reticence for indulgence, and in the course of time, may enable him to form habits of industry that will have become organized as part of his character, and prove that pauperism can be controlled by controlling the passion that tends to perpetuate it hereditarily, perhaps more than all other purposes put together.

Having passed in review all the different sections of the subject of inquiry, I now make generalizations as to the relative influence of heredity and environment in the shaping of careers: (1) the whole question of crime, vice, and pauperism rests strictly and fundamentally upon a physiological basis, and not upon a sentimental or even a metaphysical one; (2) these phenomena take place not because there is any aberration in the laws of nature, but in consequence of their operation, because disease, unsanitary conditions, and educational neglects produce arrest of cerebral development at some point, so that the individual fails to meet the exigencies of the civilization in which he finds himself placed, and that the cure for unbalanced lives is a training which will affect the cerebral tissue, producing a corresponding change of career; (3) this process of atrophy is to be met by affecting the individual by such methods as will relieve him of disabilities which check the required cerebral growth, or, where the modification to be induced is profound, by the cumulative effect of training through successive generations. These phenomena take place not where the organization is structurally modified, as in idiocy, insanity, and many diseases, but where the heredity is the preponderating factor in determining the career, and as such, is capable of marked modification for better or worse by the character of the environment. This is probably owing to the fact that these cerebral conditions depend on ante-natal organization.

The details given of the Juke family take in only a fraction of the domain of investigation into crime, its cause, and its cure. The essential characteristics of the group are great vitality, ignorance, and poverty. They have never had a training which would bring into activity the aesthetic tastes, the habit of sober industry, nor indeed, a desire for the ordinary comforts of a well-ordered home. They are not an exceptional class of people, their like, and it may perhaps be added with truth that other similar extensive families may be found in most counties of this state. It is for this reason that an exhaustive analysis of this particular family becomes valuable, because the inductions drawn from their careers are applicable to a numerous and widely disseminated class.

The study here presented is largely tentative, and care should be taken that the preliminary generalizations announced be not applied indiscriminately to the general questions of crime and pauperism, for we are here dealing mainly with blood relations living in a similar environment, in whom the order of events may be a hereditary characteristic which is peculiar to themselves, and not of universal application. The study does, however, open the way and supply the method for a study of other classes of cases, supplementing and complementing it by other distinctive categories which present a different point of departure, either as where the progeny of influential landed proprietors lose their estates and fall into crime, or the children of people of culture and refinement become felons; or again, of the converse, of children whose parents were criminals, and who have re-entered the ranks of the reputable.

fall into crime, or the children of people of culture and refinement become felons; or again, of the converse, of children whose parents were criminals, and who have re-entered the ranks of the reputable.

Different kinds of crime need special study. Thus, crimes of contrivance in their various forms, such as burglary, embezzlement; crimes of education, such as forgery; crimes of brutality, such as malicious mischief and murder; crimes of cunning, such as pocket-picking, false pretenses; crimes of weakness, crimes of debauchery, crimes of ambition, crimes of riches, and crimes of disease. Pauperism also needs a series, and this and crime need to be compared to each other and, respectively, to a third series, investigating the growth and permanence of morally developed generations. An analysis of such a series as is here indicated would form a body of evidence which would furnish accurate data, enabling us to pronounce judgement upon any scheme put forward to counteract the stream of vice and crime which grows, year by year, broader, deeper, and more threatening, and supplant the empirical method now in vogue, by one of exact and well-founded laws, derived from a patient and extensive study of the phenomena.

THE TRIBE OF ISHMAEL:
A STUDY IN SOCIAL DEGRADATION

BY

REV. OSCAR C. M'CULLOCH

PROCEEDINGS OF THE NATIONAL CONFERENCE OF
CHARITIES AND CORRECTION
(JULY 1888) PP. 154-159

The studies of Ray Lankaster into "Degeneration" are not only interesting to the student of physical science, but suggestive to the student of social science.

He takes a minute organism which is found attached to the body of the hermit crab. It has a kidney-bean-shaped body, with a bunch of rootlike processes through which it sucks the living tissues of the crab. It is known as the Sacculina. It is a crustacean which has left the free, independent life common to its family, and is living as a parasite, or pauper. The young have the Nauplius form belonging to all crustacea: it is a free swimmer. But very soon after birth a change comes over it. It attaches itself to the crab, loses the characteristics of the higher class, and becomes degraded in form and function. An irresistible hereditary tendency seizes upon it, and it succumbs. A hereditary tendency I say, because some remote ancestor left its independent, self-helpful life, and began a parasitic, or pauper, life. Not using its organs for self-help, they one by one have disappeared—legs and other members—until there is left a shapeless mass, with only the stomach and organs of reproduction left. This tendency to parasitism was transmitted to its descendants, until there is set up an irresistible hereditary tendency; and the Sacculina stands in nature as a type of degradation through parasitism, or pauperism.

I propose to trace the history of similar degradation in man. It is no pleasant study, but it may be relied upon as fact. It is no isolated case. In all probability, similar study would show similar results in any of our States. It resembles the study of Dr. Dugdale into the Jukes, and was suggested by that. It extends, however, over a larger field, compromising over two hundred and fifty

145

known families, thirty of which have been taken out as typical cases, and diagramed here. The name, "the tribe of Ishmael," is given because that is the name of the central, the oldest, and the most widely ramified family.

In the late fall of 1877, I visited a case of extreme destitution. There were gathered in one room, without fire, an old blind woman, a man, his wife and one child, his sister and two children. A half-bed was all the furnishing. No chair, table or cooking utensils. I provided for their immediate wants, and then looked into the records of the township trustee. I found that I had touched a family known as the Ishmaels, which had a pauper history of several generations, and so intermarried with others as to form a pauper ganglion of several hundreds. At the Conference of Charities and Correction at Cleveland, I reported this case. The investigations have since been extended. Year by year the record has grown. Historical data of two hundred and fifty families have been gathered, but for the purpose of this report, the number of families studied is thirty. Of these, only two are known before 1840. They are found here at that time.

The central family—that which gives its name to the tribe of Ishmael—first appears in Indianapolis about 1840. The original family stem, of which we have scant records as far back as 1790, is then in Kentucky, having come from Maryland, through Pennsylvania. Ben Ishmael had eight children—five sons and three daughters. Some of the descendants are now living in Kentucky, and are prosperous, well-regarded citizens. One son named John married a half-breed woman, and came into Marion County, Indiana, about 1840. He was diseased, and could go on no further. He had seven children, of whom two were left in Kentucky, one is lost sight of, and one remained unmarried. The remaining three sons married three sisters from a pauper family named Smith. These had children, of whom fourteen lived, and thirteen raised families, having sixty children, of whom thirty are now living in the fifth generation.

Since 1840, this family has had a pauper record. They have been in the almshouse, the jails, the House of Refuge, the Woman's Reformatory, the penitentiaries, and have received continuous aid from the township. They are intermarried with the other members of this group, and two hundred and fifty other families. In this family history are murders, a large number of illegitimacies and of prostitutes. They are generally diseased. The children die young. They live by petty stealing, begging, ash-gathering. In summary they "gypsy," or travel in wagons east or west. We hear of them in Illinois about Decatur, and in Ohio about Columbus. In the fall they return. They have been known to live in hollow trees on the river-bottoms or in empty houses. Strangely enough, they are intemperate.

In this sketch, three things will be evident: First, the wandering blood from the half-breed mother, in the second generation the poison and the passion that probably came with her. Second, the licentiousness which characterizes all the men and women, and the diseased and physically weakened conditions. From this result mental weakness, general incapacity, and unfitness for hard work. And third, this condition is met by the benevolent public with almost unlimited public and private aid, thus encouraging them in this idle, wandering life, and in propagation of similarly disposed children.

A second typical case is that of the Owens family, also from Kentucky. There were originally four children, of whom two have been traced, William and Brook. William had three children, who raised pauper families. Brook had a son John, who was a Presbyterian minister. He raised a family of fourteen illegitimate children. Ten of these came to Indiana, and their pauper record begins about 1850. Of the ten, three raised illegitimate families in the fourth generation; and, of these, two daughters and a son have illegitimate children in the fifth generation.

Returning to William, we have a pauper succession of three families. One son of the third generation died in the penitentiary; his two sons have been in the penitentiary; a daughter was a prostitute, with an illegitimate child. Another son in the third generation had a penitentiary record, and died of delirium tremens and went to the medical college for dissection. There have been several murderers; a continuous pauper and criminal record. An illegitimate, half-breed Canadian woman enters this family. There is much prostitution, but little intemperance.

I take these two cases as typical. I could have taken any other one of the thirty; or, indeed, I could have studied for reporting purposes all of two hundred and fifty families as minutely as these. The results would have been no different.

Returning now to the record, let me call your attention to the following: We start at some unknown date with thirty families. These came mostly from Kentucky, Tennessee, and North

Carolina. Of the first generation—of sixty individuals—we know certainly of only three. In the second generation, we have the history of eighty-four. In the third generation we have the history of two hundred and seventy-five. In the fourth generation—1840-1860—we have the history of six hundred and twenty-two. In the fifth generation—1860-1880—we have the history of six hundred and fifty-one. In the sixth generation—1880-1890—we have the history of fifty-seven. Here is a total of 1,692 individuals. Before the fourth generation—from 1840 to 1860—we have but scant records. Our more complete data begin with the fourth generation, and the following are valuable. We know of one hundred and twenty-one prostitutes. The criminal record is very large—petty thieving, larcenies, chiefly. There have been a number of murders. The records of the city hospital show that—taking surgical cases, acute general diseases, and cases outside the city—seventy-five per cent of the cases treated are from this class. The number of illegitimacies is very great. The Board of Health reports that an estimate of still-born children found in sinks, etc., would be not less than six per week. Deaths are frequent, and chiefly among children. The suffering of the children must be great. The people have no occupation. They gather swill or ashes; the women beg, and send the children around to beg; they make their eyes sore with vitriol. In my own experience, I have seen three generations of beggars among them. I have not time here to go into details, some loathsome, all pitiful. I was with a great-grandmother on her death-bed. She had been taken sick on the annual gypsying; deserted at a little town because sick; shipped into the city; sent to the county asylum; at last brought to the miserable home to die. One evening I was called to marry a couple. I found them in one small room, with two beds. In all, eleven people lived in it. The bride was dressing, the groom washing. Another member of the family filled a coal-oil lamp while burning. The groom offered to haul ashes for the fee. I made a present to the bride. Soon after, I asked one of the family how they were getting on. "Oh, Elisha don't live with her any more." "Why?" "Her other husband came back, and she went on with him. That made Elisha mad, and he left her." Elisha died in the pest-house. A mother and two girls, present that night, were killed by the cars.

All these grim facts; but they are facts, and can be verified. More: they are but thirty families out of a possible two hundred and fifty. The individuals already traced are over five thousand, interwoven by descent and marriage. They underrun society like devilgrass. Pick up one, and the whole five thousand would be drawn up. Over seven thousand pages of history are now on file in the Charity Organization Society.

A few deductions from these data are offered for your consideration. First, this is a study into social degeneration, or degradation, which is similar to that sketched by Dr. Lankaster. As in the lower orders, so in society we have parasitism, or social degradation. There is reason to believe that some of this comes from the old convict stock which England threw into this country in the seventeenth century. We find the wandering tendency so marked in the case of the "Cracker" and the "Pike" here, "Movin'on." There is scarcely a day that the wagons are not to be seen on our streets; cur dogs; tow-headed children. They camp outside the city, and then beg. Two families, as I write, have come by, moving from north to south, and from east to west. "Hunting work"; and yet we can give work to a thousand men on our gas-trenches.

Next, note the general unchastity that characterizes this class. The prostitution and illegitimacy are large, the tendency shows itself in incests, and relations lower than the animals go. This is due to a depravation of nature, to crowded conditions, to absence of decencies and cleanliness. It is an animal reversion, which can be paralleled in lower animals. This physical depravity is followed by physical weakness. Out of this come the frequent deaths, the still-born children, and the general incapacity to endure hard work or bad climate. They cannot work hard, and break down early. They then appear in the county asylum, the city hospital, and the township trustee's office.

Third, note the force of heredity. Each child tends to the same life, reverts when taken out.

And, lastly, note the influence of the great factor, public relief. Since 1840, relief has been given to them. At that time, we find that "old E. Higgins" applied to have his wife Barthenia sent to the poorhouse. A premium was then paid for idleness and wandering. The amount paid by the township for public relief varies, rising as high as $90,000 in 1876, sinking in 1878 to $7,000, and ranging with the different trustees from $7,000 to $22,000 per year. Of this amount, fully three-fourths have gone to this class. Public relief, then, is chargeable in a large degree with the perpetuation of this stock. The township trustee is practically unlimited in his powers. He can give as much as he sees fit. As the office is a political one, about the time of nomination and election the amounts increase largely. The political bosses favor this, and use it— now in the interests of the Republican, now of the Democratic party. It thus becomes a corruption fund of the worst kind.

What the township trustee fails to do, private benevolence supplements. The so-called charitable people who give to begging children and women with baskets have a vast sin to answer for. It is from them that this pauper element gets its consent to exist. Charity—falsely so called—covers a multitude of sins, and sends the pauper out with the benediction, "Be fruitful and multiply." Such charity has made this element, has brought children to the birth, and insured them a life of misery, cold, hunger, and sickness. So-called charity joins public relief in producing still-born children, raising prostitutes, and educating criminals.

Some persons think it hard that we say to the public, Give no relief to men or boys asking for food, to women begging, children with baskets, or the ill-clad, wasted, and wan. "I can't resist the appeal of a child," they say.

Do you know what this means? It means the perpetuation of this misery. It means condemning these children to a life of hunger and want and exposure. It means the education of the street, the after life of vice and crime. Two little boys sell flowers at the doors of church and theatre. They ring bells at night, asking to get warm. Seemingly kind people give them money. They are children of parents who could, if they would, earn enough to support them in comfort. Your kindness keeps them out in the cold. Your own children are warm in bed. They ought to be, but your cruel kindness forces them out in the street. So you are to be made a party to this? You remember the story of Hugo's "The Man who Laughs," —the boy deformed for the sake of the profit it would bring through begging? So with these children. They are kept in a life of pain, shut in to misery by the alms of cruel-kind people. And this is why our Charity Organization Society asks you not to give alms, but to give counsel, time, and patience to rescue such as these.

Do any of these get out of the festering mass? Of this whole number, I know of but one who has escaped, and is to-day an honorable man. I have tried again to lift them, but they sink back. They are a decaying stock; they cannot longer live self-dependent.

The children reappear with the old basket. The girl begins the life of prostitution, and is soon seen with her own illegitimate child. The young of the Sacculina at first have the Nauplius form common to their order. Then the force of inherited parasitism compels them to fasten themselves to the hermit crab. The free-swimming legs and the disused organs disappear. So we have the same in the pauper. Self-help disappears. All the organs and powers that belong to the free life disappear, and there are left only the tendency to parasitism and the debasement of the reproductive tendency. These are not tramps, as we know tramps, nor poor, but paupers.

What can we do? First, we must close up official out-door relief. Second, we must check private and indiscriminate benevolence, or charity, falsely so called. Third, we must get hold of the children.

MISCELLANEOUS NOTES ON GENEALOGICAL STUDIES

(1) Transmission of Criminal Traits

Green Bag

Vol. 3 (June 1891), pp. 215-216

That criminality, like moral greatness, "runs in the blood," there can be no doubt. It would in fact be a most unwonted violation of the commonest law of Nature, were we to find the children of criminals free from the moral taints of their parents. As physical disease is transmissible, and as the conditions regulating its descent are now tolerably well ascertained, so moral infirmities pass from one generation to another, and the "law of likeness" is thus seen to hold true of mind as well as of body. Numerous instances might be cited of the transmission of criminal traits of character, often of very marked and special kind. Dr. Despine, a continental writer, gives one very remarkable case illustrating the transmission from one generation to another of an extraordinary tendency to thieve and steal.

The subjects of the memoir in question were a family named Chretien, of which the common ancestor, so to speak, Jean Chretien by name, had three sons, Pierre, Thomas, and Jean-Baptiste. Pierre in his turn had one son, who was sentenced to penal servitude for life for robbery and murder. Thomas had two sons, one of whom was condemned to a like sentence for murder; the other being sentenced to death for a like crime. Of the children of Jean-Baptiste, one son, Jean-Francois, married one Marie Taure, who came of a family noted for their tendency to the crime of incendiarism. Seven children were born to this couple with avowedly criminal antecedents on both sides. Of these, one son, Jean-Francois, named after his father, died in prison after undergoing various sentences for robberies. Another son, Benoist, was killed by falling off the roof of a house which he had scaled in the act of theft; and a third son, "Clain" by nickname, after being convicted of several robberies, died at the age of twenty-five.

Victor, a fourth son, was also a criminal; Marie-Reine, a daughter, died in prison, as did also her sister Marie-Rose, whither both had been sent for theft. The remaining daughter, Victorine, married a man named Lemarre. The son of this couple was sentenced to death for robbery and murder.

(2) HEREDITARY CRIME

POPULAR SCIENCE MONTHLY
VOL. 50 (DECEMBER 1896), P. 285

An interesting investigation is reported by Prof. Pellman, of Bonn University (Germany). He has made a special study of hereditary drunkenness, which, in the case of a certain Frau Ada Jurke, he followed through several generations. She was born in 1740, and was a drunkard, tramp, and thief for the last forty years of her life, which ended in 1800. Her descendants numbered 834, of whom 709 have been traced in local records from youth to death. Of the 709, 106 were born out of wedlock. There were 142 beggars and 64 more who lived upon charity. Of the women, 181 led disreputable lives. There were in this family 76 convicts, 7 of whom were sentenced for murder. Prof. Pellman says that in seventy-five years this one family rolled up a bill in the almshouses, trial courts, prisons, and correctional institutions of $1,250,000. With such a record before it, the state seems justified in adopting measures for preventing the breeding of such characters.

SUGGESTIONS FOR FURTHER READING AND INQUIRY:

HEREDITARY DEGENERACY (GENEALOGICAL RESEARCHES AND CRIMINAL PARENTAGE)

"Heredity and Crime." *National Repository*, vol. 3 (1878), pp. 83–85.
Synopsis of a paper read by Edward H. Parker, M.D., before the New York State Medical Society on the role of heredity in the production of crime and pauperism.

"Reformation of Criminal Girls." Miss E. A. Hall. *Report of the Conference of Charities and Correction* (1883), pp. 188–199.
Of all the girls admitted to the Michigan Industrial Home for Girls, one-third had criminality in the parentage and two-thirds had intemperate parents.

"A Study in Youthful Degeneracy." George E. Dawson. *Pedagogical Seminary*, vol. 11 (1896), pp. 221–258.
A very interesting article reporting the results of an anthropometric study of juvenile criminals incarcerated in reformatories. The object of the research was to assess whether genealogical degeneration may be said to contribute to crime. The article concludes that juvenile criminals are the result of two forces at work: (1) drunken, improvident, and degenerative parental stock from which the juvenile criminals are descended, and (2) bad environments have augmented and aggravated the inherited degeneracy.

"A Study of the Stigmata of Degeneracy Among the American Criminal Youth." Eugene S. Talbot. *Journal of the American Medical Association*, vol. 17 (1898), pp. 849–856.
An outstanding example of the application of criminal anthropometry to the study of young criminals incarcerated in two reformatories at the close of the nineteenth century. The conclusion reached by the author is that juvenile criminals "belong to the degenerate class, and are so handicapped by hereditary defects that they fall ready victims to criminal tendencies."

"The Statistical Study of Hereditary Criminality." E. R. L. Gould. *Proceedings of the National Conference of Charities and Correction*, (1895), pp. 134–145.
Explores the question of whether the methods of statistical science (such as enumeration, formulation of quantitative relationships, discernment of causality, and the calculation of the probability of regularity of recurrence) can be applied to show the part that heredity plays in criminality. Contains an extensive tabular presentation of criminal genealogical statistics from Italy, Austria, Germany, and Sweden.

"Heredity as a Social Force: Traditional Traits in Well-Known Families." T. H. S. Escott. *Fortnightly Review*, vol. 70 (1898), pp. 115–127.
Evidence and arguments in support of the theory that, like degenerate and criminal traits and characteristics, admirable intellectual and moral characteristics are also hereditarily transmissible from one generation to another.

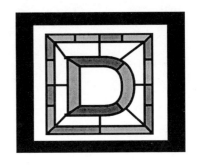

PSYCHO-
PHYSIOLOGICAL
CONSIDERATIONS

1. ALCOHOLIC INEBRIETY

INTOXICATION A SOURCE OF CRIME

QUARTERLY JOURNAL OF THE STATISTICAL SOCIETY OF LONDON
VOL. 1 (JUNE 1838), PP. 124-125

The Rev. John Clay, Chaplain to the Gaol at Preston, has for some years past collected very valuable details of the causes which have led to the offences for which prisoners confined in that gaol have been committed. They have been obtained chiefly by personal inquiry from the parties themselves, who are stated to manifest generally a great degree of candour in detailing the circumstances connected with their offences. Between the October Sessions of 1832, and the July Sessions of 1837, exactly 1,000 persons were committed to that Gaol for felonies; and of these no less than 455, or 45.5 per cent, arose from drunkenness directly connected with the crime—either from offenses which took place in public-houses and beer-shops, or when the offender or the party upon whom the offence was committed was in a state of intoxication. The cases of habitual drunkards, whose excesses have at length led them into serious violations of the law, are not included; but there can be little doubt that in a large proportion of the cases placed under the head of "Idleness and Bad Company," and in the three following classes, intoxication has been the original cause which has led to crime. Mr. Clay expresses his opinion, that if all the particulars connected with a criminal's guilt were made known, or if his general habits could be ascertained, drunkenness, which now appears to account for 45.5 per cent of the offences, would manifest itself as a little short of the universal cause of criminality.

It is surprising how few prisoners have urged the plea of want in extenuation of their offences; it might have been supposed that they would be inclined to disguise the true origin of their delinquencies, and would be prone to plead distress and poverty rather than a propensity to intoxication; but the fact is otherwise, and the proportion of offences attributed to want is only 7.5 per cent.

Drunkenness	455
Want and Distress	76
Temptation	48
Neglect of Parents	6
Combination	11
Weak Intellects	8
Idleness and Bad Company	88
Idleness and Ignorance	18
Confirmed Bad Habits	38
Alleged Innocence, and various or Uncertain Causes	252
Total	1,000

As can most clearly be seen from the following table, a comparison of the effects of drunkenness in the two principal classes of offenses, felonies and assaults, exhibits the result which might have been anticipated; the number of the latter class, arising from intoxication, considerably exceeds that of the former, and amounts to 64 percent, while in the felonies it did not exceed 34 percent.

	Felonies	Assaults
DRUNKENNESS	121	107
Idleness and Bad Company	37	7
Confirmed Bad Habits	25	2
Want	30	1
Temptation	36	—–
Combination	—–	7
Weak Intellect	4	5
Uncertain	95	38
Total	348	167

DRINK AND CRIME

Frederick W. Farrar

Fortnightly Review

Vol. 59 (April 1893), pp. 783-796

*"The alcohol madness flushes up in the
ruffian's brain, and the filthy bye-lane rings
with the yell of his trampled wife and children."*

I propose to set forth some examples of the overwhelming
denunciations of alcohol which have been uttered through
out the course of history. The most unequivocal language
has been used by learned philosophers, jurists, statesmen, and men
of the cloth to clearly establish the relationship between alcoholic
drink and crime. Let us take a look at the unanimous testimony
of men of the most unbiased judgment, the most varied experience,
and the most stainless integrity, and ponder their testimonies
concerning the destructive evils which result from alcohol.

No body of men in the world is so well qualified to form an
opinion on the *causa causans* of crime, vice, and misery as the
judges, magistrates, the coroners, and all connected with the
administration of justice. A few specimens out of many will suffice:

Sir Matthew Hale, writing in 1672, said that his position as
a judge enabled him to observe the original cause of most of the
crimes that have been committed for the space of nearly twenty
years, "and by close observation I have found that if the murders
and manslaughters, the burglaries and robberies, the riots and
tumults, the adulteries, fornications, rapes, and other great
enormities, which have happened in that time were divided into
five parts, four of them have been the issue and product of
excessive drinking at taverns and ale-houses."

The Grand Jury of Middlesex, soon after 1764, sent the
following in a powerful presentment: – "Much the greatest part
of the murders, robberies, and poverty in London may very well
be attributed to drink."

Chief Justice Coleridge:—"I can keep no terms with a vice that fills our jails – that destroys the comfort of homes and the peace of families, and debases and brutalises the people of these islands."

Mr. Justice Fry:—"The court calendar at Stafford, like so many others which came before the judges of assize, indicated most strongly the evil effects of drink in this country, and ought to make every one ask himself the question, 'Are we using our influence to the utmost to diminish this source of crime and misery?'"

Mr. Justice Denman (1874):—"He had often mentioned, and he did not know that he could do better than mention it again, a most remarkable instance of the connection between offences of violence and excessive drinking. On one occasion, in a northern county, he sat to try a calendar of 63 prisoners, out of which 36 were charged with offences of violence, from murder downwards, there being no less than 6 murders for trial among those 36. In every single case, not indirectly but directly, these offenses were attributed to excessive drinking. Drunkenness is indeed the parent of crime."

Mr. Justice Mellor:—"He thought he might express with some authority after fifteen years' experience as a judge, that most of the crimes of violence proceeded either directly or indirectly from drunkenness. It was the duty of all who valued the safety and prosperity of the country, to strive to diminish and put and end to this vice of drunkenness, and in doing this they must not be too nice about it."

Mr. Justice Fitzgerald:—"It had been the habit of the judges on the bench, and of speakers on public platforms, to address very wise observations to the public as to the crying and besetting crime of intemperance—a crime leading to nearly all other crimes—a crime which they might very well say led to nineteen-twentieths of the crimes in this country."

Mr. Justice Hayes (1869):—"Much, if not all, of the business of the criminal docket is the result of strong drink."

Mr. Justice George (1867):—"This disgraceful vice, the parent of crime."

Lord Justice Whiteside (1889):—"All the crimes we meet with on circuit are more or less directly or indirectly caused by drunkenness."

Judge Pattison (1844) to a jury:—"If it were not for the drinking, you or I would have nothing to do."

Chief Justice Sir W. Bovill (1872):—"Drunkenness is at the root of nine-tenths of the crime committed in this country."

Baron Martin (1866):—"Crime is the immediate and direct effect of that besetting evil—drink."

Mr. Justice Hawkins:—"The root of almost all crimes is the hideous tyranny of drink."

Mr. Baron Keating:—"The terrible thing is that a man often enters the public-house respected and respectable, and leaves it a criminal."

Mr. Baron Dowse:—"The amount of alcohol consumed in any district is the measure of its crime and degradation."

Learned statesmen and political leaders have from time-to-time weighed in and voiced their concern about the connection between alcohol and criminal behavior. Again, a sample of but a few of the statements on record concerning the relationship:

Sir Thomas More has observed that "tippling-houses, taverns, and other dens of iniquity, wine and beerhouses, do not all these, after rapidly exhausting the resources of their devotees, educate them for crime?"

Lord Chesterfield, Philip Dormer Stanhope, in addressing the House of Lords in 1743 commented that "the vice of alcohol is not properly to be taxed, but to be suppressed. Luxury may very properly be taxed, but the use of those things which are simply hurtful—hurtful in their own nature and in every degree – should be and ought to be prohibited. If these liquors are so delicious that the people are tempted to certain crime and their own destruction, let us at length, my lords, secure them from these fatal draughts by bursting the vials that contain them. Let us check these artists in human slaughter, who have reconciled their countrymen to ruin and sickness, and spread over the pitfalls of debauchery such baits as cannot be resisted. I find that laws allowing for the manufacture, sale, and consumption of alcoholic drinks are calculated only for the propagation of crime, vice, misery, and disease, the suppression of industry, and the destruction of mankind."

Lord Bramwell, addressing the House of Lords almost a century later said that "twice as many more crimes of violence are committed on Saturday than on any other day, and that Saturday may be considered as pay-day, drink-day, crime-day."

George Grenville, another eminent statesman, wrote in 1760 that "the common sale of intoxicating liquors is a most fruitful and prodigious source of crime, immorality, pauperism, disease, and premature death, whereby not only the individuals who give way to drinking are plunged into misery, but grievous wrong is done to the persons and property of His Majesty's subjects at large, and the public rates and taxes are thereby greatly augmented."

Mr. Chamberlain, one of England's most esteemed statesmen, has said, "Drink is the curse of the British. It ruins the fortunes, it injures the health, it is the source of the majority of our crime, and it destroys the lives of one in twenty of our population, and anything which can be done to diminish this terrible sacrifice of human life and human happiness is well worthy of all the attention and study we can give it. If we are silent the very stones will cry out."

Mr. William Ewart Gladstone, a statesman and prime minister of unimpeachable reputation, has remarked that "it has been said that greater calamities – greater because more continuous – have been inflicted on mankind by intemperance than by the three great historic scourges of War, Famine, and Pestilence combined. That is true, and it is the measure of our discredit and disgrace."

Sir William Harcourt has said, "He who knows anything of the matter knows that of all the sources of crime the most fertile is to be found in drink."

Lord Randolph Churchill spoke of alcoholic drinks as "a pernicious and mischievous article of consumption, the great obstacle in the path of human progress which darkens too many houses with sorrow and despair. We do not sufficiently estimate the amount of crime, vice, poverty, ignorance and destitution which spring up from the drinking habit of the people."

Philosophers, historians, social critics, and writers, all astute and practiced observers of human nature, have likewise not failed to notice the obvious continuity between alcohol and crime:

Pliny the Elder has said "wine drives man to the commission of a thousand crimes."

William Shakespeare, speaking through Othello, says "O God, that men should put an enemy into their mouths to steal away their brains; that we should with joy, revel, pleasance, and applause, transform ourselves into beasts. O thou invisible spirit of wine, if thou hast no name to be called by let us call thee – Devil!"

Thomas Carlyle, the Scottish essayist and historian, has expressed the opinion that "drunkenness is the most authentic incarnation of the evil principle known to man; the black throat into which wretchedness of every kind whirls down, calling all the while on crime, vice, and delirium to help it."

John Ruskin, the essayist and critic, has averred that "drunkenness is not only the cause of crime, it is crime, and the encouragement of drunkenness, for the sake of profit on the sale of drink, is certainly one of the most criminal methods of assassination for money ever adopted by the bravoes of any age or country."

It is not surprising that philanthropists and clergymen, men who have devoted their lives to the temporal and spiritual betterment of others, have also noticed the undeniable connection between drink and crime, and have raised their voices in protest.

Sir Charles Buxton, the eminent philanthropist and prison reformer has gone on record as saying "drunkenness is the most dreadful of all the manifold and frightful evils which afflict the British Isles, and the worst of plagues. The intellectual, the moral, and the religious welfare of the people, their material comforts, their domestic happiness, are all involved. The question is whether millions of our countrymen shall be helped to become happier and wiser; whether crime, vice, pauperism, lunacy, and disease, all of which are occasioned by the consumption of alcohol, shall be diminished, whether multitudes of men, women, and children shall be aided to escape from the ruin of body and soul?"

St. Augustine calls alcohol "the mother of all mischief, the root of crimes, the spring of vices, the stain of honesty, the plague and corruption of the soul."

Bishop Benson, of Gloucester, writing in 1750, said, "Our people have become what they never were before gin-drinking began to affect the masses – cruel and inhuman. These accursed liquors, which, to the shame of our Government, are so easily to be had, have changed the very nature of our people from the flower of Western civilization to debased and predatory animals. The laws authorizing the making, sale, and consumption of alcoholic drinks are founded on the indulgence of debauchery, the encouragement of crime, and the destruction of our noble race."

John Wesley said, "all who sell drams or spirituous liquors in the common way to any who will buy are poisoners. They drive men to hell like sheep. A curse is in the midst of them."

Cardinal Manning wrote to Pope Pius IX in 1878 that "drunkenness causes every year in England 60,000 deaths, and that according to the testimony of the magistrates, it is the source, directly or indirectly, of 75 per cent of the crimes committed, causing disastrous ruin of families, and destroying domestic life, together with the practice of religion and the Christian education of children."

The Synod of Roman Catholic Bishops at Baltimore wrote to the present Pope in 1891 from the Plenary Council of Baltimore that intemperance is "a perpetual incentive to crime and vice, and is the most fruitful root of all evil, plunging the families of the intemperate into the direst ruin, and dragging numberless souls down to everlasting perdition."

Contained within the preceding statements we have not a mere scintilla, but a lurid blaze of evidence, hot enough and frightful enough to make of the houses of the gin and beer-shops a perfect *borgo del incendio*. And yet, surprisingly, there remain those who stubbornly maintain that there is only a "coincidental or accidental relationship" between drink and crime! If, however, anyone wishes to estimate the truth of the astounding assertion that there is only an accidental relation between drink and crime, let him turn to the Report of the Convocation of York on Intemperance, in 1874, where he will find unvarying testimony and further endless proof of the role of alcohol in the production of crime, furnished, through more than thirty dreary pages (pp. 116-148), by the clergy, by magistrates, chief constables, governors of gaols and convict prisons, and prison chaplains; and if he will turn to the yet blacker and more patent evidence and testimony accumulated in the Report to the Convocation of Canterbury in 1869, he will see it given by judges, grand juries, magistrates, the police, &c., to the effect that "theft, fraud, embezzlement, prostitution of the young, rapes, robberies, burglaries, acts of violence in every shape (often ending in the destruction of life), by which our people are depraved and brutalised, are traceable to the passion for intoxicating drink." In the organ of the National Society for the Prevention of Cruelty to Children we are told that out of eighteen selected cases of typical fiendishness, thirteen were directly connected with drink. The more competent the witnesses the more fatal and overwhelming does the case against drink become.

And yet, there remain those who argue that the relationship between drink and crime is purely "coincidental or accidental!" Let anyone try the experiment of noting the crimes directly attributed to drink in any single year. If he does not abandon the task, disgusted, horrified, and sickened, it must be indeed the case that "damned custom" has so brazened his heart that it is proof and bulwark against common sense. Here is a summary taken in one year from a single local newspaper; and let it be observed that not one of these cases is invented by fanatics or faddists, but simply taken from the bare, bald, and colourless records of justice: "Frozen to death when drunk, 1 person; burnt to death when drunk, 2; drowned when drunk, 4; drowned in vat of hot beer, 1; death from bite of drunken woman, 1; children killed through drinking intoxicants, 2; deaths from drink other than above, 13; murders, 19; suicides (3 attempted, 8 completed), 11; maimed for life, 6; matrimonial quarrels, 8; gross cruelty to children, 5; murderous assaults on women, 42; assaults on the police, 55; ditto (most brutal and violent), 81; drunk in churches and chapels, 2; stealing drink, 14; robberies and thefts attributed to drunkenness, 36; arson through drink, 3; drunk in charge of horses, 35; permitting drunkenness and offences against licensing laws, 35; drunk and disorderly, 956; total, 1,334."

Or take _The Black Record_, published by the United Kingdom Alliance, and consisting merely of cuttings from newspapers, of the crimes directly and confessedly caused by drink for the fortnight including the two most sacred weeks of the year, the last week of 1883 and the first week of 1884. It was by no means a complete and exhaustive list, yet it proved from the mere reports of the common courts of justice that, in that fortnight, drink alone was the cause of 25 perilous accidents; 13 robberies; 5 cases of drunken insanity; 62 drunken outrages and assaults; 20 drunken cuttings, stabbings, and woundings; 5 cases of drunken cruelty to children; 52 drunken assaults on women; 13 cases of juvenile intoxication; 72 drunken assaults on constables; 94 premature, violent, or sudden deaths through drink; 18 cases of suicide attempted through drink; 15 cases of actual drunken suicide, and 12 drunken murders and manslaughters.

Is all this awful evidence untrustworthy and perjured? Can plain facts obfuscate the truth? Are the records of every-day justice falsified? Do the observations and statistics show only a "coincidental relationship" between drink and crime? What a help it would be to those blind to the experience of history and the abundant testimony of those most qualified to assess the relationship, from either first hand experience or common sense observations, if they could quote the evidence of but one judge, or magistrate, or man of sense in the whole course of our history, who ever said that if we only drank more we might shut up so much as one of our gaols!

SUGGESTIONS FOR FURTHER READING AND INQUIRY:

ALCOHOLIC INEBRIETY

"On the Effect of Good or Bad Times on Committals to Prison." Rev. John Clay. *Quarterly Journal of the Statistical Society of London*, vol. 18 (1855), pp. 74–79.

High wages during times of economic prosperity swell the prison population because the excess disposable income encourages the ignorant and dissolute to spend it on intoxicating liquors, which in turn lead them into dissipation and drunkenness, the chief cause of crime. Economic privation and distress alone, uncombined with the habit of alcoholic inebriety, are rarely operative in producing crime.

"On the Effect of Good or Bad Times on Committals to Prison." Rev. John Clay. *Quarterly Journal of the Statistical Society of London*, vol. 20 (1857), pp. 378–388.

Clay's second paper on the topic.

"Intemperance and Crime." *Proceedings of the National Prison Association* (1874), pp. 612–613.

Text of two letters from officials of the Women's Christian Temperance Union urging the National Prison Association to adopt a resolution stating that inasmuch as intemperance is the cause of nearly all the crime and degradation in society, state legislatures should abolish the manufacture, sale, and importation of all brewed and spirituous alcohol.

"The Relation of Rum to Crime." Hon. A. B. Richmond. *Chautauquan*, vol. 9 (1889), pp. 525–527.

Ninety percent of all criminal acts are directly or indirectly attributable to alcoholic intoxication.

"Origin of Criminal Impulses." *Public Opinion*, vol. 8 (1889), p. 88.

Excerpt from an article by Dr. Frank Lydston in the *Western Medical Reporter*, wherein the author argues that alcoholic liquors (as well as opium, cocaine, and hasheesh) impair the centers of reasoning and judgment in the brain, making those under the influence of alcohol prone to criminal acts.

"Phases of Crime in Paris." Hughes Le Roux. *Fortnightly Review*, vol. 50 (1891), pp. 881–895.

The hereditary alcoholist and crime.

"Influence of Liquor on Crime." *Public Opinion*, vol. 19 (1895), p. 336.

Eighty per cent of all crime is attributable to the traffic in alcohol.

"Inebriety and Crime." *Public Opinion*, vol. 19 (1895), p. 527.

Alcoholic inebriety is responsible for sixty to ninety percent of all criminality.

"The Relation of the Liquor Traffic to Pauperism, Crime, and Insanity." Francis W. Howard. *Catholic World*, vol. 64 (1897), pp. 647–654.

A scathing indictment of the distillers of spirituous liquor and brewers for their role in contributing to poverty, crime, vice, and mental degeneracy.

2. MENTAL AND MORAL INSANITY

(CRIME AS A DISEASE)

INEBRIATE MANIACS

BY

THOMAS D. CROTHERS, M.D.

POPULAR SCIENCE MONTHLY

VOL. 30 (NOVEMBER 1886), PP. 109-114

Psychologists and students of biological science have long been aware of the presence of a new division of the army of the insane, a division which is steadily increasing, more mysterious and obscure than the ordinary insane, and constituting a new realm of the most fascinating psychological and physiological interest. It consists of the alcoholic, opium, chloral, ether, and chloroform inebriates. They appear in our criminal law courts, as both principals and associates in all degrees of crime, and are called drunkards, tramps, and members of the dangerous class. In conduct, character, and motive, they constantly display many prominent symptoms of insanity, such as manias, delusions, deliriums, and imbecilities. Yet public opinion refuses to recognize these symptoms, because they are associated with intervals of apparent sanity in act and conduct. Clergymen and moralists teach that these cases are simply moral disorders, growing out of "a heart deceitful and desperately wicked," and only remedied by moral and legal measures. Scientists, who study the history and progress of these cases, find that they are diseases, following a regular line or march, from definite causes, on through certain stages of growth, development, and decline, the same as in other maladies.

Many theories are urged to explain the presence of this army of inebriates. One asserts that inebriety is evidence of the moral failure of the age, of the increasing wickedness of the times, of the triumph of the growth of evil over the good, etc. Another theory assumes that the great increase in the manufacture of all forms of alcohol and other drugs, and the ready facility with which they are procured, will fully explain the presence of this class. A third theory considers them the defective, worn-out, and exhausted victims of this crushing, grinding civilization; the outgrowths of bad inheritance, bad living, and the unfit generally, who are slowly or rapidly being thrown out of the struggle for survival. A fourth view regards them as simply coming into prominence, through the great advances in the physiology and pathology of the brain and nervous system, in which the physical character of these cases is recognized.

Inebriate maniacs have been called "border-land" lunatics, meaning persons who move up and down on the border-line between sanity and insanity, and, when studied closely, divide naturally into many classes. One of these classes, which in most cases represents extreme chronic stages, appears prominently in the daily press, in reports of criminal assaults and murders. When the genesis of the crime and the so-called criminal are studied, unmistakable symptoms of mental unsoundness appear. In most cases the victim is a neurotic by inheritance and growth. In other words, he was born with a defective brain and organism, and both growth and culture have been imperfect. Many complex influences, among which alcohol or other narcotics may be prominent, have prepared the soil, furnished the seed, and stimulated the growth of a positive disease of the brain. The higher brain-centers have slowly succumbed to a paralysis, as mysterious as it is certain in its march. The victim's capacity to comprehend his condition, and adjust himself to the surroundings, becomes less and less, and he is more and more a waif drifting with every possible influence. In appearance, head, face, and body are angular and imperfectly developed, the nutrition is defective, the eye, the voice, and every act and movement indicate degeneration and disease. Any general history of the crime reveals delirium, hallucinations, delusions, and maniacal impulses. Thus, in one day, the papers recorded the following among other cases of this class: An inebriate, of previously quiet disposition, killed his wife, supposing she had put poison in his food. Another man in a similar state shot a stranger who differed with him on the age of Queen Victoria. Another man killed his father, who remonstrated with him for overdriving a horse. Still another assaulted fatally his brother, who would not give him money. Two men, both intoxicated, mortally wounded each other in a quarrel over who should pay for the spirits drunk. Another man killed both his wife and child, supposing the former was going to desert him. Thus, day after day, the records of these inebriate lunatics appear, and each case is as positively the act of a maniac as if committed by an inmate of an asylum, whose insanity was long ago adjudged. In each case, a long premonitory stage has preceded this act; the individual history of almost every inebriate furnishes abundant evidence of this. In the court-room this insanity of the prisoner is ignored, and the legal fiction, that drunkenness is no excuse for crime, prevails. The prisoner is assumed to be always a free agent, and the use of alcohol a willful act, the consequences of which he should be held accountable for. As a result, the victim is destroyed, and the object of the law, to reform the offender and deter others from the commission of crime, lamentably fails.

The second class of these inebriate maniacs are less prominent in the press, but more often seen in the lower and police courts. They are arrested for drunkenness, minor assaults, and all grades of breaches of the peace. They use alcohol, opium, or any other drug for its effect, and their character and conduct are a continuous history of insane and imbecile acts. In appearance they are suffering from disease, and the hereditary history is prominent in ancestral degenerations and defects. They are repeaters for the same offense over and over again, and their crime is of a low, imbecile type against both person and property, characterized by profound mental and moral paralysis. In popular estimation they are simply armies of vicious, wicked persons, who are so from love of the bad and free choice of evil. This idea prevails in the court-room, and the judge, with a farcical stupidity, admonishes, rebukes, and sentences these poor victims, who are supposed to be made better by the moral and physical surroundings of the prison, and the sufferings which the vengeance of the law inflicts. The poor, diseased wretch may have appeared many times before for the same offense, and the act committed may have been particularly insane and motiveless, and yet the judge deals out justice on the legal theory that the prisoner is of sound mind, fully conscious, and completely responsible for his actions. The result is clearly seen in the records of police courts, showing that the number of persons who are repeatedly arrested for drunkenness is increasing. Another result more startling, but equally true, appears. Every law court where inebriate maniacs are tried and punished, on the theory that drunkenness is no excuse for crime, and that the victim should be treated as if he were of sound mind and his actions volitional, with free will to do differently, is a court of death, more fatal than all the saloons and beer-shops in the world. Such courts destroy all possibility of restoration, and precipitate the victim to lower grades of degeneration and degradation. It has been estimated that ninety-nine out of every one hundred men who are arrested for drunkenness for the first time, and sentenced to jail, will be returned for the same offense within two years, and appear again with increasing frequency as long as they continue to live. The report of the hospital at Deer Island, near Boston, where drunkards are sent on short penal sentences, for 1883, showed that one man had been sentenced to this place for the same offense, drunkenness, seventy-five times. Before the temperance committee of the English Parliament, in 1882, many cases were cited of men who had been sent to jails and work-houses from twenty to two hundred times for drunkenness. Practically, every sentence for drunkenness for ten, thirty, or sixty days, costs the tax-payers from fifty to one hundred and fifty dollars; and more completely unfits the victim for and removes him from the possibility of living a temperate, healthy life. Enthusiastic temperance men have drawn the most startling conclusions from these lower court records of arrests and drunkenness. Here each arrest stands for a new man and case. The nine thousand cases recorded as having been sent to Deer Island in 1883 in reality only represent a little over two thousand different men and women, and yet the number of arrests is taken as evidence of the increase of drunkenness.

A third class of inebriate maniacs are less common, and yet they often come into great notoriety from some unusual act or crime. They are known as moderate or occasional excessive users of alcohol, or they are opium or chloral takers. In most cases they are from the middle and better classes of society, and are beyond all suspicion of insanity, and their use of these drugs are considered mere moral lapses. Such persons will suddenly exhibit great changes of character and conduct, and do the most insane acts, then resume a degree of sanity that corresponds with their previous character. Thus, a prominent clergyman of wealth and high standing in the community, who was a wine-drinker, suddenly began a series of Wall Street speculations of the most uncertain, fraudulent nature. He implicated himself and a large number of friends, and finally was disgraced. A judge, occupying a most enviable position of character and reputation, who had used hard, distilled spirits and opium for years at night for various reasons, suddenly gave up his place and became a low officer-seeker – was elected to the legislature, and became prominent as an unscrupulous politician. A New England clergyman, after thirty years of most earnest, devoted work, renounced the church and became an infidel of the most aggressive type. Later it was found that he had used both spirituous liquors and chloroform in secret for years. A man of forty years, of tested honesty and trustworthiness, proved to be a defaulter. It was ascertained that he used opium and chloral in secret.

Hardly a year passes that bank defaulters, forgers, sharpers, and swindlers do not appear among men whose previous character has given no intimation of such a career. When their secret history is ascertained, the use of alcohol, opium, and other drugs is found to be common.

Another class of previously reputable, sane men suddenly commit crimes against good morals. The unusual boldness of their acts points to insanity, and it is then found that they are secret or open drinkers, using alcohol or compounds of opium. Such men come into politics with a most insane ambition for office and a childish delirium to appear in public as great men. They often become enthusiastic church and temperance men, acting along very unusual lines of conduct, and doing unusual things. Signs of mental failure are clearly traced in the childish credulity, or extraordinary skepticism, or extreme secretiveness, which are all foreign to the history of their past. Then, at last, such men leave strange wills, with strange bequests. They are contested; the expert is called in; and, while he is certain of the insanity and irresponsibility of the testator from the history, he can not make it appear clearly to the court. These cases are more or less familiar to every one, yet the history of drinking or using narcotics is concealed. In an instance of recent date, the will of a very rich man contained a large bequest to the Freedman's Bureau. This was a very strange and unusual act, but the heirs, rather than expose the secret drinking of the testator, let the will stand. To history this was a very generous deed, but in reality it was the mere freak of a man made mentally sick by alcohol, an inebriate maniac.

These persons appear to all general observation sane and fully conscious of the nature and character of their acts, yet they are in a state of intellectual delirium and mental instability, which comes out prominently in the strange and unusual conduct. The co-ordinating brain-centers are so damaged by alcohol as to prevent healthy, consistent, uniform brain-action. A certain range of thought and action may seem sane, but an ever-increasing undercurrent of disease carries them further from normal brain-health. These cases excite the wonderment of the hour, and to moralists are phases of human depravity, but to the psychologist and physiologist are explosions of masked diseases almost unknown and undiscovered.

It will be apparent to all that the most unfortunate treatment with miscarriage of justice is meted out to these victims. Thus, the inebriate maniac of the first class, those in alcoholic or opiate delirium who commit murder and assault, are not criminals to be cured by punishment. The brain of this variety of inebriate maniac is sick, diseased, and has broken down, and needs the most careful restorative treatment. He is physically and mentally sick, and can never recover except by the use of well-directed remedies and along the line of exact laws and forces.

In the second class of inebriate maniacs, the profound failure of the present methods of management should direct attention to the real means of cure. Science shows, beyond all doubt, that a system of special hospitals, where all these cases can come under exact physical care and restraint, and be organized into self-supporting quarantine stations, will not only protect the community and tax-payer, but put the victim in the best condition for permanent recovery. Here he can be made a producer, and taken from the ranks of society's parasites. If he is an incurable, he can be made self-supporting, and society and the world can be protected from his influence.

In the third class, when public opinion recognizes that the occasional or continuous use of alcohol or other narcotics is dangerous and likely to produce grave mental disturbance, these alterations of character and conduct will be no mystery. Such men will be recognized as diseased, and should immediately come under medical care and recover. Medical and scientific men must teach the world the nature and character of alcohol, and the diseases which are likely to come from its use. The moralists, clergymen, and reformed inebriates, can never do. Today these inebriate maniacs appeal for recognition and sympathy from many homes and firesides. They call for help. They ask for bread. We are deaf to their entreaties – we give them stones. In language that cannot be mistaken, they tell us of unstable brain-force, of tottering reason, of marked, insidious disease. We call it vice, and treat them as if they were of sound mind and body. They ask for help for the brain, starved, disorganized, diseased, and growing feebler by the ingestion of alcohol. We give them the pledge and the prayer, and taunt them as vile, willful, and wretched sinners. What wonder that the glimmerings of reason and the lights of a higher manhood should disappear in the darkness of total insanity brought on by alcohol and then aggravated by the manner in which our criminal courts deal with him. In the delirium of criminal assault, or the imbecilities of the low drunkard, or the strange acts and changes of character and personality in the so-called moderate drinker, they mutely appeal for aid, and we brutally fine, imprison, punish, and persecute them. These are the spirit and theory which seek support through feeble temperance efforts, through the church, and political parties, to remove an evil of which they have not the slightest comprehension. When all this thunder and roar of temperance reformation shall pass away, the still small voice of science will be heard, and the true condition of the inebriate and the nature of his disease will be recognized.

THE DEVELOPMENTAL ASPECTS OF CRIMINAL ANTHROPOLOGY

BY

THOMAS S. CLOUSTON

JOURNAL OF THE ROYAL ANTHROPOLOGICAL INSTITUTE OF GREAT BRITAIN
AND IRELAND
VOL. 23 (AUGUST 1894), PP. 215-225

The criminal has not been studied in this country on scientific lines as he has been of late years in Italy, France, and Germany. Yet three Scotsmen, Dr. J. Bruce Thomson, surgeon to Perth prison, Dr. David Nicolson, now Superintendent of the Criminal Lunatic Asylum at Broadmoor, and Dr. W. Wilson, were early in this field and did good preliminary work, apprehending the general principles that should guide investigations. Lately we have had from Dr. Ireland vivid delineations of the mental and bodily peculiarities of some great criminals ("The Blot Upon the Brain" and "The Ivory Gate"). Like a true scientific man and literary artist combined, he studies together criminals, emperors, and saints, subjecting them all to the same psychological analysis and the same anthropological tests. Dr. Bruce Thomson, in 1870, had come to the conclusion that "criminals form a variety of the human family quite distinct from civil and social men. There is a low type of physique, indicating a deteriorated character which gives a family likeness to them all," and he quotes with approval a friend's dictum that "the thief appears to me to be just as completely marked off from honest working people as black-faced sheep are from other breeds" (*Journal of Mental Science*, October, 1870).

He looked on criminality as being so "allied to insanity as to be chiefly a psychological study." He directed attention to the ugliness and deformities of criminals, their under size and weight, and other evidences of degeneration; to their great liability to diseases, especially to epilepsy, insanity, and brain disease, 12½ per cent of the whole falling into these; to the shortness of their lives, and to their many psychological peculiarities. He pointed out their frequent heredity to insanity, to habitual drunkenness, and to consumption as well as to many other bodily diseases. Finally he insisted on the fixity of all their peculiarities, so that by their incurability they proved the difference between them and ordinary mankind. As Havelock Ellis says, Thomson's papers "gave a stimulus to the study of the criminal throughout Europe." Despine in France had somewhat preceded Thomson in the same field. Dr. G. Wilson at the Exeter meeting of the British Association in 1869 read a paper on "The Moral Imbecility of Habitual Criminals as Exemplified by Criminal Measurement." He had measured the heads of 464 criminals, finding their average size less than that of the ordinary population, and coming to the conclusion that "the cranial deficiency is associated with real physical deterioration." Subsequently to these writers, Maudsley by his eloquent and forcible style, diffused a keener and a wider interest in the whole subject, especially among lawyers and medical men.

Since that time criminal anthropology has assumed a name and attained an importance unknown before. It fascinated Lombroso, an Italian man of genius, and through him has infected the minds of able observers in Italy and elsewhere. As Havelock Ellis says, "Lombroso first perceived the criminal as anatomically and physiologically an organic anomaly. He set about weighing him, and measuring him according to the methods of anthropology. Even on the psychological side he gained new and more exact results." A Criminal Anthropological Congress was held in Paris in 1885, and other Congresses have followed. The new branch of science has journals and archives devoted to its advancement. But the history, the progress, and the results of the study of criminal anthropology up to 1890 are all so admirably told by Mr. Havelock Ellis in "The Criminal," that I need only refer to that fascinating work. Few who begin to read it will lay it down again till it is finished. By its means I fully expect that the reproach of ignorance and carelessness in regard to the subject will soon be wiped out in our country; for it will certainly rouse some of our younger men to take it up. For myself, I feel it is somewhat of an impertinence to bring forward a paper on this subject at all. My excuse must be that I do so "by request" and that some recent studies of mine in regard to the nervous diseases that are apt to arise during the development of the human organism seem to have a possible relationship to one aspect of criminal anthropology. I have often directed the attention of my students and assistants to the great interest and importance of the subject; and I think the time is very near when some knowledge of it will be required of all medical men, and especially of all lawyers and the higher officials of our prisons. I trust that very soon too Bruce Thomson, Wilson, and Nicolson will have Scottish successors among its original investigators and expositors.

It is quite clear at the outset that every student of criminal anthropology must have ever before him the three great factors of:—first, the heredity of the criminal; second, his brain with its reactive and resistive qualities that may be entirely different in each case; and third, his environment, with its permanent and its immediate effects. Under the heredity must be taken into account the effects of hereditary diseases, especially nervous diseases in past generations, and the fact of their possible transmutation into other diseases in offspring; the effects of privation and innutrition, of lawlessness, of hard struggles for life, of ancestral instabilities of all kinds, and of a-social conditions: while atavism and reversions of many sorts may be the key to the problem in any individual case or family. Under the brain and its essential qualities there must be considered its receptive and its reactive power, but especially its inhibitory power against pain, against "temptation," and against temporarily agreeable and disagreeable things generally. The sensibility of the organ, mentally and bodily, to pleasurable and painful impressions; and whether it is especially explosive in its mode of working; the strength of the organic cravings for food, for stimulants, for excitement, and for sexual gratification; its educability, its imitative qualities, its intellectual force, and the vividness of its power of imagination, representation and reminiscence, are all most important to be kept in mind; as are also the moral sense and the qualities of the brain that are the basis of it; the power and natural desire to love, imitate, and admire the good, to hate the evil, to be sorry for lapses from right, and the natural strength of the social instincts in the organ.

The environment must begin with the daily life and surroundings in youth, and must go on to the education, moral and intellectual; the social, physical, and moral atmosphere breathed in youth; the motives towards good or evil presented, and how presented; the contrast example of friends and companions; the direct moral and religious precepts and examples.

Those portions of the brain cortex which have mentalization as their function are unquestionably the examples of the highest evolution of organized matter to be found in nature, the fullest of hereditary qualities, the most powerful, yet the most unstable, and by far the most physiologically valuable part of man. They undoubtedly must be regarded as the vehicle of the goodness of the saint and of the badness of the criminal. Almost all the questions that arise in the study of the criminal, according to the modern school, come to these—"Have we among us men and women whose mental cortex is of such quality that in ordinary environment their conduct must necessarily be antisocial and lawless?" And if so, "what anatomical, physiological, and psychological signs are there to distinguish this criminal and his cortex?" If there are no such signs then there is no such branch of science as criminal anthropology. It will not do to say that the sole tests are the social conditions under which the criminal lives; the thing to be tested is his mental cortex, and its reaction is his lawlessness. Lombroso, Benedikt and the whole of the school say that there are tests by which the criminal may be known; that he is a criminal, potentially, long before he is one actually. Our British laws virtually deny this, and of course take no measures to meet it. There are certain kinds of criminals, the political, the occasional, the passionate, the socially high placed cheat and swindler, who are admitted by even the most enthusiastic criminologists to be indistinguishable as yet by anatomical or other signs. It is only the criminal by habit and repute, the men and women of ever recurring convictions, and the criminal who becomes so early in life, and remains so, that we practically have to do with for purposes of scientific study.

It is not my purpose in this paper to attempt to summarize the numerous and most interesting facts that have been adduced by Lombroso, Marro, Ferri, Krafft-Ebing, Broca, Benedict and many others as to the size and shape and development of the criminal's brain, his physiognomy, his ear, his eye, and his body. One conclusion is forced on me after reading the evidence on these points. If there is no absolutely marked criminal type that all will agree on, there can be no doubt that criminals fall far below a high or ideal anatomical and physiological standard of brain, and body and mind. All investigations are at one on this point. The weak point in criminal anthropology, it seems to me, is that while criminals have been weighed and measured, observed and described, the classes of society from which most of them come, but who have not been convicted of breaking the law, have not been observed in the same way, and the same scientific tests have not been applied to them. *A priori* there would be little use in gauging the criminal by the standard of the well fed, the respectable, and the comfortably off classes of society. The really scientific method would be to apply the tests to whole sections of the lower labouring classes of society, including the criminals. As yet, to a certain extent, criminal anthropology has been in the hands of the enthusiasts, many of whom have been fascinated by its scientific and social interest, and have seen perhaps both more and less than the men of cooler judgment who will follow them. We all know that nothing in science was seen till it was looked for, but we know also that almost anything may be seen which is expected by an enthusiast.

Looking at the subject from a social point of view there must almost necessarily be a close affinity between the habitual criminal and the habitual idler and ne'er-do-well and the able-bodied pauper. Going lower down there must be a still closer connection between him and the vagrant and the tramp; and the closest of all between him and the prostitute. Up to this time there has been no very evident *pathological* nexus. But when one gets to the habitual drunkard, that element comes in along with the environment and heredity. Whatever induces it to begin with, the long continued practice of excess in drinking causes a pathological degeneration in the brain cortex that can be demonstrated by the microscope, this producing a dissolution of mental and moral inhibition, and frequently breaches of the law. There is a large class of human beings whose brains suffer manifestly and admittedly from arrested development—the congenitally imbecile. Imbecility may exist in any and every degree, and may extend to any and every mental and moral faculty. A complete idiot seems to have some connection with a criminal, but a man or a woman who is only slightly imbecile in mind has many anatomical, physiological, and psychological resemblances to him. The two conditions unquestionably overlap and intermix. Then, last of all, epilepsy and typical insanity result from a pathological change in the brain cortex, and are diseases just as much as rheumatism is a disease. Yet being diseases of the mind organ, human conduct is involved in them, and their effects are nearly always antisocial and often lead to vice, lawlessness, and criminality. Attacks of these diseases often cause permanent damage to the brain cortex, so that afterwards the subjects of them, who have before been law-abiding men and women, become addicted to crime. A man may "recover" from attacks of epilepsy and insanity so that he is not legally insane, and he may take his place in society; yet after his attacks he may, as the result of his brain damage, become addicted to habitual drunkenness, to theft, to sexual crime, or to acts of violence which he had been entirely free from before. Therefore it seems clear that a scientific criminal anthropology which is to cover the whole ground must deal with the idle, the vagrant, the pauper, the prostitute, the drunkard, the imbecile, the epileptic, and the insane, as well as the criminal. The brain and the environment respectively play very different parts in the causation of those conditions. Society has already provided counteractive environments against the conditions of the brain cortex in the case of several of these classes—in the poorhouse, the casual ward, the reformatory, the hospital, and the pauper lunatic asylum. It would follow that if criminal anthropology established physical, hereditary, and psychological bases of much criminality, the State would have to treat many criminals from an entirely different point of view than the punitive methods hitherto applied. Such in fact is the contention of the modern school of that department of study.

Without derogating from the great and arduous labours of the modern criminal anthropologists, any one in my department of medicine, whose daily experience is to see the human intellect and emotions entirely changed, and human conduct utterly perverted in highly developed and, in some cases, outwardly ideal human beings through subtle nutritional and dynamical changes in the brain cortex that after death exhibits no change of microscope appearance; such a person with such daily experiences tends to attach less importance to the gross methods of anthropometry, and to visible peculiarities in the brain convolutions. Rather one depends on facial, eye and physiognomical changes and movements, because through those we get into direct contact with the outward expressions of mind. There is no type of criminal physiognomy yet established. One instinctively attaches great importance also to the proofs of diminished sensibility in criminals given by Lombroso, Marro, and Benedikt; above all, one relies on heredity, developmental, and psychological facts to throw light on the distinctive brain qualities of the criminal. Psychometry, however, will have to be further pursued before we can fully segregate the criminal.

One physiological aspect of the criminal has not, it appears to me, obtained the observation it is worthy of. It may be called the developmental aspect. The term "degeneracy" is in the mouths of all writers on the subject since Morel's great work was written ("Traite des Degenerescences: Physiques, Intellectuelles, et Morales"), but it is clear that a degeneracy in a race or family may be a non-development in the individual. Properly speaking, the word degeneracy or degeneration as applied to a tissue or organ in an individual implies that at some former time it had been normal in constitution, like the degenerations of the cerebral cortex in extreme dementia or senility. As frequently applied in criminal anthropology it has not this sense; and when applied in the hereditary sense, it does not convey a correct meaning. It is quite clear that many criminals are so, through the environment having changed in the present generation from that of the former, though their brains are the same as their non-criminal ancestry. We all know that there are districts of the country where there are actually no criminals. It cannot be supposed that there are not in those districts persons with all Lombroso's marks of criminality, and all Benedikt's "atypical confluence" of the brain fissures. We know that when some of the inhabitants of such districts go to live in our great cities they become habitual criminals. We know also that there have been tribes of men who were all reasonably social and none of them criminal before a different race came among them with a different standard of morality and different social conditions, after which they all became drunkards and criminals together.

It seems clear to me that one of the great factors of the causation of criminality is the same as I laid down in 1889 for certain forms of insanity. If the environments and conditions of life were good, and the same in any race from generation to generation, we should have a complete adaptation of the organism to these environments. The continual process of too sudden adaptation to new environments and new conditions that is going on in our modern life constitutes in my opinion one of the great causational factors of criminality as I believe it does of certain forms of insanity ("Clinical Lectures on Mental Diseases," by the author, 3rd Ed., p. 287). In the course of the development of the brain I think it is a certain fact that the later years of adolescence are those in which the great inhibitory, moral, and social faculties that fit men and womenkind to live in a well ordered, modern, civil society, attain such perfection as they are capable of in most men and women. If we take the twelve years between 13 and 25 as the average period of adolescence, it is in the latter six that most criminals develop into that condition. The maximum of criminality falls after 25. By far the greater part of the habitual criminals become so in fact before the moral and inhibitory faculties have attained full physiological perfection. The difficulties of earning a livelihood and the antisocial temptations are not then greatest. Yet the habitual thief is then developed. There is only one kind of temptations then strongest and these are connected with the sexual nisus. Looking to the psychological peculiarities of the criminal, it is very striking that they appear in most instances at the age when the moral faculties have not yet attained perfection, but in the normal man and woman are taking a special start in growth. The conclusion seems supported by many facts that most criminals become so at that period through a non-development of cerebral qualities which should then be getting normally strong in normal individuals. Most habitual criminals are never developed intellectually too in any sort of all-round way. Their reasoning power is apt to lack backbone. They stop short at the narrow intellectual range of puberty, not going on to that of full adolescence. A certain arrest occurs before the brain cortex attains its highest qualities, but after the man has attained a sort of legal responsibility. He is not technically imbecile, but such arrested brains, being subjected to the conditions and severe temptations of a highly organized modern city life, cannot exhibit qualities that they do not possess. Their owners to a large extent become the professional criminals and prostitutes of our large cities, and the tramps, idlers, paupers, and stupid unenergetic denizens of our country places. Given this quality of an undeveloped brain in its higher intellectual and moral qualities, the environment then determines the class to which it gravitates. The brain has attained almost its full size and weight but its cells have not reached perfection in their physiological qualities, notably not in the most valuable quality of all, that of inhibition. It is a striking fact too that the early years of adolescence which immediately succeed puberty between 13 and 18 years of age, are those in which epilepsy arises in the greatest degree; these six years producing one-third of all the cases of this disease. Now most authors are disposed to attribute epilepsy to a certain kind of diminished inhibition in the motor centres of the brain. Motor centres nearly always precede mental centres in development. The great outward likeness of the epileptic and the criminal brain is one of the most striking of Benedikt's observations.

It is in the later years of adolescence that the peculiar form of insanity incidental to this period of life is most seen, and there occur at this period also a series of lesser mental and moral changes and perversities which are unquestionably allied to criminality in all classes, and often take the form of criminality in the lower social grades of society. They lie between insanity and criminality. Drunkenness, amounting to uncontrollable craving (dipsomania), is one marked form of this moral disturbance. They consist in some cases of stupidity and lethargy, so that the girl or lad cannot be interested in anything, especially in duty; or they consist in an a-social or antisocial development at this, normally, one of the most social of all ages; or they take the form of a causeless aversion to father, mother, sister, or brother, intolerance of control and utter disregard of duty and the ties of affection; or they take the form of general incompatibility of temper, or of impracticable visionary scheming and want of common sense; or we have sudden immoralities contrary to the bent of the former life; or perverted sexual and reproductive trains of thought dominate the mind and affect the conduct. All these mental and moral symptoms I have seen in the adolescent members of neurotic families, some of whom went through such phases of life and recovered from them as they might do from measles, and they were therefore proved to be pathological. What were "symptoms of disease" to me would certainly have been to the policeman and the magistrate evident proofs of "criminality." What were controlled and cared for in the members of a well-to-do family would probably have been neglected in a poor one. In the one instance the doctor looks after the "case," in the other the policeman locks up the "criminal;" yet they are both equally phases of the same kind of pathological brain development due to hereditary weakness.

There is a curious and in itself an unimportant change in the hard palate, which is found with such frequency in criminals in common with idiots, congenital imbeciles, epileptics, and the adolescent insane, to whom I have just referred, as compared with the general population, that it seems strongly to confirm the theory that certain criminals labour under an essential defect of develop-ment of the brain. As can be readily seen the hard palate has a very close relationship to the base of the anterior lobes of the brain in man. No doubt the base of the skull there follows, and is directly controlled trophically by the development of the brain that it encloses and protects. If the brain base is narrowed laterally so is the skull base, and that would imply a contraction of the hard palate which hangs from it, and is in reality an integral part of it. But why does not the palate arch in that case simply become a narrow arch of the normal form? There are two reasons against this. In the first place the palate is a part of the alimentary system, and follows the development of that rather than the nervous system. Secondly, if the brain base was arrested in growth shortly before or after birth while the palate bones were growing fast like the rest of the alimentary system, then they would not have room for expansion, and would be thrown into a high vaulted or V-shaped arch. The palate bones continue to grow and develop normally in fact, while the skull base does not expand proportionally. If again the anterior lobes of the brain—and they are in my opinion the chief higher mental centres—do not grow in antero-posterior size, then the palate bones are confined antero-posteriorly, and we have a high deformed arch in that direction (see diagrams and photographs in "The Neuroses of Development," by the author, pp. 42, 48). These conditions are found in every degree, shading up into the normal palate arch. I divided the palates I examined into the "Typical," the "Neurotic," and the "Deformed"; and the following table shows the results in the general population, among criminals, in the insane (acquired insanity), in epileptics, in those suffering from adolescent insanity, and in congenital imbeciles and idiots.

So far as this indication goes, if indeed it is an indication, many criminals suffer from a developmental brain defect, analogous to that form which we know epileptics, the adolescent insane, and those congenitally weak-minded suffer. I look on adolescent insanity as being clearly a developmental instability due to hereditary weakness. It occurs in greatest frequency during the last stage of development, between 22 and 25, the mind cortex being the highest of all, and the last to attain perfection.

Frequency of the Three Types of Palates in Various Classes of Persons Examined

Classes of Persons	Typical	Neurotic	Deformed	Number Examined
The general population	40.5	40.5	19.0	604
Criminal (the degenerate)	22.0	43.0	35.0	286
The insane (acquired insanity)	23.0	44.0	33.0	761
Epileptics	20.0	43.0	37.0	44
Adolescent insanity	12.0	33.0	55.0	171
Idiots and imbeciles	11.0	28.0	61.0	169

I have scarcely touched on the anthropology (using the word in its wide sense of the study of man in structure and function, in body and mind) of the juvenile criminal who becomes so under the age of puberty. He no doubt may be a criminal by environment and by education, just as other children become diligent attenders of church or readers of good books. But there are many cases on record, and I have seen and studied several others, where this explanation will not explain all the facts, and in whom, therefore, I had to assume an original, inherent non-development of inhibition and moral faculty, where crime was truly "instinctive" and normal to the particular individual, and where no responsibility, legal or moral explanation could be attached to the subjects of these crimes or vices. In such cases morality does not exist because its brain basis does not exist. I have no hesitation in placing in the "developmental" anthropological species of criminals the child in an educated family about whom I am consulted, who at 7 or 8 cannot be made to see the difference between right and wrong, truth and falsehood, who steals, breaks crockery and furniture, tortures and kills animals, has not the elements of the virtues of reverence, respect, and obedience, and does all this surreptitiously and perhaps with cunning, blaming others for his transgressions, and resenting punishment as an injustice. I often see no essential difference between this child and the criminal of 11 or 12 whom I am asked by the Crown agent to visit in prison where he or she lies under the charge of deliberate murder of a little brother, or of setting fire to the house. It scarcely admits of a doubt that criminal anthropology is on a sure basis of physiological fact when it pronounces such a case a criminal through its organization and not through its environment.

The considerations to which I have directed attention seem to point to two great sources of criminality. First, the not fully evolved man who might do his work well enough in a primitive society, but who cannot accommodate himself to the conditions of a highly organized and largely artificial modern society. Secondly, the non-developed man, whose development has been pathologically arrested towards the end of the period of adolescence, just before the inhibitory and moral faculties had attained normal strength, there being in him often a slight intellectual impairment also.

THE INSANITY OF THE CRIMINAL

VOL. 79 (NOVEMBER 1898), PP. 50-55

When society was startled by the recent attempt in open court on the life of a judge, the inevitable question of the insanity, and, as a necessary corollary, the irresponsibility of his assailant was at once raised. It is almost impossible to exaggerate the importance, to the community as well as to the accused person, of this problem of criminal responsibility, and at the same time realize the difficulties which embarrass its solution. For not only has the law to decide whether mental health or its antithesis is present, but in those frequent cases in which insanity and crime co-exist, combined in an infinite variety of proportions, it is compelled to disentangle the complex skeins of rational and responsible acts from those which represent the outcome of mental disease. The question is still further complicated by the fact that in many respects the criminal bears to the insane person a physical and psychical relationship which is so intimate as to be almost indistinguishable. To such an extent is this the case that one is tempted to ask if any criminal who commits a serious crime can be called sane. I propose to draw attention to the remarkable coincidence of attributes in the criminal and in the victim of mental alienation, for I believe that only on a recognition of this coincidence can a correct estimate of responsibility be based and from it alone a rational system of criminal treatment evolved.

By the term criminal I do not mean the occasional thief induced, almost compelled to break the law through the influence of his surroundings, or the criminal by passion, the homicide, who earns his title to the brand of Cain in a moment of ungovernable rage; but the instinctive wrong-doer, the result partly of hereditary anti-social instincts and partly of vicious environment and example, who at the time of his offence is as incapable of distinguishing right and wrong as a blind man is of distinguishing light from darkness. If the lunatic is mentally blind or defective in vision, the criminal is morally so. The born delinquent possesses an instinctive propensity to crime which is sometimes called moral insanity, and it is this psychical defect combined with a stupendous selfishness, a self-seeking which in it gratification completely ignores the feelings, the property, even the lives of his fellow men, that especially distinguishes the criminal.

A well-known victim of moral insanity was the German girl, Marie Schneider, who was sentenced to eight years' imprisonment for murder. This child, who was twelve years of age at the time of the crime, was born in Berlin in 1874. She proved lazy at school but could read and write, understood the Ten Commandments, and the significance of theft, deceit, and murder. The girl was cruel towards animals, and confessed to sticking forks in the eyes of live rabbits and afterwards slitting them open. Greed and deceit complicated the sum of her faults. One day, dispatched by her mother on an errand, she met in the street a little friend (aged three years and a half) who happened to be wearing a pair of ear-rings which excited Marie's childish cupidity, not for their intrinsic value, but because the acquisition of the trinkets would lead to their conversion into money and finally into cakes. In a flash came a suggestion of evil to her; she determined to take the child to a second floor of her mother's house, get hold of the ear-rings and then kill her, on the principle that dead men tell no tales. "I went with her to the window," said Marie afterwards, "opened it wide and set her on the ledge. Then I heard some one coming down; I quickly put the child on the ground and shut the window. The man went by without noticing us. Then I opened the window and put the child on the ledge, with her feet hanging out, and her face turned away from me. I did it because I did not want to look in her face, and because I could push her easier. I pulled the ear-rings out. Grete began to cry because I hurt her; when I threatened to throw her out of the window she became quiet. I took the ear-rings and put them in my pocket. Then I gave the child a shove and heard her strike the lamp and then the pavement." The little murderess then quickly ran down-stairs and completed her errand. She was quite aware that her action meant death to her companion, but she felt no sorrow, no remorse, and denied the crime until a policeman appealed to her sense of physical pain by threatening to box her ears if she did not tell the truth.

Of Thomas Wainewright, the famous English poisoner who was another moral idiot, another instinctive criminal, Mr. W. C. Hazlitt writes in his publication *T. G. Wainewright's Essays and Criticisms* (London, 1880): "His two salient characteristics were an unconsciousness, actual or feigned, of his true character. This was he who, with smiling face and jewelled fingers, could infuse the deadly venom from his ring, by stealth and without a qualm, into his friend's coffee, into the cup of the man who had offered him an asylum! This was he, who, with his wife at his elbow, she not a whit less guilty than himself, could watch demon-like the convulsive tortures and dying struggles of the fair and trusting girl, who leaned on his love, and idolized his every action and word!"

On the other hand, in most forms of insanity the morals become altered or lost; but there is undoubtedly a definite moral insanity, as a result of brain-mischief, similar to that which we observe in criminals. Its origin may be contemporary with the birth of the individual, or it may come on in later life; it may be cured or may persist, exactly like any other manifestation of mental disease. Dr. Thomas S. Clouston relates in his *Mental Diseases* (London, 1887), the case of a lady, who eventually died of softening of the brain, in whom the first indication of this organic disease was an attack of moral insanity. After living a blameless and useful life for thirty-seven years she suddenly and entirely changed, morally and affectively, and embarked on a career of imposture and swindling. She developed withal a special predilection for astute lying, with the result that several benevolent gentlemen, who failed to estimate the statements of this poor, mad, female Munchausen at their true worth, were heavily mulcted.

A consideration of the relative intelligence of criminals and insane persons will reveal the fact that, while in ordinary transactions the former class (with the exception of certain forgers, sharpers, and other professional rogues) exhibit an extreme stupidity, so much so that they are occasionally literally unable to distinguish the right hand from the left, they are past masters in a certain low form of cunning. Conversely, I have heard it stated by a distinguished expert in mental diseases that, unlike the legal delinquent, the average intellectual standard of insane patients (excluding the idiot) is comparatively high. Yet the same authority has borne witness to the intense cunning which the inmates of asylums exhibit, thus in one other respect resembling the criminal class.

The principles of altruism are not incomprehensible to the man of crime, and he is capable of evincing signs of family affection; but nevertheless he is as a rule permeated throughout with intense egotism, coupled with an egregious vanity. "There is not a set of people in the world," writes George Barrow, "more vain than robbers in general, more fond of cutting the figure whenever they have the opportunity, and of attracting the eyes of their fellow creatures by the gallantry of their appearance." Booth, the man who killed President Lincoln, protested indignantly against the depreciation which his deed suffered in the papers, and after giving an inflated account of his prowess, he exclaimed: "I am here in despair. And why? For doing what Brutus was honoured for, and what made William Tell a hero!" Wainewright remarked in prison: "They pay me great respect here I assure you. They think I am in for 10,000 pounds sterling." The real amount for which he was incarcerated was less than 3,000 pounds sterling. When he was later a degraded convict lying under the stigma of fraud, and with the guilt of murder and other crimes upon him he said: "I have been determined through life to hold the position of a gentleman. I have always done so, and I do so still!" It is easy to find examples, in the unfortunate inmates of asylums, of individuals who, like the criminal class, have formed an exaggerated estimate of their own importance. If a mentally afflicted person has any delusions about his personality he usually believes himself to be a sacred personage, or a royal individual who has figured in some epoch of ancient or modern history; seldom is he a person of indifferent rank. Puerile attempts at self-decoration not unfrequently supplement the ideas of aggrandizement, and complete the picture of pitiable vanity. Coupled with exaggerated self-esteem in the legal delinquent is a certain childishness. The criminal in most instances is essentially infantile, particularly in his reasoning process, his frank egotism, and his want of forethought. The insane are notoriously childish and are managed with much greater success if we assume such juvenility.

Again, even a superficial acquaintance with the inmates of an asylum for the insane will convince the observer of the existence of a crude eroticism which occupies the minds of the many patients. Criminals also give abundant evidence of this form of moral perversity.

A further point of interest is the emotional instability of both criminals and the insane; the tendency to "break out," to throw off all restraints and, under the stimulus of an intense excitement, to commit the most terrible crimes. Mr. Havelock Ellis in *The Criminal* (London, 1895) has quoted for us the following species of dialogue and attendant result, which, according to its source, Miss Mary Carpenter, is said to occur not unfrequently: "I am going to break out to-night. Oh, nonsense; you won't think of any such folly; I'm sure. I'm sure I shall. What for? Well, I've made up my mind, that's what for. I shall break out to-night, see if I don't. Has anyone offended you or said anything? N-no. But I *must* break out. It is so dull here. I'm sure to break out. And the breaking out often occurs as promised; the glass shatters out of the window frames; strips of sheets or blankets are passed through or left in a heap in the cell; the guards are sent for, and there is a scuffling and fighting and scratching and screaming that Pandemonium might equal, nothing else."

Compare these outbursts with the brain-storms which take place in epilepsy, in homicidal madness, and in other forms of brain-disease. There is a strong family likeness, and an added point of resemblance is the *aura*, or presentiment, that commonly precedes the attack. The criminal, we have seen, may give notice to the warder; the epileptic, experiencing a warning of the awful cataclysm that is about to overwhelm him, flies from a position of danger; the diseased victim of homicidal impulses, when the summation of stimuli, inciting him to destroy, has resulted in such an aggregate of resistless force that it is on the point of bearing down reason, will, and power, shrieks out to the bystanders to hold him, to deprive him of weapons, to save him from himself. We have known, among the insane, women who, in their intervals of sanity, were quiet, gentle, conscientious, and good; but who, even while praying with bitter tears that their chalice might pass from them, have been attacked by some brain-tornado which has immediately transformed them into veritable Furies. Such a patient is perhaps quietly reading or talking, when suddenly she springs from her chair, hurls the volume through the nearest window, makes a rush at the attendant and endeavors to strangle her. The lips may pour forth a perfect flood of iniquity, or she may be silent, with teeth clenched, and eyes fixed and staring. Thus the poor creature fights on until nature becomes exhausted, and she gradually returns to the normal condition as the storm in her brain subsides. Dipsomania and kleptomania are other forms of irresistible impulsiveness which are, like the foregoing outbursts, external evidences of marked emotional instability, of that loss of self-control which distinguishes alike the criminal and the lunatic.

Those characteristics, common both to criminals and the insane, to which allusion has been made, may be noted by the term *mental*; but there are similarities and agreements in the physical peculiarities of the two classes which appear to point to a common origin in defective or disordered brains. Professor Benedikt has investigated the subject of the criminal brain, and he found that it was characterized by the excessive development of the depression on the surface of the organ which are known as fissures, and by the inter-communication, or confluence of these fissures (*Dictionary of Psychological Medicine*, edited by D. Hack Tuke, M.D., London, 1892). Neither of those phenomena occur in connection with the fissures of the normal brain, but it is significant that the same peculiarities are seen in the brain of the weak-minded and of idiots. An anatomical ridge running along a portion of the centre of the forehead on the inner surface of the skull is frequently stronger and more prominent in criminals. "It is also larger," writes Mr. Havelock Ellis, "in the insane and lower races, and relatively larger in orang-outangs. It may signify precocious union of the two parts of the frontal bone with consequent arrest of brain development." Chronic inflammation of the membranes covering the brain is extremely frequent in criminals, even more so than in lunatics, although it is very common in idiots and is also encountered in two other forms of mental disease. Defects of the roof of the mouth and small undeveloped teeth often occur in both criminals and idiots. Various deformities of the ear are prevalent in criminals, lunatics, and idiots. The power of moving the ear, which is somewhat rare in normal individuals, is possessed by an equal percentage (approximately) of legal delinquents and lunatics. Further, the criminal shares with the insane patient the privileges of abundant hair on the head, comparative immunity from baldness, the faculty of ambidexterity, and, with many idiots, the Mongolian or Negroid type of face. I have not observed in the physiognomy of the insane the fierce and feline expression which certain observers have noticed in the instinctive law-breaker, and which they believe to be, like most of his other specific attributes, congenital. "We rarely hear," writes Mr. Ellis, "of a baby who looks round from his mother's breast with fierce and feline air." Nevertheless, a baby predestined for crime may have an anatomical physiognomy which approximates closely to that of the infant with the seeds of mental disease in his brain; and, similarly, the adult configuration of the anatomical elements of the face may and do resemble each other in the criminal and the insane patient, while the expression remains dissimilar.

Disease of the heart and arteries is another ground on which delinquent man and insane man can meet on comparative equality. The intimate connection between the brain and the heart, apart from disease, is very apparent. A feeling of comfort follows entry into a bright room because of the light causing more blood to flow to the brain. A sensitive man suffers a real or imaginary insult. Hardly is the offence committed than the arteries are flung wide open by a lightning impulse from the mind; on rushes the angry torrent of blood spreading rapidly over face and neck in a dull red sheet, suffusing the eyes and flooding the brain, and the intenser degrees of feeling retreating as quickly as it had advanced and leaving a countenance pale and distorted with passion. The brain is held together, as it were, by a net-work of blood vessels, and it is not surprising, therefore, that disturbances in the supply of blood, due to organic disease of the heart, have a profound effect on the mental processes. Criminals are exceedingly prone to disease of the heart and of the blood-vessels; so are the insane; and it is probable that irregularities and deficiencies in two such important organs as the brain and heart react upon each other, in each case, to the great disadvantage of the intellectual functions.

A study of the question of heredity reveals a number of facts which indicate that instinctive criminals and the insane are frequently branches of a common genealogical tree. The abnormality of some immediate ancestor is reproduced in his descendants, and the inherent brain-weakness which made the father an incurable drunkard may produce an offspring who is either an instinctive law-breaker or insane. It is probable in the case of the criminal that he does not spring forth, like Minerva from the brain of Jupiter, fully armed with all the impulses of wickedness, but that he enters life a peculiarly fit subject for the contagion of vice and crime to which he is but too frequently exposed; and the absorption of the poison helps to consummate his partly atavistic and partly acquired nature. If both parents possess deteriorated brains, either in the direction of alcoholism, insanity, or crime, the progeny are liable to prove a veritable brood of vipers. Thus Dr. Jules Morel quotes a case in which the father was alcoholic and the mother insane, with the result that of their five children two were criminals, two insane, and the fifth committed suicide.

Mr. Ellis has quoted various statisticians dealing with the heredity of crime. Of the inmates of the Elmira Reformatory in America, 13.7 per cent were of insane or epileptic heredity. "Rossi found five insane parents to seventy-one criminals, six insane brothers and sisters, and fourteen cases of insanity among more distant relatives." Dr. Clouston says that the children of the insane should be carefully educated on physiological lines to repress the unnatural tendencies and anti-social tendencies of such individuals, for it is from these members of the community that the insane, the dipsomaniacs, and the motiveless criminals arise, with a poet or a genius to redeem the class once in a century and to vindicate nature's law of compensation in the world.

It is probable that the moral insanity (moral idiocy or imbecility) which has been referred to is the most salient feature in the composite character of the criminal, and this, coupled with other considerations, leads us to believe that, of all forms of mental disease, cases of mental deficiency or idiocy most nearly resemble the cerebral condition of the instinctive law-breaker. The criminal seems almost to have arisen from a different stock to the normal man. It is as if his first parents did not eat of the Tree of Knowledge and knew not good from evil. On conviction he is, to state it paradoxically, innocent of morals, frequently debilitated in body, and with a mind which, if it can be compared to a blank sheet, is not a very clean one. The process of manufacturing from such rough material a being who shall not only fail to be a nuisance and a menace to society, but who shall succeed in proving a useful addition to it, has been accomplished in many parts of America by regarding the convict as a moral idiot. His length of sentence depends largely upon himself, but cannot exceed a certain limit. His bodily functions are first rehabilitated; he is taught school-work and a trade; lastly, he enters the class of Practical Morality, where he is taught to appreciate the good in life and to despise and avoid the evil. He is treated on similar lines to the mental idiot. The result of this is that bodily, mental, and moral improvement follow quickly on each other's heels; and as a practical proof of the value of treating the instinctive criminal for his mental deficiency, or *disease*, rather than merely punishing him, it may be noted that of twenty-three hundred convicts who have been let loose on the world from the Elmira Reformatory, only 15.2 per cent have returned to criminal practices.

But it is only the instinctive criminal, for the diagnosis of whom there are now so many signs and symptoms, whose complete responsibility can be called into question. The criminal who understands the wickedness and the social immorality of his act, and the criminal by passion are as responsible for their wrong-doing as is every one in the world who has a perception of what is right and what is wrong.

SUGGESTIONS FOR FURTHER READING AND INQUIRY:

MENTAL AND MORAL INSANITY

"The Problem of Crime." Francis Gerry Fairfield. *Appleton's Journal*, vol. 15 (1876), pp. 15–19.
Habitual criminals, like the insane, are readily identifiable by readily discernable physical indicia and nervous traits and conditions that they share in common.

"Are All Criminals Insane?" *New Englander*, vol. 35 (1876), pp. 323–340.
Very fine discussion on the ramifications of punishment consequent on adopting the notion that all criminals are mentally diseased and morally insane, and therefore should not be punished because they lack free will.

"Madness and Murder." William A. Hammond. *North American Review*, vol. 147 (1888), pp. 626–637.
Most perpetrators of murder are not mentally diseased, and although murderers may have a morbid impulse, the perpetrator is a reasoning maniac deserving of death.

"The Moral Imbecile." I. N. Kerlin, M.D. *Proceedings of the National Conference of Charities and Correction* (1890), pp. 244–250.
A fine discussion of mental disorders as manifested by kleptomaniacs and habitual prevaricators.

"Is Crime a Disease?" *Public Opinion*, vol. 8 (1890), p. 340.
If crime is indeed a disease, then, given the fact that the percentage of reformed criminals is discouragingly small, it would appear to be an incurable one.

"The Revival of Phrenology." *Saturday Review*, vol. 69 (1890), pp. 500–501.

Very fine discussion of recent medical investigations into the functional and pathological topography of the brain and the psycho-physiological dynamics of mental and moral disease.

"The Malady of Crime." *Saturday Review*, vol. 72 (1891), PP. 466–467.

A fine synopsis of Dr. S. A. K. Strahan's argument that criminals are the victims of mental disease or defect.

"Responsibility in Crime From the Medical Standpoint." Sanger Brown, M.D. *Popular Science Monthly*, vol. 46 (1894), pp. 154–164.

An outstanding article by a professor of medical jurisprudence at the Rush Medical College, Chicago, Illinois, which lays the modern foundation for the biomedical approach to criminological etiology.

BIOLOGICAL
POSITIVISM
AND
CRIME CONTROL
POLICY

THE STAMPING OUT OF CRIME

BY

NATHAN OPPENHEIM, M.D.

POPULAR SCIENCE MONTHLY

VOL. 48 (FEBRUARY 1896), PP. 527-533

It is only a short time since civilized nations abolished slavery and already we look back with wonder at our own and other countries, and are barely able to realize that the world could have borne such an unspeakable institution – that it could have steadily progressed while weighted with the breaking load of such a burden. Nevertheless, for thousands of years, and even at times of exquisite culture, men thought that slavery was inevitable, or even necessary, or at any rate that it could never be done away with. Now there is an equal steadfastness of opinion in the opposite direction. We regard with horror the social condition which justified bondage; we are astounded that we could have lived in such an atmosphere.

There are other similar examples in the history of civilization. Until the present century drunkenness was almost universal, and the gentleman who did not drink himself under the table was thought at best to be a poor sort of man. Our present attitude in the matter is just as great a revolution as our change in regard to slavery. Likewise is there an equally great difference so far as the interests of society are concerned. Again, until the middle of this century there was a constant succession of wars among the principal nations; but within a few years conditions have so changed that the man who dared to precipitate a war would be utterly overwhelmed with universal abhorrence.

If we look into the future, we may see as great a change, which is beginning to assert itself in regard to the necessity of crime. Indeed, the above analogies are well carried out, from the fact that so many people at present think crime is inevitable – that because society has always sweated under this burden it follows that the burden must ever be carried. On the contrary, because society has always been oppressed with crime there is good reason to suppose that changed conditions must alter the present facts, and that we may look for a season when crime as a constant and unvarying social element will have ceased to exist; when it will show itself in minor and individual cases, as drunkenness is beginning to do, as plagues and epidemics are beginning to do.

One of the best indications for hope is the growing effort to study crime accurately; not merely to regard it as an excuse for confining lawbreakers in self-inflicting herds, where they may undisturbed pollute one another, but, on the other hand, to seek for the causes of crime, to ascertain all its concomitant conditions, to recognize and classify the criminal in sociological and psychological ways—in the ways of anatomy and physiology. The recent congresses of criminal anthropology in Paris, Rome, and Brussels have opened a new world of information, have shown how misty have been our ideas on the subject, how primitive our methods have been and are, and what little hope for the future lies in a continuance of them.

This much, at least, we have learned: that the criminal forms a class by himself, no matter whether he is born so or grows into vice; that not only in his acts but likewise in mind and body does he vary from the healthy normal. For his tendency, as that of all organic life, is to reproduce his kind. This fact should be regarded as a rule that is as widely applicable and as unvarying as any law of biology. It can not be otherwise, for every child is a summing up and a manifestation of the traits and blood of his ancestors. And so, in spite of our present efforts, each confirmed law breaker becomes an ever-fruitful fountain for wrong—a moral plague spot —the limits to whose contagion are bounded only by the amount of material that can be contaminated. The most superficial glance will show how true this is, for if it were otherwise one would rightly suppose that the vast efforts for social amelioration throughout society must surely result in an increase of the better and a decrease of the worse elements. But as a matter of fact this is not the case. We spend tremendous amounts of time and money and effort in the attempt to eliminate the need of crime; we strive to the last extent to do away with destitution, unsanitary conditions, ignorance, and depressing moral influences, and undoubtedly these efforts have accomplished much good. But in spite of all this, in spite of aid societies for discharged convicts, in spite of educational possibilities that are as free as air, in spite of college settlements, protecting associations for children, reformatories, and lavish charities of all kinds—in a word, in spite of vastly improved social surroundings—the criminal remains as he has always been. Crime does not lessen, but on the contrary increases with the growth of our cities, or even increases beyond the proportion which we should naturally ascribe to it.

The strange thing about all this is that the development in crime does not necessarily depend for its beginning and growth upon elements which are popularly held responsible. Many people believe that with the wider diffusion of knowledge, wrongdoing must necessarily shrink away—that mental enlightenment and moral darkness are incompatible. But this is merely a supposition, for the most part based on our admiration for education. And, as a matter of fact, concrete examples constantly remind us that the educated person, if wrongly minded, does not as the result of his mental training become a law-abiding citizen, but rather becomes a dangerous and capable criminal. Moreover, this is true not only of individuals, but also of masses as well. We have to prove it the statistics of Dr. Ogle, in regard to the English population at a time of steady increase of crime: "Eighty five percent of the population were able to read and write in the years 1881-1884, and as this represents an increase of ten per cent since the passing of the Elementary Education Act, it is probably not far from the mark to say that at the present time almost ninety per cent of the English population can read and write. In other words, only ten percent of the population is wholly ignorant." In spite of this general diffusion of knowledge, in spite of compulsory education in the most critical and formative years of childhood, there was no decrease, but on the contrary an increase of crime.

Again, it has been conclusively proved that destitution, that specter which frightens the hearts of men, which covers and obscures with its sodden wings every wrongdoing in human life, is not in any way the real cause of crime; it is true that often it is the excuse. But it is only the excuse, and even in that capacity it serves for the want of something better. However, relying upon this excuse, one would naturally think that men with the greatest burdens would be the most liable to lawbreaking, and that times of profound destitution would be those most deeply marked with crime. As a matter of fact, both of these suppositions are false, so that we find criminals, as a rule, to be those persons having almost no responsible burdens, and, strangest of all, the times of prosperity show the greatest flourishing of crime. Therefore,

Morrison, a reliable writer, says: "It is a melancholy fact that the moment wages begin to rise, the statistics of crime almost immediately follow suit, and at no period are there more offenses of all kinds against the person than when prosperity is at its height." Again: "It is found that the stress of economic conditions has very little to do with making these unhappy beings what they are; on the contrary, it is in periods of prosperity that they sink to the lowest depths."

In like manner it can be fully and plainly proved that the other fortuitous and external conditions which are usually blamed for the wrongdoing in the world are either quite innocent or merely accidental. Thus, climate is said by some to be a guilty factor; but we all know how easy it is to show that there is no part of the world untainted. Seasons are responsible, say others. Here again, a strange fact confronts us: for it is in the pleasantest seasons of the year, when people have least in Nature to contend with, when they are most abroad and mingling together, that crime is commonest. Some well-intentioned men say that certain foods, especially "strong" and animal foods, so inflame the tendency to viciousness that evil instincts flare up, and as a result we have the criminal. It is quite unnecessary to spend time in exposing this fallacy in physiology; we need only refer to the Italians, whose food is very largely vegetable, and whose percentage of crime is among the greatest. The native inhabitants in India are another case in point; for their diet is likewise almost entirely a vegetable one, and yet, if it were not for the interference of the carnivorous English, they would even now be addicted to the almost universal practice of infanticide. So also is it that social rank, while setting metes and bounds in every other direction, fades away in the domain of evil. The criminal may be high or low, he still is the criminal; and, reasoned about broadly, there are as many offenses among the socially exalted as the socially debased.

Thus from every side we are driven away from the fortuitous, the occasional, the accidental, the cosmological, and the social environmental, as the controlling cause. We are forced, as a necessary resort, to something more reasonable, more stable, something which we can work on and understand. And as soon as we look on the matter with such eyes, it becomes plainer, more tangible, holding out hopes for amelioration if not entire cure.

In a problem like this, which has so many ramifications, we should seek for constant factors of divergence from the normal;

or better still, let us decide what is the healthiest development, so that we may better be able to understand the abnormal, the deficient in human character. "The perfection of man," says M. de Laveleye, "consists in the full development of all his forces, physical as well as intellectual, and of all his sentiments; in the feeling of affection for the family and humanity; in a feeling for the beautiful in Nature and art." Now we have something really definite. We have a clear idea of what is essential to the highest growth of human worth, and immediately we recognize that in the criminal we have a being more or less utterly removed from this standard, and thus representing what is abnormal, twisted, or diseased. What is more, this divergence is a constant one, which reproduces itself over and over again in successive generations of wrongdoers. It is rarely necessary for a man to commit crime at the present time, even though he is laboring under adverse circumstances; and it is never necessary for him to continue such a career. Therefore, when he does, it is a matter of choice or temperament. Very often the amount of ingenuity and talent exhibited would be sufficient, if rightly applied, to bring him comfort if not greater rewards in the regular lines of effort.

The majority of us exhibit a strange lack of logic in thinking about hereditary transmissions. We recognize the necessity of breeding and the duty of selection in regard to animals; we are perfectly willing to follow well-known ideas on the need of weeding out undesirable traits in cattle; moreover, the world has for a time shown its belief in the existence of hereditary genius, otherwise Galton's painstaking work on the subject could never have reached its present popularity, nor should we now possess our admiration for "good blood." But when you speak of the more unfavorable traits and the deadly certainty of their reproduction in descendants, our lips falter, we quickly hide the unpleasant sight with a capacious covering of charitable forbearance. We constantly meet with startling examples of transmitted crime, such as the famous or infamous Jukes family; every day in the more unfortunate phases of metropolitan life we see children following in the wake of parents and grandparents in the wide sea of vice; even do we see the same manner of crime reproduced in straight family lines, and yet we dare not look the plain truth full in the face; under the mask of a specious system of correction we hide our fear of facts and our incapacity to act for the criminal individual as well as the noncriminal public.

It is time for us to see that punishment will not abolish crime any more than a whipping will change a lunatic into a sane man. Until the citizens of a community are really healthy in mind, body, and soul, crime will and must continue in its concomitant ratio. For crime is merely the expression of the action of ordinary social conditions upon distorted and diseased organisms. The symptoms of this pathological state when occurring singly may, as in the common sicknesses, mean but little. But when they come together in recognized groups they point to definite degrees of degeneration. For this reason, anthropologists have been trying to classify criminals, to put in their proper places symptoms of weakened will and industry, overweening egoism, a failing respect for consequences, deficient domesticity, insensibility to the higher impulses, as well as the merely physical traits of facial and cranial asymmetry, misshapen heads, epilepsy, idiocy, and the tendency to disfigurement, as in tattooing. It is on the permanency of such traits that Bertillion's system of measurement is founded, as well as Galton's theory of finger markings. The main idea which these facts should impress upon us is the absolute stability of these peculiarities and the inevitable surety of the results which flow from them. The criminal is not necessarily without good impulses; on the contrary, he may have them more or less constantly, but he is unable to act them out. Where the will is thinned out almost to the vanishing point, or where the faculty of concentration has been progressively weakened, it is practically impossible to make up for them, and the unhappy offender is quite at the mercy of circumstances which bring him time and again before the criminal courts. In this connection it is interesting to read from Sir John Strachey's quotation of an official report from India: "When a man tells you that he is a Bodhak, or a Kanjar, or a Sonoria, he tells you what few Europeans ever thoroughly realize—that he, an offender against the law, has been so from the beginning and will be so to the end; that reform is impossible, for it is his trade, his caste—I may almost say his religion—to commit crime."

The belief in the inevitable steadfastness of these personal and family traits will finally clear our moral atmosphere, for we shall and must see that the safety of society lies in right methods of development based upon normal marriages and normal breeding. As population increases and the complexities of life increase, the burdens put upon us become heavier in proportion. We need more mental and moral backbone than we have; we are becoming progressively unable to stand the strain, it has become absolutely necessary to raise men to a higher level. For our present standard in character even more than in brains is a pitiably low one. Just as it is practicable to improve a breed of animals, so it is possible to increase our own worth. It is in this belief that Francis Galton said: "I argue that, as a new race can be obtained in animals and plants, and can be raised to so great a degree of purity that it will maintain itself, with moderate care in preventing the more faulty members from breeding, so a race of gifted men might be obtained, under exactly similar circumstances."

Here we have the gist of the matter. There is a consensus of opinion in the competent that crime is not fortuitous; likewise that there is, in the words of Galton, one sure method for betterment: *"in preventing the more faulty members of society from breeding."*

Scientists have known this for a long time, but the mere fact that the opinion was a scientific one kept it from the active appreciation of the many people who go to make up the intelligent class. Now it is time for us to understand the full bearing of the matter, as we certainly must do if we follow to their logical conclusion the teachings of great minds like Darwin and Wallace, like Wilson, Prof. Oscar Schmidt, Dr. Maudsley, and Jonathan Hutchinson; if we would rightly follow the meaning of the brilliant Weismann when he says that heredity is "that property of an organism by which its peculiar nature is transmitted to its descendants. And not only are the characteristics of the species transmitted to the following generation, but even the individual peculiarities." Besides all this, we have the evidence of men of authority, specialists in criminal anthropology, whose conclusions point in exactly the same direction, men like Cesare Lombroso, Ottolenghi, Rossi, Zucarelli, Virgilio Morselli, and Marro; to these let us add the names of the eminent Lacassagne, of Kocher, Raux, and Bournet. And even then we shall have only a part. The teaching of science all over the world echoes again and again the words of Galton, that the way to a better race lies "in preventing the more faulty members from breeding."

We need this reform more than any other that has been proposed in our present time. We should look forward to it as we do to the noblest and best aspirations which crown our lives with light, yea, as we look with uplifted eyes for the hope of our best salvation in this world. The earth is reeking with the sweat of evil, injustice, and moral sickness; the means for relief are easily within our reach; they will bring injustice to no one, they will put a stop to millions of wrongs, they will guarantee to our posterity the possibility of a higher career in every way, without the burdensome disadvantages which crowd us to low planes of life. There is no room with us for the confirmed criminal; and there is less room for his offspring, for they pollute the places whereon they stand.

ASEXUALIZATION OF CRIMINALS AND DEGENERATES

BY

DAVID INGLIS, M.D.

MICHIGAN LAW JOURNAL

VOL. 6, NO. 1 (DECEMBER 1897), PP. 298-300

We have among us many human beings who are morally defective—these constitute a criminal class, the existence of which is a perpetual menace to the rest. Not only does this class constitute a menace to the safeguard of society but it is an increasing burden upon the industrious and normal citizens. We spend almost as largely for courts, jails, and police as we do for schools, colleges, art museums, and training schools. It costs as much to look after the wrecks of one generation as it does to build the naval fleets of the next.

There are two ways in which we may regard these wrecks of society. We may call them "the wicked," hold them up for condemnation, and inflict upon them "punishments." The vindictive idea has varied in ferocity but remains the same in essence as ever. Even in our modern and more temperate forms of punishment lurks the old idea of vengeance. Outbreaks of ferocity such as lynch-law are the natural outcome of such a way of regarding criminals.

There is, fortunately, a second and more humane view, it is that certain of our fellows start life handicapped. They are usually defective from the influence of hereditary taint. They are born of blood which condemns them to failure sooner or later. Others grow up to a similar fate as the result of damage to their nervous apparatus caused at birth or by disease in early infancy. These unfortunates do not and cannot conform to the average type of their race and time. These we term degenerates.

We have all come to agree that those degenerates whom we class as imbeciles, or insane, are free from all responsibility. No idea of punishing them would be tolerated, notwithstanding that these persons constitute a burden or a menace to those about them.

But these are not the only degenerates. Just as some men are born color blind, others are born morally blind. As some children of impaired nervous organization develop uncontrollable muscular activities, others, from similar defect, cannot develop normal control over their passions or animal instincts.

It is a law of psychology that when individuals degenerate those functions of the brain which were last acquired are the first to be lost. The same law applied to the race. Man was an animal first—the higher attributes, which are the glory of the race, were laboriously acquired by later generations—when degeneration begins in the race the higher attributes fail, and the animal tendencies assert themselves uncontrolled. Our habitual criminals represent the product of this process. As the unfortunate products of degeneration they are no more justly worthy of punishment than the insane. Among the insane we recognize varying degrees of responsibility—so it is with the criminals.

The insane respond, in a certain degree, to the ordinary influences which control conduct. So do criminals.

So close is the parallel between the insane and the criminals that the facial expression, the bodily habits, and the physical defects are strikingly similar. Mount, on a large card, photographs of 100 prison convicts and on another, 100 photographs of the insane at an asylum (omitting those who had lost all mental power), and it would be difficult to tell which group was insane, and which was criminal.

Accepting, as I do, the view that habitual criminals are degenerates, it at once follows that I entirely eliminate the vindictive idea. Having done so I then have no hesitation in advocating the castration of habitual criminals. To advocate castration as a mode of punishment would be barbarous. It is to be advocated on two safe grounds: first and foremost as a means of preventing the propagation of a degenerate criminal class; and second, for its deterrent effect upon such degenerates as are still capable of being acted upon by those influences which generally control conduct.

As to the first ground this is to be said: Inasmuch as the great majority of degenerates are victims of hereditary defect there can be no doubt that a degenerate is specially likely to transmit to his children a degenerate inheritance. This is not a theory only, but abundantly confirmed by the facts set forth by Richard Dugdale, Oscar M'Culloch, and others. Again, as the degenerate represents a relative preponderance of the animal over the intellectual and moral functions, the degenerate does not lose the power of propagating. Indeed, the sexual impulse is usually the strongest impulse, the one most uncontrolled. We cannot trust nature to promptly end the generation of degenerates. It is the duty of the state to step in and end it.

At this point comes up the eternal conflict between the individual and the socialist. The individualist will claim that the state has no right to maim a person who is not fully responsible. The socialist on the contrary maintains that the welfare of society takes precedence over the rights of the individual. This principle is already fully recognized in practice—we confine the insane not as punishment, not, in many cases, as a means of possible cure, but for the protection of society.

We confine criminals—we ought to confine them not as punishment, not as a possible means of cure, but above all for the protection of society. The castration of habitual criminals is advocated on the same grounds. Society has a right to protect the next generation from the tainted blood of degenerate criminals. Similarly, just as many criminals are reformed by the discipline and training of modern reformatories, so the effect of castration might well have, in many cases, a curative effect. The entire change of temper and disposition effected in the horse by castration is strikingly suggestive.

As regards the restraining influence of castration for habitual degenerate criminals, this is to be said. There are many criminal degenerates in whom the possession of immoral tendencies is so strong that fear of any punishment or discipline has no restraining influence. Such would not be deterred by the prospect of castration. There are, however, many who are still able to control conduct if stirred by some powerful influence. Inasmuch as, in the criminal class, the sexual impulse plays such a predominant part of the prospect of being unsexed, it would undoubtedly exert a most powerful restraining impulse. Those familiar with the criminal class would, I feel certain, corroborate the statement that this would be something to be evaded by them, far more carefully than a term of imprisonment. For these reasons then, it ought to be adopted.

As regards the details, it ought not to be resorted to for a first crime or for a petty one. But if a many is convicted of a serious crime for the third time, we are safe in regarding that man as a degenerate habitual criminal, and his children will almost certainly be degenerates. To allow such a man to bring children into the world is cruelty to his own children, for they will be born to sorrow, misery, and degradation—humanity forbids it—to allow such a man to propagate is suicidal to society itself, for it is sowing the seeds of the disruption of society.

Since man, living in isolation, is a barbarian, since all the finer qualities of the race are the product of social forces, the preservation of society is of prime importance to every individual in it. The idea which commends the unsexing of degenerate habitual criminals is not hatred of the criminal, but love for our race. It should be adopted.

SUGGESTIONS FOR FURTHER READING AND INQUIRY:

BIOLOGICAL POSITIVISM AND CRIME CONTROL POLICY

"Repression of Crime." *Public Opinion*, vol. 8 (1890), pp. 360-361.
Convicts, the children of convicts, and the vicious poor should be under permanent medical supervision, and the hereditarily diseased and degenerate habitual criminal should be confined in prison for life.

"Artificial Selection and the Marriage Problem." Hiram M. Stanley. *Monist*, vol. 2 (1891), pp. 51-55.
A truly enlightened government would intervene and assist nature to do what she cannot do by herself: selectively enhance the breeding stock of mankind and elevate civilization by preventing criminals, paupers, and the defective from marrying and procreating.

"The Breaking up of Vicious Families." *Public Opinion*, vol. 11 (1891), p. 353.
Given the assumption that heredity and the influence of evil familial associations are largely responsible for the size of our criminal population, then just how far ought government properly go in the matter of interfering with domestic concerns to lessen both the present and future amount of criminality?

"Preventive Legislation in Relation to Crime." C. H. Reeve. *Annals of the American Academy of Political and Social Science*, vol. 3 (September, 1892), pp. 223-234.
Society is best protected from hereditarily degenerate criminals by the passage of legislation prohibiting them from marrying.

"Survival of the Unfit." Alice Bodington. *Open Court*, vol. 6 (1892), pp. 3327–3329, 3337–3339.

For the general protection of society, insane and degenerate criminals ought not to be allowed to procreate.

"The Survival of the Unfit." Henry Dwight Chapin, M.D. *Popular Science Monthly*, vol. 40 (1892), pp. 182–187.

The author argues that preventive as well as protective measures should be adopted to protect society from the depredations of hereditarily defective and degenerate criminals. Preventive measures include the passage of legislation to bar them from marrying and propagating, and as a protective measure, he advances the idea of a "three-strikes and you're out" law, arguing that habitual criminals, upon their third conviction, should be permanently quarantined and isolated in prison for life.

"Natural Selection and Crime." Edward S. Morse. *Popular Science Monthly*, vol. 41 (1892), pp. 433–446.

Crime, vice, and degeneracy are the result of hereditary transmission from one generation to another; therefore, the government should pursue a common sense crime control policy that first quarantines those who belong to the vicious and criminal class, and then prevent them from breeding.

"Restrictions on Marriage." *Public Opinion*, vol. 14 (1892), p. 156.

To safeguard society against the propagation of hereditary taints, Dr. William M. L. Fiske has laid before the New York Legislature a proposed law which would require both parties contemplating marriage to secure a medical certificate attesting to the fact that they are not criminal, insane, or degenerate.

"Crime and Marriage." *Public Opinion*, vol. 16 (1894), p. 459.
Discussion about the difficulties of imposing celebacy on convicted criminals who are not disposed to obeying the law.

"Can the Social Residuum be Stamped Out?: Extermination the Only Remedy." James Oliphant. *Public Opinion*, vol. 22 (1897), p. 202.
The indisputable law of natural selection logically suggests that an enlightened government crime control policy is one that is directed toward the extermination of the criminally unfit.

"The Regulation of Marriage." *Public Opinion*, vol. 23 (1897), p. 398.
Commentary on a paper read by Dr. E. T. Rullison before the Buffalo, New York, Academy of Medicine, arguing that the hereditarily diseased, delinquent, and criminally vicious should not be allowed to marry and breed.

"A Bill for the Regulation of Marriage." *Public Opinion*, vol. 24 (1898), p. 208.
Short description and commentary on a bill introduced into the Ohio legislature that would ban those with criminal records from marrying.

"The Improvement of the Race." *Public Opinion*, vol. 25 (1898), p. 460.
Criminals, inebriates, and paupers are biologically unfit, and should therefore not be allowed to marry and breed.

"Marriage of Defectives." *Public Opinion*, vol. 29 (1900), p. 654.
Short but interesting note regarding the steps taken by the medical associations of Tennessee, Alabama, and Georgia to secure legislation to regulate or prohibit the marriage of habitual criminals, drunkards, and users of harmful drugs.

SOCIAL AND PHYSICAL ENVIRONMENTAL EXPLANATIONS

ARGUMENTS AGAINST THE CRIMINAL ANTHROPOLOGICAL AND HEREDITARY DEGENERACY PERSPECTIVES OF BIOLOGICAL POSITIVISM

CRIMINALS NOT THE VICTIMS OF HEREDITY

BY

WILLIAM MARSHALL FITZ ROUND

FORUM

VOL. 16, (SEPTEMBER 1893), PP. 48-59

One of the difficulties in the way of ethical culture to-day is that the believers in the cult feel bound to find an explanation for everything, and that nothing is worth attention that cannot be explained into importance, and nothing worth dropping until it can be explained away. In this way the materialists have felt obliged to account for the criminal, and they have gone so far in their efforts at explanation that, if one may judge from their writings, it is logical to suppose that you might take the worst possible man, give him enough Turkish baths to keep his pores open and his skin generally healthy and sufficient massage to develop the muscles, watch over the condition of the liver, by systematic exercise get his heart's action under full control, straighten his spine by military drill and exercise, cultivate his ear for music and his eye for beauty, educate his intellect, and that having done all this you would have eliminated the criminal tendency from his life, or if you had failed in one generation, you might expect that each child he should beget would be a paragon of virtue.

In order to account for the criminal type, physical defects have been supposed to tally with moral defects. An examination of actual inmates of our prisons, however, has shown me that of one thousand men inspected, a trifle more than one-fourth had not only a fine, but an exceptionally fine physical basis of life and strength. The other three-quarters were rather below the average of the people one finds outside the prisons. This, I believe, only goes to show that the criminal is rather more largely drawn from among those who are physically degenerate or disheartened and weighed down by burdensome physical conditions, than from other classes.

I have begun to examine systematically one thousand prisoners and to keep a record of the examination. This examination is not yet complete up to the thousand, but so far as I have gone about three-quarters of the way—it shows conclusively to my mind that much more weight has been given to heredity as a predisposing cause of criminal life than fairly belongs to it. If the figures of the remaining three hundred prisoners bear out the record of the seven hundred already examined, they will show that there has been no such transmission of moral qualities as has previously been claimed, except such as might be traced directly to physical conditions. The resistance to temptation is truly not so great in a man physically weak as it should be, when his physical weakness results from vices in a previous generation; in other words, the conditions likely to promote criminality may be inherited. But vices themselves solely as the result of moral impulse I do not believe to be inherited. Nor do I believe virtue to be inherited. I have seen repeatedly the most virtuous children of the most vicious parents; and, on the other hand, I have known children of the most virtuous parents to turn out the most hardened criminals and the most troublesome social subjects to deal with. There is rarely a popular axiom without some truth at its foundation; and since I have made a careful examination of criminals, the old adage as to ministers' sons has come forcibly to my mind. Physical conditions likely to promote criminality aside, I believe that the child of a thief, apart from his environment and possible training, starts well-nigh as fairly in the race of life as the child of the average citizen. It is environment and training, not heredity, that give the most favorable condition for the development of the criminal impulse.

I wish to put myself on record, after a study of the criminal, and contrary to my previous utterances, as going squarely back to the doctrine of Free Will as laid down by our fathers, and I wish to be understood distinctly and squarely to hold the doctrine of moral responsibility as applying to every sane individual; at the same time making all allowance for such physical conditions as may weaken the will and in some cases destroy it. I do not believe for one moment that crime is a disease, nor by any necessity the result of disease in some instances. I do not believe that crime and disease are identical, and I am almost afraid of the analogy between them, lest humanity's heritage of Freedom of the Will be misunderstood. Of the seven hundred criminals I have examined,

I have found that more than five hundred had a clear motive and a sane motive, though a perfectly understood dishonest one and a criminal one; that in the conduct of their affairs they showed intelligence, and in the pursuit of their avocation a determined and controllable will. I do not believe that one-fifth of this number were ever in a condition when they could not have turned around, had they determined to do so, and lived virtuous and upright lives.

For a long while I hardly dared broach this opinion, fearing it might be considered to argue a want of proper charity in me toward my erring brothers. I am now emboldened to utter it quite fearlessly because I find that I am borne out in this feeling by most of the close students of penology in my own country. I find that of the practical penologists fully half have rejected the old theories of heredity as laid down by Lombroso and his followers; and there is a pretty general and settled conviction among scientific criminologists that moral qualities, purely and simply as moral qualities, either for good or for evil, are not transmitted.

The effort has been made repeatedly by writers of more or less standing, men so eminent in anthropological science as Lombroso, to account for the criminal on purely materialistic grounds. The hands of criminals have been measured with others, and a standard called "the criminal hand" has been apparently established. One can believe that most pickpockets and adept thieves have delicate hands, because otherwise they would not be successful; but that a man has a delicate hand of a certain formation I do not believe is an indication that he must be a pickpocket or a criminal of any kind. Even the "criminal thumb" has been defined, and while I was in attendance at the International Penitentiary Congress in Rome, impressions of ten thousand thumb-marks of criminals were displayed, intended to show that the thumb-lines were different in the criminal class from any others. I am bound to say in explanation that this was merely the vagary of a mild and inoffensive theorist, and had no official weight in the Congress or in the exhibition. As there were not ten thousand thumb-marks of honest people at hand for comparison, the theory advanced did not gain many followers.

The criminal head has been measured and a criminal type supposed to be established. But the criminal type of head is a very near approach to the *cretin* or idiotic type, which I believe simply goes to show that crimes of a certain kind are more likely to be committed by a class that usually have such heads than by others—

a class with small brains who will not take the trouble to trace out intellectually the logical consequences of their acts, but who could do so if they would. Not long ago I saw an instance narrated where a man who had committed a crime was held to be not responsible for it on account of the conditions of his heredity and environment, though he showed an amount of cunning, an intellectual grasp of the situation and will-power to evade examination, four-fold as great as were necessary to have withheld him from the commission of the crime. In the one case he simply chose to commit the crime; in the other he chose to exercise his intellect and will to escape punishment. The motive was clear in both cases, and I do not think heredity had anything to do with it in either.

One of the most eminent leaders of liberal thought in this country, a man who has done more than almost any other to promote ethical culture of the highest order, said in talking with me, "It is time the materialists among penologists called a halt. They do not at present make an allowance for a soul; and if it is true that criminals have no freedom of the will, they are hardly worth the trouble that is spent upon them." I believe that most criminals are criminals because they wish to be criminals; that they deliberately choose the profession and follow it for so long as its excitements and rewards are adequate to the effort they make; and that they can and do abandon it when such rewards are not equal to the effort, or when the penalties are too great an opposing force, or when, gaining a higher view of life and of their own weakness, they come to desire the things that make for righteousness and virtue. In other words, I believe that the criminal is generally a criminal because it pays him to be a criminal, and becomes virtuous when it pays him to be virtuous. The moment that he understands that "honesty is the best policy," the average professional criminal becomes honest.

The criminal, as I wish to study him in this little paper, is the man who deliberately chooses a life of law-breaking, who serves term after term in our prisons—if he chances to be caught at his acts of law-breaking—and who comprises one of the great number of a well-organized class whose business it is in life to prey upon society, regardless of its laws. Burglars, pickpockets, professional thieves of all kinds, professional forgers and counterfeiters, illicit rum-sellers, prostitutes, gamblers of every description, and other smaller rogues, comprise what I consider the active criminal class. This class—though there is a difference in the figures obtained by different census-workers, varying with the local nomenclature of crime—numbers in this country, I think we may fairly estimate at three hundred thousand persons. The latest census, if the figures should ever be entirely complete, will no doubt show a much larger number than this. But the conclusions deducible when we consider an army of even three hundred thousand criminals are sufficiently appalling, and I have chosen the lowest estimate that I may not be accused of using alarmist statistics. One does not need to be a great social economist to see in a moment that, by adding to the value of all the prison "plants" in the country the enormous expense involved in sustaining these people and in protecting ourselves from them, in trying them, and in keeping them in prison, we reach a sum such as makes this subject of sufficient importance to demand the attention not only of social scientists and philanthropists, but of the whole public. And no man has a right to complain, if burglars enter his second-story windows or blow up his bank safe, or if he be garroted in the street or his name be forged to a check, who has not taken his part as a citizen in eradicating this dangerous class.

The criminal is undoubtedly an outcast from society. He certainly deserves to be. But aside from this I do not believe him to be a man apart from others. I fail to see wherein he is lacking in any of the faculties, mental, moral or intellectual, of other men. We find him standing apart as an enemy to society; but this is his only distinction, and we are bound to protect ourselves against him as against any other enemy. It would be interesting to investigate the extent to which he is also a victim of society and the extent to which he is an enemy of society because he is a victim. But placing all discussion as to causes aside, the one question which we will try to answer is: What are we to do to protect ourselves against our enemy the criminal? At present, society fails adequately to protect itself. As I have already said, just as soon as the criminal finds that the rewards of criminal life are not commensurate with the risks and the labor involved, that his chances of great gains are lost, he will cease to be a criminal. Society therefore plainly has to concern itself with measures that shall increase the risk of a criminal life and reduce its gain to a minimum. Penal measures are the corrective to the criminal class. These measures, to be efficient, must possess three elements: certainty, severity and publicity. If the active criminal knew that the chances of escaping after any violation of the criminal code were infinitesimal, and that imprisonment was absolutely certain to follow the detection of crime, he would feel that he would much rather, much better, spend his life out of prison than in it, and would, doubtless, soon cease to be a criminal.

A large class of our criminal population, on the contrary, are not only unmolested by our city police authorities, but are, in fact, protected by them. Thanks to the power of money and political "pulls," the criminal is often perfectly well aware that at the very threshold of his relation to the law he stands a good chance of escaping arrest or punishment. Citizens of New York City and Brooklyn see every day, and especially every Sunday, flagrant violations of the law with the full connivance of the police. The criminal understands this perfectly and knows how to calculate to a nicety the chances of his arrest if he enters upon any criminal exploit. Going a step further, and considering the enormous number of cases that are pigeonholed and forgotten, that never come to trial, and never will come to trial, the criminal sees still another avenue of escape if he does not find the police sufficiently corrupt to screen him in the first instance.

If, however, he should be weak enough in his "pull" on the police force or in the manner of "influence" to entangle himself in the meshes of the law so as to be arrested and brought to trial, he knows perfectly well that legal technicalities may be so juggled with by shrewd lawyers hired with his stolen or ill-gotten money, and that the mind of the intelligent juror may be so befogged by cunning sophistry, that he stands a good chance of acquittal even after he has got into court. If, moreover, he should be so unfortunate as to be found guilty, the long delays through possible appeals still give him a reasonable chance to escape punishment. He takes every one of these things into consideration with every criminal act. They are the study of his life, no less than the criminal practices by which he gains his livelihood. If we see our criminal class increasing, it is not alone because of the feebleness and of the ill-judged scheme of our prison system, but because one of the factors in an efficient penal system, that of certainty, is reduced to a minimum.

But suppose the criminal is found guilty and is sentenced to a State prison or to a penitentiary. Then what do we do for him and for ourselves by keeping him in prison? As I have said before, punishment to be effective must have severity for one of its elements. Your standard of severity, and mine, is not the standard that has been set by the criminal. The most severe punishment for the criminal is to make him do that against which every day of his criminal life is a protest. He is determined that he will not earn his living by honest labor, or at least he is determined that he will live in violation of the law. The most severe thing that can be done for him is to bring to bear upon him all the ordinary conditions of society, so thoroughly intensified that he will feel their pressure and gradually come to yield himself to the habit of obedience to them. He must be made to feel that he is part of the body politic, with an obligation to earn his living and obey those laws that have been thought to be good for the common weal. In fact, he must be brought back from the exceptional conditions which he has chosen for himself to the ordinary conditions which society necessarily imposes upon every individual. If he is to earn his living, we must teach him some trade, and his faculties must be trained to some occupation with which, by a given amount of labor, an honest livelihood can be honestly earned. Or, if an income is already assured to him, he must be made to feel that that income is worthless to him and that the State will make it worthless to him, unless he lives under such conditions as will make him a desirable citizen of the State. In fact, the one idea of the State in the treatment of criminals must be to train the man so that the criminal tendency will be obliterated from his character and the traits that make for a righteous life developed to the highest degree. If this can be done, the State will protect itself from the criminal; if it cannot be done, we shall continue to increase our criminal class in precisely the same ratio to the population, or shall even raise it by the influx of foreign criminals.

So as long as the criminal remains a criminal, he is a source of danger and a moral contamination. It is not practicable to kill him—though from a purely economic standpoint, eliminating all Christian feeling and the duty of philanthropic effort for his reclamation, the very best thing that could be done for society would be to kill every ten years all who had placed themselves distinctly in the criminal class. But society must be protected against the criminal so long as he is a criminal; and for that reason we isolate in prisons those who are convicted of crime. It has sometimes been vaguely supposed that imprisonment pure and simple had a deterrent effect, and the theory has been hinted at, rather than distinctly expressed, that the judges of our courts are so gifted with prescience that they can mete out the exact amount of time required for a criminal's reformation. Yet under the old system of imprisonment, with limited time-sentences—a system still in vogue in all our States, but gradually giving way to a more rational one—not more than eighteen per cent of the people sent to a State prison come out with the ability or intention to earn an honest livelihood; that is, out of every one hundred prisoners discharged there are only eighteen reformed, and a good many of these are not reformed criminals but are first offenders, men who do not belong distinctly to the criminal class and who would not have committed a second offence if they had not been in prison at all. If we expect perhaps one-tenth of the really criminal class whose criminal operations are at least modified or done away with by their imprisonment, society, under the old system of time-sentences and under the present system of prison-labor, is protected against the criminal only while he is locked up. This is a small showing for a large expenditure. Under the old system, it was perfectly well known that a criminal came out of prison just as much a "crook" as he went in, and it became the immediate business of the police to watch him, they showing no confidence in the effect of imprisonment for his good by an expectation that any day he might fall into crime and renew his criminal associates. There is not very much satisfaction in locking up a burglar for three years to meditate and plan other burglaries in the fourth year. To protect society by locking up criminals is a mere palliative. Some of the States of the Union have long recognized this fact and have made the remedy rather more radical by instituting the "Habitual Criminal Act," by which a man on his third conviction for certain offences is judged a "habitual criminal" and is locked up for life.

There remains yet a fourth way in which society may be protected from the criminal, and it is the only radical and true measure which Christian society has a right to insist upon. This is to put him under such conditions of training and surveillance that he will come to recognize the fact that in the long run it pays better to be an honest man than a criminal; that is, to show him so plainly the advantages of an honest life that his will may be roused in the direction of an honest life; in other words, to reform the man, to make him feel the pressure of the law so severely and so persistently that he shall come to understand that the mere chance of a reward for criminal practices is only to be got at a tremendous risk; to train him to the "habit" of honest labor, so that his mind will be fixed on getting an honest livelihood in an upright manner rather than by criminal practices; to cultivate in him an ethical sense and a spiritual impulse for righteousness; to raise him as far as possible to such a bodily condition as will remove depressing physical influences from his life, and will overcome the effect of inherited physical taints that might reduce his power of resistance to evil.

And here is proper place to insist that there is such a thing as the "criminal habit," as much as the "clerical habit," or the habit of honest industry; and that this criminal habit must be considered and obliterated. I know well a reformed pickpocket, a man who has led a pure and spotless life for the last five years, a faithful and humble Christian, who told me that during the first year after his reformation the habit of thieving was so strong upon him that oftentimes in a street-car or in a shop his hand had almost grasped a purse or watch before he could bring the power of his untrained higher will upon it, and he found himself many a time in a cold sweat in recovering from such a shock. It would be an interesting thing to consider what would have been the result on this man's life and character if he had yielded to a habit of years before his sluggish will could act.

The feasibility of converting criminals into honest citizens long ago dawned upon the older penologists, and in the councils of the Prison Association of New York plans were discussed for the establishment of a Reformatory which should be at once a prison and a training-school, a place where a young man far enough advanced in criminal practices to have become a felon should be taken and trained toward an honest life. The late professor Theodore W. Dwight drafted the bill for such a Reformatory, and it was established in Elmira in 1877. I cannot go into details as to the treatment of felons in this most wonderful prison. I need only say that every prisoner sent there is treated individually, that he is "sized up" according to his mental, moral, and intellectual qualities and his physical condition; that the depths of his character are probed for him and to build him up is to bear upon him. The rewards of the place are to be gained only by good behavior. All progress is expected to be achieved through intense application of the sternest discipline. Men are sent to the Elmira Reformatory, first, that they may be made to understand that it does not pay to be a criminal; second, that they may learn that it is for them to be other than criminals; third, that they may be made other than criminals. The fact is never lost sight of that the inmates must presently go out into society again and be subjected to the test of daily temptation.

In our old prisons, the conditions of life were entirely different from the conditions of life outside. At the Elmira Reformatory the conditions are made as nearly like the outside conditions as possible, but every condition is intensified to its utmost degree. I can hardly conceive a more beautiful sight in life than to watch the enkindling manhood as the processes of training at Elmira continues. Men find they have faculties of mind and soul that they never dreamed of. They find they have abilities they did not suspect. They walk with a new purpose in life because a new purpose has been shown to them. The very wisest feature of the Elmira Reformatory is that a man is sent there to be cured of his enmity to society, to be made to understand that he can grow on his own roots and need not be a human parasite; and under the Indeterminate Sentence he is kept until he does learn that and is released when it is learned; he is released not to become again a menace to society. He cannot go until he has acquired some means of honest self-support, and he cannot leave the institution until a place is found for him to work and earn his living. He remains a ward of the State, under its direct control without process of law, within the maximum term of the statute under which he has been sentenced, until he is released by the Board of Managers on their judgement that he is a reformed man. "Nothing succeeds like success." The Elmira Reformatory has shown a reformation of more than eighty per cent of those who have been trained there.

If this system established at Elmira in 1877 was a good one, why not apply its principles to the entire prison-system of the State? This was the question that the Legislature of 1899 asked itself, and to which it found an answer in the present prison law of the State of New York, which is doubtless the best in the world, though the original law was modified somewhat to suit the not altogether reasonable demands of the labor reformers. The law makes it permissive that any judge sentencing a prisoner shall sentence him on the indeterminate plan, his release on parole being the subject to the judgement of a Commission made up of prison officials. The new law also provides for a graded prison-system based on age and on progress in crime. Although the law was passed in 1889, there had been last January only a score of men sentenced under its operation on the Indeterminate plan, and a graded system had not been established owing to the fact that the prisons of the State were so much more engrossed in politics than they were in the treatment and reformation of men.

It is beyond question that New York's three State prisons are dominated entirely by political influences and run for political ends, that the Superintendent of Prisons dare not place himself squarely upon penological principles as against the wishes of the political bosses. It is a significant fact that the people of the State are willing to trust the custody of a dangerous class of men, about three thousand in number, to those who avowedly regard the prisons as a part of the political machine. It is a fact, lamentable, easily proven, that the prisons of the State of New York are not today conducted with the sole idea of the reformation and uplifting of men. They are run solely to make political capital for the dominant party, they are run in fear of the labor element, they are run to make places for "lowdown" politicians and rewards for political leaders. In the State of New York we have seen during the last two years an efficient prison warden of high standing in the National Prison Association of the United States thrown out of one great prison to make place for a politician whose training had been more in the caucus than in the prison; and we have seen another warden thrown out after thirteen years of service, with only forty-eight hours' notice, to make place for a man whose training had been in the press-room of a daily newspaper. It is fortunate for the State that neither of these two new wardens, however inexperienced, is a bad man; but they were not appointed with reference to their character or to the conduct of the prisons, but purely as a reward for political service and that minor officers might be controlled and drilled into line by their superior knowledge of political management. When we run our prisons to reform prisoners, we shall reform them, and we shall then reduce our criminal class. We need not hope to do it before.

The theory of the proper treatment of criminals may be summed up in a few straight-forward propositions:

1. A criminal is like any other man.

2. Too great importance has been attached to the manner of heredity, both in the judgement of criminals and in their treatment.

3. Moral traits are not inherited, except in so far as they are directly traceable to physical conditions.

4. The ratio of punishment to crime is so small as to give the criminal such a chance of escape as he distinctly counts to his advantage.

5. The criminal is a criminal of his own volition, and feels that he has an adequate motive for being a criminal. This applies, of course, to the professional criminal who commits crime against property and only incidentally against persons.

6. We cannot reduce the criminal population until we can remove the motive for crime.

7. The criminal when he becomes a ward of the State must be treated with severity, but under an intelligent method making wholly for his reformation.

8. We cannot reform our criminals until we reform our prisons.

9. We cannot reform our prisons until we take them out of politics.

10. We cannot take our prisons out of politics until special Civil Service rules are fully enforced in our prisons or so long as any prison office may be filled as a reward for political service.

11. In conclusion, to purify our prisons, to save ourselves from criminals, we as Christian citizens must throw our prayerful interest into the matter of purifying our politics and saving ourselves from politicians.

INSTINCTIVE CRIMINALITY AND SOCIAL CONDITIONS

BY

ERNEST BOWEN ROWLANDS

LAW QUARTERLY REVIEW

VOL. 13, NO. 49 (JANUARY 1897), PP. 59-69

Among the great fallacies which have taken a lasting hold of both tutored and untutored minds, and as the groundwork of systems of philosophy which startled the world, is the idea of a golden age. Long before Rousseau wrote of a social contract, long before Zeno taught the individual duty of resistance to passion, the intellectual fathers of the past dwelt fondly on an age in which man, freed from all earthiness, lived pure and peaceful. That period, whose ruling spirit was loving co-operation, has been discussed from time immemorial. It has proved of immense service to the speculative scientist, and subserved the purpose of the labour leader. Philosophers, whose philosophy is evident in superabundant untenable theories, have joined the cynic in denouncing society, its modes, and its progress. It matters little to them that one believes in the fact of an evolution from good to evil, the other in a change from bad to worse. Both regard the past as a standard from which the world has departed only to deteriorate.

Professors of religion lament, have always lamented, and must necessarily always lament, the decadence of peoples. Even the old time squire, with a soul centred in sport and fox-hunting, babbles about the "good old times," and bemoans the disrespectful temper of degenerate sons of men. And yet for two centuries, at least, the wise have taught the lessons of history. And to some extent in vain: for the "golden age" is a pleasing formula; it is full of agreeable associations, and appeals to the artistic temperament with the force of an undraped statue or a flaring yellow flower.

And, further, the idea is a powerful antiseptic to the stern reality of a world where railways abound and athletes are worshipped. As a plaything it may be tolerable, but as a basis of practical conduct it is absurd. I do not intend to deal with those who countenance the idea and its appropriate appurtenances further than to deny categorically that there ever was such an age as "the golden age." That is sufficient for my purpose.

And now to briefly inquire into the conditions of early mankind. A fitting resort to the historical method of inquiry has proved conclusively that the state of primitive man was one of internecine disputes, imprudent selfishness, and deified violence.

Going far beyond the period at which—to quote Sir Henry Maine's pet phrase—the "family was the unit of society," and even previous to the establishment of an exogamous regulation, right back to the time when man, four-footed, hairy, and donkey-eared, had his being in the cave, and lived on what he could find in the ground or the spoils of his encounter with another beast, we see man as he was in his primitive condition, before he lived in association with his fellow men. It may not be pleasant looking backward, but it is inevitable.

History laughs at the idea of a golden age, and enjoins the student of sociology to date as the first stage of society the time when man was many steps lower in the progressive scale than the hairy ainu, the intellectual inferior of the educated ape of the itinerant organ-grinder.

From an age of filth, and not from an age of gold, it is historically necessary to trace the career of man. The principal stages in that career can be shortly summarized as follows: Primeval man lived in a state of pure individualism. He was a law unto himself and the women and weaklings whom in his sensual wanderings he met. His morality was measured by his creative wants and the strength of his foe. His habits were those of the beast amongst whom he lived and with whom he fought. He killed and ate, chattered and quarreled, ravished and slept. He lived for himself, a creature repulsive in appearance and abominable in habit. Then, at some period which it is impossible to exactly define, he began to associate with his fellow man. This fact of association is the evidence of his first progressive step, the commencement of the reign of civilization.

Directly man consorted with man, he necessarily became in a degree social, and the cultivation of self was considerably affected by his altered position. For the convenience of the associates—settled or nomadic—rough rules were laid down as to the division of the chase or of war, these rules being greatly increased when the nomadic was superseded by the stationary mode of life. At this period the age of morality had begun, and the inception of law was foreshadowed.

The primary rules which had served the wandering hunters would not suffice for permanent co-dwellers, and thus in the process of time they were refined, expanded, and materially added to in point of number. Each particular rule infringed somewhat the license of the associates, this being a necessary consequence of that subjection of the individual desire to the paramount interests of the associated, which association implied.

The imposition of restraint on the individual for the benefit of the many marks the era of liberty, which had now become an accomplished fact. In all the changes and alterations in the rules rendered necessary by ever-changing circumstances, the principle of change and the modification of existing license and individualism were the necessities of men living together in a state of peace. It was the adoption, conscious or unconscious, of this principle which from an aggregate of fortuitously collected individuals caused the development of society, each member of which is compelled to regard the convenience of his co-members and harmonize his conduct with the requirements of others. To say that individuals were thus actuated is to say that they had attained some measure of civilization. For civilization, in its fullest meaning, is but a succinct method of expressing the result of the adoption as a principle of conduct, both individual and national, of the permanent good of a community. The nations which have consciously adopted this principle as a basis of action most consistently and most thoroughly are those who are now the rulers of the world.

It would be outstepping the proper limits of such an article as this aims to be to analyze the various causes which have contributed to the practical development of this principle, but it will not be out of place to say that, whatever from a cosmic and theological standpoint may be the shortcomings of Christianity, the religion which taught that man lives not for himself alone had much to do with the evolution from a system of gross imperfect selfishness to a municipal creed whose fundamental doctrine is a prudent self-regard.

And now, having dealt with man, his primitive notions and methods, my foregoing statements may be adequately summed up as follows: Man, considered as a member of a community, is naturally imprudently selfish, is naturally lawless, and consequently is naturally anti-social. Or, to put it in another way: Man, until he is taught what regulations he has to obey, is necessarily unable *knowingly* to obey or offend against those regulations.

And this will serve to make it clear that *I am not on the side of those who labour to prove that the criminal is merely an abnormal person, or one who is morally insane.* On the contrary, I consider—putting the truly insane out of the question—that the criminal *is* normal; that criminality is the result of causes external to the criminal himself and totally unconnected with the influences of heredity. In my opinion it is as absurd to say that the criminal is born *not* made, as it is to ascribe criminality to the possessor of certain physical attributes.

Now, I have already stated that man is naturally anti-social. At his birth, he is either capable of *appreciating* the teaching of the state or not. If his mind is so singularly weak as to render him either absolutely unintelligent or (perhaps) destitute of self-control, or if he is unable to distinguish between right and wrong or cannot appreciate the nature and quality of a certain act, he is called "idiot" or "lunatic." Between this condition of mental unsoundness and sanity there can reasonably be no intermediate condition, whether it be called moral insanity or by any other high-sounding title.

But, for all that, let us shortly in the light of the preceding analysis look into this question. It is claimed that there is such a thing as an instinctive criminal, a person who is born into this world the unfortunate possessor of an innate peculiar and abnormal disposition to break the laws of the country he happens to reside in. Now, bearing in mind that a crime is simply a particular infringement of the law obtaining in a community, the sanction of which is enforced by the sovereign power in that community, and further that laws are constantly changing, and the character of crimes consequently frequently varying, it surely seems unreasonable to argue that a babe may be a victim of a desire to infringe the Factory Acts or evade the postal regulations of his country.

Is it reasonable to argue that a child may be born with a disposition to break a law which has received the royal assent at the very moment of his birth? Assuredly no! Yet those who advocate an innate criminality theory are forced to do this or admit the untenability of their views. They may, however, object that what is meant by innate criminality is an abnormal disposition to override all laws and not the tendency to commit a specific offence. Well, to that it may be replied, that as the greater includes the less, the child cursed with such a disposition is innately constrained to carry off wards in chancery, refuse to give stamped receipts for money paid, and negligently allow his chimney to take fire.

And again, it may be pointed out that "torts"—or actionable wrongs independent of contract—are in every case intimately connected with, and in some cases inextricably mixed up with, crimes – differing from crimes only in point of procedure. Still, in order to preserve consistency, the advocates of the "innate tendency" theory must aver the existence in the criminal not of merely natural anti-social tendencies but of an innate abnormal disposition to be guilty of all torts, including those of libel and nuisance.

According to my view (I think it better to sum up my foregoing remarks before discussing the view of a leader of the opposite school of thought), every person is naturally anti-social, in that he will naturally prefer himself to all others; but that any particular person will, *when he ascertains* the state and subject-matter of the regulations affecting him and the people amongst whom he lives, be actuated by innate more or less irresistible forces derived from his own peculiar mental and/or physical character to disregard those regulations seems to me to be opposed to the teachings of science and reason. Further, I contend that man is the creature of social circumstances, and is dependent on heredity only for those qualities which may be described as physical.

Mr. Havelock Ellis, whose work titled *The Criminal* champions and reflects the views of Professor Cesare Lombroso and his unique school of philosophy and practice known as criminal anthropology, is of a different opinion. According to Lombroso and his followers the criminal is an "abnormal man," a "monstrosity," and "a person who is by his organization directly anti-social." It is difficult to see how any one can be naturally social, but that is a question for later consideration. Mr. Ellis also lays down that "to be a criminal a deed must be exceptional in the species, and must provoke a social reaction among the other members of that species." Following the tenets of Lombroso's school, Ellis also divides criminals into the following classes: the political, the occasional, the habitual (created by social conditions —at least, I presume that is what he means), and the born, or instinctive criminal. This last is the class worthy of our consideration in this discussion, for other criminals are but petty bunglers in comparison with those who are born to commit every available kind of crime.

That every criminal (meaning thereby the instinctive criminal) is born a criminal is the keynote of Mr. Havelock Ellis's highly ingenious work, taken together with the fact that every criminal can be distinguished at once by the competent eye. One waits with some curiosity to see what the marks of distinction are, but for now, let us delineate the more important ones advocated by the criminal anthropologists: Receding forehead; lack of cranial symmetry; sugar-loaf head; and, it seems also, a low skull. In the cerebral department, inasmuch as Gambetta's brain "resembled in shape that of a micro-cephalic idiot," it is not altogether surprising to note that neither the convolution, shape, nor development of the brain are at present valuable as indicia to the criminal anthropologist. In the face: prominent chins denote great, and receding chins petty criminals. Other criminal facial marks are prominent cheek bones; wrinkles; pallor of skin; rectilinear nose; abundant hair; scanty beard; dark eyes; and in sexual offenders, light eyes. While it may surprise many of those who practice in criminal courts to learn that "a pleasing, well-formed face is never seen in a prison," the fact that the eminent physiognomist Lavater once mistook Herder's portrait for that of an executed criminal will reassure those who feel nervous as to the portentous aspect of their own countenances and "hirsute appendages." But, I digress. Let us continue our inventory of those supposed characteristics by which criminal anthropologists claim the born criminal may be distinguished. In the body: the distinctive marks are long arms; pigeon breasts; bad chests; stooping shoulders; and among other indicia denotative of the criminal are great physical agility; bad olfactory sense; ill-developed sense of taste; good eyesight; and bad hearing.

Moral insensibility, we are also told, is an important index to the criminal, though one might be pardoned for thinking that early training was not altogether unconnected with its cause. Physical insensibility is another index; vanity is another—and this perhaps accounts for the ever increasing number of female criminals. Immaturity in the parent, or decadence of the father often produces the criminal; fathers over forty-one years of age being especially likely to beget idiots and murderers. The criminal is further to be recognized by his tastes and occupation; he is fond of alcohol, cards, and sexual vices; he dislikes regular work, and is sentimental, religious, or superstitious; he is given to write poetry on the walls of his cell or on the kitchen utensils; he is both stupid and cunning; he is frequently tattooed, and generally justifies his misdeeds on high moral principle. And, finally, the typical criminal would have "projecting ears, thick hair, and thin beard, projecting frontal eminences, enormous jaws, a square and projecting chin, large cheek bones, and frequent gesticulation," and would in type resemble the Mongolian or sometimes the Negroid.

The above being the indicia which denote the criminal, if the *fact* that the human face and body varies very slightly in the inhabitants of defined regions does not prove the absurdity of the theory, indeed, a week passed at the Old Bailey Criminal Courts or in a Cardiff or Liverpool Assize Court would effectually demonstrate the shakiness of Dr. Cesare Lombroso's and Mr. Havelock Ellis's generalizations. But on this score it is not my part to quarrel with those gentlemen, for having anticipatorily dealt with the theory of innate disposition, I am only concerned with the theory that underlies their writings, namely that of an hereditarily acquired criminal disposition. Mr. Havelock Ellis and other criminal anthropologists may object that their views do not necessarily demand an adherence to the doctrines of heredity, and although I do not for a moment suppose they would put forward such an objection, it will be as well to anticipate it. Ellis and others of Lombroso's ilk labour to show that criminals are born and not made, and that they bear on them the physical marks which denote a criminal mental tendency. This then establishes an identity as between body and mind, or if not an identity, at least a close relationship. Now, it must be conceded by the greatest stickler for "circumstances," that physical construction does largely depend on the influences of heredity, and so, if a certain physical construction is eventually co-existent with a certain mental tendency, it must follow that heredity necessarily plays an important part as an element in the theories of Dr. Cesare Lombroso and Mr. Havelock Ellis. And assuming that it does, I have dealt already with the doctrine of innate tendency, and now I will briefly consider it again in relation to heredity.

Briefly, the points at issue are: (1) Can a human being come into the world endowed with a disposition anti-social in the sense that he has a tendency to break the laws of his country, and *not anti-social* in the sense that he will do his best for himself according to his lights? Mr. Havelock Ellis says, "Yes"; and I in the preceding pages of this article have said "No"!; and (2) Assuming there is such a disposition, can it be communicated by parent to child? On the second point, let us look at it from a practical standpoint. Would any competent breeder of the lower animals breed to obtain mental results? In short, to quote concrete cases, is it likely that a sane breeder would breed from a performing pig or a calculating horse, in order to obtain increased qualities of intelligence in their progeny? Having regard to the history of mankind, the researches of biologists, and the various processes of consciousness, it is hard to say in what essential respect the animal world differs from mankind. But, coming directly to the case of man, no educated person would expect a brilliant child to result from the union of a senior wrangler and the foremost mathematician at Oxford.

It is, we believe, not asserted by any competent person that intellectual qualities can be transmitted from ancestor to descendant, and it passes all rational understanding why a criminal disposition should be included among inherited qualities. It would take up too much space to enter minutely into an analytical disquisition on the subject, but I assume that it is capable of proof that the only inherited qualities are those dependent on physical characteristics. This, at least, is the conclusion to which I have been led by a study of the available data. I admit that such capacities as are indicated by musical skill, oratorical power, and others of an essentially similar kind are inheritable, for they are intimately related to physical conformation, but I can see no sufficient reason to justify the inclusion among inheritable qualities those capacities which are properly styled intellectual.

Take an ordinary child, and put him in a bassinette with another child of the same age, e.g., six-months, who is the possessor of a toy. How long will it be before the envious ordinary child attempts to commit robbery with violence, disturbs the public peace by brawling, and is engaged in the highly anti-social act of losing its temper. Again, when at home, what is there dearer to that ordinary child, in the intervals of feeding, than hurting a kitten or killing a fly, unless it be the doing of malicious injury to property in breaking its bottle. This child is a type, and he is *ex hypothesi* the child of ordinary parents and the representative of a very ordinary ancestry. Is it then to be assumed that the child is a *born* criminal? True, he acts criminally, and will continue to act criminally, until he is taught by a rigorous system of punishments and rewards to realize how impossibly anti-social he is.

Mr. Havelock Ellis and his school might say that notwithstanding all teaching the born criminal continues his vile career. To that it may be replied that experience does not warrant the supposition in the case of any human being, and Mr. Ellis himself in advocating ameliorative measures destined to reform the criminal is attacking his own theory with inconsistent reasons. The truth is that both of Mr. Havelock Ellis's theories, and likewise, those of other criminal anthropologists, are fallacious; they are pretty, but they lack a sensible basis.

And now finally to state the conclusions of the opposite school. Every one, being instinctively anti-social and naturally individualistic, endeavours to obtain for himself the maximum of good, regardless of others' rights and others' convenience. If *having been taught* how to mould his conduct so as to accord with the views of the community of which he is a member, he continues to transgress the regulations, he either does so intentionally or unintentionally. If the latter, he is not responsible for his actions, and is insane. If, not knowing what rules are laid down by the community, he offends, but he is clearly not criminal in mind, – though criminal in fact, according to some unscientific systems of law. In short, criminality, or the disposition to commit a crime or crimes willfully and intentionally, is the result of a conflict of desires. Criminality implies comparison, and therefore cannot be unconscious or innate. The causes of the existence of a permanent tendency to crime in man are lack of education, miserable surroundings—implying poverty, and in England and some other countries, the prevailing penal system; and the habitual criminal, who in this classification takes the place of Mr. Havelock Ellis's instinctive criminal, is the victim of circumstances. He is the victim of circumstances in that the causes above specified render the desire to break the law greater and more operative than the desire to avoid punishment and gain the rewards which honesty is supposed to bring in its train.

Education, the improvement of the social conditions of life, and an improved penal system will alone reform the criminal. It is the habitual criminal who can be dealt with and reformed; it is the occasional criminal, the slave of passion, who is the standing pest of civilization. The forces of education and worldly wisdom are powerless to prevent the crime of the paederast and the poisoner, and society will ever stand mute periodically at the commission of some brutal crime, the work of educated men whose motive is revenge or lust.

But the habitual criminal, about whom books are written and treatises composed, *is* curable. He is driven to crime by circumstances which are not unchangeable; he is the slave of a vicious social system which is not ineradicable. The report of the Departmental Committee on Prisons bears out my contention. In 1893, whose judicial statistics are given in the report, the total number of persons convicted at Assizes and Quarter Sessions was 9,694, of whom 5,335, or 55 per cent, had been previously convicted. Of this number again, 2,988 had been previously convicted on indictment, and 2,3447 on summary process. In the different classes of offences given below, the proportion of recommittals varies as follows:

Offences against the person	30 per cent
Offences against property with violence	66 per cent
Offences against property without violence	64 per cent
Malicious injury to property	42 per cent
Forgery and coining	32 per cent
Other offences	25 per cent

As regards these data the Committee has made the following remarks: "The proportion is highest where the offence offers to the habitual criminal the best means of obtaining a livelihood. This is further illustrated by the fact that for the offence of larceny from the person there were 79 per cent of recommittals, and for simple larceny 78 per cent. The majority of recommittals are in respect to larceny;" and this invites the suggestion that as instinctive criminality can hardly be claimed as a privilege of the poor, the rich, whom larceny as a means of earning a livelihood would not excite, are singularly fortunate in the division of criminal dispositions. I have not sufficient space at my disposal to suggest how best to deal with criminals. But one thing is certain, and that is that every increase in our population, unless it is accompanied by prudential measures for the improvement of the masses of the people, means an increase in the number of recidivists. Mr. Havelock Ellis, and those criminal anthropologists who think with him, wear out their energy in discussing how such luxurious agencies as Turkish baths and gymnastic training may be used to convert the instinctive criminal. Would it not be better to give up putting the so-called instinctive criminal on the rack as a pretty problem, and, looking facts squarely in the face, advance to the relief of those whom poverty and misery will inevitably lead to crime. Though day by day, in accordance with prevailing sentiment, new Acts of Parliament are made and new offences consequently constituted, it is gratifying to note that the proportion of criminals to the population is ever being lessened. This in itself is a significant fact, and it speaks volumes in favour of the beneficial influence of education, and the action of a progressive community.

Prevention is better than cure. A useful Act of Parliament couched in a democratic spirit is worth a myriad of such remedial forces as prison visitors and Turkish baths. Educate, educate, educate, should be the everlasting cry of the legislator, and the improvement of social conditions for the mass of the people should be the aim of the statesman. It is idle to preach the doctrines of religion to a man whose life outside the prison walls is a living hell. "If I do not steal," the habitual thief may ask, "what am I to do? My record is known, the police are ever anxious to distinguish themselves, my past life is a barrier to an honest livelihood." He may commit suicide, it is true, but if he tries to kill himself and fails, he will get maybe six months' hard labour for attempting to deprive the state of a potential soldier. It is in the case of such a man that the difficulty arises, and it must be grappled with. To treat the victim of social circumstances as a romantic plaything is both cowardly and intolerable.

The instinctive criminal is but the habitual criminal—which term must include those who, having made up their minds to a career of crime, are prevented, e.g., by death or altered conditions of life, from continuing in their criminal course beyond the first crime—after all, the man whose original fall was, in the large majority of cases, caused either by social misfortunes, or lack of education, or both causes acting in combination, and whose after career was guarded by the demons of police supervision and ticket-of-leave.

But, although it may be comparatively easy—dismissing as untenable the theory of innate criminality—to spy out the means of dealing effectually with the "criminal or dangerous class," and although the philanthropist may confidently anticipate the time when that class of poverty-stricken wretches whose ignorance is on a par with their miserable surroundings, shall be so depleted as to be almost non-existent, it is presently impossible to cope with the criminals who are actuated by motives of revenge or lust. These criminals are generally occasional, but inasmuch as some of them —especially sexual offenders—are permanently involved in the commission of crimes, they should be termed *habitual criminals*, were it not for the fact that that term customarily denotes gain as the object of the crime. The paid catamite would thus be included among habitual criminals, but not so the paederast, the motive of whose crime was lust. Dr. Cesare Lombroso, Mr. Havelock Ellis, and other criminal anthropologists might include him among instinctive criminals, but hardly, for it is clear that such a criminal is either the victim of too much or too little education. Besides, the crime of unlawful and unnatural connection with men or beasts is of a curious origin and character, and would not support their theory.

Without entering into further detail, I think I may assume this. The criminals whose fault is born of revenge are distinctly occasional. These criminals who commit the foulest crimes are not touched on by writers on criminal anthropology. They are so ridiculously normal as it were, and all preventive and remedial human agencies seem to have failed in their case. What is then to be done? Here, indeed, is a fine field for the criminologist. The occasional and not the habitual criminal opens up a huge mass of possibilities to the prospective philosopher. The output of habitual criminals, not including the sexually vicious, can be materially lessened, I firmly believe, by the efforts of the wise. It remains to be seen whether the most severe punishment or any other human agency can alter the course of those who have committed sexual offences, or prevent the commission of crimes by men acting suddenly and in obedience to an overwhelming passion, since every human being is a potential criminal by passion.

SUGGESTIONS FOR FURTHER READING AND INQUIRY:

ARGUMENTS AGAINST BIOLOGICAL POSITIVISM

"The Treatment of Crime as Affected by the Doctrine of Evolution." J. H. Hyslop. *Unitarian Review*, vol. 29 (1888), pp. 139-147.
Discussion of the ideas concerning the best method for the treatment of crime that logically flow from the theoretical perspectives advanced by the Italian school of criminal anthropology, and how advocates of hereditary criminal predisposition are wrong in lobbying for major revisions in the prevailing practice of punishment grounded in the free-will model.

"The Modern Frankenstein." George M. Gould. *Open Court*, vol. 3 (1889), 1745-1748, 1754-1758.
In this paper read before the Medical Jurisprudence Society of Pennsylvania, the author condemns Lombroso's Italian school of criminal anthropology as a wearisome absurdity.

"Jukes Again." *Saturday Review*, vol. 72 (1891), pp. 241-242.
Commentary on Dr. S. A. K. Strahan's condemnation of the hereditary influence in the production of criminals and paupers as utterly without foundation, and therefore unbelievable.

"The Social Factor in Crime." James H. Pershing. *American Law Review*, vol. 28 (1894), pp. 368-375.
A fine overview of the three broad and commonly accepted families of criminological etiology (biological, social environmental, and cosmicological) and a discussion concerning the relative impact each has on crime. The thesis is advanced in that the nature and relative importance of the various constituent elements of the social environmental perspective of crime causation (e.g., urban decay, economic social

inequality, and uncertainty of detection and punishment) are of paramount importance to the criminologist, because these factors can be most readily addressed and be made to regulate and neutralize biological and cosmicological influences.

"Can the Criminal Be Reclaimed?" H. S. Williams. *North American Review*, vol. 163 (1896), pp. 207–218.

The central question in regards to criminological etiology is not why some people commit crimes, but rather why all people do not commit crime. The article advances the thesis that the criminal differs from the law abiding person not in an inherited predisposition to depravity and crime, but in a lack of cultivated powers to resist the universal desire we have all had to infringe upon the personal and property rights of others. The cultivation of the powers of resistance is to be achieved through reform of the social environment (e.g., slum eradication), education, and early reformatory intervention of young criminals.

"Is There a Criminal Type?" Gustave Tarde. *Charities Review*, vol. 6 (1897), pp. 109–117.

A scathing rebuke of the criminal anthropological theory of crime causation, and an argument for the social and physical environmental perspectives. Written by the Director of the French Bureau of Statistics (Ministry of Justice, Paris, France), and one of Cesare Lombroso's fiercest European critics.

"The Evidence for and Against the Transmission of Acquired Characteristics." *Public Opinion*, vol. 27 (1899), p. 527.

The full text of an address read by George Archdall Reid before the British Medical Society, wherein he presents an outstanding summary of the evidence to date.

"Typical Criminals." Samuel G. Smith. *Popular Science Monthly*, vol. 56 (1900), pp. 539–545.

Report of an interesting experiment, the results of which are offered to refute Lombroso's contention that criminality is chiefly attributable to atavism and that criminals possess distinct physical anomalies and abnormalities.

THE FRENCH
AND
BELGIAN
STATISTICAL SCHOOLS

(OF CARTOGRAPHY
AND SOCIAL ECOLOGY)

GUERRY ON THE STATISTICS OF CRIME IN FRANCE, BEING AN ABSTRACT OF HIS *ESSAI SUR LA STATISTIQUE MORALE DE LA FRANCE, AVEC CARTES*

WESTMINSTER REVIEW
VOL. *18, NO. 36 (APRIL 1833), PP. 353-366*

A knowledge of statistics was sought with avidity in France at an early period of the first revolution. Napoleon did not neglect the subject, but he was too well aware of the arguments which it afforded against his system, to permit the free extension of inquiry; and at the restoration of the Bourbons, it was for a time still more rigorously checked. In 1816, a vote of money was required to pay for statistical returns, which shortsighted royalists opposed.

From 1825 inclusive, yearly accounts of criminal justice have been made with great care in France and printed. In 1829 an officer was appointed to make full collections and improve arrangements of facts, for the double purpose of stimulating the public functionaries, and of framing tables of the moral statistics of Paris. This establishment was broken up in 1831, and is not yet revived in the same form; but in October last, a fifth class was added to the Institute of France, upon the original plan of 1790, which comprehended statistics.

M. Guerry, the officer appointed in 1829 to collect the moral statistics of Paris, was before known as the colleague of M. Balbi, in publishing a statistical map, showing the extent of education, compared with the extent of crime, in France. A letter upon the same subject by the same author, was published in 1831, by M. Quetelet of Brussels, in a curious statistical work with maps, entitled *Researches in the Disposition to Commit Crime at Different Ages of Life*. M. Guerry has therefore had good training to his task of writing this new work on the *Moral Statistics of France*.

A peculiarity in recent inquiries of this kind, is the addition of pictorial illustrations. Maps showing the distribution of crime and education have been used by the author, by his coadjutor Balbi, by Quetelet, Duchatelet, Dupin, and others. In the present work that vehicle of information is much improved in execution, and applied to several more subjects than before. In the words of M. Guerry, "In order to place the results in a more striking light, several maps have been framed which have peculiar advantages, not found in tables or figures. The shades of colour present comparative views of facts more rapidly to the mind than could be gained from tedious calculations. The comparative amounts are expressed without the least incorrectness, and the eye instantly receives from the outlines a lasting impression of the truth."

The materials upon which the inquiry is mainly founded are six quarto volumes of documents, entitled '*Comptes Generaux de L'administration de la Justice Criminelle,*' and prosecuted every year since 1825 by the Garde-de-Sceaux to the King of France. The accuracy of these documents has been questioned in England, but probably without reason. They are drawn up from quarterly returns prepared, in all parts of France, by public prosecutors, who are provided for that purpose with uniform printed forms; and when occasional inaccuracies are discovered, they are corrected under the double supervision of local superiors, and of the chief administrator of criminal prosecutors in Paris.

Out of the subjects comprised in these high official documents, M. Guerry selects the number of commitments, not the number of convictions, for the basis of his calculations. The ground of M. Guerry's selection deserves to be noticed. "Some errors," he says, "must arise as to the real amount of crime in the country, whichever basis is chosen. But the number of accusations is nearer the truth than the number of convictions. Except in political charges, the public prosecutors in general give way to few circumstances which produce any want of uniformity in their prosecutions; whereas the verdicts of juries vary surprisingly, both according to the neighborhood where the trials take place, and also according to the subject matter of the trials."

To an objection, that the distribution of crimes throughout France in maps divided into departments must be incorrect, on account of the probability of the criminals having been strangers and not natives, M. Guerry replies from the *Compte General* of 1828, in which year the point was first specially inquired into, that it is ascertained that seventy-two in every hundred of the accused are uniformly natives of the departments where accused, and that ninety-seven in every hundred of those accused in all France are natives of France. The foundation therefore for comparison is sure.

As soon as the comparative uniformity of crime in short intervals, as for instance from year to year, shall have been established as indicated in what next follows; the interesting subsequent inquiry will be to find how it varies in longer periods, and to connect this with moral and political causes. All of which must be supposed to have been in the author's mind. According to M. Guerry, "When facts shall once be fully and clearly established, and divested of all accidental circumstances, criminal statistics will become equally certain with other sciences which depend upon observation. Results will be seen to recur steadily, uninfluenced by chance. Every year will produce the same number of crimes, in the same order of succession, in the same districts. There will be a uniform distribution of offenses, according to the differences of age, sex, and seasons; the whole being regularly attended by collateral circumstances, of little apparent force, and difficult to be explained. It will be easy to give proof that facts, hitherto thought to be too subtle for any fixed law, thus steadily recur. Let France be supposed to be divided into five great regions, namely, the north, south, east, west, and centre, each composed of seventeen departments, and containing respectively, 8,757,700; 4,826,493; 5,840,996; 7,008,788 and 5,238,905 inhabitants. Then, if the whole of the crimes committed in all France in a year be called one hundred, the proportions for the five regions will stand thus: (See tables on following page)

"These tables show how little the average amount of the number of crimes is ever exceeded, robberies and murders recurring with more uniformity than the harvests. The like regularity exists as to sex. Out of every hundred criminals, the average number of men is 78, of women 22. The actual number of men in five years ending in 1830 being 79, 79, 78, 77, and 78, and 78; and the actual number of females for the same period being 21, 21, 22, 23, and 22."

Crimes Against the Person

	1825	1826	1827	1828	1829	1839	Average
North	25	24	23	26	25	24	25
South	28	26	22	23	25	23	24
East	17	21	19	20	19	19	19
West	18	16	21	17	17	16	18
Centre	12	13	15	14	14	18	14
	100	100	100	100	100	100	100

Crimes Against Property

	1825	1826	1827	1828	1829	1839	Average
North	41	42	42	43	44	44	42
South	12	11	11	12	12	11	12
East	18	16	17	16	14	15	16
West	17	19	19	17	17	17	18
Centre	12	12	11	12	13	13	12
	100	100	100	100	100	100	100

"So, as to age; out of every hundred accused of theft in 1826, there were 37 in number between sixteen and twenty-five years of age; in 1827, 35; in 1828, 38; in 1829, 37; and in 1830, 37; the average of 37 being very little exceeded. And out of every hundred also accused of theft in 1826, there were 31 between 25 and 35 years of age; in 1827, 32; in 1828, 30; in 1829, 31; and in 1830, 32; the average of 31 being also never much exceeded."

"So, as to the seasons; out of every 100 attacks for the purpose of violation (*attentats a la pudeur*), there were committed in the three summer months of 1827, 36; of 1828, 36; of 1829, 35; and of 1830, 38; (*nearly double the average left for all the other quarters of the year*). In 100 cases of wounds, there also happened in the three summer months of 1827, 28; of 1828, 27; of 1829, 27; and of 1830, 27; giving the same steadiness of average."

"Now, if the infinite variety of circumstances which lead to crime be reflected upon, together with the extraneous or personal influences which constitute its greater or less depravity, these unvarying results are what nobody would have dreamed of; and it is a matter of astonishment that acts of free will should rigorously assume so uniform a character. On such a view there is no reasonable ground to deny that moral as well as physical events are subject to invariable laws, and that in many respects judicial statistics afford a sure guide to the judgment. In spite therefore of the frequent misuse of statistics by some reasoners, and of the objections of others whose speculations this science does not bear out, it has naturally attracted general attention, and given a new direction to criminal legislation, and to the inquiries of the moral philosopher."

The substance of the volume is distributed into tables and remarks under the following heads: 1. The crimes committed in France every year, arranged according to their nature and number; 2. The influence of sex on the commission of the various crimes; 3. The influence of age on the same; 4. The influence of the seasons; 5. The motives of capital crimes; 6. The motives of crimes against the person; 7. Account of the map in which the crimes against the person, committed in France in a year, are distributed by departments; 8. Account of a similar map for crimes against property; 9. Account of a map showing the distribution of education in the departments of France; 10, 11, and 12. Accounts of three other maps, showing the distribution of natural children, of charitable donations, and suicides, in the same departments. The 13th section describes another map, showing, in waving lines, the different ages at which various crimes are committed, and the text closes with a statement of certain general results. The maps, handsomely executed with copper plates, are annexed in the book.

The great question upon the increase of crime in modern times is thus described by M. Guerry. "It is often asserted," says M. Guerry, "that the darker offences have become alarmingly more numerous of late than heretofore in France. But no means of comparison exist for any years before 1825. It is therefore only by opinions, not proofs, that the point must be decided. Probably crimes against the person have not increased in number. Formerly courts of justice were secret, and beyond their walls everything was imperfectly known. Now, the public have access to the courts, and newspapers are everywhere full of law reports in all stages of prosecution. Advantageous as this publicity is for other reasons, it gives to society at present an unfair appearance, which has misled many, of crimes being more prevalent. Others maintain that morals have improved, and that since the restoration of the Bourbons crimes are lessened. This opinion is founded on the doubtful fact that the number of criminals condemned to the galleys is diminished; and also on the decrease of the expense incurred for keeping prisoners. But the absence of documents render the former ground of argument weak, and as to the latter, it is forgotten, that the saving has arisen from improved management of gaols. Indeed, truth can be ascertained only by a rigorous examination of facts. The returns for the years 1825 to 1830 show a gradual diminuation of the worst crimes against the person, from the number of 2,069 committed in 1825, to 1,666 committed in 1830; but the same returns show a gradual increase of the worst crimes against property, from 5,018 to 5,552. One of the great causes of the increase in France, as in England, is the want of good prisons for reforming young offenders. Gaol discipline was long despised by governments as the reverie of benevolent men in their closets. And when adopted, it was adopted more upon chance than upon system. Thus it still remains, and the consequence is that every third criminal is one who has been punished before. Incredible as it may appear, gaols said to be well regulated have actually produced more second commitments than the gallies. The existence of these evils has been demonstrated by judicial statistics; and it remains for governments to correct them. The first step is to abandon all prejudices, and to collect all the facts extant respecting prisons, in order to consider all the improvements needed in them. Probably such inquiries would save enormous expense in making experiments, which must be given up as soon as made."

M. Guerry's work affords some remarkable inferences on the effect of poverty in reference to crime, and he takes great pains to point out the true use of the common sort of education, and to expose the error into which many have fallen in thinking that merely teaching the people to read, write, and cast accounts, is enough to repress crime.

He first gives two tables, which show that in every hundred of young men entered upon the military service of all France, the number of those who can read and write in the eighty-six departments ranges from twelve per cent to seventy-four per cent; and also that on an average of six years from 1826 to 1830, the number of persons accused of great crimes against the person, in all France, ranges for the eighty-six departments, from one in 2,199, to one in 36,014. These tables correspond with two maps coloured in departments, with shades from white to black according to the extent of education, and the amount of great crimes. Upon these M. Guerry observes the following: "It has been said that ignorance is the main cause of crime, and that to make men better in happiness, education only is wanted. This opinion has been pronounced in the Chambers, repeated at the Royal Prison Society, and is adopted throughout France. Since the results of criminal justice have been published, it has been repeated with so little hesitation and in so many shapes, that it has become one of those common places which no man thinks of proving. M. Malte Brun first noticed (in 1823) a fact worthy of serious attention, that a distinction exists in regard to the extent of education, between what have been since denominated _dark_ France and _enlightened_ France. The only ground of M. Malte Brun's observations was the number of boys at school. Those who have repeated the observations have confined themselves to this ground. But it was probably an incorrect basis, and since 1827 the Minister of War has caused all the young men liable to serve in the army to be examined as to their being able to read and write. This examination has been made during three years, and as the young men belong to all classes in society, the number in every hundred who can read and write affords an exact scale of the comparative state of education throughout France. According to this sure test, the educated or _light_ departments are the thirty to the North East. Those of the Meuse, the Doubs, the Jura, the Haute-Marne, and the Haut-Rhine are the lightest. There nearly three-fourths of the young men can read and write. It is not however in the South that the most ignorance is found; it is in the West and Centre, in Brittany, in Berry, and in the Limousin, where a twelfth, a thirteenth, and even a fourteenth only can read and write. In

Corsica, which was supposed to be greatly behind in education, half can read and write, which is beyond the proportion of sixty other departments. But more crimes are committed in Corsica, in Alsace, and in the South East, than in any other part, being the parts of France where there is the least ignorance. On the contrary, the fewest crimes are in the West and Centre, where there is the most ignorance."

"The geographical distribution of crimes, however caused, is now exactly known, and its course is uniform every year. That some other cause than the difference of education must be resorted to in order to explain the inequality of the distribution, will be clear upon the inspection of the three following tables."

Education

Young men classed for the Army. Number out of every hundred who could read.			Number of every hundred of the criminally accused who could read.			Boys at school in proportion to the whole population
1827	1828	1829	1828	1829	1830	1829
East 51	56	58	East 52	52	53	East .... 1 in 14
North 48	53	55	North 49	47	47	North .... 1 in 16
South 32	33	34	South 31	28	30	South .... 1 in 43
West 26	27	27	West 29	25	24	West .... 1 in 45
Centre 24	25	25	Centre 25	23	23	Centre ..... 1 in 48

"By two of these tables the eastern region of France is twice as well educated as the centre, and by the third the proportion is three-fold, so that it is demonstrated that the comparative amount of crime does not depend on education."

"The argument in favour of popular education, hitherto thought irrefutable, deserves consideration. It is this: both in England and France, half, or even two-thirds of all the prisoners cannot read. But to give force to this argument it should be known whether the rest of the people were better taught, and this fact is quite unknown. If three-fourths of the prisoners could neither read nor write, but four-fifths of the whole population of the same age and sex were equally illiterate, then the culprits would be proportionately better instructed, and ignorance could not be held to be the cause of their crimes. It has been said very lately that the number of young criminals has gone on decreasing since 1828, when the accused under twenty-one years of age in France were 1,421; in number; in 1829 they were 1,243; and in 1830, 1,275; and in these years the education of the young has greatly increased. The public returns, however, show that in 1826 the number of the same class of criminals was only 1,226; and in 1827, it was 1,258, so that the numbers have gone on increasing."

"The same result has been recognized in other countries where education is highly appreciated, but where additional remedies are earnestly desired to lessen the ills which afflict society."

"It would, however, be a new error to suppose that instruction is proved by statistical inquiries to have a tendency to increase crime. Instruction, meaning thereby reading, writing, and casting accounts, is only an instrument of which a good or bad use may be made accordingly as the morality of the people stands high or low from other causes. It is an excellent instrument in regard to the material advancement of popular interests, and if its uses have sometimes been exaggerated, those uses really understood, and applied to improving men's minds and destroying prejudices, deserve all the care which they have received of late years."

The degree of connexion between education and the frequency of crime is likely to turn out a more complex affair than was expected. It would have been very grateful to the friends of education, that among other good consequences, all crime should have vanished on the apparition of *Reading Made Easy*. But as it does not, they must not therefore give up the case, or cease to watch it narrowly. There are several sources of erroneous conclusion, which it seems necessary to guard against. If Corsica, for instance, produces a large amount of crime, and a large proportion of Corsicans can at the same time read and write, this is no evidence that reading and writing produce crime in Corsica, for it is well known that crime in Corsica arises from perfectly distinct sources. What would really point to that conclusion would be the evidence that reading and writing had increased in Corsica, and with them crime. Again, if it was established that an extraordinary proportion of thieves could read and write, this would not prove that reading and writing were the cause of theft. The real question would plainly be whether, since the introduction of reading and writing, thieving had increased. For example, if since the extension of reading and writing the number of thieves in proportion to the general population was reduced one half, but every thief was found to be a perfect clerk, would this go to prove that reading and writing had increased thieving, or to prove directly the contrary? The pictorial representations of M. Guerry afford an excellent opportunity for a *coup d'oeil*, which, there can be no doubt, may be pursued with advantage into the details. The gross or general inference seems to be that the connexion between the arts of reading and writing and crime is in a state of chaos— that the inferences from one part are contradictory to the inferences from another, and though it is most probable that the average, if pursued throughout, would fall on one side or the other of zero or neutrality, such a result would be of small practical importance, on whichever side it fell. The first striking fact is that the reading and writing portions of France lie to the north-east of the line drawn from somewhere about St. Malo to Geneva. In the matter of crimes against property, this part of France as a whole is certainly not brilliant. On the contrary, though, there is a considerable quantity of thieving in other departments, it must be allowed to be rather dark. In the matter of crimes against the person, on the contrary, it is of the average lightness of the comparatively harmless parts; the south and south-east of France appearing to be the places where criminality of this kind concentrates itself. It certainly does look as if "Thou shalt not steal" was the commandment to be impressed with double vigour on all the subjects of public or charitable education. At the same time there are some exceptions. Meuse for instance is the very brightest department in the matter of instruction, and it holds a very respectable rank in the scales both of thieving and murder, being 65 from the climax of guilt (out of 86) in the first, and 62 in the other. A great number of very tolerably instructed departments seem also to be very tolerably clear of crime in both kinds. The only part where the balance turns decidedly against the instructed people is in the matter of thieving in the departments around Paris, and in Alsace and Lorraine. Crimes against the person, as before intimated, concentrate themselves in the south and south-east; and in point of instruction, though not of the very darkest, these portions are of the next shade to it. A dark portion in the matter of instruction, in the direction of Ushant, is of average badness in theft, though rather clear of murder. The dark and uninstructed patch in the centre of France has a leaning to murder, especially on the south and south-east, and to theft on the north-west. But one department of this region (Creuse) is made to exhibit the phenomenon of being as dark as midnight in the matter of instruction, and as white as milk in the matter of crime of both kinds, while it displays a blacker spot than any of its neighbors in the affair of *enfans naturels*. It must be the terrestrial paradise of the *freres ignorantins*.

The chart of suicides exhibits some remarkable results. The instructed parts, in the main, are those which produce suicides. The ignorant portion in the centre of France attack other people's throats, but take especial care of their own. On the subject of suicide, they present a great white patch.

Some other parts of this visual arithmetic present curious results. A greater quantity of crimes against the person are committed in summer; of crimes against property, in winter. Men begin to commit crimes earlier than women, but leave off rather sooner. Of men who shoot themselves, considerably above a quarter are between the ages of 20 and 30; of such as hang themselves, above a quarter are between 50 and 60, and nearly another quarter between 60 and 70. Nevertheless, gentlemen above 80 seem to die by pistol. The probability is, they were unable to get upon a stool.

The killings or attempts at killing that arise out of adultery present remarkable results. A *mari adultere* is never killed at all. Out of 1,000 cases, 22 are where the *femme adultere* is killed by her husband, and 11 by her partner in sin. 437 are where the *mari outrage* is killed; of which 77 are by the wife, 177 by her partner in sin, 166 by the wife and partner together, and 17 by the wife and some strange hand. 282 are where the injured wife is killed, of which 177 are by the peccant husband, 55 by his helpmate in adultery, and 50 by the two together. In 34 the guilty husband's partner in sin is killed, of which 17 are by the offended wife, and an equal number by the relations of the discreditable husband. In 138 the seducer of the wife is killed, of which 110 are by the affronted husband, 11 by the faithless wife and some strange party, and 17 by the relations of the faithless wife. 39 are where the children of adultery are killed, of which 22 are by the adulterous mother, and 17 by the affronted husband. 16 are of legitimate children, of which 5 are by the adulterous mother herself, and 11 by her and her partner in guilt conjointly. 21 are of other parties, of which 16 are by the wife's partner in adultery of somebody who was in the way, and 5 by the injured husband of somebody he conceived to be an accessory.

The section upon the crimes of poisoning and other murders committed or attempted in consequence of debauchery, seduction, and concubinage contains the following commentary by M. Guerry upon a table in which these crimes are analysed.

"More than three-fourths of the numerous murders committed or attempted in consequence of debauchery, seduction, and concubinage are upon females. The wish to stifle complaint and to escape the scandal and risk of prosecution is the most common motive. One sixth portion are committed against females who are either faithless in a culpable connexion or want to put an end to it, and another equal portion, to get rid of women who are in the way of the marriage of their former acquaintances. One seventeenth portion are committed without intending to do more than procure abortion. In marriage, the infidelity of the wife does not cause more than one twenty-third portion of the attempts against her life; in concubinage, infidelity of the female causes one-sixth of the cases that arise. The vengeance taken by the offended relations leads to half the attacks upon the seducers. About a thirty-third portion of the attacks on the lives of men take place in a house of ill-fame. Add to these consequences of personal profligacy, one fourteenth of the cases of incendiarism of which the motive is known, a great number of duels, of cases of insanity, particularly among the women who live by prostitution, all the cases of infanticide, and almost all the suicides of young women, and a true picture will be afforded of the evils arising from immorality of this kind. It is but too common in modern times to think lightly of irregular connexions between the sexes. The principles of duty have been weakened in this respect, and it is become of the first importance to bring to their support considerations of interest and utility, to prove that the consequences of such irregularities will be inevitably the same, whatever may be our opinions of their innocence or guilt. So true it is, that examined deeply, views of true utility and of moral duty will ever be found inseparable and identical."

M. Guerry's remarks upon the influence of different degrees of poverty are curious and cautious. In proportion to the numbers of the people, he says, crimes against property are commonly more frequent in populous towns than in the thinly inhabited districts. Hence it has become thought that a condensed state of the population tends to increase crime. The conclusion is too hasty. In the departments in which the great towns of Nantes, Bordeaux, Nimes, Toulouse, Montpelier, and Marseilles are situated, fewer crimes are committed against property than in the departments in which Troyes, Chalons, Arras, Evreaux, and Chartres, less populous towns, are situated. The error has arisen from effects being attributed to a condensed population which are attributable to some other concurrent, but not necessarily connected, circumstances. There is considerable difficulty in distinguishing from each other results which have had a simultaneous origin. *Wealth indicated by the amount of direct taxation* is more frequently than a condensed population coincident with an increased proportion of crimes against property. It would therefore seem to be indirectly the cause of these crimes. If the maximum of wealth occurs in those northern departments where the greatest number of crimes are committed against property, and the minimum in the central departments where they are fewest, and if also in the south the mean amount of wealth is almost on a level with that in the north, how does it happen on this principle of wealth being the indirect cause of crimes against property that the crimes in the south are not equally numerous with those in the north? It would not perhaps be very illogical to conclude that extreme poverty is *not* the chief cause of crimes, when the poorest departments are found to contain the fewest criminals against property. But while I do not absolutely reject this conclusion, further direct proofs are necessary to establish the point beyond all doubt. The poorest departments may not be those in which there are the greatest number of poor inhabitants, and certainly where there are the greatest private fortunes, there usually is at the same time a portion of the people in the deepest misery. It is a more difficult question than at first appears, what degree of influence wealth or poverty may exercise upon crime. In order to resolve it, the comparative numbers of the needy and of the beggars in each department must be ascertained much more correctly than has yet been effected. The results of inquiry are noted upon the maps which accompany the work, in reference to the distribution of *patents* over France, and it will be seen that wherever there are the most patents taken out, there the greatest number of crimes are committed against property, except in Corsica, and where the fewest patents are taken out, the fewest crimes are committed. There are but a few exceptions to this last remark, as in a part of Brittany, where with little means of employment, thieving is very common, and on the contrary, in Ardennes, in Meuse, in Côte-d'Or, with great activity of trade, there is little thieving. This apparent general relation of crimes against property to the greater or less degree of industry and trade in a country, requires further and more careful examination than it has yet received. It is not in France alone that it has been noticed. In various reports of the British House of Commons curious details may be found respecting it (*Report from the Select Committee on Criminal Commitments and Corrections*, July 1828, p. 5. *Ib.* on *Secondary Punishments*, 1831, p. 103, and *ib.* June 1832, p. 64). In Paris and the neighbourhood, and also in all the great commercial towns and sea-ports, a large proportion of the crimes against property are committed by people who make thieving a business. In all France there are more than thirty thousand people of this kind. Among them are many young persons who took their first lessons in the infamous trade in what are called Houses of Correction. The criminals who have undergone their sentences in the Bagnes rarely commit the more atrocious crimes after their release, as is commonly supposed. They know the law too well to risk capital conviction by being guilty of capital offences, but they become regular plunderers of property.

Enough has been given of the work of M. Guerry to prove that the contents are of substantial interest and importance. It may not be useless to add that without being expensive, it is from its size and plates entitled to rank among "show books," and on the whole eminently calculated to lie on the tables of members of parliament and others, who to the possession of competence unite a taste for legislative inquiries.

QUETELET ON THE LAWS OF THE SOCIAL SYSTEM

LITTELL 's LIVING AGE

VOL. 21, NO. 260 (MAY 12, 1849), PP. 241-244

Greater attention has, perhaps, been paid to social questions during the present year than at any recent period. Civil perturbations naturally produce, with other effects, a disposition to devise rules for their governance, or remedies against their recurrence. There will, of course, be great differences in the character of the remedial measures proposed; still, it is always best to look boldly at the evils with which humanity is afflicted, and in this regard honest endeavors to systematize social aberrations, to explain their laws, may find acceptance.

Among the writers who have occupied themselves with this subject, M. J. L. A. Quetelet of Brussels is already favorably known to many readers by his treatise on *Man*, and the development of his faculties, published about twelve years since. This was followed, in 1846, by *Letters on the Theory of Probabilities Applied to Moral and Political Science*; and now, as the compliment of these, we have the work titled *Du Systeme Social, et des Lois qui le Regissent* (Guillaumin et Co., Paris, 1848). In the *Letters*, &c., was originated the law of accidental causes, and this law is shown to be reducible to calculation in common with physical or mechanical laws. *Many social phenomena, including crime, which appear to be accidental and random in their nature utterly cease to be so when the observations of their occurrence are extended over a very large number of incidents*, and as Quetelet remarks, "the liberty of choice (free will), whose results are so capricious when individuals only are observed, leaves no sensible traces of its action when applied to multitudes." Hence the important law is deduced, "that social facts, influenced by liberty of choice, proceed with even more regularity and predictability than facts submitted simply to the action of physical causes." Although the tracing out involves certain difficulties, yet analogies are to be found between moral and mechanical laws; and on these various considerations it is urged by Quetelet that "henceforth the collection by the government of a broad range of moral statistics (including those relative to crime) ought to take its place among the sciences of observation." It will thus be seen that the aim of his most recent work on the laws of the social system is something beyond mere political economy; it is to develop the laws of equilibrium and movement, and especially the preservative principles existing between different parts of the social system.

The law of accidental causes is not one of mere hypothesis, it may be proved by physical facts; for instance, the height of the human frame. By aggregating the heights of the population of the country, a mean is obtained which gives the standard, and the departures or variations from this mean range symmetrically above and below it; "as if," observes M. Quetelet, "nature had a *type* proper to a country, and to the circumstances in which it is placed. Deviations from this type would be the product of causes purely accidental, which act either *plus* or *minus* with the same intensity." The groups on either side of the average are the more numerous the more they approach to or resemble the mean; and the more widely they deviate, so do they terminate in rarities, as giants and dwarfs. Every portion of the scale, however, has its value, and "there exists between them a mysterious tie, which so operates that each individual may be considered as the necessary part of the whole, which escapes us physically only to be seized by the eye of science."

The conclusions to be drawn from the statistical observation of this and other physical phenomena as well are intended to bear on the great moral view of the subject. M. Quetelet shows that many of the erroneous opinions to which writers on social questions have come, have originated in their regarding man in the individual rather than in the mass; that which defies calculation in the one is easily established in the other. Moral are distinguished from physical phenomena by the intervention of man's free choice, and the exercise of this prerogative is found rather to restrict than to disturb the limits of deviation. Marriage is adduced as affording the best example of the direct interference of free choice. Generally speaking, it is entered on with great circumspection. Yet, during the past twenty years, the number of marriages in Belgium, regard being had to the increase of population, has remained annually the same. Not only has the number proved constant in the towns and the country, but also as respects marriages between young men and young women, young men and widows, widowers and young women, and widowers and widows. The same fact holds, too, with regard to the ages at which marriage is contracted; and the great discrepancies sometimes observed in ill-assorted unions, are neither to be considered as fatalities nor mere effects of blind passion; like giants and dwarfs in respect of growth, they constitute the remotest deviations in the law of accidental causes. The same results also obtain in other human actions as well as that of marriage; there is a certainty of predictable regularity in crime, in suicides, in mutilations to avoid military service, in the sum annually staked on the gaming-tables of Paris, and even in the unsealed, undirected, and illegibly-addressed letters deposited yearly in the post-office.

"With such an assemblage of facts before us," asks Quetelet, "must man's free choice be denied? Truly I think not. I conceive only that the effect of this free choice is restrained within very narrow limits, and plays among social phenomena only the part of an *accidental* cause. It therefore ensues, that making abstraction of individuals, and considering circumstances only in a general manner, the effects of all accidental causes ought to neutralize and destroy themselves mutually, so as to leave predominant only the true causes of virtue or vice existing in society. The possibility of establishing moral statistics, and deducing instructive and useful consequences therefrom, depends entirely on this fundamental fact, that man's free choice disappears, and remains without sensible effect, when the observations are extended over a great number of individuals." In predicating, however, on the number of marriages to take place in any given year, it is important to distinguish between the *apparent* and *real tendency* to the conjugal state. These may exhibit great differences. "Thus one man may have all his life a real tendency for marriage, without ever marrying; while another, from fortuitous circumstances, may marry without experiencing any inclination for wedded life." It is possible to represent these tendencies by curved lines, which, for males, commencing at the age of 20, and ending at 80, shows the maximum to be between 35 and 40. For females, the curve terminates ten years earlier, and reaches its highest point in the years from 25 to 30. *The distinction between the apparent and real is essential*; for although we are able to establish a law for the mass, we can prove nothing beforehand of the individual.

The same real and apparent tendency or inclination exists also with regard to crime, and nearly all other moral actions; for it is clear that a person may have a great inclination for crime without once committing it; another may abhor crime, and yet become culpable. "It is thus possible," says M. Quetelet, "to state, from continued observations, the relative degrees of energy which lead men to execute certain facts. Thus, if I see a million men of 25 or 30 years of age produce twice as many murders as a million men of 40 to 45 years of age, I should be disposed to believe that the inclination to murder among the former has twice the energy of what prevails among the latter. It is important, therefore, to have a number of observations sufficient to eliminate the effects of all fortuitous causes from which differences may be established between the real and the apparent inclination to be determined. So long as the march of justice and that of the repression of crime remain the same, which can scarcely be possible, except in one and the same country, constant relations are established between these three facts:—First, crimes committed; second, crimes committed and denounced; and third; crimes committed, denounced, and brought before the tribunals." An investigation of criminal tables has shown "that the law of development of the tendency to crime is the same for France, Belgium, England, and the grand-duchy of Baden, the only countries whose observations are correctly known. The tendency to crime toward the adult age increases with considerable rapidity; it reaches a maximum, and decreases afterwards until the last limits of life. This law appears to be constant, and undergoes no modification but in the extent and period of the maximum. In France, for crimes in general, the maximum appears about the 24th year; in Belgium, it arrives two years later; in England and the grand-duchy of Baden, on the contrary, it is observed earlier. Considering the circumstances," continues M. Quetelet, "under this point of view, we shall better form an opinion of the high mission of the legislator, who holds to a certain extent the budget of crimes in his hands, and who can diminish or augment their numbers by enlightened, informed, and instructive understanding of the operation of the general moral laws of society, combined with more or less of prudence."

In addition to the foregoing, the law of accidental causes admits also of application to derangements of the mental faculties. "Moral maladies," says Quetelet, "are like physical maladies; some of them are contagious, some are epidemic, and others are hereditary. Vice is transmitted in certain families, as scrofula or phthisis. A great part of the crimes which afflict a country originate in certain families, who would require particular surveillance—isolation similar to that imposed on patients supposed to carry about them germs of pestilence.

Besides the points we have noticed, M. Quetelet's work contains many valuable inquiries and suggestions which may be recommended to those interested in the betterment of society through thoughtful legislation which has a basis in science. M. Quetelet's work must be taken as a valuable contribution to moral science, the cause of justice, law, and order. Whatever differences of opinion may be entertained, it is impossible not to be impressed by M. Quetelet's earnestness. Who will be the other Newton to come forward and fully expound for our enlightenment and understanding the natural laws governing this other celestial mechanism, the social system?

SUGGESTIONS FOR FURTHER READING AND INQUIRY:

THE FRENCH AND BELGIAN STATISTICAL SCHOOLS

"An Inquiry into the Statistics of Crime in England and Wales." Rawson W. Rawson. *Quarterly Journal of the Statistical Society of London*, vol. 2 (1839), pp. 316–344.
The first published research using official English statistics to ascertain whether crime in England obeys the same general laws of periodicity as suggested by the results of Guerry in France and Quetelet in Belgium. The author concludes from his statistical analyses that a universal law is at work that influences not only the periodic nature and frequency of criminal offenses, but that there do indeed in England exist differentials with respect to sex, age, and place (i.e., urban/rural patterns).

"Notice on Periodical Phenomena." Lambert Adolph Jacques Quetelet. *Quarterly Journal of the Statistical Society of London*, vol. 4 (1842), pp. 208–213.
A fine overview of the Belgian statistician's researches and interpretation of the data.

"Criminal Statistics Remarkably Even Where Accurately Kept." *Frank Leslie's Popular Monthly*, vol. 15 (1883), pp. 382–384.
The criminal statistical differentials with regards to age, sex, season, and place (i.e., urban versus rural) are remarkably consistent across a thirty-year period.

HUMAN AGGREGATION, URBAN DECAY, AND MORAL DEGRADATION

(THE RISE OF THE CRIMINAL, VICIOUS, OR DANGEROUS CLASS)

ON CRIME AND DENSITY OF POPULATION

BY

JELINGER SYMONS

TRANSACTIONS OF THE NATIONAL ASSOCIATION FOR THE PROMOTION OF SOCIAL SCIENCE

(1857), PP. 265-270

I have striven to make this a paper of facts, which, together with the conclusions from them, I have also endeavoured to condense within the narrowest limits, aware how often time is wasted in journals by pleonastic statements and diffuse reasoning. The importance of the subject I have chosen must not, however, be judged by the brevity of its treatment. It is rather in inverse proportion to it. It aims at exhibiting the chief proximate cause of the greater criminality of one district over another. This disparity is immense. Taking into account *all* crimes and offences, whether committed for trial or disposed of by summary conviction, it ranges from 1 in 98 of the population in Middlesex to 1 in 1849 in Merionethshire.

I quote from Mr. Redgrave's accurate and admirable table of relative criminality, in page 18 of his last *Return of Judicial and Criminal Proceedings*, published by the Home Office, and from which I have collected all the criminal statistics in this paper.

It is a common belief that crime is the concomitant of gross ignorance. It is not so. The relative proportion of those who possess different degrees of instruction among persons committed for offences have stood nearly thus for twenty years:

Degree of instruction	per cent
Totally uninstructed	33.1
Who can read or write imperfectly	53.8
Idem, well	05.4
Superior instruction	00.3
Unascertained	07.4

Even at Liverpool, where the Irish swarm, the proportion per cent of all offenders in 1855 who could neither read nor write was only 44 per cent.

Those who have received a smattering and superficial instruction therefore furnish the bulk of criminals. They who have most thoroughly investigated and probed the education given during the last dozen years in our common schools, will scarcely question the fact that such is the general character of the instruction given to the great bulk of the scholars who have passed through them. I may almost say in *all* of them, except that mere fraction of their number who are in the first two classes of the really well-taught schools. And if we were to test the subject-matter of the knowledge imparted even to these favoured classes, I fear we should have a good deal of chaff to winnow before we came to grain fruitful of good living and useful labour.

The Census of Education of 1851, compared with the criminality of each corresponding county as scheduled by Mr. Redgrave, enables me to put this to a statistical test. I have arranged all the English counties, together with Galmorganshire and the rest of South Wales and North Wales, separately – first, in order of their *ignorance or dearth of schooling*; secondly, in the order of their *criminality*; and thirdly, in the order of their *density of population*. The kind reader will find the arrangement of these data in the Table I have appended to this article following my concluding remarks.

And now, as to the results. I find little correspondence between the ignorant and criminal counties. As you may readily discern for yourself, those which stand at the top of one column are sometimes near the foot of the other. On the other hand, when I compare counties as regards crime and density of population, I find the correspondence most striking indeed. Of the six most criminal counties – *viz.*, Middlesex, Lancaster, Surrey, Warwick,

Northumberland, and Stafford – none are among the six most ignorant, but every one (except Northumberland) are among the six most densely peopled; and the four first, comprising a population of five millions, stand in the same order, whilst there are no less than twenty-four counties, including nearly all the large ones, which almost exactly correspond in density and crime. Of the whole category, however, North and South Wales (without Glamorganshire, which has peculiar industrial and moral features) stand foremost for ignorance, innocence, and sparsity of population.

The criminality of counties seems also to be greatly determined by the *rapidity* of the growth of their populations. Of the twelve most criminal counties—viz., those above named, together with Glamorgan, Durham, Kent, Chester, Hants, and Monmouth – the increase in population averaged no less than 19 per cent between 1841 and 1851, whilst that of England and Wales was only 13 per cent. The converse holds good equally. The twelve least criminal counties are South Wales, Cornwall, North Wales, Cumberland, Rutland, Norfolk, Lincoln, Derby, Suffolk, Cambridge, Dorset, and Wilts. Of these the population has increased only by 7 per cent instead of 19 in the same period.

Again, Durham, Northumberland, Monmouthshire, and Glamorganshire have increased their population by 23.2 per cent, and their crimes by 53.2 in the same period, although those of England and Wales had barely increased at all, or only by 0.72 per cent.

I have selected these four counties as presenting the greatest rapidity of increase. It is a noteworthy fact that the chief industry in each is mineral. This is a useful index to another, and one of the most fruitful causes of low moral condition—I mean disregard of the physical agencies of civilization. In few places of labour are they so recklessly neglected as in the mineral districts. The intermixture of the sexes at work—the total absence of the means of decency, and of that vital necessity, public baths—the prevalence of dirt, and slovenly squalid habits, are painfully manifest in most of those districts, even to the casual observer. Such habits, together with the crowded dwellings and sleeping-rooms without separation of sexes or families, notoriously prevail more or less in all densely-peopled localities.

In order to test these conclusions I have, since writing the foregoing remarks, applied to the Town Clerks of the most crowded provincial towns, who have favoured me with the committals for trial and summary convictions *last year* within their respective boroughs, and comparing these urban offences (in relation to population in 1851) with the aggregate returns given by the Home Office for the *counties* in which those towns are situated, we have the following striking results:

In Manchester there were 4,134 offences (of which 826 were committals for trial and 3,308 summary convictions), giving an aggregate of 1 offender to every 73 of the population, whilst in the county of Lancaster there was 1 only in 118.

In Birmingham, 511 committals and 1,347 convictions, being 1 in every 125 of the population, whereas in the county of Warwick there was 1 in every 167.

In Leeds, 300 committals and 1,157 convictions, being 1 in 117, while in the county of York there were 1 in 257.

In Bristol, 217 committals and 1,318 convictions, being 1 in 89, while in the county of Gloucester there were 1 in 216.

In Sheffield, 162 committals and 2,150 convictions (including persons "held to bail," thus the number is somewhat unduly swollen), being 1 in 58, while in the county of York there were 1 in 257.

In Portsmouth, 100 committals and 517 convictions, being 1 in 117, whilst in the county of Southampton they were 1 in 186.

In Plymouth, 64 committals and 925 convictions, being 1 in 53, while in Devonshire there were 1 in 225.

In Norwich, 104 committals and 208 convictions, being 1 in 218 of the population, while there were in the county of Norfolk 1 in 380.

In Liverpool the returns of last year are only made up for nine months, and those which are perfect for 1855 exhibit such an appalling state of vice and crime that they require special mention, particularly as the number summarily convicted is not given separately, but is merged in the larger number of those returned as "summarily punished," and which exceeds those sent to gaol. The committals for trial were 448 in 1855, and the summarily punished 15,053, being together no less than 1 offender in every 24 inhabitants; though the number slightly decreased last year among children, owing, it appears, chiefly to the beneficial effect of the Reformatories, and the fear of the parents lest they should become chargeable for their children if convicted, who now try to prevent offences they previously encouraged. The following abstract from the head constable's able report for 1855 exhibits a state of vice and crime in Liverpool scarcely equaled, I believe, in this or any other country: Twelve persons were committed for murder by verdicts of the coroner's juries, though on trial found guilty only of manslaughter. It is rare that coroner's juries find a verdict of willful murder without due cause and sufficient evidence. It is rare that assize juries find the same verdicts on the same evidence! For cutting and maiming there were 45 apprehensions. Common assaults, 1,131: on police officers, 873. Robberies from the person, 860. Of drunkenness the head constable says, "The degrading vice of intemperance is unhappily not confined to men, there being 3,617 drunk and disorderly females, and 1,203 drunk and incapable, making a total of 4,820 taken into custody during the year. But it is right to add that the number of apprehensions for the various offences does not represent so many persons, in many cases the same individual having been taken into custody again and again. During the year, 103 boys and girls _under ten years of age_ were taken into custody by the police, two of whom destroyed their companion, and afterwards threw his body into the canal; whilst a very large majority of the rest were charged with serious offences—felonies, for example. There were 251 boys and girls between ten and twelve years charged with stealing, &c.; 756 boys under eighteen years of age were charged with being drunk and disorderly, and 12 girls under fifteen years of age were charged with the same offence; whilst from above fifteen years, and not completing eighteen, there were 642 females taken into custody for being drunk and disorderly. "This," says the report, "will go far to show that females are led into habits of intemperance at an earlier age than males, as it will be seen that of the entire number of females charged with drunkenness, nearly one-half are under twenty one years of age.

Now for the proof that these towns are densely crowded: An average town of 12,935 inhabitants in Great Britain stands on an area of 3.88 square miles, and there are 3,337 persons to a square mile of an average town. (As an aside, it might interest the reader to know that in Great Britain there are on average 1.1 families to a house; 5.7 persons to a house; and 4.8 persons to a family).

From a table in the _Census Returns_ (volume 1, page 111) reproduced below, of the persons to a square mile, there are:

TOWN	PERSONS
Liverpool	74,446
Birmingham	41,853
Leeds	30,886
Bristol	22,858
Plymouth	20,441
Manchester	11,557
Norwich	10,091
Sheffield	6,263

The London Eastern District would give similar results both as to crime and density. Thus, after carefully analysing a mass of statistics, and testing all the generally alleged sources of crime, I arrive at these conclusions:

First, that in whatever degree other causes operate, densely-packed communities invariably generated crime in nearly like proportion; second, that this proportion is increased in large seaports frequented by foreign sailors, such as Liverpool, Bristol, Cardiff, &c.; and third, that all such places should be plied *first* with the preventives of crime.

These conclusions lead me to suggest, but with great deference to better judgments, these chief remedies:

First, the immediate repeal of the vile Act for multiplying beer-shops without the restriction of magistrates' licenses, the rigorous suppression of all ill-conducted public-houses, and the increase of a more efficient, better paid, and trusty police; second, an Act rendering it penal, by summary conviction, for any publican to have an intoxicated person on his premises. It is better to fine sober people who profit by making men drunk than to fine the drunkards; third, the compulsory erection by local rates, in all towns where the population exceeds 10,000 to the square mile, of sufficient and well-organized lodging-houses, public baths, and washhouses, all under strict sanitary regulations and municipal inspection; and fourth, an Act rendering it penal in any person to let lodgings by the day or week, where adults of different sexes, not being members of the same family, sleep in the same room.

TABLE
Counties in order of

IGNORANCE IN 1851	CRIME IN 1856	DENSITY OF POPU- LATION
1. South Wales	Middlesex	Middlesex
2. Glamorgan	Lancaster	Lancaster
3. North Wales	Surrey	Surrey
4. Monmouth	Warwick	Warwick
5. Hereford	Northumberland	Stafford
6. Bedford	Stafford	Chester
7. Middlesex	Glamorgan	Durham
8. Lancashire	Durham	Kent
9. Warwick	Kent	Worcester
10. Stafford	Chester	Gloucester
11. Cornwall	Southampton	Notts
12. Worcester	Monmouth	York
13. Salop	Herts	Derby
14. Devon	Worcester	Leicester
15. Notts	Gloucester	Herts
16. Bucks	Berks	Monmouth
17. Somerset	Oxon	Somerset
18. Norfolk	Essex	Beds
19. Chester	Hunts	Glamorgan
20. Gloucester	Beds	Cornwall
21. Suffolk	Somerset	Berks
22. Northumberland	Northampton	Southampton
23. Leicester	Devon	Oxon
24. York	Notts	Sussex
25. Surrey	Hereford	Suffolk
26. Northampton	Salop	Cambridge
27. Durham	York	Bucks
28. Derby	Bucks	Essex
29. Essex	Sussex	Devon
30. Lincoln	Leicester	Northampton
31. Cumberland	Westmoreland	Norfolk
32. Cambridge	Wilts	Wilts
33. Berks	Dorset	Dorset
34. Dorset	Cambridge	Hunts
35. Wilts	Suffolk	Salop
36. Sussex	Derby	Rutland
37. Oxon	Lincoln	Northumberland
38. Kent	Norfolk	Lincoln
39. Huntingdon	Rutland	Hereford
40. Hertford	Cumberland	North Wales
41. Southampton	North Wales	South Wales
42. Rutland	Cornwall	Cumberland
43. Westmoreland	South Wales	Westmoreland

ISHMAELITES OF CIVILIZATION: OR, THE DEMOCRACY OF DARKNESS

BY

BENJAMIN ORANGE FLOWER

ARENA

VOL. 6, NO. 31 (JUNE 8, 1892), PP. 17-39

I.

There is to-day in all populous centres of civilization a world of misery, where uninvited poverty abounds; a commonwealth of victims whose wretchedness fills the heart with mingled sorrow and indignation. No more pathetic scene can be imagined than the daily battle waged by this battalion in retreat, who yet struggles for a foothold on the granite of honesty and virtue. There is, however, another spectacle still more soul-sickening, because of its added blackness. Below the social cellar, however, where uninvited poverty holds sway, is yet a darker zone: a subterranean, rayless vault – the commonwealth of the double night. In the upper stratum we find gloom, here perpetual darkness. Above, the closing door of opportunity to live, the frightful pangs of hunger, and the ever-present dread of sickness shut out the sunshine of external enjoyments; still, so long as virtue and integrity remain, the inner temple is illuminated. In the sub-cellar, however, even the soul's torch goes out; hence there is twofold darkness. So long as the fires burn on the altar of morality, the soul knows an exalted pleasure, even in the bitterest want; for the mystic power of the Divine impearled in every mind holds supremacy, and the spirit stands erect. When, however, this light disappears, the soul grovels in the mire, and the incentive to walk is less strong than that to crawl and wallow in animality. In this under-world vicious crime and degenerate vices mingle with poverty; bestial passion is the goddess of its denizens; here the acme of pleasure is reached in sensual gratification; here men do not look you in the eye; the glance, even among one another, is furtive when not defiant. *This is the real inferno*. No need to wander into other worlds to experience hells of God's creation.

Man has made an under-world, before which the most daring imagination of poet or seer staggers. Over its portals might well be blazoned Dante's soul-freezing legend: "All ye who enter here give up hope."

If its inhabitants came hither voluntarily, their conditions might merit less concern, even though they would in no less degree be a menace to society. But the truth is, the vast majority are driven hither by relentless influences over which they have no control; such, for example, as the cupidity and avarice of powerful individuals, the selfishness of a short-sighted and indifferent civilization, reinforced by the intangible but potent influence of heredity, on the one hand, and the still more irresistible power of the social environment on the other.

And in this subterranean world, as in the world of hope, we find men, women, and children plying their trades and eking out an existence as fate or inclination dictates. Here, however, schools, universities, and libraries contribute little to the satisfaction of man's appetites and aspirations; but in their stead we find the omnipresent saloon with its ancillary contingent of prostitutes, catering to all that is worst in frail humanity.

Yet it must not be understood that all pleasure is exiled; a certain kind of enjoyment remains; it is a counterfeit coin, which, however, in the absence of that which is real, passes current. It possesses none of the pure essence which endures and is refining and elevating. Moreover, the pleasures known here consume the life of their votaries, and are mingled with bitterness, which increases with each hour of indulgence. They end also in death, prefaced by an existence loathsome to even the depraved souls who reap their certain fruitage.

II.

Would you glance at the pseudo-pleasures current in this lower zone of life? Come with us as we skirt this realm, and see what it has to offer those who have recently crossed its threshold. We are in Boston, within rifle-shot of the gilded dome of the State House and the palaces of Beacon Hill, and yet we are entering this under-world. It is Monday night. At the station-house we are politely received by the police officer in charge, who observes that we have chosen the worst night of the week. Saturday and Sunday, he explains, are always a kind of Saturnalia for great numbers of people in this part of the city; but on Monday night there is little to be seen because these people are "resting" or "broke." While he is speaking, a drunken man is brought in—a searcher for pleasure and gratification—who, losing reason, has been overtaken by the law. "Do you make many arrests daily?" we asked. "Oh, yes, here is the record. For Saturday, fifty-six cases; yesterday, thirty-five, mostly drunkenness. Ah, here is the officer who will go with you." We set off, threading our way through the commonwealth of poverty, crime, and vice. Here are thousands of people, Ishmaelites of civilization, herding in crowded quarters where dwelt, only a few decades ago, the very elite of the "Boston Hub."

We have now reached a nest of old buildings with an unsavory record, a veritable nursery of crime and vice such as is found nowhere else but in your most populous cities. Here we find the poorest and most degraded of the whites mingling together in the most shameless promiscuity with negroes. The creaking stairways are worn and carpeted with filth. The walls and ceiling are blistered with the foul accretions of months and perhaps years. It is a noisy spot; snatches of low songs, obscene oaths, coarse jests, and the savage voices of poor wretches whose brains are inflamed and tongues made thick with rum, meet our ears on every side. The air is heavy with odors of spoiled fish, decayed vegetables, urine and feces, smoke from old pipes, and stale beer.

From one room loud and angry voices proceed, a note of fear mingled with a threatening tone; the room seems perfectly dark. With a quick movement the police officer lifts the smoking lamp from a stool in the hall, and opens the door. The scene is sickening in the extreme, one of the most disgusting spectacles in the underworld, none the less terrible because it is so common. A filthy den of prostitution, occupied by a young girl whose career has not yet brought upon her unmistakable signs of debauchery, save in a certain expression of the eyes and a brazen smile, which speak volumes against the liability of restoration. A wealth of black hair falls in great waves over her head; she has a deep olive complexion; a large head, arching brow, and eyes which once must have been extremely beautiful, for even yet, though slightly dimmed by dissipation, they are yet very expressive. On her countenance one detects something inexpressibly sad: the sunshine of girlishness blending with the shadow of vice. A few years before she must have been a remarkably beautiful child, richly endowed by nature with those physical charms so dear to womanhood, and which to-day are a fortune to a maiden in easy circumstances. This girl, surrounded in early life by healthy influences, schooled in virtue, and given a fair chance, would probably have graced society and added to the dignity of American womanhood. But the accident of an unkind fate willed otherwise, and now we find her in a filthy den of inequity, the air of which is heavy with fumes of liquor and other nauseous odors, and her male companion, whose loud and angry voice originally attracted our attention, we find to be none other than a low-browed, thick-necked, and thoroughly brutish and ignorant looking fellow.

Heart-sick, we turn from this spectacle, too common to the police officer to even call to his face a momentary shadow of disgust. In this child of a dark fate we see a type of thousands of poor girls who seem doomed to wed despair. They may have entered life in the social cellar, where they have never seen, with anything like clear-cut vision, the line of demarcation between right and wrong. They may have drifted to the city for the purpose of making an honest living, but have been driven into vice and crime, in order that soulless greed might flourish and they still live. Or they may belong to the commonwealth of betrayed maiden-hood, who, being betrayed, have found all society's doors barred against them, lest, perchance, they contaminate innocence, brush too closely against undiscovered sin, or annoy the lepers who have accomplished their ruin, and who still move unabashed in the upper world. In any case, to them the circumstances into which they were born were a calamity, life a bitter cure, death their sweetest heritage.

We leave this rookery of vice and crime, having caught a glimpse of life's sad quest for pleasure in the modern metropolitan inferno, and traverse a street filled with brilliantly lighted saloons. The counters are thronged with scores of men seeking pleasure in guzzling beer. At the corner of the street a striking picture is presented. In the front window of a large saloon sit a company of young men and girls, laughing hilariously over their liquor. The men are boyish in appearance. One of the three women present is not a novice. Her face is typical, and carries a significant history: brazen eyes, steeled and slightly dimmed; countenance stamped with the unmistakable history of reckless indulgence, doomed to grow more terrible as she is pushed, with ever accelerating speed, toward her frightful end, a premature death brought on by the physical and mental dissipations which are the end-products of a morally bankrupt life and the diseases of sexual promiscuity. They are well dressed; a rosy flush suffuses their brows, born of excitement rather than rouge; their eyes, not yet dimmed by debauchery, sparkle brilliantly; their voices also posses a silvery ring. They seem happy, as, with rapid words, jests pass from lip to lip over the clinking glasses.

Behind this partitioned compartment, the bar, thronged with men, is the scene of that coarse merriment which is ever found in saloons in low parts of great cities. We turn the corner, and, passing the rear of the same establishment, catch another kaleidoscopic view of the pleasures of this dismal life. Here, in a rudely partitioned box, which partially shuts it from the bar, but which opens on the street, are a half-dozen withered women, some aged before their time; others, though still young, appear haggard and corpse-like; their faces, like their ragged gowns, are faded, their voices harsh and rasping, their laugh barren of all merriment and carrying notes of defiance and despair. In the front of this saloon is laughing and careless girlhood; in the rear besotted and fallen womanhood. The difference is that these poor creatures have pursued the *ignis fatuus* a little longer than their younger neighbors —they are several rungs lower on the ladder —that is all. As we momentarily pause before this pathetic picture, one poor woman whose dull eyes are sunken far into their sockets, and whose face is of an ashy hue, rises, and, extending her long, bony finger, beckons to our company. The grin on her toothless face, which in childhood was doubtless a smile, is so ghastly that we are thrilled with horror. Ah! Poor Ishmaelites of our nineteenth-century civilization, terrible is your fate.

Of another pastime we catch a glimpse in passing a basement poolroom. Here is a certain fascinating excitement which games of chance ever possess for the human mind, but here also we find the atmosphere which seems everywhere present in this subterranean world; fumes of liquor and tobacco are as omnipresent as coarse profanity, and still more repulsive jests and gestures.

This scene suggests another I witnessed some time ago in going through a wretched rookery in the north end of Boston. We were in search of a poor sick woman, said to be in a starving condition. Passing one room and hearing loud voices, my friend, who spends his life in relieving the suffering of the poor, quickly opened the door. Around a rude table were seated four men playing cards; the revolver by one and the omnipresent whiskey flask by another were as symbolic of the lives of these young men as their hardened, depraved countenances and red eyes. There was a certain animal ferocity in the expression of their faces. In one corner of the room I noticed a man hastily throwing some things he had been handling into an old box. The moment the door opened, all the gamblers sprung to their feet, defiant and yet uneasy. Their furtive glances wandered from us to the box. My impression was that they were whiling away the day gaming for the booty or spoils acquired during a robbery or burglary the previous night. "Does Mrs. so-and-so live in this building?" inquired my friend. "We don't know," grumbled two or three voices sneering at us as we quickly closed the door and made a hasty departure.

Such are the pleasures of this under-world—as false as they are short-lived; utterly spurious; a counterfeit coin; bearing small if any resemblance to true enjoyment, whose influence is ever refining and uplifting. Pure pleasure is a sun which warms into life all that is noblest in nature, calling out that which is sweetest and richest, developing the flower and fruitage of a noble character; while the pleasures of which our nineteenth century inferno boasts, bears precisely the relation to its victim which the candle does to the moth: it dazzles with its light, it warms with its heat, it fascinates with its radiance, but it destroys!

III.

Let us now examine some facts relating to this commonwealth of darkness, where crime and vice mingle with misery and want. It is with the great cities that we are chiefly concerned in the present discussion, although its baleful influence has, sadly to say, already extended to some of the smaller cities and towns situated on the outskirts of our large metropolitan areas; for a nation takes the tone of life largely from her metropolitan centres. Dr. Lyman Abbott has well observed that "The whole country is affected, if indeed its character and history are not determined, by the condition of its great cities."

In the outcropping of the lower world in our courts, we catch a glimpse of one aspect of this problem, although it must not be forgotten that the records of our criminal courts represent only a small proportion of the crime committed. Thus, for example: The prison returns for Great Britain for 1889 showed that there were fourteen thousand seven hundred and forty-seven known thieves at large, to say nothing of seventeen thousand and forty-two suspected persons. With this thought in mind, let us take up the records of New York City. In 1889, we find there were eighty-two thousand two hundred arrests; in 1890, eighty-four thousand five hundred and fifty-six arrests. Of the number of persons apprehended in 1889, over five thousand were taken on the charge of theft or robbery, and more than five thousand for assault and battery. Another fact in this connection worthy of thought is the enormous expense required to keep in partial check the dangerous classes in this commonwealth of darkness. The police department of New York City costs yearly four million eight hundred thousand dollars (_Darkness and Daylight in New York_, p. 499).

And what is true of the criminal records of New York City is, to a certain extent, also true of some of our smaller but rapidly growing cities. Take, for example, Detroit, Michigan. In 1890 we find there were eight thousand six hundred and ninety-three persons arrested, of which over nine hundred cases were for murder, rape, assault and battery, burglary larceny, or robbery. In speaking of these returns, Commissioner Robinson observes: "The whole number of arrests for the six years 1885 to 1890 was fifty-one thousand eight hundred and seventy-six, a yearly average of eight thousand six hundred and forty-six. According to population, there was one arrest for every twenty-three persons; but as four hundred and seventy-three persons were recidivists and figure in two thousand three hundred and sixty-three arrests, it appears that one person in every thirty-one was a prisoner for some cause or another in 1890. The citizens of this once quiet town have now become numb to the frequent occurrence of crimes of the most frightful nature perpetrated by a class of vicious men, women, and children whom the community would not have tolerated in years past." If we take the somewhat smaller but rapidly expanding town of Saginaw, Michigan, we find in 1891 there were two thousand six hundred and twenty-four arrests, in writing of which Commissioner Robinson observes: "The number of arrests in the city of Saginaw for 1891 was two thousand six hundred and twenty-four, a great increase over former years when crime was the rare exception rather than the daily rule. No allowance being made for reconvictions, one person in every 17.6 of the population was a prisoner in the year ending March 22, 1891. Clearly, I am convinced that as our smaller burgs increase in population and begin to take on more and more the character of metropolitan areas, the amount of crime and vice which one may reasonably expect to see in these once peaceful and serene hamlets is not at all a pleasant picture of what the future holds in store (*Ninth Annual Report of the Bureau of Labor Statistics of Michigan,*"p. 401)."

These facts merely hint at the nature and extent of the waste of wealth in our cities, caused chiefly by the subterranean vaults of social life. The financial aspect, however, is unimportant in comparison with the ethical significance. Whatever adds to the sum of human misery, increases the volume of crime, lowers the standards of morality, entails physical weakness, mental imbecility, or moral degradation, rises above all financial considerations, and is of supreme importance.

In descending into the under-world of our metropolitan centres, we find no monotony or sameness in life. The filthy and overcrowded rookeries are infested with many gradations of crime and vice. Here we find in great numbers the murderer, the thief, and the burglar; the gambler, the courtesan, and the confidence man; the bully, the sneak thief, and the common drunkard, who, like a maniac, is always a possible murderer. Here also we find pedagogues in crime, as well as, what is still more soul-sickening, traffickers in vice. Some striking illustrations of these phases of life which are a distinguishing characteristic of certain districts in metropolitan centres are necessary, in order to impress terrible facts vaguely believed but not realized by the great majority of our thoughtful people; for a typical case pictures in miniature a particular class or condition more impressively than any amount of generalizing. Doubtless few people realize that there are Fagans in real life to-day no less terrible than Dickens graphically pictures in his fiction; and we need not go to London or Paris to find them; they are flourishing at our own door.

A most striking illustration of this character was given to the public in the well-known case of David Smith, which was widely discussed at the time of his apprehension and conviction, a little over two years since. The story, briefly stated is as follows: Edward Mulhearn, a youth of fourteen years, who lived in a neighboring, yet still rural, town and was rather wild, ran away from home to seek his fortune in New York City. After he had exhausted his resources, and while debating in his mind the advisability of returning home and his probable reception from a somewhat stern father, he was accosted by David Smith, who cordially invited him to his miserable lodging-house in one of the foulest districts of the city. Delighted at the prospect of supper and bed, the boy accepted the invitation, was taken into one of the worst lodging-houses in the city, introduced to Smith's friends, and by his newly found protector flattered and cajoled. "I will make a man of you in less than a week," exclaimed Smith. The next week was one of license; the modern Fagan determined to "show his little country friend the city," with all the terrible significance of that expression when uttered by one hardened by years of crime and vice, and who is determined to thoroughly compromise his victim, while firing all that is worst in his nature. Next, Edward was shown how carelessly the women carried their purses; how often they were merely slipped into the outside pocket of their wrap. Edward was assured that it was an easy thing to take them. He was induced to make the attempt. He succeeded, and was a few dollars richer. The boy was complimented by Smith and lionized in the den, where the easily acquired wealth was squandered. His self-appointed guardian soon psychologized the youth. The friend and protector now became the iron-hearted master, and the boy a servile slave. He was next taken or sent on several thieving raids. When, however, Smith was not present to direct him, he rarely returned with any booty. This was naturally very unsatisfactory to his master, who saw little revenue to be gained from a poor thief. His fertile brain, however, soon hit upon another expedient. One morning when Edward returned penniless, our modern Fagan deliberately locked the door; the boy was then securely bound, after which his arms were horribly burned with heated irons pressed deeply into the flesh. The frantic shrieks and pitiful entreaties of the poor lad produced no effect upon his callous and vicious master, who into the wound then poured acid which greatly inflamed them. He was now ready for Smith's purpose, and, after being assured that he must beg money and beg _effectively_, if he did not wish his arms _burned off_, he was sent into the street. Smith, however, did not allow him to get beyond his sight. He was compelled to tell all who were willing to listen a most pitiful story of how, while hard at work in a factory, he was crippled by having some poisonous acid fall on his arms. Edward begged faithfully each day under the close surveillance of his master, and at night turned over a goodly sum, in return for which he received scanty food and a filthy bed. Smith, meantime, was spending his nights in the reckless abandon characteristic of an old debauche who has sounded the lowest depths of vice. One day, however, Edward's father, who was searching New York City street by street, discovered his boy. Smith was arrested and sent to the penitentiary.

This is doubtless an extreme case, and yet events are constantly coming to the surface which show how prevalent is this pedagogy in crime. Inspector Thomas Byrnes some time ago observed that during the last two or three years, at least four hundred boys and young men had been arrested for crimes originating in low lodging-houses, which are the headquarters for our modern Fagans.

There is another pursuit distinct to this under-world even more terrible than this systematic schooling of the young in theft, —a crime so revolting that it is seldom mentioned, especially in polite society, and for this reason is gradually growing to enormous proportions in our large cities. I refer to the traffic in girls. The terrible revelations of the *Pall Mall Gazette*, a few years since, sent a shudder through all civilized lands, because, in addition to the horrors of the crimes depicted, they revealed two startling facts: the prevalence of this polluting white-child slavery, and secondly, that at the head of fashionable society stood the battalions of social lepers, for whom these wretches plied their infamous trade. The author of a recent work titled *Chicago's Darkest Places*, which examines the dark side of Chicago life, commissioned a number of earnest, high-minded persons to investigate this phase of evil in his city. The results were appalling. These commissioners found that many women were engaged in this loathsome traffic. Incoming trains are frequently boarded. The young, naive, and unsophisticated country girl was readily recognized; her acquaintance easily made, after which friendly conversations elicited all the procuress desired. If the girl proved to be travelling alone and had no one to meet her, she usually fell an easy victim. This, however, was only one of many methods employed to decoy and ruin the innocent. It has, until recently, been the custom of some of these procuresses to obtain visitors' tickets, by which they were enabled to enter the wards of the County Hospital at Chicago at all times. Here they watched for attractive girls who were convalescent. The fact that they were in the County Hospital proved that they were without resources; and with false promises of lucrative pay for easy and honorable employment, they led them to a fate more terrible than death. The author of the work referred to above states that he has been authoritatively informed that the warden of the County Hospital had recently called in several visitors' tickets, and now demands a more thorough examination into the standing of those who apply for tickets, because of having discovered the terrible work going on.

I have only room for one case cited; but it will illustrate the horrors of this traffic in human virtue, and should prove a warning to parents. The noblest and purest girls of to-day may be ruined, in spite of themselves, in our great cities, and owing to that false sentiment which would conceal from the onward-moving victims the pitfalls which lead to death, armies of pure and noble girls year by year fall into snares hidden from view until too late. Here is the story to which I have referred:

A girl, not yet fifteen years of age, came up from a small town in a neighboring state. She had been a clerk in a grocery store in her native town, and things not being so comfortable at home as she desired, the thought that in Chicago work could be found and an independent living made, urged the child to leave home and come here. After she had been here a few days, the weather being cold and frosty, she slipped on the curbstone and broke her ankle. Helpless and alone, without home and money, there was but one place for her to go, the County Hospital, and thither she was sent. Just as she was about to be discharged, a woman came, and, passing through the ward, spoke to her, and asked if she wished a good position as a nurse-girl. A glowing account was given to her of the sweet and beautiful children and their elegant home, surrounded by all refinements; and the poor child, her imagination thus worked upon her, asked the doctor if she might be discharged. The physician gave her the permit to leave; a hack met them at the hospital door, and she was then brought by the woman into the darker quarter of the metropolis, to a house of shame, where she was kept under lock and key for a lengthened period. A lady commissioner, visiting the house, was heard by the imprisoned child pleading with another of the girls to leave her life of sin; and the final plea struck the attentive ear of the commissioner: "If you do get tired of this place, come to us and we will care for you!" The young prisoner determined, if possible, to escape, and a few days later, her door being accidently left unlocked, she ran out, and, escaping detection, found her way to the house of refuge run by the lady commissioner, where loving hearts were ready to welcome and help her.

Thus far we have caught a few glimpses of the horrors of the metropolitan abyss, have heard some distant plaints from the inferno of our civilization, some notes from the symphony of despair; only enough, however, to hint at the measureless misery of this world of crime, vice, and gloom, where bloom no fragrant flowers, and from whence hope and joy, inseparable companions of the uncrushed soul, have forever departed, the democracy of the damned, typified by the bat, the lizard, the jackal, the wolf, and the dull-eyed serpent. Ah! poor Ishmaelites, your sins are many; but you also have suffered from the weight of the world's selfishness, and you have been denied justice and education, which are the handmaids of progress. Can you, dear reader, for but one single instant, imagine the presence in any of our small, quiet, and peaceful towns of a dark quarter inhabited almost exclusively by the vicious, wanton, and depraved, where the pestiferous lodging-house is home to hoards of criminals, where dark and sinister saloons attract the lowest grade of customer, and where prostitution flourishes? Or could you imagine the fair people of such a small town tolerating for one day such goings-on? I think not, because these states of affairs are exclusively the domain of populous centres of civilization.

IV.

I now come to notice a few basic causes of the appalling frequency and nature of crime and vice at the social nadir. Now, it must be evident to even the most casual observer, that there are certain potent causes operating in such a manner as to increase the borders of this commonwealth of social night. Space prevents my touching upon more than three or four which seem to me to be most immediate in their baleful effects on our metropolitan centres.

First, *unjust social conditions, especially as they relate to taxation.* What is true of the evil suffered in the social cellar is almost equally applicable to the sub-cellar; for the crowding of people in squalid dens brutalizes and criminalizes, and so long as landlords have comparatively low rents to pay for old, rickety, disease-laden, and vermin-infested rookeries, they will not replace them with clean, healthful, or more commodious buildings; and while vacant lots adjacent to a city are lightly taxed, land speculators will hold them out of the reach of the poor. Thus, our present system of taxation acts as a two-edged sword: it encourages the landlord to preserve as long as possible the most wretched old buildings, and it practically bars the poor from securing homes near the outskirts of the city. A recent writer on social problems has pointed out the important fact that frequently wealthy people buy tracts of land on which live poor tenants, tear down the buildings, displacing the lodgers, and leave the land vacant, because they do not want the poor near them. Thus the gulf is even in environment, widening day-by-day between the rich and the poor, and as one author suggests, Fifth Avenue loathes the slums, and the slums hate Fifth Avenue. The present system of taxation is essentially unjust: it places a fine on industry; it favors the avarice of landlords; it adds to the misery of the slums, and increases our criminal population.

A second and equally fruitful source of crime in our large cities is *unrestricted immigration*. Says Inspector Thomas Byrnes: "It has frequently been stated to me by thieves that a large number of foreign criminals have their passage paid to this country by the authorities in their native lands or by somebody else. When they land here they have no money, or very little, and they immediately seek a cheap lodging-house, where they can live for almost nothing, meet people congenial to them, and be put in the way of again engaging in criminal pursuits. Once so esconced, they seldom if ever leave the district, and hence, they swell the ever increasing ranks of the dangerous classes in our cities" (*Darkness and Daylight in New York*). To what extent this is true, we cannot say. Certain it is, however, that large numbers of criminals, who are closely pressed by the authorities in the older civilizations, or who view the New World as an El Dorado for daring souls, do drift penniless to our shores, and thus immensely aid in swelling the inordinate volume of crime in our great cities. Our immigration laws should be more stringent. Our nation should cease to be the asylum for the moral wrecks of the world, at least until we have better facilities for reformation than those in operation at the present. As the case now stands, the crimial emigrants, as well as thousands of penniless incomers, drift to cheap lodging-houses in our cities, which are already swarming with the lowest and most vicious of our people. And thus the Dead Sea enlarges its banks;

crimes increase; prisons, jails, almshouses, public hospitals, and insane asylums are crowded to overflowing.

Third, great as is the reinforcement given to the lower world by immigration, its influence in this respect is meagre compared to the *cheap lodging-houses*, which, as one careful writer avers, more than counterbalance in evil all the good resulting from free lectures, reading-rooms, and all other agenices of reform. In the city of New York there are two hundred and seventy of these houses. The price of a night's lodging is from twenty-five cents down to three cents a "spot." At most of them the price is below fifteen cents a night; and in these very cheap quarters we find filth, vermin, foul odors, and everything repulsive—nothing inviting. Here congregate the most vicious, wretched, degenerate, and dilapidated specimens of humanity. In some of these lodging-houses men and women pay for a hammock, in other for a bench; while still others pay a few pennies for a spot on the floor. Inspector Byrnes declares that "they have a powerful tendency to produce, foster, and increase crime. They are," he continues, "largely the resorts of thieves and other criminals of the lowest class, who here consort together, and lay plans for crime. During the last two or three years, hundreds of young men have been arrested for crimes that originated in these places. In many cases it was the first step in wrong-doing." He then recounts the following significant facts, which illustrate the legitimate fruits springing up from the poisonous atmosphere of the cheap lodging-houses: "Lying on my desk are two tintypes of the cheapest sort, evidently taken in the Bowery. They represent two young 'toughs,' each holding a pistol at the head of the other. They were taken from the pockets of the young fellows, who were brought into my private room on charges of robbery. These photographs interesed me, and I asked the boys how they came to be taken in that style. 'Oh,' they answered, 'we held a pistol up to the head of a man one night and got his money, and we just thought we would like to see how we looked when we did it.' They seem proud of their achievement. I mention this as an illustration of the sort of young criminals the cheap lodging-houses turn out" (*Darkness and Daylight in New York*).

That we may gain a more comprehensive idea of the magnitude of this evil in our great cities, both here and in Europe, let us note some facts in relation to the lodging-houses of New York City. According to the official report of the police department, there were in 1890 four million eight hundred and twenty-three thousand five hundred and ninety-five lodgings given in New York's two hundred and seventy lodging-houses. Of this number one million four hundred and fifty-two thousand and twenty were given in the sixty-four lodging-houses in the eleventh precinct, which embraces the district where the vast per centage of all crime in the city occurs! Thus, we find thirteen thousand two hundred and fifteen people on an average huddled together and sleeping in these nurseries of criminal and moral contagion each night.

And lastly, we notice _the saloon_ as the supreme curse of the nineteenth century, because its influence extends in all directions, and wherever it is felt, human misery, degradation, and moral eclipse follow. It is the devil-fish of our present civilization, whose every tentacle crushes to death. It pollutes politics; it degrades manhood; it fills the slums of our cities with want and wretchedness; it crowds to overflowing our jails and prisons; it is a leading factor in populating insane asylums, almshouses, and the Potter's Field; it destroys the physical strength; it beclouds the intellect; it obliterates moral integrity; _and it is the single most visible landmark in slum areas._ In many a low district in our great cities there are to be found a ridiculous number of saloons, sometimes so many in the area covered by one square block that they exceed by many times the total number of churches, schools, libraries, and coffee-houses found in the immediate area.

_V._

What, then, is to be done? In my judgement the initial step to practical and enduring reform is the patient, exhaustive study of the social cellar by both the criminologist and the sociologist. We must systematically examine into the great root causes of poverty, crime, and vice, and also the bearing of the social cellar to the world above. We must accumulate statistics and facts, not for the purpose of proving any special claim, but that we may arrive at the truth, and thus show precisely where the root of the evil which infests the criminal districts of our metropolitan areas lie, and the relation of each to the sum total of the appalling rates of crime, vice, and misery which we find there. Armed with these facts, an agitation can be inaugurated which will result in a revolution of measureless importance, and rid what ought to be the jewels of civilization, our large cities, of the present insidious cancer which is now such an integral part of them.

SUGGESTIONS FOR FURTHER READING AND INQUIRY:

HUMAN AGGREGATION, URBAN DECAY, AND MORAL DEGRADATION

"Moral and Physical Evils of Large Towns." *Foreign Quarterly Review*, vol. 19 (1837), pp. 338-357.
A very detailed summary of the pioneering research by A. J. B. Parent Duchatelet on urban degradation and prostitution in Paris, France, contained in his classic work titled *De la Prostitution dans la Ville de Paris*.

"On the Dangerous Classes of the Population in Large Towns." *Monthly Review*, vol. 155 (1841), pp. 486-495.
A very fine overview of H. A. Fregier's classic 1838 treatise on the moral and criminal topography of Paris titled *Des Classes Dangereuses de la Population dans les Grandes Villes, et des Moyens de les Rendre Meilleures*." Fregier was for many years the Bureau Chief of the Seine Prefecture (i.e., the chief of the Paris police).

"Paris - Its Dangerous Classes." *Quarterly Review*, vol. 70 (1842), pp. 1-44.
Another more lengthy and very detailed review of H. A. Fregier's classic 1838 treatise.

"Causes of the Increase of Crime." Archibald Alison. *Blackwood's Edinburgh Magazine*, vol. 56 (1844), pp. 1-14.
The most powerful restraints on human conduct — interpersonal relationships and a sense of neighborhood and community—are lost with escalations in the density of population.

"The Night-Side of Civilization." *Tait's Edinburgh Magazine*, vol. 20 (1853), pp. 165-171.
Discussion of the phenomenon that in virtually all large, metropolitan areas there can be found districts populated almost entirely by the criminal class.

"Dangerous Classes of London." *British Quarterly*, vol. 35 (1862), pp. 352-360.
The deterioration of the social fabric in the congested and filthy quarters of London that promote vicious, degraded, and criminal behavior.

"In the Five-Points." Wirt Sikes. *Harper's New Monthly Magazine*, vol. 36 (1868), pp. 223-226.
A fine first-hand account of "the hot-bed of American crime and degradation" in the Five Points section of New York City.

"Dangerous Classes of New York City." C. L. Brace. *Appleton's Journal*, vol. 3 (1870), pp. 211-212; 226-229; 277-278; 434-435; 496-498; 577-578; 631-632; vol. 4 (1870), pp. 45-47; 222-224; 490-491; 667-668; vol. 5 (1871), pp. 18-19.
A truly classic and outstanding series of articles treating upon the nature of crime and vice occasioned by the unique social conditions in large metropolitan areas. The enumeration of the series of articles contains a misprint. The series consists of eleven articles, not twelve. What should have been article eight in the series is incorrectly numbered article nine.

"Night Rambles in the East End." Alexander Strahan and Richard Rowe. *Good Words*, vol. 12 (1871), pp. 276-282.
A very fine first-hand description of the social dynamics driving crime and vice in the notorious East End of London.

"The Dangerous Classes." W. Chambers. *Chambers's Edinburgh Journal*, vol. 52 (1875), pp. 113-115.
A fine description of crime, vice, and moral degradation in the overcrowded and filthy slum districts of New York City.

"Homes of the Criminal Classes." Hugh E. Hoare. *National Review*, vol. 1 (1883), pp. 224-229; 824-831.
An outstanding two-part article describing from direct observation the social conditions and everyday life of the criminal class in London slum districts.

"Nurseries of Crime." Thomas Byrnes. *North American Review*, vol. 149 (1889), pp. 366-362.
A very interesting article written by the famous Chief Inspector of the New York Police Department, wherein he argues that cheap lodging houses located in slum areas are a major, predisposing source for both adult as well as juvenile criminality.

"Town-Life as a Cause of Degeneracy." G. B. Barron. *Popular Science Monthly*, vol. 34 (1889), pp. 324-328.
Abstract of a paper read at a meeting of the British Association which argues that the city dweller (as compared to his country cousin) is inordinately exposed to opportunities for bad associations and bad habits, both of which work to produce the onset of physical as well as moral degeneracy.

"Cancer Spots in Metropolitan Life." Benjamin Orange Flower. *Arena*, vol. 4 (1891), pp. 760-777.
Crime, vice, and degradation in slum areas.

"Wellsprings and Feeders of Immorality." Benjamin Orange Flower. *Arena*, vol. 11 (1894-95), pp. 56-70, 167-175, 399-412; and vol. 12 (1895), pp. 337-352.
A very lengthy article in four parts treating on the social, economic, and political dynamics of large metropolitan areas that contribute to prostitution and inordinate levels of crime.

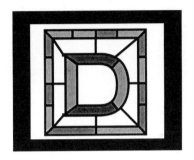

CRIMINAL TYPOLOGY

THE PROFESSIONAL, HABITUAL, AND CASUAL THIEF

CHAMBERS'S EDINBURGH JOURNAL

VOL. 31, NO. 265 (29 JANUARY 1859), PP. 84-87

It is an old and trite saying, that "half the world knows not how the other half lives;" but, like many other saws, so familiar that it is almost impertinence to quote them, it contains a great deal more of latent truth and wisdom than meets the ear of those who hear it, or touches the sense of those who quote it. We will not pretend to enter at present into more than one of its manifold meanings. But it may be interesting to many of our readers to be reminded of its reference to the varieties, habits, and condition of a class whose numbers and importance are known to few, except those who have given very special attention to the subject. Were it not that unseen dangers are easily neglected, and not seldom disbelieved, it would seem strange that any should be unaware of or indifferent to the presence among us of a large and distinct body of persons who are by habit and profession enemies of society; engaged in ceaseless war with the community in the midst of which they dwell; against whom an internal army of more than twenty thousand men is constantly kept on foot, and who, in one way or another, cost the public revenue more than 1,000,000 pounds sterling annually; to say nothing of the loss and damage inflicted on individuals by their predatory incursions on their neighbors.

Certainly, however, more than "half the world" has very little idea about the distinct varieties of criminal thieves and the nature of their lives and "labours" among them who are described in the aggregate as our Criminal Classes. They imagine that the prisoners who appear at the bar of our tribunals, from those of the Scotch sheriff or the English stipendiary magistrate, up to the Central Criminal Court itself, are individual members of the ordinary working-body of society, whom idleness, or want, or vicious habits have led into guilt; and that most of whom will, perhaps, after suffering the punishment assigned to their offence by law, be reabsorbed into the mass of the population, and lost to the eye of the police. They may be confirmed in this opinion by observing that the number of second convictions recorded in the statistical tables which are now annually compiled by our country as well as France and Belgium, form but a small proportion of the total; and still more by observing how very few of the sentences passed are of that severe description which is alone just or reasonable, in the case of the notorious and habitual plunderer of his neighbours. Even of the latter, not a few of us probably conceive of a man engaged like other men in some daily avocation, and who is only less able or less willing than his neighbours to resist the temptations to sin which fall in his way. It is no doubt to some such ideas as these that we owe the excess of sympathy which induces good and wise men too often to speak of and to deal with criminals as persons afflicted with some disease of conscience, or mental malformation; who should be placed in a prison as in a kind of moral hospital, and regarded by their happier brethren in a spirit of pure charity and compassion. If they were told that an enormous proportion of the crimes committed are the acts of men with whom crime is as much a profession as is law with the advocate, or medicine with the physician; and that of the remainder, the great majority are perpetrated by persons who, in the phrase we have heard employed by a policeman, "work a little, and steal a great deal," they might perhaps be inclined to take a different view of the matter.

That such is really the case is certain. The experience of officers of police has well established that a very large proportion of the number apprehended in a year for crimes against property —for larceny, burglary, highway robbery, and the like—are persons either having no other profession or occupation than that of plunder, or who combine with the pursuit of thieving some other and less profitable employment, often affording them special opportunities for the exercise of their more lucrative talent, and who steal both while employed and in the intervals when they are out of work. We may fairly estimate these two classes to furnish one-half of the number apprehended for any of the various kinds of theft. The other half will then consist of persons habitually honest who, from weakness of principle, or from force of temptation, have been misled into isolated acts of guilt, and who are often, and, we believe, generally, detected in their first or second offence. The number of these "casual offenders," apprehended will probably not fall very far short of the total number of offences committed by persons of this class; but if we suppose them to be on average detected only in the second offence, we have for every hundred apprehensions among this class of culprits only two hundred crimes. But in the class of habitual pilferers, and still more certainly among the higher order of professional thieves, every apprehension may be taken to represent at least thirty offences; and every hundred apprehensions will represent about 3,000 separate thefts. For every two hundred arrests for theft, then, we may calculate that 200 crimes have been committed by casual, and 3,000 by habitual offenders; or, out of every 3,200 such offences, 3,000, or fifteen-sixteenths, are perpetrated by persons constantly, willfully, and deliberately persisting in the practice of dishonesty. By far the largest number of serious breaches of the law fall under the head of crimes against property; so that, if we take nine-tenths of the total number of crimes committed to be the work of habitual criminals, we shall certainly be guilty of no exaggeration.

All offenders against the law, then, and especially offenders against the law of property, who form an overwhelming proportion of the inmates of our prisons—such as robbers, burglars, forgers, or thieves—are not of a single, homogenous class, but may be divided into three types, or distinct classes, each with their unique characteristics and attributes, under the respective denominations of *professional*, *habitual*, and *casual*.

The first type constitutes a body perhaps not exceedingly numerous in comparison with the others, but far more dangerous to society and mischievous to individuals than either. The professional thieves are those who follow no other ostensible calling – who live solely, and we might say avowedly, by pilfering or defrauding their neighbours. They are a class or trade altogether apart from the rest of the community of thieves. They have their own dwellings generally in quarters where few honest people are to be found; they associate principally or solely with one another; they have, like men in other occupations, their own houses of call, their own specialized instruments and tools, their own rules and "maxims of the trade," their own organization and division of labour; their especial recreations and amusements (though in this they are less exclusive), wherein the ill-gotten gains of their profession are squandered as lightly as they are earned. There are, in all large towns certain neighbourhoods which are their headquarters, and to which they resort from all the various regions round about, where they may have been carrying on their operations. These streets are narrow, dingy, and most unpleasant to traverse; the houses are tall, rickety in construction, and unsafe in appearance; the windows glazed with coarse green glass; and when that is broken, in a row, or by some drunken passer-by, the place is filled with the first dirty piece of cotton rag that comes conveniently to hand. In many of these streets every other dwelling is a low beer-house, whose upper rooms serve the purpose of a lodging-house, and are filled with closely packed beds of a most uninviting aspect. Above, all is dirt, darkness, and squalor; below, at the time when these places are most crowded, there prevails an uncomfortable, cheerless, riotous gaiety; the inmates of these hovels assembling round a dirty table, on a floor innocent of washing since first it received the contributions of beer-dregs and tobacco-juice, which are every evening augmented. Here the plunder of the congregated class of professional thieves is spent in the coarsest kind of dissipation; in drinking beer, or, less often, gin and brandy, in the lowest condition of adulteration; in gambling with filthy dominoes, or filthier cards; or in other amusements of a nature still more coarse, debasing, and criminal. But if there be one feature which is common alike to the professional class of thieves and their dwellings, it is the all-pervading appearance of comfortless squalor which distinguishes them, above the very worst of the orders from which this variety of thieves chiefly come. Honest labourers, even when very poor, would shrink from the utter wretchedness of these miserable abodes. Yet, for the sake of the dissipations which they here enjoy, these professional thieves choose a life of dishonesty, with the constant prospect off severe legal punishment before their eyes, rather than earn their bread by honest industry. True, they have meat every day, and a quantity of drink, in which the honest man can happily but seldom find leisure, even if he has the money to indulge. But they have neither home nor wife; they can never enjoy security even for an hour; and cleanliness and comfort are absolutely beyond their reach.

For the professional thief, probably the greatest attraction of this kind of life is the wild freedom which they enjoy, and the total absence of hard and persevering labour. For though many of their thefts require much ingenuity, patience, and skill, they do not call for a tenth part of the steady hard work that would be required to make a living in a respectable calling. The professional thief chooses his own time of rising and of going to rest; his own hours of work, and his intervals of laziness. He is under no necessity of regular attendance in mill, or foundry, or warehouse; he roams whither he will, and returns when he pleases. If he be disposed to indolence, he can spend the day in listlessness, and the night in debauchery, without fear of fine or dismissal from an indignant employer. A few days spent in a career of successful thieving may furnish him with the means of enjoying, for weeks, unlimited riot in the luxuries he best understands – drink and idleness. When his purse filled with filthy lucre is exhausted, he sallies forth again in search of fresh plunder.

All this time, his character, his habits, and his person are perfectly well known to the police. They will enter his haunts, and speak to him as to one notoriously engaged in the professional trade of thieving; and he will not attempt to deny it. They can point him out in the street, and say: "That man is a thief; he is now out on such and such a track. He is going to see what he can get at this crowded meeting, or at that fashionable assembly." Or they may see him take his seat in the train that starts for a neighbouring town on the day of some attractive fete, and be perfectly aware of his errand. In a day or two, he returns with the fruits of his expedition, and spends them merrily under the eye of the guardians of the law, who have no hold upon him. Such a life has no doubt great attraction for the thoroughly idle and habitually dissolute, and while youth and vigour remain, it is from this crowd that the ranks of thieves whom we have styled as professional are filled. In advancing age, we should expect to find it less obstinately adhered to, its charms diminished, and its inconveniences more keenly felt; and this accords with the fact, which we know from statistical evidence, that a vast majority of the total number of thieves committed annually are under thirty years of age, and that only about one-sixth are more than forty.

The professional thief chooses, indeed, "a short life and a merry one," and generally, according to the evidence of men well qualified to judge by long knowledge of this class of thieves, closes it at an early age by a wretched death on his dingy bed, amid the riot and debauchery in which he can no longer take his share. But it cannot be supposed that an ignominious death from physical exhaustion and disease is the only agent which typically cuts short the career of the majority of professional thieves before they have reached forty years of age. The disproportionately small number who pass that period must be attributed, at least in part, to a change of life in those who find themselves no longer fitted by physical power or mental vigour for the risks and activity of their previous career. Drink, dissipation, and squalid discomfort have told upon a frame probably diseased from birth, inherited from vicious and dissipated parents, and educated in the hardships of the streets by day, and of the lodging-house by night, until the young professional neophyte was able to provide for himself at the expense of society. So the broken down professional turns either to some easier branch of his own trade—as to the stay-at-home and comparatively safe business of the "resetter" or receiver of stolen goods—or finds some occupation which, compared to his former one, may be called honest. The cases of genuine reformation of professional thieves, when left to themselves, are few indeed. The besetting temptation of drink, to which they have been for a lifetime accustomed; the habit of idleness, which they have never learned to overcome; the irreparable loss of character, which renders it almost impossible to find employment that will afford an honest livelihood—all these difficulties, which in part characterize the class of thieves we have delineated as professionals, stand in their way, and oppose at every point their approach to the path of rectitude.

Besides this class, whose only occupation is the plunder of their neighbours, there is a much larger group who may be described as thieves by habit and repute, but who are nevertheless in employment more or less regularly, and who are chiefly differentiated from the professional thief by their dependence in a far larger degree upon their labour for their principle means of subsistence. They comprise the numerous class of dishonest workpeople, disreputable hawkers, rag-pickers, and others; many of them work in factories, and others as porters, or in occupations generally of a somewhat irregular and uncertain character. Many of them work while trade is good, and turn to thieving only when it becomes slack, and when they—as the hands with whom the master will most willingly part—are thrown out of employment. Others purloin small articles or stores from their places of work; iron from the foundry, cloth from the warehouse, and cotton from the factory. They seldom reach such a post of trust as would give them a chance of robbing the till, or embezzling the moneys of their employer. The small shopkeepers who are unfortunate enough to employ the habitual thief suffer severely from the petty depredations of this class, especially as, being in work, and known by their neighbours merely as working-people, it may be some time before they become marked by them, as suspected characters. Habitual thieves have no particular quarter of their own, like the class of professional thieves, but are scattered, in the poorest neighbourhoods, especially among struggling and industrious families. In great part, because of these differences from their brethren, the professional thief, habitual thieves are less accurately known to the police. By way of further distinction, their operations are conducted on a much smaller scale, their skill greatly inferior, and their detections, we are inclined to believe, proportionally more frequent. In idleness, profligacy, and absolute want of any shame in their evil trade, they differ only degree from the former type. Lacking the same opportunities for the indulgence of vice, rather than the same depravity of character, there may be more hope of their reformation, inasmuch as they have found less success and enjoyment in a career of crime; but the effect of punishment or exhortation upon them is seldom great, and cures are far from frequent.

It is not so, we would hope, with the third type, casual thieves, those whom strong temptation or momentary weakness have led into sins opposed to the whole habits and feelings of their lives. The clerk, born of honest parents, reared in comfortable domestic surroundings, and brought up a respectable man, who has appropriated money which he intended to replace in time, and cannot; the servant-girl, whose father's gray hairs are bowed to the dust by the shame, when he learns that his darling has bought some coveted ribbon with the pinched sovereign her master's carelessness left loose on his dressing-table; the wee lad who has snatched a penny-whistle hung temptingly outside the door of a toyshop; the child who has purloined a bun from the baker's shop to satisfy the cravings of hunger – who can doubt that these thieves are cut from a wholly different bolt of cloth than the professional and habitual thieves, and may be, and should be, saved from deeper sinking into the mire? The casual thieves are not of the same criminal class; these are not the enemies of society by choice, but by circumstances. For these, we need a discipline which may serve as a warning and example, without inflicting degradation or urging to despair; against those whose life is that of the beast of prey, the sons of Ishamel, whose hand is against every man, we need stringent barriers and stern coercion; not forgetting the while, however, that even among these are many, very many, "more sinned against than sinning;" and that it belongs not to us to administer retribution for sin, but merely to protect ourselves and them against the probability of their return to a life of depredation, and against the continual recruitment of the ranks of this army of crime, engaged perpetually in an intense warfare with the community.

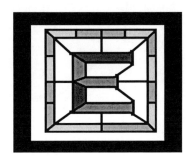

EVIL ASSOCIATES
AND
LEARNED CRIMINALITY

PROFESSIONAL THIEVES

CORNHILL MAGAZINE

VOL. 6, NO 35 (NOVEMBER 1862), PP. 640-653

Thieving, considered as an art, is only just beginning to be understood in this country; it is scarcely thirty years since honest men turned their attention to the subject with a determination to master it, and their investigations have been hindered by the fastidiousness and false delicacy of society, even more than by the obstacles opposed by roguery and rascaldom. But, obviously, crime will never be cured until its origin and career are thoroughly understood. Chaplains, governors of prisons, and heads of convict stations could give valuable information and assistance; but the so-called interests of the service require their silence. Many of these gentlemen entertain advanced opinions on the subject, but are in the position of those who can instruct but dare not. Yet great improvements have been effected in dealing with crime during the last thirty years. There is less brutality and ignorance among criminals, crime has perceptibly diminished, and therefore there is every reason to persevere, and less justification for discouragement.

In turning to the *Judicial Statistics* for 1860, we are struck with the extent of official knowledge displayed. The variations, the agencies, and the results of crime are detailed in a very instructive manner. In 1860, it seems, the total Police and Constabulary force amounted to 20,760, and their cost for the year amounted to 1,531,111*L.*, 5*s.*, and 7*d.* We had one policeman for every 870 of the population. The following are the numbers of thieves and depredators then known: Under sixteen years of age, 4,028 males, 1,467 females—total, 5,495. Above sixteen years of age, 25,407 males, 7,012 females—total, 32,419. Suspected persons, in round numbers, 35,206. But those in prison should be added to the numbers of those at large, and this done, we have a grand total of 155,145, or one in every 115 of the population.

In the vast aggregate of criminals there are many who are only occasional and temporary offenders. These are obviously neither the most difficult, the most injurious, nor the most costly section of the criminal class; that distinction is enjoyed by the habitual, or *professional*, thieves. How numerous the class of professional thieves is, it would be impossible to say. They count by many thousands. Scattered throughout the country, they form a network of veins by means of which all criminal knowledge circulates. In prison and out of it, in the lowly village lodging-house, and in the Bay of Bermuda, "doing their separates" at Pentonville and among the rocks of Gibraltar, wherever they are they develop and increase criminal tendencies, and spread criminal knowledge. They are the preachers of thieving, the schoolmasters of dishonesty, and the expounders of roguery. They give the countryman finishing lessons as reward for his putting up jobs for them. The police have their *Hue and Cry* to prevent crimes; but the professional thieves are every one of them a *Hue and Cry* for the diffusion of criminal knowledge and for the spread of crime. In the convict stations, the old professional thief is venerated by the young thieves in their first conviction. They gather round him to listen to his boastful stories, and as he tells of this neat trick and that, many a laugh rings over Bermuda Bay, and many a young hand resolves to be a hero in crime—a second Jack Sheppard. The old thief will teach the young one almost all he knows, if he will be only docile and "pal" with him. It is no uncommon thing for a young thief, during the term of his penal servitude, to write down the lessons in the art which he receives from some old thief. He will read these explanations and study them until the tutor assures the pupil that he is master of the trick. In fact, the Advertisement Supplement of *The Times* is not half so useful a medium for commercial affairs, nor yet so successful for the diffusion of information, as are the professional thieves as sources and means for the spread of criminal knowledge, and for the facilitating and encouragement of crime through all the land.

Now how are we to understand and conquer professional thieves? Police reports, reports of trials, and Blue-books help us a little. These are valuable aids, but still they are official, and so of necessity limited and one-sided. Chaplains and prison officers could communicate much valuable information, and in many instances they have done so. Still this is only part of the question; it is only the thief under sentence, with as much of the thief at large as the criminal chooses to let out. Mr. Mayhew's book about "those who won't work" is very useful, and although the nature of its topics excludes it from the family circle, it entitles its author to much consideration. The thieves told him something of their art, but they by no means gave him all their secrets; his book rather sketches the external life and circumstances of crime than dissects the system, so that the public may be prepared to grapple with the vast and subtle machinery of thievedom.

Would that the professional thieves could be induced to come forward, and candidly tell us all about it. We shall never fully understand them until they explain themselves. Police, prison discipline, fence-masters, penal servitude, on each of these subjects a conference of old thieves, earnest and out-spoken, would speedily teach the public more than they can ever learn from associations for the promotion of social science, parliamentary committees, government commissioners, prison inspectors, and police reports.

Believing that we cannot understand people of any class or character unless we go among them, see them in their open hours of unreserved communication, and hear what they have to say for themselves, I have for some time past made the most of every opportunity of becoming acquainted, as a clergyman, with the origin, character, acts, and habits of professional thieves, and I shall give my readers the benefit of what I have been able to gather. Conversing with thieves from different parts of the country who were unknown to each other, I have been able to test their truthfulness by various independent testimony, and I have found far more veracity and openness than could have been expected from such a class of vicious and degraded men. By degrees I have got from them the greater portion of their craft and mystery, from "pricking the garter" to "drilling a safe," and from the sale of a stolen shirt to the disposal of the valuable booty which they occasionally obtain from the jewellers. Will they not be enraged by being shown up too much? The answer is, "No, so long as you do not hurt us _individually_. There always have been plenty of flats to plunder, and there always will be. There will be enough thieving to be done in our time, whatever you may write, and the next generation must shift for themselves as we have done."

In reference to their origin, professional thieves may be classed as follows: 1. Those who have been trained to it from their infancy. 2. Those who have taken to it through the connivance or neglect of their parents. 3. Those who have been driven to it from ill-usage. 4. Those who, from their childhood, have evinced a propensity to thieving, and taken to it because they liked it. 5.

Those children who have forsaken their homes, have been forsaken by their parents, and have fallen into the hands of habitual thieves. 6. Youths whose parents have been imprisoned or transported, leaving their children entirely destitute. 7. Idle and dissolute labourers and mechanics. 8. A few broken-down tradesmen and clerks who were once respectable. 9. Others who are very changeable and restless, are too idle to work, and have a strong passion for the adventures of crime. 10. Those who, after a first imprisonment, are forsaken by their friends, and can obtain no employment. 11. A few who, by degrees, get into it by the terrible pressure of poverty, and having once got into it, go on to the end. 12. A few from the stern severity of honest parents, who when a son or daughter has been led to a solitary act of theft, have shut the parental door upon them when they came out of prison, with the distinct intimation that they should not darken their father's threshold again: a poor way, indeed, of wiping out the family disgrace.

Young hawkers, both boys and girls, frequently become professional thieves. They are first tempted to steal bits of metal or trifling articles of wearing-apparel which they see lying about the houses where they go to vend their wares, and having once begun, the descent is easy. A thief told me – "I have often sat in our public-houses of an evening in company with other thieves. We have been in one of our better moods, and have talked about what first caused us to become thieves, and I have heard many a pitiful story. Many of them would say, 'I never knew anything else. I have been at it all my life, and as I have lived, so must I die.' Another would say, 'I could get no work after my first conviction; nobody would look at me; I could not starve, and was obliged to go on the cross.' Another would say, 'I began to sell oranges when I was a boy, or what fruit might be in season. I could not always sell all I had, and sometimes I used to eat them. I durst not go home without the money. Then I used to steal something, and take it to the marine store dealer's. The man would encourage me, and tell me to bring what I liked, and he would buy it of me. As I got on in thieving, I left home, and was soon polished off into a first-class wire.'"

A few of what the thieves call the more respectable members of their fraternity, fence-masters, and the better sort of publicans in the thieves' quarter, do all they can to keep their children out of crime, by sending them to school, or getting them into honester company as early as possible. But while these unfortunate children do remain at home it is next to impossible to keep them out of mischief. They inevitably see and know a great deal of what is going on around them, and they soon long to be at it, and doing what they consider the clever and manly thing. Too often this ambition is industriously encouraged. Not unfrequently entire families are trained to dishonesty, and it has happened that nearly the whole of them have been in prison at the same time. The ragged schools do much to check those children whose parents incite them to steal, and a few beautiful instances have occurred in which the poor ragged-school scholar has refused to obey the unrighteous behests of his parents.

The origin of female professional thieves is, in many respects, similar to that of males, and yet there is something in it sufficiently distinctive to merit a passing notice. They are the offspring of prostitutes, thieves, beggars, poor, cruel, and drunken parents, low shopkeepers in the thieves' quarter, and hawkers. They get into it by degrees, much the same as boys do. The young girls begin with the little things, and pass on to greater as they acquire confidence and skill, and as opportunities increase. If they have no one to train them in the first instance, they have not to wait long for their criminal education. They soon get known to the older female thieves, and any signs of superior cunning and audacity they may show are never neglected. By-the-by the novice pairs off with some established thief, who completes her education, but generally she has suffered a great deal, and been in prison many times before it comes to this. Her end is generally the same as the man's; consumption through drink, imprisonment, and unhealthy habits.

In the days of old Fagan and Jonathan Wild young thieves were trained by means of wearing-apparel suspended on a line in a room with a bell attached to the cord, so that if they did not perform the exercise very adroitly the detector bell would ring. Now this method is antiquated and obsolete. The progress of intellect has made itself felt among professional thieves, and they go a much readier way to work with their pupils, adopting a simpler and more natural course of training. But thief-culture is not so distinct and systematic a branch of criminal life as some imagine. A few do little else except train boys and girls, but these are very few in number compared with the hosts of juvenile thieves who are constantly feeding the criminal market. Thief-trainers are something like dog-trainers. Here and there men keep kennels for the sole purpose of educating all sorts of dogs, sporting, fancy, house-dogs, and others. But where one dog is trained in this way, there are thousands of dogs who are simply trained by their owners, or their owners' keepers, while many dogs manage to go through the world without either education, manners, or style. It is just so with thieves. A few are trained by professional educators, the majority are trained by some thief who takes a fancy to them, or they are educated for crime by their parents. The ordinary and general training which boys and girls get refers to stealing small things from houses, shops, street stalls, warehouses, and neglected premises. They are taught to go two or three together, so that they may be of mutual assistance to each other. One will act as a "stall" to cover the working thief, and will run away with the booty, so that should the pilferer be detected, the stolen goods are not found upon him. These will also try pocket-handkerchiefs, and soon become expert in taking them.

For a superior education the professional trainer, or coaching by a first-class thief in full practice, is necessary. On this head I am informed by an adept that, "the juvenile is generally committed to stealing habitually before the professional thief will take him in hand. A boy cannot be thieving long without the fact becoming known to some established thief. In a theatre, in a shop, mostly in a crowd, the old thief sees the boy at work, and watches him very carefully. If the boy is sharp and steady over his business and is at all good-looking, the old thief will make friends with him. An arrangement is soon come to, and the boy goes to reside with his new friend. The first thing is to dress the boy very respectfully, and teach him politeness and good manners as far as such a thing can be done. We try all we can do to make him up so that he will pass for a very respectable school-boy. This pays best. It would never do to have him rough. People would be on their guard in a minute if he were not smooth and nice. We sometimes succeed in getting them up beautifully, and then we have what a thief likes, a young, innocent-looking, and lucrative deception. Pocket-picking is the boy's first lesson, and he practices on his instructor, and on the women who may reside with the thief. When he can quickly and quietly pick the pocket of his new friends, the woman takes him out, generally into some crowded shop. Here he probably succeeds well, gets pleased with his success, and warms to his work. After practicing shops and crowds for some time, the woman ventures to take him out for single-handed and open work. He goes with her into the streets, and does a few easy cases in stealing pocket-handkerchiefs and purses. The woman has nearly always most to do with the education of the boy. When she has done with him, the man takes him in hand, and they go out together. The boy has now become a single-handed street wire, and works with front and back stalls, _i.e._, a man before and a man behind to cover him, to take the purses from him, and to get him out of trouble if he is suspected. They are always kind to the boy, for if not he would leave them. They feed him and clothe him, and he wants for nothing. They give him a little money, but not too much, lest he should be foolish with it, and attract the attention of the police. The boy often gets sent to prison, and when he is liberated the thief meets him and takes him home. As the boy gets older, he becomes independent of his trainers, and so he in turn pairs off and leaves them." If the boy should attempt to leave his trainers too soon, they will frighten him by threatening to set the police upon him; nor do they scruple to carry out their threat. There is very little difference between the training of boys and girls. Some idea of the amount of juvenile crime may be formed from the fact that in 1860, there were under sixteen years of age 4,208 boys who were known thieves and depredators; and 1,467 girls of the same age and character.

There is a thieves' quarter in all large towns well known to the police, and better known to the thieves. They flourish, with kindred infamy, amidst a congeries of small rag-shops, Irishing shops, coffee-houses, beer-houses, spirit-shops, and lodging-houses for single men, with, of course, a tripe-seller, a bird-fancier, a fiddler to pay at the thievedom carnivals, and a ragged school within hail. As the reader passes into the quarter in the day-time, he is struck by the strange physiognomy and attire of men and women, boys and girls. The children don't play like other children; they lounge about, looking very suspicious and preter-naturally sharp. The adults look seedy and sleepy, as if they had been up all night. They lounge about the doors, indulging in subdued laughter, and now and then call to one another across the street, or saunter listlessly through the quarter with their hands in their pockets. It is not often that depredations are committed here, unless some stranger chances to present a temptation too strong to be resisted. There are fights and brawls sometimes, but not often. Half-a-dozen policemen are always about, sometimes looking as excited as sportsmen who have just flushed a woodcock, or wearing an air of languid weariness as if exhausted by expectation of a prize that never meant to come. In the afternoon, a few men and women, habitual thieves, drop in from different parts of the country—perhaps they are returned convicts, fresh from Gibraltar, Western Australia, or Bermuda. Nearly the whole of the houses hereabouts are nests of crime, notwithstanding the dinginess and quietude of their exterior. If a stranger enters one of their public-houses, and calls for a glass of ale, it will be given to him reluctantly; and if he is not off as soon as he has drunk his beer, some of the thieves will insult him, and drive him away, or they will go to the landlord and say, "What is that man? Is he square? If he is, send him away. We don't want him, and we won't have it. If square people are allowed to come here, we shall take our money somewhere else." If circumstances should be favourable, the stranger will perhaps be cheated and gambled out of all his money, and then sent out of the house insulted as well as plundered. These public-houses are always, with scarcely an exception, kept by persons who have formerly belonged to the thieves' organization in some one of its many departments. According to the judicial statistics for 1860, there are 4,938 beer-houses and public-houses resorted to by thieves and the infamous of the other sex. The thieves resort to these houses for the sake of society, security, and enjoyment. In the afternoon, very few of them are drunk; they pass away the time in gambling with dominoes, dice, and cards. Two detectives, perhaps, come in quietly, look round the rooms, and then pass out, without anything being said. Should a man whom they want be present in the rooms, they will give him a tap on the shoulder, and say, "You are wanted; come with me." The professional thief will generally accept this invitation to prison without any ado, making inquiries as he goes along as to what they want him for. Should there be an individual in the room, a stranger to the detectives, they will bid him stand up, and then, "Take off your hat, sir." This they do that they may know him another day, and the thief obeys them as though he were a soldier under inspection on parade.

The thieves are mostly dressed in a mean and slovenly way when they are off work; but when they go out on their criminal business, they dress well and become animated and brisk in their manner. There is very little plunder kept in the thieves' quarter; they seldom take their acquisitions to their own houses, nor are the burglar's tools often found about them; they are quietly stowed away in some unsuspected quarter and are brought out again only when they are wanted. Should a thief go into one of their public-houses with a stolen watch upon him, the company present would be very angry, and request him to leave them at once. "Don't come here with it. Go and put it off. You may get us all into trouble if you stay here with that thimble upon you." And away the thief goes to the fence-master, and the watch is turned into money probably in less than an hour after it has been purchased; and in another hour or two the "fence" can, if he likes, melt the gold down, and dispose of the works. The thieves think it perfectly fair to cheat one another in gambling, and they are proud of the feat. Sometimes they lose fifteen or twenty pounds at a sitting. They never carry much money about with them; they make the publican their banker, and he is generally faithful. No amount of success induces them to desist. However large the proceeds of a burglary or garotte, they still go on until they are caught and imprisoned.

The majority of habitual thieves profess to believe in the Bible, and to respect religion. They are not all drunkards. A few of them are moderate, steady, and even abstemious. In some instances they conceal their wickedness from their parents, if still living—visiting them occasionally and giving them money. Generally they are true to each other, but sometimes they are treacherous—though "rounding" or treachery is always spoken of very indignantly by them, and often severely, and even murderously punished. Their character in respect of violence and cruelty has been much ameliorated during the last fifteen or twenty years. They do not like resorting to violence if it can possibly be avoided. When the stolen property is on them, they will fight to get away, but they do not in these times put old men and women on a blazing fire, and keep them there until they tell where their money is. The modern thief depends upon his skill for finding the cash, and, in fact, often knows where the stake is before he enters the house. Pistols are seldom carried by them; the weapon of choice is generally a "neddy," or life-preserver. The professional thieves admit that they are wrong, but try to make out that they are no worse than some other folks, such as fraudulent bankers, for instance. A constant study of the newspapers, and especially the reports of criminal cases, convinces them that they are rogues in every sphere of life, and that thieves are not much worse than their neighbours. Professional thieves are not capable of sustained reasoning. Their intellects confuse rules and expectations. Blinded by their own passions, they cannot see the difference between an honest life, and the exceptional instances which come under their notice in the courts of law. With the view of obtaining some insight into their moral nature, I sought out a large number of their favourite criminal songs. It is not necessary to say anything about the obscene ditties, because these thieves relish in common with many fast young men who are not thieves. "The Female Transport," "When I Go Flimping Through the Night," "The Transport's Farewell," "Young Tyler and Robinson," "The Female Smuggler," "Roger O'Hare," "The Famous Adventures of John Scott," "Bold Nevison the Highwayman," "Sketch of Roguery," "Mary Martin," "Stark-Naked Robbery," "Poly Oliver's Rambles," "Jack Sheppard's Songs," "The Cruel Miller," "The Robbers of the Glen," "Brennan on the Move," "The Bloody Gardener's Cruelty," "Death of Parker," "The Female Poachers of Nottinghamshire," "Barnet Races," and "Rufford Park Poachers" – these are their principal songs. An analysis of their sentiment is easily made; they all more or less invest crime with false glory, colour it with unreal happiness, and give it by far too much good luck. It is some consolation to find that the more vicious songs are chiefly sung by the elder members of the guilty fraternity, and are slowly and surely passing into disuse. The younger thieves prefer sentimental airs such as "Gentle Annie," and "Why Did She Leave Him Because He Was Poor." "Little Nell" was for a long time a prodigious favourite. With the progress of this sentimental turn in musical matters we may fairly connect the fact that out of 836 cases of burglary and house-breaking committed or bailed for trial in 1860, only eight were attended with violence.

The female thieves keep to picking up, pocket-picking, and the various methods of robbing shops and offices in the day. They are always connected with male thieves. How the male and female thief first come together is a question which need not occupy our attention. They meet and become acquainted in the course of criminal life, and are more constant to each other than one could expect. Great enmity subsists between female thieves and another class of vicious women. They spoil each other's trade, and are nearly always quarreling, and trying to set the police upon one another. A female thief prides herself on having her "mate" dressed well and showily, with plenty of money to spend, and she will keep him in clover if she goes in rags. She drinks a good deal, and especially if she has not children, but she will only drink with her own partner: this is a point of honour among them. When he is in prison, she keeps to herself, if not caught, and when he comes out, it is the delight of her heart to have some money ready for him. They often quarrel, and as often make it up again, but when either gets a long sentence, the other takes to some one else. Women are useful to the men in taking booty to the fence-master. Occasionally they assist at a burglary, and carry the instruments, though they never enter the house— remaining instead outside and keeping watch; they are then called crows. They are considered to make good scouts in the night, as less likely to attract the suspicions of the police. Female thieves are made more use of than formerly by the men in various ways of pilfering and concealment. Passing base coin, shop-robbing, pocket-picking in places of worship, streets, crowds, and railways, are their chief employment. Sometimes two women work together, or a man and woman, or two men and one woman, or one woman with one or two girls or boys.

The professional language of thieves is peculiar to themselves. They use it for the sake of secrecy, from pride, from the influence of custom, and from the necessity of the case. Their own language conveys their meaning in many instances more clearly and fully than the modes of expression common among honest people. For instance, they have a technical use of the word "sweet." If they are attempting to rob, and the victim has no suspicion, they say he is "sweet." If a person's suspicions are roused, then they try "to sweeten him," and to "keep him sweet" until their object is accomplished. If a thief wishes to tell you that you know all about a thing he will say, "You have got the full strength of it." Their cant contains some very old words, but it changes somewhat with each succeeding generation. The London thieves are the fountain and authority for all new cant. Some thief utters a comical and queer word when in a state of excitement, and it is taken up and used by others. Here is a short cant letter written by a thief:

"Start, Jan. 27, 1862.

Jerry, old chap, we have just been thundering lucky. We have just touched for a rattling stake of sugar at Brum, of a titman while he was getting on his prod. It is all in single pennifs on the England jug. The coppers were dead on sneaking for it. We shall get away as soon as we can. I think I shall let old Abraham the Sheeney have it, at four punt and a half a nob. If you like, Jerry, I will send a few thickuns to bring you and your tamtart up to Start. When we touched for it, we had to get on the finger and thumb a few miles. We durst not get on the rattles in eir."

The following is a translation of the foregoing letter:

London, Jan. 27, 1862.
Jerry, old chap, I have just got a large stake of money at Birmingham, from a farmer on horseback. It is in five pound notes on the Bank of England. The police were on our track, and expected to take us for it. But we shall come away as soon as we possibly can do so. I think I shall take them to Abraham, the Jew, and let him have the notes at four pounds and 10 shillings each. If you like I will sent you a few pounds to bring you and your Mrs. to London. When we got it we had to walk along the road for a few miles. We durst not get on the rails in the town.

The professional thieves are so accustomed to their own words and phraseology that they cannot help using them, if engaged in a long conversation with an honest person or a stranger. Nothing pleases the habitual thieves better than to make the ignorant convicts from the rural districts stare and wonder by rattling off their cant and slang. The back slang of the costermongers is said to have been in use about eighteen years, and for the last few years the professional thieves have had the use of it. This back slang consists in spelling and pronouncing the words backwards; for instance, woman is pronounced "namow." They also alter a letter or two, and add something to the end of the words. These endings seem like the recollections of an uneducated person, who has heard French and Italian spoken. Here is an example of the way in which they sometimes write to one another in prison when they succeed in corrupting the warders:

Eenjary, Edesla; Oljau Hutbo. I iteri ease yew inesli ot hoo ingopetho attha is the yam indfi althaw indgo eritspir evesle all elware at esentpre. I alsha omecoo antha isitva hoo torromow, and ringbra omeso axma ithmewa, antha omeso nose, antha omeso uggersho. Ialsha ivitga toayeth screw ewe hatgawu iteri rofyou ewe hav unghimslow emaja, – Yours, Ned.

Being interpreted, this letter reads thus:

Leeds, January. John Bull, I write these few lines to you, hoping that this may find you in good spirits, as it leaves us all well at present. I shall come and visit you tomorrow, and bring you some rum, some tobacco, and some money. I shall give it to the officer we have got to rights for you. We have given him one pound.

What with this mongrel back slang and their own cant, the old thieves can talk for hours without the uninitiated being able to form the slightest idea of what it is all about. The thieves are very fond of their own proverbs and sayings. They have not many maxims, but they are in constant use. A garotter says, "The bigger the man the better the mark." "Flats graft for guns," *i.e.*, honest men work for thieves, "Honest people maintain thieves in prison, and when they are at large," and "Show a parson a shovel and he will begin to cry; Ask a thief to work, and he will feign to die."

Every professional thief is considered to belong to the branch of thieving in which he excels the most. And he is named after it. A wire, a flimper, a snyde pitcher, a magsman, or a cracksman, as the case may be. But while he generally keeps to his own line of business he by no means confines himself to it. An habitual thief knows the whole round of crime. Pickpockets and burglars are the steadiest to their own department.

All professional thieves are great travellers, especially the pickpockets, who, in some instances, work very hard indeed, being up for the earliest trains in the morning, and out for the latest at night. The first class thieves do not confine themselves to Britain. They work the Dover packets, and visit the Lakes of Killarney. They go on the Manchester Exchange, and sleep in the hotels of New York. They know the way to the Liverpool Docks, and "wire" in the streets of Paris. They generally go on the Continent in the spring, and remain there until the races and fairs are coming off in England. The London mobs go down to Manchester in December, there being a large number of commercial men about the town at that time. The Manchester men will go to London when they are outlawed; —the Liverpool mobs to Manchester; —the Birmingham mobs to Bristol and Wales. Scotch thieves go into the

North of England. Irish thieves come into England in the summer for the fairs and races. In the latter end of April and the beginning of May, the London mobs do the May meetings of Exeter Hall and other places, and then start for Wales and the Midland counties, as the fairs are coming on about that time. The pickpockets are always at work, travelling night or day, or both as it may suit them. The migration of thieves into Wales takes place from March up to May, the time of the fairs. Cardiff is the last place visited for Llandaff fair. The thieves are fond of royal progresses, and follow the Queen everywhere. After the races and fairs are over, the magsmen, or thieves' gamblers, go to different towns, and make up mobs for the winter.

The formation of the mobs or gangs can soon be explained. In the case of boys, they are thrown together by accidental circumstances, or from a casual acquaintance, or live near to each other, or meet when coming out of prison together. They work with each other until broken up and scattered by sickness, imprisonment, death, change of residence, or their locality getting too hot for them. The adult mobs will number any thing from four to twenty. They get to know each other in prison, on public works, on the convict ship and foreign stations, or by passing their leisure hours in the public-houses. A gang will include all sort of thieves. They will work one town until the police press them too closely, and they, becoming too notorious, are obliged to make themselves scarce; or perhaps the gang will break up by some going to one town and some to another. Occasionally the whole gang will move about from town to town, and keep together for a long time. When they go to races and fairs they settle beforehand what part each shall take, and where their meeting places shall be. They will work with no strangers. They must be introduced by some one known to both. They will not work with occasional thieves if they can help it; or if they do they will put the heaviest and dirtiest work upon them. The gangs are broken up in a variety of ways. Sometimes they betray one another to the police and so get dispersed. Sometimes they quarrel about the spoil. "What do you mean?" said I once to a thief, as he talked of these quarrels. "Why," said he, "it is shameful work; they play Ananias and Sapphira, and whip the Apostles." "What do you mean by that?" I replied." "Keeping back part of the price, sir." Wandering like shoals of fish, responsible to nobody, scattering and changing by a thousand accidental circumstances, we can learn little of these gangs. In their wanderings they fall in with other shoals, and some get lost, and some are famished to death, and some are poached, and some get hooked. I suppose I must say a word or two about the *black-faced mobs*. They are chiefly navvies and second-class thieves who blacken their faces. First-class thieves never do it except occasionally when it is a "put-up job" and there is a heavy stake of money, jewellery, or plate. In these cases they use crapes, arm themselves, and will resort to violence, though not with intent to murder. When the different mobs are moving about in large towns they occasionally meet, and cross each other's path, when the salutation is as follows: "Are you out on speculation? Where are you going?" The answer: "We are going a flimping, cracking, tooling, wireing, and away we go." This means they are ready for anything that turns up. Each gang has its *esprit de corps*. There is a great deal of rivalry among them, and they are envious and jealous of one another. All their ambition is focused on which among them can do the most profitable, the quickest, the cleverest, and the most daring thing. A thief once said to me, "Sir, they would send out advertisements challenging one another, if they durst. They would be as fond of puffing and running one another down as the shopkeepers are."

The first-class thieves, or "tip toppers," never enter the thieves' quarter if they can help it; they take furnished apartments in some quiet and respectable part of the town. Towards their neighbours they are fair-spoken, civil, honest gentlemen, and go on quietly and steadily until they change their residence, quarrel with their wives, or are disturbed by the police. These first-class thieves always "go in" for very high stakes, and will have nothing to do with petty affairs. They will not associate with thieves of the second or third order. A first-class thief will wear no stolen clothes. He is naturally clever, has received most of his education in prison, and rises to be A-1 by his talents, moderation, and polish. He does his work quietly and neatly, and leaves no more traces of his handiwork behind him than he can possibly help. He knows all the detectives, but he takes care that they don't know him. He will have nothing to do with goods, clothes, and provisions. Plate, jewellery, cash, or bank-notes alone tempt him. He is clever enough to pick a pocket without the assistance of either front or back stalls. He can take a pocket-book from the inside of your waistcoat as quick as lightening, and get a long way out of danger before the treasure is missed. He delights "to go on change," where his respectable appearance and quiet bearing enable him to pass without suspicion. He goes to the bank, takes a genuine 10 pound Bank of England note, and asks for change, and puts his name on the back in a business-like manner; but he contrives to rob somebody by means of the insight into people's purses which he obtains while he stands carelessly changing his note, and seeming to be looking at nobody. The first-class thief knows a good bottle of wine, and a good hotel; if he can help it he will drink no inferior stuff, and stay at no inferior place. He likes to keep a few diamonds by him as a resource in extremity. If your house has been robbed, you can easily tell whether a first-class thief has been there. He will not break and tear down everything that comes to his hands. He will unlock everything he can, but if a lock is refractory and awkward, he will only then break it open. He will not stay eating and drinking in the house he has burglariously entered, though he will have pleasure in cracking a bottle of good wine, and drinking the health of his sleeping host and the family up-stairs. But he goes for plunder, the filthy lucre of his nefarious art, and not for eating and drinking. He does that after the booty has gone to the "fence," and he is safe-housed in his quarters. There, before a good blazing fire, and a tankard of good ale, he will talk fast enough about the exploit, as a sportsman does about his first of September, or the soldier about the last battle, or a Member of the House of Commons in the smoking-room, quizzing the last debate.

When a first-class thief is disabled, either by accident, bad health, or nervousness, brought on by habitual drunkenness, he can still be of use to the thieves. He is the go-between for those who escape from a robbery, and those who are apprehended in consequence of it. He will communicate between the one and the other, see the lawyer, get ready for the trial, and look up the "snyde witnesses." He can also attend the different criminal courts, and carry and fetch any information that may be of use.

Close to the first-class thieves, and yet not of them, is another class of men. Broken-down respectable people, artists and tradesmen, lawyers' clerks, and commercial clerks, who, although they can never thoroughly learn the art of thieving, nevertheless get among the thieves, and are of great use to them. This class of men make very good "stalls." They have no thieves' ways or manner about them, and therefore people are off their guard. They are good assistants at forging, drawing up false scrip and sham commercial bills; they are equally useful in passing cheques, bills, and bankers' drafts.

The professional thieves have a miserable time of it. They spend half their time in prison, and always reckon on doing so. They are never sure of safety for an hour altogether. The very next policeman they meet may apprehend them, out of that apprehension there may grow for them ten or fifteen years of penal servitude. In 1860, 1,030 males, and 618 female thieves, had been five times previous in prison. Seven times, and above five – 1,122 males, and 857 females. Ten times, and above seven – 622 males, and 584 females. Above ten times – 825 males, and 2,584 females. This last item shows an enormous number of females. It is partly, if not chiefly, made up of cases of drunkenness and abuse of the police. But these statistics are poor guides for ascertaining the number of times a professional thief has been in prison. He wanders all of the country, and gets many sentences, of which nothing ever is known to the police, so as to enable them to bring all his convictions home to him. A professional thief of any standing has been in all the leading English prisons. He can tell the character of the chaplain and officers, recite the prison rules, knows all about the diet, and many other things, which must not be recorded here.

The criminal knowledge of habitual thieves is astounding. They know something of every notorious culprit, every important trial or robbery for the last five-and-twenty-years. So far as their own practices are concerned, they are well informed on criminal law; but that avails little to mitigate the ills of a life which, from its nature, must be very much made up of hardship and misery. Thieving is always a losing game. The money they get never does them any good; it never stays with them. It all goes in gambling, debauchery, and law expenses. They betray and are betrayed. All men shun them, and if many could have their way they would make short work of the professional thieves by having them all shot. They are miserable and accursed in their relation to society, and they are miserable and accursed in themselves. Few ever reform, or ever mean to do so. We have already explained why they persevere in a course that must and does lead to destruction. For the most part they can do nothing else, they have learned no trade, except of course, that of thieving. In 1860 there were no fewer than 18,949 persons committed to prison who described themselves as having no occupation. Even if people would employ them, they are too idle, nor could they get money by honest means fast enough to satisfy their wants. Nearly all habitual thieves, male and female, die of consumption, and under or about thirty-five years of age. Drink, debauchery, irregular hours, the sudden transitions from luxuries to a low prison diet – these things soon kill them off. The largest decrease in the number of persons committed to prison is among those who are between thirty and forty years of age. In 1860 there were in prison 19,555 persons who were from thirty to forty years old; but there were only 11,448 persons in prison who were from forty to fifty years old, showing a decrease of 7,807. Again, in 1860 there were 33,048 persons in prison who were from twenty-one to thirty years of age. But in that same year of 1860, there were only 2,685 persons in prison above sixty years of age, showing a falling-off between the ages of twenty-one and sixty of no less than 30,363. What has become of all these people, and how is this great falling-off to be accounted for? In a few instances reformation sets in, and the offenders break the laws no more – in the majority of others, death doubtless comes according to the course of nature.

Alas, it is hoped, dear reader, that you now see the wisdom and profit of supplementing our knowledge of criminals garnered from official reports by going about them and learning first hand about the nature of their lives and activities.

POVERTY,
DESTITUTION,
AND
ECONOMIC
PERTURBATIONS

THE RELATION OF ECONOMIC CONDITIONS TO THE CAUSES OF CRIME

By

CARROLL D. WRIGHT

ANNALS OF THE AMERICAN ACADEMY OF POLITICAL AND SOCIAL SCIENCE

VOL. 3 (MARCH 1893) PP. 764-784

The criminologist, in his search for the causes of crime, cannot, in the nature of things, accept any blanket theory. The fall of man and the doctrine of total depravity may satisfy his theological views as to the origin of evil, but they cannot satisfy his sociological views. He must, as a criminologist, be able to develop specific causes more or less in harmony with his theology. He cannot be a criminologist without being scientific. He must study anthropology –the biology of the human race – and through this study he will classify, scientifically, the causes of crime. His theology will teach him the results of a criminal career, and these results will be in accordance with his theological views; but his scientific classification must be based upon his scientific researches. He will find that, to some extent, men are criminals through their psycho-physiological organization, and such a criminal commits crime without regard to his environment. Prosperity, or the lack of prosperity, good or bad training, under all conditions, a man with an abnormal psycho-physiological organization of a certain type not only commits crime, but defends it.

Another type of man, even with a normal psycho-physiological organization, commits crime through the influence of environment, or of an uneducated and an untrained conscience, or of a conscience naturally dull. The recent researches into the relation of the formation of the brain in certain parts to criminal tendencies are among the most valuable studies of scientific men; yet should their researches prove beyond doubt that certain brain formations lead directly to criminal courses, such demonstration could not fully account for all criminal lives, in all degrees. If they did, there would be no use of wasting time over the discussion of the influence of heredity, environment, economic conditions, or of any of the other causes which, related or unrelated, lead men to criminal courses. Whatever cause the scientific criminologist may find and even establish, it is true, and must always be true, that a weak conscience will be lulled by necessity or desire to the point of criminal action, and that conditions surrounding a man will at times stimulate such action. Personally, I am very much in sympathy with the views of scientific criminologists, and with some of the views expressed by the celebrated Doctor Despine. I am rather out of sympathy with the idea that a criminal becomes such through the loss of moral attributes which he once possessed; with the idea that he started in life a comparatively good man, but that he has willfully and maliciously broken the laws of the State. I believe the criminal is an undeveloped man in all his elements, whether you think of him as a worker or as a moral and intellectual being. His faculties are all undeveloped, not only those which enable him to labor honestly and faithfully for the care and support of himself and his family, but also all his moral and intellectual faculties. He is not a fallen being: he is an undeveloped individual.

The reverse of this idea leads men to adopt many illogical conclusions, and also leads into considering all the convicts of a State as belonging to the same class. Notwithstanding these statements, I believe it is true that men even with fairly sound consciences can and do become habituated to the idea of crime through their necessities or their environment, and even degenerate from a reasonably good life to a bad one. Such conditions have much to do with the commission of crime.

So while the scientific view of crime attracts me more than any other, I am yet aware that the penologist must govern himself by the doctrine that men commit crime, or refrain from it, as they wish; that crime is the result of some craving, some want, some unsatisfied desire, and that the basic action or motive of crime is to be found in some physical or mental condition. Whether it suits our views or not, therefore, we are obliged to consider the criminal as acting under free will, and while we need not lose sight of all the scientific conditions which are alleged as primarily necessary to constitute criminal action, we must deal with the criminal as a free, moral agent; as one committing his act to satisfy his want or desire, which he feels he is unable to satisfy through the ordinary or legitimate conditions. Hence the discussion of economic conditions in their relation to the causes of crime becomes legitimate.

All great social questions, on careful analysis, resolve themselves, in a more or less degree, into some phase of what we call the labor question, and certainly the causes of crime, in a sociological sense, cannot be studied without considering the status of man in the prevailing industrial order, for among all the causes for criminal action, or for the existence of the criminal class, we find that economic conditions contribute in some degree to their existence. This, however, is only a phase of criminology. It is the phase which has been given me as a subject for discussion.

The world has seen three great labor systems – labor under slavery, labor under the feudal system, and labor under the wage or the prevailing system. Crime was not so fully recognized under the slave and the feudal systems as it has been under the modern system of labor. Ownership came naturally through conquest. Possession was the clear title to property. Conflict and conquest were the prime causes of private ownership. Hence, under slavery, crime assumed a different relationship to the body-politic than it assumes under the modern system, where the right of free contract prevails. The feudal system was only an advanced phase of slavery, and so intermingled were the conditions that it is sometimes difficult to clearly define the life of the individual man under the two. These conditions existed prior to the general adoption of the wage system, and in the study of the relation of labor conditions to criminal conditions the earlier systems of labor become interesting. The peasants under the feudal system had no hope, for they had no land and no chance of bettering their condition. With no comforts or even necessaries of existence, life was to them a perpetual hardship. These conditions continued in many countries, the result usually being seen in vast herds of thieves, robbers, and vagrants that desolated the land. Even in the time of Henry VIII., and during the course of his reign of thirty-eight years, no fewer than seventy-two thousand persons were executed for crime. History has not begun to tell the story of the sufferings of labor prior to the advent of the modern industrial system, or of the necessities which drove men into criminal lives. All were in misery, with the exception of the few who constituted the families of the feudal lords. All the conditions surrounding labor were abject. Pauperism, as we understand it, was unknown, to be sure, because all were paupers. Pauperism, therefore, did not attract legislation, and crime, the offspring of pauperism and of idleness, was brutally treated; and these conditions, betokening an unsound social condition, existed until progress made pauperism and crime as well, the disgrace of a nation, and it was then that pauperism began to be recognized as a condition which might be relieved through legislation. Of course, intellectual growth began to have some influence. This is illustrated by one of the statutes of England passed against laborers during the worst days of her feudal labor, upon the complaint of lords and commons, and men of the Holy Church, who in their complaint state that "they do come there in great routs and agree by confederacy that every one shall aid every other to resist their lords with strong hands. And so they seemed, partly by law and partly by force, to resist all claims due of their bodies and of them as land-tenants." These efforts, marking the first results of intelligence among the laborers, constituted probably the first strikes for industrial progress in history. They were contemporaneous with those great upheavals on the continent which were traced up through the Anabaptist revolt and along up to the revolution of '89, when the French nation sought to rid itself of the lingering burdens of feudalism; but it was through all these efforts in the great countries of Western Europe that the distinguishing features between prosperity and poverty became prominent. Carry industry to a country not given to mechanical production or to any systematic form of labor, employ three-fourths of its inhabitants, give them a taste of education, of civilization, make them feel the power of moral forces even to a slight degree, and the misery of the other fourth can be gauged by the progress of the three-fourths, and a class of paupers and resultant criminals will be observed.

We have in our own day a most emphatic illustration of this in the emancipation of slaves in this country. Under the old system the Negro slave was physically comfortable, as a rule. He was cared for, he was nursed in sickness, fed and clothed, and in old age his physical comforts were continued. He had no responsibility, and, indeed, exercised no skill beyond what was taught him. To eat, to work, and to sleep were all that was expected of him; and, unless he had a cruel master, he lived the life that belongs to the animal. Since his emancipation and his endowment with citizenship he has been obliged to support himself and his family, and to contend with all obstacles belonging to a person in the state of freedom. Under the system of villeinage in the old country it could not be said that there were any general poor, for the master and the lord of the manor took care of the laborers their whole lives; and in our Southern towns, during slavery, this was true, so that in the South there were few, if any, poorhouses, and few, if any, inmates of penal institutions. The South to-day knows what pauperism is, as England learned when the system of villeinage departed. Southern prisons have become active, and all that belongs to the defective, the dependent, and the delinquent classes has come to be familiar to the South.

To the industrial system, therefore, which was changed by the Civil War, the presence of some features of crime in the Southern States must be traced. The Civil War was, indeed, a labor war, whether it was instituted as such or not. The slave of the South could not compete with the skilled artisan of the North, and the conditions in the former had to give way to the conditions in the latter section of the country. The progress of the wage system, the increasing intelligence of the men who work under it will, as time advances, correct these crude conditions. They do not cause them: they only bring them into prominence. But so far as the modern industrial order superinduces idleness or unemployment, in so far it must be considered as having a direct relation to the causes of crime. I believe, however, that whatever tendency in this direction exists under the modern industrial order is of far less degree, not only in extent, but in severity, than the conditions which were superinduced by the industrial order which preceded it. In a treatise written by Richard Hakluyt, of England, in 1584, on the religious, political, and commercial advantages to be derived by England from the attempted colonization of America, entitled _A Discourse on Westerne Plantinge_, recently discovered, and published for the first time in 1877, by the Maine Historical Society, the familiar question of how to employ the unemployed was discussed by the author, and in terms which remind one forcibly of the oft-repeated fears and the chimerical schemes of reformers of the present time.

In urging upon his government the undertaking of voyages, Hakluyt uses this language (the spelling being modernized), after referring to the prosperity of Spain and Portugal: "But we, for all the statutes that hitherto can be devised, and the sharp execution of the same in punishing idle and lazy persons for want of sufficient occasion of honest employment, cannot deliver our commonwealth from multitudes of loiters (tramps we call them), and idle vagabonds. Truth it is, that through our long peace and seldom sickness, two singular blessings of Almighty God, we are grown more populous than ever heretofore; so that now there are of every art and science so many that they can hardly live one by another; nay, rather, they are ready to eat up one another; yea, many thousands of idle persons are within this realm, which, having no way to be set on work, be either mutinous and seek alteration in the State, or, at least, very burdensome to the commonwealth, and often fall to pilfering and thieving and other lewdness, whereby all the prisons of the land are daily pestered and stuffed full of them, where either they pitifully pine away, or else at length are miserably hanged, even twenty at a clap out of some one jail. Whereas, if this voyage were put in execution, these petty thieves might be condemned for certain years in the western parts." And then follows a glowing picture of results, which the writer concludes as follows: "There need not one poor creature to steal, to starve, or to beg, as they do."

The quotation refers to a time only a quarter of a century prior to the permanent settlements on our coast, while in 1629 John Winthrop, the first Governor of Massachusetts, before he left the old home, stated, among others, these reasons for leading emigrants out of the overburdened England, which Hakluyt described:

"This land grows weary of her inhabitants, so as man, who is the most precious of all creatures, is here more vile and base than the earth we tread upon, and of less price among us than a horse or a sheep. Many of our people perish for want of sustenance and employment; many others live miserably and not to the honor of so bountiful a housekeeper as the Lord of heaven and earth is, through the scarcity of the fruits of the earth. All of our towns complain of the burden of poor people, and strive by all means to rid any such as they have, and to keep off such as would come to them. I must tell you that our dear mother finds her family so overcharged as she hath been forced to deny harbor to her own children, – witness the statutes against cottages and inmates. And thus it is come to pass that children, servants, and neighbors, especially if they be poor, are counted the greatest burthens, which, if things were right, would be the chiefest earthly blessings."

These conditions of labor, as I have already stated, were all attended with a great volume of crime, and it was crime, to a large extent, which grew out of individual physical wants. Guizot has said that labor is a most efficient guarantee against the revolutionary disposition of the poorer classes. He might have added that labor, properly remunerated, is an effective guarantee against the commission of crime. Certainly hunger leads to more crime of a petty nature, perhaps, than any other one cause.

In the study of economic conditions, and whatever bearing they may have upon crime, I can do no better than to repeat, as a general idea, a statement made some years ago by Mr. Ira Steward, of Massachusetts, one of the leading labor reformers in that State in his day. He said: "Starting in the labor problem from whatever point we may, we reach, as the ultimate cause of our industrial, social, moral, and material difficulties, the terrible fact of poverty. By poverty we mean something more than pauperism. The latter is a condition of entire dependence upon charity, while the former is a condition of want, of lack, of being without, though not necessarily a condition of complete dependence."

It is in this view that the proper understanding of the subject given me, in its comprehensiveness and the development of the principles which underlie it, means the consideration of the abolition of pauperism and the eradication of crime; and the definitions given by Mr. Steward carry with them all the elements of those great special inquiries embodied in the very existence of our vast charitable, penal, and reformatory institutions, "How shall poverty be abolished, and crime be eradicated?" The discussion is a very old one, and neither modern professional labor reformers, nor philanthropists, nor criminologists, nor penologists have any patents upon the theme. The progress of the world may be read as well by statutes in the humanity of law, in the existence of prisons, in the establishment of charitable institutions, and by the economic conditions which surround labor, as by written history; for, as the condition of labor rises, pauperism and crime must fall in the general scale.

To say that pauperism, and crime as an attendant evil, follow the unemployed more mercilessly than the employed, would be to make a statement too simple in its nature to invite serious consideration. Yet the history and the statistics of labor and the conclusions resulting from their study in their relation to pauperism and crime present most interesting and valuable features. Criminal conditions, the evils we are considering, have always existed, no matter what the social or legal status of men; under the most favorable as well as under the most unfavorable conditions; under liberal and under despotic government; in barbarous and in enlightened lands; with heathenism and with Christianity; under a variety of commercial systems: and yet they are, in a philosophic sense, a rebuke to a people living under constitutional liberty.

Employment of the unemployed will not crush pauperism and crime, even if every able-bodied man in the country could be furnished with work tomorrow. Universal education will not. The realization of the highest hopes of the temperance and labor reformers will not. The general adoption of the Christian religion will not. But all these grand and divine agencies working together will reduce them to a minimum, and make that community which tolerates them indictable at the bar of public opinion, the most powerful tribunal known. Physical agencies, without all the higher elements, can do but little. The early history of this country and the history of all countries where civilization has made any headway teach this truth.

The proposition that pauperism and crime are less frequent in cultured communities will not, I suppose, be debated. It is true that the intelligent, skilled laborer is rarely found either in a penal or charitable institution; nor is the person who has the elementary education sufficient to enable him to read, write, and make his own calculations so liable to become a charge as the one who has not these qualifications. I am, of course, aware that the full accuracy of these statements is oftentimes questioned; yet it is statistically true that enough of knowledge to be of value in increasing the amount and quality of work done, to give character, to some extent at least, to a person's tastes and aspirations, is a better safeguard against the inroads of crime than any code of criminal laws. I must, of course, consider this point as a fact, and shall not weary you with the oft-repeated arguments and the usual array of figures used to convince legislators that it is wise economy to foster our educational institutions. This being conceded as to intellectual or mental acquirements, including elementary book-learning, how does the fact affect the matter under consideration? Simply that the kind of labor which requires the most skill on the part of the workman to perform insures him most perfectly against want and crime, as a rule.

This statement is fortified by such statistics as are available. Of 4,340 convicts, at one time, in the State of Massachusetts, 2,991, or 68 per cent, were returned having no occupation. The adult convicts numbered at that time 3,971. Of these 464 were illiterate; and the warden of the State Prison, for the year in question, stated that of 220 men sentenced during that year, 147 were without a trade or any regular means of earning a living. In Pennsylvania, during a recent year, nearly 88 per cent of the penitentiary convicts had never been apprenticed to any trade or occupation; and this was also true of 68 1/2 per cent of the convicts sentenced to county jails and workhouses in the same State during the same year. In Mr. Frederick H. Wines' recent report on homicide in the United States, in 1890, it is shown that of 6,958 men, 5,175, or more than 74 per cent of the whole, were said to have no trade. The full statistics relating to convicts in the United States, when Mr. Wines makes his full report, will, I have no doubt, corroborate these statements.

These statistics represent the conditions in other latitudes, and show what is true everywhere, that it cannot be claimed that any very desirable working material can be found among convicts. If we except the large number that are unable to work, we shall by no means find workers remaining. We shall find some with trades, able and ready to work, but the greater number unpossessed of a self-supporting occupation, and many unwilling to work. I believe that the unfitness for productive labor, whether it springs from lack of a trade or occupation, or from personal antipathy to work, is a great and predisposing cause of both pauperism and crime. Furthermore, it is true, so far as the statistics which I have been able to consult demonstrate, that during periods of industrial depressions crime of almost all grades is increased in volume. The difficulty of demonstrating this feature of my subject to any full extent lies in the fact that our criminal statistics are given for periods, and not year by year. Could we have annual statements of the convictions in all our States, so that such statements could be consulted relative to economic conditions, I feel sure that we should find a co-ordination of results that would startle us all. We should find that the lines of crime rise and fall as the prosperity of the country falls and rises.

The law of political economy comprehending supply and demand is brought into prominence in this thought. It is an economic principle, always stated by all writers on political economy, that the highest cost makes the price. This is true only so long as demand is superior to supply. If the supply is superior to the demand, then the lowest cost makes the price in the market, and it is this condition that brings about what is popularly called "over-production," resulting in stagnation of trade and competition for work. This competition for work throws out the weaker elements in the industrial system, drives them to necessity, increases the want, and decreases the means of its satisfaction. Larceny, burglary, and all the forms of theft come into play, and the volume of crime increases. It is this principle, too, that influences the working man in his antagonism to the employment of convicts upon productive labor.

Political economists and all writers upon antagonistic commercial systems are fond of saying that if labor cannot be profitably employed at one trade or in one locality it should seek another. This was the favorite remedy offered by a certain class of political economists during all the great industrial depressions which existed in England during the first half of this century. Depression was to be relieved by a mobilization of labor. Now labor is not so mobile as these writers would have us believe. Great bodies of men employed in Lancashire in the cotton factories cannot, when sudden depressions come upon the industries, mobilize themselves so as to take up work in some other locality in England. The shutting down of the mines in Pennsylvania, or the reduction of work therein, throws large bodies of men out of employment, and it is utterly and physically impossible for those bodies of men to be mobilized or for them to take up other callings in life so as to keep the wolf from the door. These conditions make tramps and able-bodied beggars. Crime is the result, and the criminal statistics swell into columns that make us believe that our social fabric is on the verge of ruin. Hungry stomachs, again, at such times, are at the base of the enlarged figures. Ignorance of work, the lack of some technical training prevents the mobilization of labor and compels men with a weak conscience to commit crime.

Doctor Schaffle, in his excellent work on the *Impossibility of Social Democracy*, says: "We cannot do enough in the endeavor to abate and avoid the misery of these trade stoppages: it hangs like the sword of Damocles over the heads of non-propertied laborers; it embitters the existence of every one of them who reflects and who has the care and nurture of a family to provide for."

All idleness, whether induced by economic conditions, or by a lack of inclination to work, or by a lack of knowledge of how to work, leads directly to crime – not, of course, in all cases, but such conditions aggravate and irritate and drive men to criminal courses. The idle man's brain is, indeed, the devil's own workshop. Political economy, which has dealt so largely with the acquisition of wealth, must, sooner or later, deal with other features of wealth, and teach the world what conditions will largely relieve society of crime or largely lead to a reduction of its volume, through teaching the power of moral forces in the adjustment of industrial forces. My chief quarrel with political economy, which, to my mind, is one of the grandest departures of human knowledge, lies in this very thought, that it does not recognize as one of its elements the power of moral forces in society which really make or mar healthy commercial conditions.

Under the new political economy, sanitary conditions are shown to be a necessity to true economic conditions. The material prosperity of a community depends much upon the health of its workers, and the health of workers depends in a very large degree upon sanitary surroundings. It is that the physical condition of the people may be improved by every means, that social economy deals with the subject of sewerage, tenement houses, light, and ventilation; and in this respect social science teaches valuable lessons to political science, for the health of the workers of a community is essential to their material prosperity, and the health of a community has much to do with the volume of crime.

In this connection I cannot refrain form weaving in a few thoughts from W. R. Greg, an English writer, with some of my own. Dwelling upon the physical and moral development of the race as essential to prosperity, it may be asked – What may we not rationally hope for when the condition of the masses shall receive that concentrated and urgent attention which has hitherto been directed to furthering the interest of more favored ranks? What, when charity, which for centuries has been doing mischief, shall begin to do good? What, when the countless pulpits, that so far back as history can reach, have been preaching Catholicism, or Anglicanism, Presbyterianism, or Calvinism, or other isms, shall set to work to preach Christianity at last? Do we ever even approach to a due estimate of the degree in which every stronghold of vice or folly overthrown, exposes, weakens, and undermines every other? Of the extent to which every improvement, social, moral, or material, makes every other easier? Of the countless ways in which physical reform reacts on intellectual and ethical progress and the prosperity of our industries? Under the constant teaching of a moral philosophy which shall embrace the political economy of the labor question, what a transformation—almost a transfiguration—will spread over the condition of civilized communities, when, by a few generations, during which hygienic science and sense shall have been in the ascendant, the restored health of mankind shall have corrected the morbid exaggerations of our appetites; when, by insisting upon the healthy environment of our toiling masses, the more questionable instincts and passions, which, under such rule as I have indicated, shall have been less and less exercised and stimulated for centuries perhaps, shall have faded into comparative quiescence, and have come under the control of the will; when, from the expulsion of vitiated air, disordered constitutions, whether diseased, criminal, or defective, which now spread and propagate so much mischief, and incur so much useless expense to taxpayers, shall have been largely eliminated; when sounder systems of educating the young shall have prevented the too early awakening of natural desires; when more rational, higher, and soberer notions of what is needful and desirable in social life, a wiser simplicity in living, and a more thorough conformity to moral law shall have rendered the legitimate gratification of our appetites more easy and beneficial, and when that which is needed for a happy home shall have become attainable by frugality, sobriety and toil! These conditions, so desirable to be reached, are not impossible ones, and are not to be reached by revolutionary schemes of any party or sect, but by the gradual adoption of sanitary laws in the dwellings and homes of the laboring people; and the new school will teach that the secondary, and often primary, causes and encouragements of intemperance are bad air and unwholesome food, which create a craving for drink; bad company, which tempts it; undue facilities, which conduce to it; squalid homes, which drive men forth for cheerfulness; and the want of other comfortable places of resort, which leaves no refuge but the publican's parlor or den. And if, on the other hand, we find that the consequences are poverty, squalid homes, brutality, crime, and the transmission and perpetuation of vitiated constitutions, who can say they cannot be prevented by the sound administration of sanitary laws, which shall prohibit the existence of bad air, of unventilated dwellings, the undue multiplication and constant accessibility of gin and beer shops, and the poisoning of wholesome food and drink?

You cannot discuss the labor question from either the ethical or economical side without consideration of the temperance question; and from the results of such consideration it is perfectly clear to my own mind that the solution of the temperance question is largely in the control of the employers of labor. The interests of capital as well as of labor, the interests of religion itself, demand a sober and industrious community; and, when the employers of labor shall demand abstinence from alcoholic drinks as a qualification for employment, the ugly problem, so far as the working masses are concerned, will be far on the way to settlement. What will bring the employers to the same issue is perhaps a knottier problem. The presence of crime works a direct injury upon the welfare of the workingman in many ways. It costs him more to live because of it; it disturbs his sense of justice because the convict works at the same occupation which furnishes his support; but, while the labor reformer cries for the abolition of convict labor, the political economy of the labor question cries for the reduction of the number of criminals by the prevention of crime as the surest and most permanent remedy for whatever evils may grow out of the practice of employing convicts in productive labor. We make criminals now; for three-fourths of the crime committed is by young men who are temporarily led astray, and the fact that fifty per cent of all the convicts in the State prisons of the United States are under twenty-six years of age only confirms the estimate. These accidental criminals we make into positive convicts, to be fed upon the production of men outside. We shall learn better methods in the future civil state, in which wise and effective legislation, backed by adequate administration resulting from a sound public sentiment, which will not hesitate to punish when necessary with that punishment which is most dreaded by the offender, shall have made all violation of law, all habitual crime, obviously, inevitably and instantly a losing game, and when the distribution of wealth, and its use, shall receive both from the statesman and the economist the same sedulous attention which is now concentrated exclusively upon its acquisition.

It is perfectly true that unsanitary conditions, and all conditions that work a deterioration in the health of people, lead to uneconomic conditions. Bad air, bad housing, bad drainage, lead to intemperance and want. It requires no argument to show that these are precursors of crime. Anything that brings about a higher rate of mortality among the children of the poor leads to crime, and is perfectly deducible from facts that are known that any occupation which insures a high rate of mortality among the children of its participants tends to conditions most favorable to the prevalence of pauperism and crime.

The displacement of labor through the application of improved machinery temporarily, and to the individual, produces a condition of want which may or may not be remedied by the increased labor demanded through invention. Society can be easily answered by stating the benefits which come to it through inventive genius, but it is a poor answer to the man who finds the means of supporting his family taken from him. But with the progress of invention and the consequent elevation of labor both pauperism and crime, so far as society is concerned, have correspondingly decreased. This is true in more senses than one. The age of invention, or periods given to the development and practical adaptation of natural laws, raises all peoples to a higher intellectual level, to a more comprehensive understanding of the world's march of progress.

But the question of the removal of poverty and the suppression of crime is not wholly with the workingman; the employer has as much to learn as he, and he is to be holden to equal, if not greater, responsibility. Ignorant labor comprehends ignorant employer. Insomuch as the profits of labor are equitably shared with labor, insomuch is poverty lessened, and, insomuch as poverty is lessened, insomuch is crime decreased. The employer should always remember that if conditions become ameliorated, if life becomes less of a struggle, if leisure be obtained, civilization, as a general rule, advances in the scale. If these conditions be reversed, if the struggle for existence tends to occupy the whole attention of each man, civilization disappears in a measure, communities become dangerous and the people seek a revolutionary change, hoping by chance to secure what was not possible by honest labor.

In a State in which labor had all its rights there would be, of course, little pauperism and little crime. On the other hand, the undue subjection of the laboring man must tend to make paupers and criminals, and entail a financial burden upon wealth which it would have been easier to prevent than to endure; and this prevention must come in a large degree through educated labor.

Do not understand me as desiring to give the impression that I believe crime to be a necessary accompaniment of our industrial system. I have labored in other places and at other times to prove the reverse, and I believe the reverse to be true. Our sober, industrious working men and women are as free from vicious and criminal courses as any other class. What I am contending for, relates entirely to conditions affecting the few. The great volume of crime is found outside the real ranks of industry.

The modern system of industry has reduced the periods of depression from the long reaches extending over half a century under older systems. These periods have been reduced to decades and half decades of years. The time will come when periods of depression will occur only for the few months of a single year, and when this time comes the columns of the statistics of crime will show a receding quantity. Infinitely superior as the modern system is over that which has passed, the iron law of wages, when enforced with an iron hand, keeps men in the lowest walks of life, often on the verge of starvation. As intelligence increases and is more generally diffused, the individual man wants more, has higher aspirations for himself and his family; but, under the iron law of wages, at times, all these desires and aspirations are hard to satisfy. The modern system produces mental friction; a competition of mind has taken the place, in a large measure, of mere muscular competition, and the laggard in the industrial race may lose his mind or his conscience, in the latter case causing him to develop into the criminal. The economic condition or environment of this particular man leads him inevitably to crime. But system gives way to system, and the present industrial order will be suspended by one vastly superior to it. As the establishment of the wage system reduced crime and its attendant evils, so that which is to come will still further benefit the human race ethically and economically.

Does some one inquire—Can it be possible that more civilization means more crime? Yes, and no. For a time under improved civilization, under improved mechanical methods, and under the march of invention, competition, as I have said, is mental to a larger degree than under the simpler methods and cruder civilization. The residuum of society is more easily observed and more thoroughly claims the attention of philanthropists and of legislators; but to say that more civilization means more poverty and more crime is a reversal of truth in every sense. I believe that with elevated civilization there come conditions of labor which will largely relieve society of crime, or, at all events, largely reduce its volume. This must come through a more just and a more equitable distribution of the profits of production. It has always proved true, and it always will prove true, that wherever there is a sincere desire to secure a just and equitable distribution of the rewards of production, or even to make headway in some measure, fruits, rich and abundant, have been the result. The experience of the Briggs brothers in their attempts at profit-sharing, converted a turbulent and intemperate community, given to theft and rioting, into a sober and orderly body of people. The experience of Robert Owen, at New Lanark, is the record of one of the most prominent experiments in the Old World for the bettering of industrial communities. This experiment was made by Owen before he became imbued with socialism. At the period of his Lanark experience (1819), Owen gained respect and renown in distant lands, was sought by the great, was consulted by governments, and counted among his patrons princes of the blood in England, and more than one crowned head in Europe. The main cause of Owen's success began with the practical improvement of the working-people under his superintendence as manager, and afterward as owner of the cotton mills in New Lanark. He found himself surrounded by squalor, poverty, intemperance, and crime. He determined to change the whole condition of affairs. He erected healthy dwellings with adjacent gardens, and let them at cost price to the people. He adopted measures to put down drunkenness and to encourage the savings of the people. The employees became attached to their employer, took a personal interest in the success of the business, labored ably and conscientiously, and so made the mills of New Lanark, in Scotland, a great financial success. He turned a community given much to law-breaking into one happy as a law-abiding people.

The experience of the Cheney brothers at South Manchester, Connecticut, of the Fairbanks Company in Vermont, of hundreds of others who have recognized the great fact of the Decalogue, testifies to the soundness of the thought that with improved conditions which result in a more just economic environment, crime will be reduced.

All these considerations lead us to weigh well the practices which should be resorted to. Trade instruction, technical education, manual training—all these are efficient elements in the reduction of crime, because they all help to better and truer economic conditions. I think, from what I have said, the elements of solution are clearly discernible. Justice to labor, equitable distribution of profits under some system which I feel sure will supersede the present, and without resorting to socialism, instruction in trades by which a man can earn his living outside a penal institution, the practical application of the great moral law in all business relations—all these elements, with the more enlightened treatment of the criminal when apprehended, will lead to a reduction in the volume of crime, but not to the millennium; for "human experience from time immemorial tells us that the earth neither was, nor is, nor ever will be, a heaven, nor yet a hell," but the endeavor of right-minded men and women, the endeavor of every government, should be to make it less a hell and more a heaven.

RELATION OF CRIME TO ECONOMICS

BY

SAMUEL G. SMITH

LEND A HAND

VOL. 17 (JUNE 1896) PP. 408-419

If three of the best prison chaplains of the United States were adrift in a open boat upon the high seas without food it would only be a question of time when these Christian gentlemen would cast lots as to which of them should be killed and eaten. If three of the best prison wardens in the United States were in the same situation, it is probable, but not certain, that they would neglect the formality of casting lots and the two stronger would sacrifice the weakest to their needs. This illustration would tend to show that the criminal instinct is latent in us all; and if I am right about the chaplains, they would represent a more orderly process as the outcome of a higher evolution, while the wardens would represent more perfectly the natural struggle of existence, but in both cases the result would be practically the same.

We may recognize that there is a remnant of saints and heroes who have reached a spiritual development that properly lifts them out of the domain of our investigations, but the average good citizen owes at least a large share of his good conduct to the inherited social advantages in which civilization has placed him. Remove the advantages, increase the stress, and the good man breaks.

In considering the phenomena of crime, I wish also distinctly to dismiss from this study the congenital criminal. If Lombroso and his school have discovered and have delineated a criminal type, there seems to be no question but that the criminal anthropologist has but a very small section of the criminal community as the material for his science. It is probable that 95 per cent of all crime is preventable, or at least 95 per cent of all criminals are salvageable.

In recent studies the criminal type has received attention far out of proportion to its legitimate importance. Given a criminal type, the members of the class should of course be imprisoned for life and made sterile by confinement, so that their class would tend to perish. But in any event, anthropological studies have not reached such scientific exactness, that even their boldest and most pronounced exponents would dare to take the responsibility of incarceration after the scientific examination and measurements of their subjects instead of after judicial determination by the courts. In other words, the criminal type thus far remains to be discovered in the prisons and not outside of them; and if the criminal anthropologist should be let loose in society to pick out criminals before their crimes, with a full table of indications and a complete set of measurements, there is not telling who of us would escape. Relegating with a word, therefore, these voluminous and very important scientific investigations to their proper place, let us address ourselves to the more practical question of what can be done with the ninety and nine good sheep who have gone astray, rather than spend our strength upon the one black sheep who never deserved a fold. Nor do I propose any complete study of the causes of crime, but rather to call your attention to some considerations which may perhaps indicate that the economic relations of crime are the most pressing for study, the most vital in importance and the most promising in their practical application.

The criminal has been defined as the anti-social man. In order to discover his characteristics and to find out how to prevent him, or to cure him, some adequate conception of what the society is which he fights against, would seem to be essential.

It may be broadly stated that the social order consists of various permanent manifestations of the property instinct. The civilized man has multiplied his wants and has found out how to satisfy them. When his wants cannot be satisfied by his environment, he seeks to modify his civilization. This effort may result in further evolution, a revolution, or it may manifest itself in the slow processes of decay. There is here a key to the history of civilization. Should any one be disposed to question the validity of the propositions that the property idea is the most comprehensive social foundation, he must be referred to the history of development of primitive peoples. It will be found, that not alone has the organization of a home been perhaps the most influential incentive to industry, but it will be found that the marriage relation, fine and spiritual as we now regard it, is only a transformed property right. Religion, even in its high development among the Hebrews, found its strength in the thought that Jehovah would make his people rich.

And the doctrine of immortality is the most colossal property dream that has ever haunted the soul of man. Nor in these considerations do I mean at all to encourage a merely materialistic explanation of man or of his history, for the Infinite Life teaches us to read the everlasting Gospels by the aid of visible symbols, just as the child begins to read his Bible and his Shakespeare, when learning his letters from pictured blocks in his playroom.

The property instinct consists of two parts: First, a consciousness of wants; and second, an effort, more or less successful, to satisfy them. The greater the range of wants which are recognized by men and the more successfully they are satisfied, the higher the civilization.

As the entire social order may be said to be built upon the property instinct, so it may be broadly said that all crime resolves itself into crime against property, for, not only do crimes against property outbulk all others, but crimes against persons are very frequently merely incidental to crimes against property, and crimes against public order, such as indecency and intemperance, are simply degenerate manifestations of human wants. It would seem, therefore, that in efforts of education in the schools, and of reformation in the prisons, attention should be directed to enabling the human object to satisfy his wants by means of successful and remunerative labor, and to enthroning the will and the conscience so that the wants may be reduced to the limits of possible and lawful gratification. So much by the way of statement in brief of a general theory of the relation of crime to economics.

It is now time to consider some of the phenomena presented to us by the activity of criminals in their anti-social struggle, in order to see how far the propositions heretofore stated are maintained. The much discussed words "heredity" and "environment" may really be made to include all the conditions of the criminal, if, for the sake of convenience, the word heredity be used to include all the psychical and physical elements of the individual, and the word environment be used to include all his relations, both social and material. Where the environment, whatever it is, permits a productive and satisfying activity for the heredity, whatever it may be, the social bonds are strong.

It is necessary further, for the clear understanding of our problem, to remember the uses of the modern doctrine of subjective values, and to remember that wants are antecedent to satisfactions. The supply is created in answer to the demand.

The difficulty in securing adequate statistics for the study of crime problems has already been pointed out by various distinguished investigators; but, even if these statistics were carefully collected with the utmost intelligence and patience, the proper use of them in deducting conclusions would still be impossible without the most careful consideration of differences in government and in race. A scientific method is required to show what statistics really mean. The number of arrests does not indicate the prevalence of crime, but the vigilance of police administration. The number of convictions in proportion to the number of arrests by no means indicates the wisdom of police activity, but indicates the thoroughness of the courts and the popular recognition of the majesty of law. And there are other considerations equally important with those already stated. A high standard of living in a complex civilization places before the weak and unskilled temptations whose strength is utterly unknown to men and women living under conditions more simple and of a lower grade. But given a high standard of living and a complex civilization, and a great difficulty upon the part of the average man in reaching that standard of comfort, then the flood-gates of crime are thrown open.

There seems to be little doubt but that crime is increasing both in Europe and America. There has been a wide spread opinion that crime has really decreased in England, while it has been increasing in America; but whereas, in 1840 there were twenty thousand convictions for indictable crimes, in 1880 there were more than forty thousand of the same class of crimes. In other words, while the population increased 60 per cent, indictable crime increased 102 per cent. On the other hand, twenty-seven thousand crimes were dealt with by magistrates and not in Courts of Assize in 1880, owing to change in the statutes. Beside, there is the effect upon the statistics of the various industrial schools, which have received the juvenile offenders, and there are three times as many juvenile offenders as formerly. Moreover, the length of sentence decreased twenty-six per cent in the double decade between 1870 and 1890.

The relation of the administration of courts to crime is also a subject for special investigation. For example, murder in three great countries, Germany, England, and the United States, varies year by year in a similar proportion to the conditions of those who are accused of murder; that is to say, Germany convicts most of those who are tried, England next, and the United States is the most lax, and murders are most frequent in the United States in proportion to the population and less frequent in Germany.

Some studies have been made in the relation of pauperism to crime; but these are by no means decisive, for the economic relation, when badly adjusted, is usually broken by crime rather then pauperism. The pauper is a degenerate, requiring quite special investigation. M. Monod arranged to give 727 beggars a letter of recommendation by which they could obtain work at four francs a day. Of those who applied for aid, 415 never came back for the letter, 138 who got the letter never presented it to secure the work. A few worked one day, a few half a day, and out of an experience with this number of persons, extending over eight months, there were only found eighteen who worked three days or more. It is quite evident that the problem of the beggar is one that must be commenced at a little earlier in his career in order to reach an adequate solution.

It might be supposed that if there be a vital relation between crime and economic conditions, that crimes would be more numerous in periods of financial depression, but this does not seem to be the fact. In English statistics we have the bad year of 1872, in which there were 80,000 crimes against property and 183,000 misdemeanors; in the good year of 1877 there were 88,000 and 194,500, while in 1884, which was a bad year, there were 81,000 crimes against property and 182,000 misdemeanors. The five years ending 1874 were prosperous, and, according to William Douglas Morrison, they show more crime against property than the five depressed years ending 1888. Drunkenness and dissipation tend to increase crime in good years, the wages being larger than the recipients are quite equal to bear. Need and idleness increase crime in bad years, the wages being too small for virtue. I am sure that this statistical reference is too slight for the deduction of a general law, but it is at least sufficient to indicate the problem.

It would seem also to be doubted that the better classes of society commit more rather than less of their share of crimes against property. Now, on the other hand, it ought to be said, that in the report of the Commissioner of Prisons for England and Wales, we find a table showing the number of able-bodied paupers in receipt of indoor relief from 1849 to 1885, together with a table showing the average number of persons in the local prisons in England and Wales for the same period, and the chart shows that as the number of paupers decrease during the period, so, in a broad way, the number of prisoners decrease, the range being between 16,000 and 26,000 paupers and 15,800 and 20,200 prisoners. These figures are given, with the discussion upon them, by Gordon Rylands in his "Crimes, its Causes and Remedy."

I wish now to call your attention to the comparative statistics between the various countries in Europe with reference to crimes against property. It surprised me to find that Spain presented the lowest number, being 74 out of 100,000 of the population, and Scotland the highest number, 289 out of 100,000 of the population; that France has 121 out 100,000, while Germany has 262, ranking next to Scotland. Ireland has 101 in 100,000 while Italy has 221. Consider in connection with these facts, the statement that the total crimes in Christian England is one to every 42 of the population per annum, while in heathen India there is one criminal to every 195 of the population, and the question at once arises whether we can simply dismiss these statements with the assertion that the lower the percentage of crime, the better is the character of the population. I venture to affirm the opposite and to urge my conviction that it will be found that the most moral races are also the most criminal. Strong races have strong passions, appetites, and desires. Their abundant life flowers out in manifold attempts to secure all that seems to them good and worthy. Ambitious life seeks to find an environment more and more fit for the exercise of its power. In the case of such a people, the struggle for existence becomes more and more intense. The high standard of living upon the one side is paralleled by the strong arm of greed upon the other, which beats down the weak and the unworthy. India has a civilization many thousand years old. The fiercer passions have worn themselves out. The people who are to be destroyed by intemperance have already been eliminated. Those who are left are without thirst or the danger. The East Indian has grace, gentleness, and good manners, but the good manners of the Orient have been won at the fearful expense of the sturdy strength, which still exists in more recent and more vigorous peoples. The contrast of the various European nations will show that where the standard of living is high and the energy of the people is great, there is also a larger proportion of crime. Great achievements are accompanied by great defeats. The strong win and some of the weak steal. The distinction found among primitive peoples, between the military and the industrial types, indicates a lasting quality of race. It is true that military types are compelled by and by to go to work, but under this industrialism there still lurks a great deal of untamed savagery. The Scotch Highlanders, who used to steal cattle from English lowlands, learned, indeed, to sing Psalms and made sure of heaven, but in view of their history, it is not to be wondered at that they still show the highest record for stealing in Europe. But let no one suppose that the Spaniard is a better man than the Scotchman because he does not steal. The poor Spaniard has practically ceased the struggle for existence and has few crimes against property, because the instinct of property creation in Spain is well-nigh extinct.

Let me ask you to notice for a moment the relation of occupation to crime. I find, for example, in the state of Minnesota, that about two and one-half per cent of our crime is committed by the farmers, who are about half of our population, while persons engaged in trade and transportation, who constitute about ten per cent of our population, commit about twenty per cent of the crime. Now are we to believe that the farmer is intrinsically a more honest man than the railroad clerk? Must we think that working in the earth is a more moral occupation than working in an office? I think not. I have here introduced into our problem the great modern American question, *viz.*, "What to do with our cities." The complex life of the city, the comparative high standard of living which it maintains, the intensity of its manifold struggles, makes it the crucial testing place of our civilization. Here is the battle of life; here are won the greatest victories, here are suffered the most stinging defeats, here is found the highest virtue, and here skulks also the darkest crime and shame. The standard of living makes the temptations more strenuous, and the fierceness of the struggle makes weakness the more helpless. It is not alone a matter of municipal government, it is not alone a question of a very mixed population. The struggle is of the very essence of the situation. The increasing sense of duty upon the part of municipalities is doing much to alleviate the situation, although, as yet, there is no real effort to solve the problem; but the better sanitary conditions, a pure water supply, the condemnation of unwholesome dwellings, are among the measures of amelioration, and will tend, not alone to lessen crime, but also insanity and pauperism.

But if, as I have argued thus far, the right of personal property leads to nearly all the crimes in the world, the question may at once boldly be asked, why continue the cause of human wickedness and human misery? Why not abolish private property and in the millennium of socialism find peace from all our evils? The answer is equally bold; of all crimes, the crime of socialism is the least to be endured. Better a thousand times the struggles and the defeats; better even the rags and misery, the heart-ache and sin which pollute society, rather than that the incentive for personal achievement and personal development, which has driven the world thus far, should be sacrificed to an ideal at once fair and false. Socialism is the paradise of fools, the asylum of the lazy man, the heaven of the worthless, but it is the purgatory of industry, the destroyer of high effort, and the hell of character. Into this struggle, therefore, the human life, fiercest among the greatest and best races, darkest and most uncertain in the midst of our cities, intensified a thousand fold by the complications and perplexities of modern life, with its machineries and new processes of toil, – into this struggle, I say, the race must go with the fierce joy of warriors into battle. To the conception of scientific charity upon the one side, which says to mere sentimentalism, you shall not rob even the weak of the necessity of exerting all his strength, there need to be added other mandates of social reform. There must be an education which will prepare our youth for the civilization, which they are compelled to inherit.

Fine idealisms about culture for culture's sake are all very well, but men who still live in the body, must walk with their feet upon the solid earth, and our education, which has too often satisfied itself with the mere blossoms of beauty, must also ripen into fruit of actual service for practical life. It is a terrible thing to teach a boy Latin and not teach him how he must earn his bread. The illiterate are in excess out of all proportion in the ranks of the criminal but the proportion of unskilled boys and young men, who have no knowledge of any wealth-producing business, is vastly more. And do you ask me, if the conscience has no place and if there is no moral side to this question? I respond by asking you what you mean by morals? If morals be not right conduct, both leading to and manifesting right character, I know nothing of the subject. The fine memories and beautiful sentiments are not morals. Man is made of sterner stuff. There is nothing more moral than hard work. There is nothing more invigorating to character than hard work, successfully and adequately paid, for successful work not alone produces the means by which the desires of the body and mind are gratified, but is in itself restraining of unlawful desires, and a means by which the will is enthroned and the conscience given voice. The application to the training of the young is so manifest that it need not be pursued. Equally manifest is the application to the entire *regime* of prison discipline. Toil, obedience, intelligence, skill, and physical development, are the results required at the hands of the prison authorities.

The boy who has committed his first offense should not step out of the prison doors until he is so taught that he is fitted for successful labor, and so instructed and reorganized, that it will be easier for him to be social than to be anti-social. This is reformation. The great trade schools of the Elmira Reformatory in New York are a model in the economic adaptation to the criminal. The prisons of Paris in the variety of their industries and in the success with which they are pursued, have also many lessons to teach us on the subject of productive prison labor. I cannot close without saying that not alone is it necessary that men should be trained to toil, it is also necessary that society be so constructed that toil shall receive its adequate reward. It has been discovered that as governments become steadily free and are participated in by the people, their institutions become secure. There is no European life so in danger as that of the most irresponsible monarch. The same law is universal. Let those who would silence the voice of public discontent; who would down mob rule; who would secure public order, simply see to it, that it is to the highest interest of the vast majority of the people, to maintain existing institutions, and those institutions will be secure. But if the time ever comes when the social order stands for injustice, if the time every comes when the people believe that the greatest thieves live in palaces rather than in the jails, the day of doom is not far. The industrial fabric to be secure must also be just and free.

Society can never eliminate the ordinary criminal, or reform him, if she is suspected of being essentially criminal herself. Instead of a battle between organized labor upon the one side and trusts, monopolies, and corporations upon the other, the time has come when all our people should study the first principles of self-government. It still remains true, "that righteousness alone exalteth a nation." Reverence for the private rights of some can never obtain, unless there be also reverence for the private rights of all. When it becomes a part of the public consciousness that every man's desires must be limited to his fair share of the common production of labor, we shall have created a social condition less fruitful in breeding criminals.

SUGGESTIONS FOR FURTHER READING AND INQUIRY:

POVERTY, DESTITUTION, AND ECONOMIC PERTURBATIONS

"The Desperate System: Poverty, Crime, and Emigration." William Maginn. *Fraser's Magazine*, vol. 1 (1830), pp. 635–642.
Poverty is, without a doubt, the fountainhead of crime.

"On Variations in the Price of Food as They Affect the Ratio of Crime at Given Periods." *Journal of Prison Discipline and Philanthropy*, vol. 8 (1853), pp. 33–41.
Very fine statistical analysis of the relationship between economic perturbations and the nature and frequency of crime.

"Crime and Pauperism." Robert Everest. *De Bow's Commercial Review*, vol. 19 (1855), pp. 268–285.
A statistical analysis and discussion of the relationship between poverty and crime.

"The Increase of Material Prosperity Compared with the State of Crime and Pauperism." J. H. Elliott. *Hunt's Merchant Magazine and Commercial Review*, vol. 61 (1869), pp. 339–366.
A statistical examination demonstrating the relationship between crime and depressed economic conditions in the United States and Great Britain.

"Capital, Poverty, and Crime." Edward Roscoe. *Victoria Magazine*, vol. 21 (1873), pp. 561–569.
A statistical analysis of the relationship between economic depressions and crime in Great Britain.

"Breeding the Huns and Vandals." *Public Opin-ion*, vol. 2 (1887), p. 459.
Poverty as the principal cause of crime and social decay.

"Poverty and Crime." Harold Thomas. *Westminster Review*, vol. 145 (1896), pp. 75–77.
This sets forth a long list of legislative protocols for addressing the problems of crime, vice, and moral degeneracy caused by poverty.

IGNORANCE
AND
ILLITERACY

THE RELATION BETWEEN IGNORANCE AND CRIME: OR, STATISTICS SHOWING THE REIGN OF IGNORANCE AMONG THE CRIMINALS OF THE WORLD

WESTERN JOURNAL AND CIVILIAN
VOL. 8, NO. 5 (AUGUST, 1852), PP. 297-308

In 1846, the number received into the Jails and Houses of Correction in Massachusetts, was 6,544, of whom 953 were debtors. Of these, 4,381 were unable to read and write. It is probable that most of the debtors could read and write, so that the proportion among the really criminal who are thus ignorant is still greater. Suppose 700 of the debtors could read and write, and 253 could not, we must deduct them from the aggregate, because it is too late in the day to call a debtor a criminal. We shall thus have 1,716 who could read and write, and 4,128 would could not —or nearly one of the former to two and a half of the latter. In 1847, the number in the Jails and Houses of Correction in Massachusetts was 7,009, of whom 1,060 were debtors. Of these, 3,270 were able to read and write. If one supposes that 800 of the debtors could read and write, there would then be 1,570 able to read and write, and 5,179 of the criminals who could not read and write—being nearly one of the educated to three and a half of the ignorant. In 1840, the number of people in Massachusetts who could read and write was 403,761—and the number of those who were unable to do so was 4,448—a little over 1 to 100. Were not ignorance the cause of crime, there ought to have been only 58 in the Jails and Houses of Correction who could not read and write, instead of 4,128; and in 1847, there ought to have been only 68 instead of 5,179. We have in these cases from 5,000 to 7,500 per cent in favor of Education as a preventive of crime.

Of the 9,979 committed to the Jails and Houses of Correction in Massachusetts in 1850, only 3,175, or less than one-third, could read and write—and that too, while only one in one hundred of the people of the State could not read and write, making about 10,000 per cent in favor of Education!

In the Ohio Penitentiary in 1847, there were 445 convicts, of whom 297 were reported able to read and write. Of the 297, about 100 were taught to do so while in the prison, so that really 248 of the whole number are from the class of the totally ignorant. In 1840 the number of the population of Ohio who could read and write was 638,649—and the number of those in the State who could not do so was 35,394, being 1 to 21—that is, there ought to have been twenty-one times as many among the convicts who could read and write as could not. Here we have 2,100 per cent in favor of Education.

In 1843, of the 1,778 convicts in the Eastern Pennsylvanian Penitentiary, 906 could not read and write. The population of Pennsylvania in 1840 who could read and write was 765,917, and the number that could not read and write was 38,296 – being 1 to 20 of the former, while more than half the convicts mentioned above were from the latter. Were not education effectual in staying the hand of crime, 1,690 should have been able to read and write, and only 88 should have been without this ability. Here again, we have nearly 2,000 per cent in favor of Education. The whole number of convicts received in the Eastern Penitentiary of Pennsylvania, from the first up to 1844 was 1,916. Of these, 945 could read and write, 447 could read only, and 524 could not read and write at all.

In 1844 there were in the New York Penitentiary at Auburn 778 convicts, of whom 164 are reported to have been unable to read; how many more could not write is not stated. In 1845 the number was 683, of whom 131 could not read. Of the 1,653 sent to that prison during from the first up to 1844, the following was reported as their educational standing:

Of Collegiate Education	7
Of Academical Education	14
Could read, write, and cipher	482
Could read and write only	400
Could read only	380
Could not read the Bible	373
Whole number	1,653
Could not cipher	1,171

What a commentary is this upon ignorance? —showing that nearly all are from the ranks of the uneducated. In view of these facts the Inspectors of the New York Penitentiary say: —"These statistics present facts showing the connection of ignorance and crime, and that should prompt every philanthropist to renew efforts to multiply the facilities to properly educate and discipline every youthful member of our wide-spread population." And yet it seems that the people will not believe, though one rise from the dead to tell the terrible truth.

In 1846 the number in the Auburn Penitentiary was 606, of whom 112 could not read, 9 had an Academical and 3 a Collegiate Education. In 1847 the number was 504, of whom 79 could not read, and 9 had pursued Academical studies. In 1848, there were 452 convicts in this penitentiary, of whose Education the following is reported:

Unable to Read	170
Learned to Read in Prison	105
Could Read and Write, and knew some Arithmetic	247
Had a good English Education	31
Had a Classical Education	4
Had some Religious Instruction	239
Had no Religious Instruction	213

In 1849 the number in the New York Penitentiary at Auburn was 609, distributed with respect to education as follows:

Unable to Read	126
Could Read Indifferently	87
Could Read, Write, and Cipher	360
Had a Good Education	30
Had a Classical Education	6

Of the 1,121 people convicted in the Courts of Record in New York in 1850, we find the following with respect to education:

Could both read and write	687
Could read only	86
Could neither read nor write	215

In the cities of Albany, Brooklyn, Buffalo, New York, Schenectady, and Troy, 3,176 people were convicted at the Courts of Special Sessions in 1850, of whom we note the following:

Could both read and write	1,746
Could read only	240
Could neither read nor write	1,003

The number of commitments to the various Jails of New York City in 1850 was 21,299, of whom:

Could not read	9,449
Could read only	1,646
Could both read and write	7,284
Well Educated	2,737
Classically Educated	25
Unknown	164

In view of such facts, the Warden of the Ohio Penitentiary, in a special report on Prison Discipline recently made in 1851, said: "When it is considered that a very fruitful cause of crime is ignorance, the importance of the Penitentiary schoolmasters will be rendered at once apparent. In no other way than by giving them the rudiments of a common English Education can we hope that convicts, when discharged, will attain to any considerable degree of usefulness or virtue. Intellectual and moral culture are co-workers together for the reformation and elevation of man."

During 1847 and 1848 there were 335 people received into the convict department of the Philadelphia County Jail, of whom one hundred and twenty-six could neither read nor write; ninety could "read a little;" one hundred and sixteen could read and write imperfectly; and three were what we would call well educated. Of twenty-one persons in this County Jail under conviction of riot on the 19th of December, 1849, eight could not read; three could read, but not write; seven could read and write, but knew nothing of arithmetic; and three could read, write, and cipher. No one of them had a good elementary education. Of 237 boys over 13 years of age received into the White Department of the Refuge between January 1st, 1847, and December 17th, 1849, 42 could read well; 153 could "read a little;" and 42 could not read at all. The Clerk of the Philadelphia Court of Special Sessions says that a large majority of the persons held to bail in the Court for riot and other offences involving a breach of the peace are "destitute of Education, being unable to write their names to the bail bond." Messrs. Wharton, Webster, and Reed, who have in turn prosecuted the pleas of the Commonwealth in this county for the last five years agree that, with few exceptions, this class of offenders are "almost utterly uneducated."

It is proper to remark here that an ability merely to read is of little service in a moral point of view. Indeed, we might say the same of the ability merely to read and write, for an effectual Education must go to the thoughts and feelings of the individual —it must give him the complete command of himself, enable him to comprehend the true object of life, and understand the momentous import of his existence and his duty to society. Viewed in this light, we shall not find even a small per cent of educated criminals in our Jails and Penitentiaries. The ability to read and write is of little service in morals and good citizenship, unless that ability be exercised, and we shall find it not a singular fact, that of all the convicts who can read and write, but the smallest number have used the acquirement as a channel for information and improvement. This being the case, they are as if they could not read and write, and all should be included among the totally ignorant. The Warden of the Eastern Pennsylvania Penitentiary says that not one in twenty of the convicts "can write a fair and connected letter." The Board of Prison Inspectors for Pennsylvania reported that only one out of four could write more than merely their own names!

If we turn to the Old World we shall find our pathway full of facts enforcing the doctrine which we now announce, that *a true Education—such as every one is entitled to by the rights of his existence—will banish crime from the earth.* As shall soon be demonstrated for the benefit of our readers, the relationship between Education and crime pertains not only in the United States, but, indeed, appears to be a universal social law applicable in all civilized Western nations. France furnishes the following four excellent tables showing the state of Education among her criminal populations for the five year period beginning with 1828 and ending with 1832:

UNABLE TO READ OR WRITE

	1828	1829	1830	1831	1832	Total
Crimes against the Person	1,009	1,063	990	1,144	1,833	5,539
Crimes against Property	3,157	3,460	3,329	3,456	3,416	16,818
Total	4,166	4,523	4,319	4,600	4,749	22,357
Number Acquitted	1,589	1,696	1,654	1,918	1,883	8,729
Number Convicted	2,627	2,827	2,665	2,652	2,856	13,637

ABLE TO READ IMPERFECTLY

	1828	1829	1830	1831	1832	Total
Crimes against the Person	505	496	465	568	150	2,884
Crimes against Property	1,353	1,451	1,361	1,479	1,606	7,250
Total	1,858	1,947	1,826	2,047	2,456	10,134
Number Acquitted	715	787	776	1,000	1,162	4,430
Number Convicted	1,143	1,160	1,060	1,047	1,294	5,704

ABLE TO READ AND WRITE WELL

	1828	1829	1830	1831	1832	Total
Crimes against the Person	215	185	174	234	292	1,100
Crimes against Property	566	544	514	533	483	2,639
Total	780	729	688	767	775	3,739
Number Acquitted	342	325	330	428	373	1,796
Number Convicted	438	404	358	341	402	1,943

RESPECTABLY EDUCATED					
	1828	1829	1830	1831	1832	Total
Crimes against the Person	36	46	37	98	169	386
Crimes against Property	82	124	92	92	88	478
Total	118	170	129	190	257	864
Number Acquitted	77	89	82	132	162	542
Number Convicted	41	81	47	58	95	322

From these four tables we find that crimes in France during the period in question are distributed with respect to Education as follows:

Unable to read or write	22,375
Able to read imperfectly	10,134
Total of Ignorance	32,491
Able to read and write well	3,739
Respectably Educated	864
Total of Education	4,603

These are the aggregates of crimes charged against individuals. Those proved, or the number convicted, are as follows:

Unable to read or write	13,637
Able to read imperfectly	5,774
Total of Ignorance	19,341
Able to read and write well	1,913
Respectably Educated	322
Total of Education	2,265

Of the crimes charged, we find the proportion between Ignorance and Education as 8 to 1; and of crimes for which convictions were obtained as 8.5 to 1. The average population of France over the course of the five year period adverted to in the statistical tables was 32,561,563, and the proportion who could read and write, was, to those without this ability, 38 to 90. In these facts we have about 700 per cent in favor of Education. Indeed, this would be a much greater per cent if we could deduct from this class of ignorance the children who cannot read, and are not upon the criminal lists.

If we cross the channel into Great Britain, we shall find the facts equally gratifying in support of our thesis about the relation between ignorance and crime. In the reports of the Prison Discipline Society, we find that Rev. James Brown, Chaplain of Norwich Castle, Norfolk, England, says that "From January, 1825, to March, 1826, 400 prisoners came under my examination. Of these, 183 could neither read nor write; 28 merely knew the alphabet; 49 could read very imperfectly, so as not to be able to comprehend or obtain any information by it; 51 could read only; and 99 could both read and write." He also states that "among those who have learned to read and write, there exists a lamentable ignorance of moral, religious, and civic duties."

In Porter's work on the Progress of the British Empire, we find the following facts: In twenty counties of England and Wales, with a population of 8,724,338 persons, there were only 59 instructed convicts for 1840, while in the 32 remaining counties there was but one instructed convict – that is, who had received more than the rudest elements of instruction. Middlesex, the metropolitan county, with 1,576,616 inhabitants, did not furnish a single educated convict. Among the 59 mentioned above, 15 were political offenders. In 1841 fifteen English counties furnished only 17 instructed convicts out of a total population of 9,569,064, while the remaining counties of England and the whole of Wales did not furnish one convict out of a population of 6,342,661 who had received more than the mere elements of instruction. It must be remembered, to the credit of Education, that out of the 109 accused persons who had been educated, but one was female, while among the uneducated convicts one-fourth were females.

The following are the criminal returns for England and Wales from 1836 to 1841:

1. Convicts Who Could Neither Read nor Write

	Males	Females
1836	5,598	1,435
1837	6,684	1,780
1838	6,342	1,601
1839	6,487	1,709
1840	7,145	1,913
1841	7,312	1,908

2. Convicts Who Could Read Only, or Read and Write Imperfectly

	Males	Females
1836	8,968	2,015
1837	10,147	2,151
1838	10,008	2,826
1839	10,523	2,548
1840	12,151	2,958
1841	12,742	2,990

3. Convicts Who Could Both Read and Write Well

	Males	Females
1836	2,016	199
1837	2,057	177
1838	2,051	206
1839	2,201	261
1840	2,038	215
1841	1,839	214

4. Convicts Who Received Instruction Beyond the Elementary Branches of Reading and Writing

	Males	Females
1836	176	16
1837	98	3
1838	74	5
1839	74	4
1840	100	1
1841	126	0

The number for 1841—126—was found afterward to be only 109. Besides these, 500 per year of males, and 100 of females, were undetermined as to Education. In England in 1841, the proportion of criminal offenders to the general population was 1 to 573, while in Scotland they were in the proportion of 1 to 742, the difference due to the superior Education in Scotland. To complete the record for all of England, let the following table (reported in percentages) be given:

Degrees of Instruction	1842	1843	1844	1845	1846	1847	1848
Unable to read	32.35	31.00	29.77	30.61	50.66	31.59	31.93
Read Imperfectly	58.32	57.60	59.28	58.43	59.51	58.57	56.38
Well Educated	06.77	08.02	08.12	08.38	07.71	07.79	09.83
Superior Education	00.22	00.47	00.42	00.37	00.34	00.28	00.27
Not Ascertained	02.34	02.91	02.41	02.30	01.78	01.60	01.59

From this table we notice that an average of 88 per cent of all the criminals of England were among the uneducated! Reading imperfectly is equivalent to no Education, and accordingly, the first two classes are included among the uneducated. It is noticed also that an average of only about 8 per cent were well Educated, while but a third per cent possessed a superior Education! Let these facts tell in favor of the greatest of all the agencies for human improvement and advancement. About two-thirds of the males of England are "well Educated," as it is called, and yet 88 per cent of criminals are from the 33 per cent of the uneducated and ignorant population—about 2,000 per cent in favor of Education!

In Porter's work, to which we again refer, we find the following satisfactory statement in relation to the regenerating power of Education: "In the island of Iceland, there is no such thing to be found as a man or woman—not decidedly deficient in mental capacity—who cannot read and write, while the greater part of all classes of the inhabitants have mastered several of the higher branches of education, including a knowledge of modern languages and an acquaintance with classical literature. Every account of this people that has been published, agrees in describing them as gentle and peaceable in their dispositions, they being to a person sober, moral, and religious in their habits. Crimes among them are hardly known. The House of Correction at Reickiavich, the capital of the island, after having stood empty for years, was at length converted into a residence for the Governor, by whom it has since been occupied. The island is subject to the penal code of Denmark, which awards the penalty of death to murder and some other heinous offences. It is said that on the island only three or four capital convictions have occurred during the last two centuries. The last of these happened in 1810. It was of a peasant for the murder of his wife, and on that occasion it was not possible to find any one on the island who could be induced to perform the office of executioner, so that it became necessary to send the man to Norway, that the sentence might be carried into effect."

We extract the following interesting particulars from Mr. Frederick Hill's eleventh report on the Prisons of Scotland, presented to Parliament in 1848: "Of about 18,000 prisoners received during the year ending 30th June, 1845, rather more than 2,600 convicts were under seventeen years of age; nearly 3,300 were between seventeen and twenty-one years of age; nearly 11,000 from twenty-one to fifty; and about 1,100 above fifty. As a general rule, the prisoners, especially the young, are found on admission to be inferior to the general population in mental and physical development, and the amount of knowledge they have acquired, this owing, no doubt, to the unfavorable circumstances of their birth and early training, and to frequent exposure to cold and want, often alternating, as the age advances, with the effects of dissipation. Many who are committed and liberated while young probably die before they reach manhood; but the same general inferiority is observable, to a greater or less extent, in prisoners of all ages. In many cases, indeed, the degrees of weak-mindedness and the want of self-control often pass the boundary of sanity, and a lunatic asylum would often be a more appropriate receptacle than a prison."

"The record of the state of education of the prisoners, on their admission, as shown by their knowledge of reading and writing, agree with what might be expected under such circumstances. Of upward of 15,000 prisoners examined last year, only 1,003, or one in fifteen, were found able to read and write well; only 262, or one in sixty, knew more than mere reading and writing; while upward of 3,000 could not read at all, and upward of 8,000 could not write at all."

"It will be found, by a comparison of the foregoing summary with that given by Mr. Redgrave, in the criminal returns from England and Wales, that, although the general state of education in Scotland is usually considered to be superior to that of England, the criminal population of Scotland is quite as low in education as the criminal population of England and Wales, showing clearly, that in Scotland as well as in England, it is among the uneducated that crime abounds, potent as may be other causes than the want of education in producing crime. "

We respectfully request our readers to re-peruse and carefully consider the foregoing facts. They are full of instruction touching a subject in which the interest of every individual in the community is deeply involved. From a comparison of the statistics of crime in the United States, France, and Great Britain, it appears that about three-fourths of all criminals belong to that class who are totally uneducated, or whose education has been so limited as to be of but little or no advantage to them. No amount of wealth, no degree of intelligence or civic-minded virtue, no calling or station, can place a citizen above the reach of those evils which we believe flow from ignorance. Ignorance is the handmaiden of crime, and as such, it serves to endanger the safety of both one's person and one's property, and may properly be regarded as the chief cause of almost all the mental anxiety and inquietude that afflict the human family today. Assuming ignorance to be the principal source of crime, as it is proven to be by the foregoing facts, it robs and steals away the very life-blood of our society, while it taxes the community to pay for the investigation, apprehension, and prosecution of criminal offenders, and for the building and maintenance of Jails and Penitentiaries to confine and punish the ignorant wretches. We have not the data from which we can make accurate estimates, but are persuaded, nonetheless, to the conclusion that it will not cost the community as much to prevent crime by a judicious system of public education as to provide for the erection of Jails and Penitentiaries for the punishment of delinquents and malefactors.

SUGGESTIONS FOR FURTHER READING AND INQUIRY:

IGNORANCE AND ILLITERACY

"An Inquiry into the Conditions of Criminal Offenders in England and Wales, with Respect to Education; or Statistics of Education Among the Criminal and General Population of England and Other Countries." Rawson W. Rawson. *Quarterly Journal of the Statistical Society of London*, vol. 3 (1841), pp. 331–352.
A classic statistical study in the style of the French ecological school.

"Prevention of Crime by Popular Education." Henry Rogers. *Edinburgh Review*, vol. 86 (1847), pp. 512–523.
Advances the thesis that compulsory state education is the surest and most certain way to prevent crime.

"The Influence of Education, Shown by Facts Recorded in the Criminal Tables for 1845 and 1846." G. R. Porter. *Quarterly Journal of the Statistical Society of London*, vol. 10 (1847), pp. 316–344.
A replication of the earlier statistical study conducted in 1841 by Rawson.

"Moral and Educational Statistics of England and Wales." Joseph Fletcher. *Quarterly Journal of the Statistical Society of London*, vol. 10 (1847), pp. 193–233.
This and the following three articles by Fletcher constitute the most monumental statistical report of its kind produced during the nineteenth century on the relationship between education and crime. A true classic in every sense of the word.

"Moral and Educational Statistics of England and Wales." Joseph Fletcher. *Quarterly Journal of the Statistical Society of London*, vol. 11 (1848), pp. 345–366.

"Moral and Educational Statistics of England and Wales." Joseph Fletcher. *Quarterly Journal of the Statistical Society of London*, vol. 12 (1849), pp. 151–176.

"Moral and Educational Statistics of England and Wales." Joseph Fletcher. *Quarterly Journal of the Statistical Society of London*, vol. 12 (1849), pp. 189–335.

"Relation of Education to the Prevention of Crime." *De Bow's Commercial Review*, vol. 18 (1855), pp. 409–421.
Report of a statistical study examining the relationship between crime and education in Europe and the United States which concludes that overall crime rates could be lessened through enhanced educational opportunities for children.

"On the Relationship between Crime, Popular Instruction, Attendance on Religious Worship, and Beer-Houses." Rev. John Clay. *Quarterly Journal of the Statistical Society of London*, vol. 20 (1857), pp. 22–32.
An interesting study of the relationship between crime and ignorance, and how they stand with respect to some additional variables.

"Illiteracy as a Source of National Danger." *Popular Science Monthly*, vol. 27 (1885), pp. 118–126.
An expression of the view that education is the foundation of a stable, productive, and law-abiding society.

"Education and Lawlessness." F. D. Huntington. *Forum*, vol. 4 (1887), pp. 133–142.
Bad citizenship, as exemplified by lawless behavior, is a function of ignorance and illiteracy.

"Public Schools as Affecting Crime and Vice."
Benjamin Reece. *Popular Science Monthly*, vol. 36
(1890), pp. 319–328.
   A most curious and interesting article that argues that
   education does not elevate the moral standards of a
   generation, but rather works to the opposite direction, in that as the minds of the masses are increased
   in knowledge, there is an equal if not more rapid
   increase in crime and vice.

"Education and Crime." Allen Walton Gould. *Popular
Science Monthly*, vol. 37 (1890), pp. 211–221.
   A well-argued refutation of Reece's contention that
   compulsory public education is a root cause of
   elevated crime rates in modern society.

"Crime and Education in Saxony." *Public Opinion*, vol. 9 (1890), pp. 555–556.
   An interesting statistical report from Germany tending to suggest the causal nexus between crime and
   education.

"Popular Education and Crime." *Public Opinion*,
vol. 17 (1894), pp. 841–842.
   The text of the opening address by Sir John Lubbock
   at the International Institute of Sociology in Paris,
   France wherein he discusses his findings regarding
   the relationship between education and crime in
   England.

"Cornwall, England: A Puzzle to the Sage
Criminologist." *Public Opinion*, vol. 25 (1898),
p. 399.
   A very interesting report concerning the enigma of
   Cornwall, England, where the theory that lack of
   education is a precursor to crime obviously does not
   hold true.

COSMICOLOGICAL INFLUENCES

(TEMPERATURE, HUMIDITY, AND BAROMETRIC PRESSURE)

CRIME AND THE WEATHER

PUBLIC OPINION
VOL. 22, NO. 16 (APRIL 22, 1897), PP. 494

Considerable attention has been given of late to the effect of weather on crime. The theory that a connection exists between the one and other is not exactly new, and now that there is an up-to-date installment of calculations to support it, many citizens are ready to say "I told you so." Some sorts of crime are perennial. An English statistician, Mr. Troup, has just demonstrated to his own satisfaction the dependence of crime on the temperature. He has made this question a study for years, and bases his belief on the criminal statistics of several years previous to 1895. He gives figures, and also diagrams to throw light on the subject.

The first diagram is arranged in this way: The years from 1881 to 1895 are represented by perpendicular lines. Upon these lines is a scale of degrees each representing tens. Just above the twenty-third degree representing, therefore, more than 230 and less than 240, a line starts to cross the line of years. This line is labeled "all crimes," and it tells the eye that the proportion of all crimes to 100,000 of the population in 1881 was 233. The line takes an upward course and reaches 240 as it crosses the year 1882, then it gradually descends till it reaches 1887, where we find it at 202. It rises and falls a little in its passages across the other years, but in the main takes a downward tendency stopping in 1895, well under 170—a small figure gives 167 as the exact proportion. Here then in one line you have vividly brought before you the course of crime in fifteen years—a satisfactory course of diminuation. But it is only a small part of the uses of the diagram. Its chief value is for the purposes of comparison. Another line just below is made to trace the course of a particular class of crimes – larcenies – and it is found that at a lower level it follows with marvelous exactitude the same directions as the other, bringing out clearly, as Mr. Troup says, the fact that the total of all indictable offenses is completely dominated by the figures for larceny, which enormously outnumber all other crimes. This shows the necessity of examining separately the chief heads of crime; and then we have a series of other diagrams, all teaching their lessons in the same vivid way.

Having reached this point in his demonstration he applies the same method of comparison to temperature and crime in 1895. The writer says: "Mr. Troup traces a line across the months of 1895 showing the great depression of February in that year, when the average temperature was 28.9. The line rises rapidly in June, takes a tolerably even course till September, then falls smartly in October, rises slightly in November, and drops again in December. With this line Mr. Troup compares the lines of crimes and apprehensions for crime in the same period. It is most curious to observe how many of these lines make a violent dip just where the temperature line did, that is, in the month of February. Some clever reader will bethink himself that February is a short month, and that this is the explanation. But Mr. Troup was not so simple as to be trapped by his own lines in that way. He made allowances for that. The figures were corrected so as to apply to months of thirty days, the actual figures for February being increased by one-fourteenth, and the actual figures for the months of thirty-one days being diminished by one-thirty-first. Therefore, the comparison is not vitiated by any irregularity in the monthly divisions represented in these diagrams." Mr. Troup has a diagram showing also by the fluctuations of a line what was the average number of persons in receipt of relief in the months compared. It naturally shows a rise in the severe 1895 February, special distress and poverty accompanying the cold weather. But the line of crime does not follow this poverty and distress line. It moves, as we have said, in the same direction as the temperature line, that is, downward. From the dip in February the lines showing the upward or downward movement of crimes reported and persons apprehended move generally upward. There is just a little wavering at midsummer and again in September; then the line shoots rapidly upward in November. Now from October to November the weather, instead of continuing its normal course toward a lower temperature, took an upward tendency and was much above the average. Then came the drop again in crime as the cold weather set it.

THE INFLUENCE OF WEATHER UPON CRIME

BY

EDWIN GRANT DEXTER

POPULAR SCIENCE MONTHLY

VOL. 55 (SEPTEMBER 1899), PP. 653-660

The relation between general climatic conditions and the prevalence of suicide has been somewhat exhaustively studied by students of criminology, the results being a considerable accumulation of data and the formulation of a number of more or less tenable theories. From these studies we may safely conclude that the homicidal tendency, as shown by self-destruction (suicide) and the destruction of others (murder), is stronger in the temperate climatic zones than in the torrid or frigid, and that in the late spring and early summer months more of these offenses have been recorded than for any other period of the year. To these few facts the seeming effects of cosmical forces upon such tendencies has apparently been limited.

In fact, it was the oft-repeated statement that nothing was known of the exact relations of the more definite meteorological conditions with the prevalence of suicide – a statement to be found in most treatises upon the subject – that has given rise to this paper. Realizing that the science of climatology must include, and in fact be based upon, a study of the meteorological conditions prevalent, and that the study of these definite conditions for the exact times when suicides or murders occurred might throw some light upon the question, this problem was undertaken.

In the preparation of the accompanying charts, from the study of which the conclusions herein stated were deduced, the record of crime for Denver, Colorado, for the fourteen years ending with June, 1897, was made use of. Superintendent Howe, chief of the city detective service, has kept such a record with the greatest care, and we wish here to acknowledge the many courtesies of his office.

No attempt has been made in this paper to compare the conditions for Denver, either meteorological or social —and each is somewhat unique—with such conditions elsewhere. In fact, such a comparative study is at present impossible since data are wanting.

In the actual preparation of the charts each murder, suicide, or attempt at suicide—which, for our purposes, is equally important—was set down chronologically in the left-hand columns of large sheets of paper ruled for the purpose. These sheets were then taken to the office of the United States Weather Bureau, F. H. Brandenburg, director, where were recorded in the proper columns the maximum and minimum barometer readings, maximum and minimum temperature, maximum and minimum humidity, maximum velocity of the wind, precipitation, and character of the day for each day during the fourteen years on which a crime of either class occurred. When several took place upon the same day the fact was taken into consideration. From the sheets thus filled out, the curves on the accompanying charts were plotted by computing the per cent of crimes of each class committed under the definite meteorological condition indicated.

The curves marked "normal" were constructed by tabulating in a similar manner the conditions for every day in a sufficient number of days to secure a fair average. Five years were so tabulated for Figures 2, 3, 4, and 5, and the records for the nineteen years used in Figures 1 and 6.

The whole number of suicides recorded is two hundred and sixty; murders, one hundred and eighty. It may be noted that this number of suicides, for a city averaging hardly one hundred thousand inhabitants for the fourteen years, is largely in excess of the rate recorded for American cities, but it must be remembered that some of these were unsuccessful attempts, and also that the social conditions of Denver tend to swell the number—containing, as it does, so many disappointed in the last struggle for health.

Figure 1 shows the occurrence, in per cent, of crimes of both the classes considered for each month of the year, together with the monthly meteorological means, computed from the records for nineteen years. The expectancy curve in the occurrence table is based upon the supposition that the months of the year are all of the same length, and that the numerical expectancy would be one twelfth, or eight and a third per cent for each. It will be seen that the crime curves are for the most part below the expectancy for the winter months, and above it for the summer (except for April, and suicides for June), showing the maximum for the latter class in May and for murders in March. Morselli, in his volume in the International Science Series titled *Suicide*, shows that for most European countries suicides are at the maximum in June, though

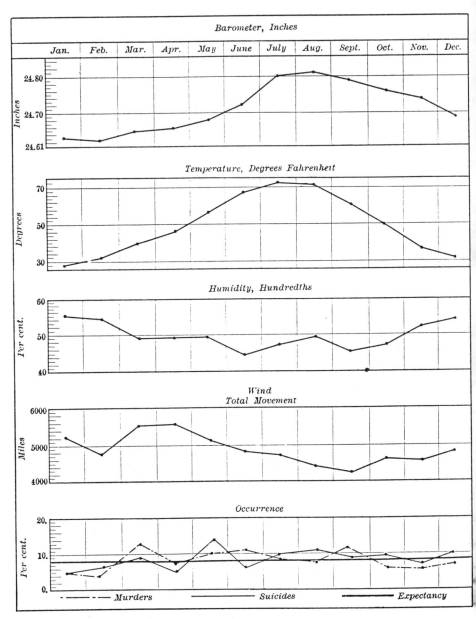

Fig. 1.

a considerable number show that condition for the later spring months. A study of the general meteorological means, shown upon the same plate as the occurrence table, fails to indicate any good reason for irregularity of the crime curves. The "month" columns read from the top to the bottom of the chart, and by following that for May, for instance, which month shows the maximum for suicide, we find that the meteorological condition for each class of data is about halfway between the extremes for that class for the year, while for January (minimum suicides) each class is by far more divergent. Yet a mean, like those considered in this table, is but the average of the extremes, and those months which show great per cents of crime also present great extremes of condition, which fact, interpreted in light of those disclosed by the charts yet to be considered, make the occurrence curve more explicable.

WIND.—An explanation of the various curves in Figure 2 may serve for the series following, so I give it in some detail. The vertical distances from the base line indicate per cents, and the distances from left to right, divided into columns, the maximum velocity of the wind per hour for the days tabulated. In the "normal" curve every day for five years was considered, and it was found that seven per cent of the days for that period showed a maximum velocity of between one and ten miles (first column),

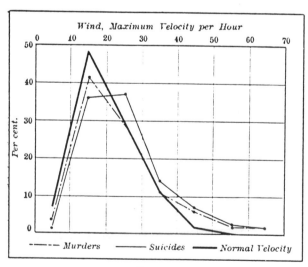

F ɪɢ. 2.

forty-eight per cent a maximum velocity of between ten and twenty miles (second column), nineteen percent a maximum velocity of between twenty and thirty miles, and so on, as indicated by the curve. Now, it can readily be seen that this normal curve may also be considered the expectancy curve – *if the wind has no effect.* That is, if forty-eight per cent of the days of the year show a maximum velocity of the wind, between ten and twenty miles an hour, the law of probability would give us the same per cent of the crime for the year on such days if this meteorological condition were not effective.

What we do find, however, is indicated by the other curves, and any increase of crime over expectancy may in this case be ascribed to the wind. We notice that for slight velocities (one to twenty miles and hour) the crime curves below that of expectancy, but we can see that if the sum of all the per cents for any one curve is one hundred, and one is forced above the other at any part, there must be a corresponding deficiency at some other part. So we may, perhaps, with justice suppose that these mild velocities do not exert a positively quieting effect emotionally, but simply a less stimulating effect than the higher ones. For velocities of between twenty and thirty miles a marked effect is noticeable, and under those conditions the proportion of suicides to that expected is 37 : 29; velocities of from thirty to forty miles, 14 : 11; of forty to fifty miles, 7 : 2; of fifty to sixty miles, 0.4 : 2.6; of sixty to seventy miles, 0.2 : 2. The curve for murders shows the increase to be slightly less than for suicides, but the same general relation is preserved throughout. The value of such curves is, of course, somewhat proportional to the number of observations made and recorded, and we must confess that two hundred and sixty (suicides) and one hundred and eighty (murders) is a hardly sufficient number from which to deduce a definite law, but we can hardly doubt, even considering this somewhat limited number, that the wind is, in our problem, a factor of no mean importance.

TEMPERATURE.—Figure 3 is intended to show, in a similar manner, the relation between expectancy curves, based upon conditions of temperature, and the actual occurrence of the crimes in question. With this class of data, as well as that for the barometric readings and humidity (Figures 4 and 5), both the maximum and minimum readings are considered. This was done instead of taking the mean of both for the day, since in many cases the latter might be quite normal, while one or possibly the former might exhibit marked peculiarities. All the curves were constructed precisely as in the chart just considered, and those marked "normal" are again the expectancy curves. An inspection of the chart shows no marked discrepancies until we reach the higher temperatures. For the lower the coincidence for all the maximum and all the minimum curves is not exact, but somewhat similar. When, however, we reach for the minimum curves, temperatures of from 40 to 50 degrees and from 50 to 60 degrees, which means that for the per cent of days indicated, the temperature did not go below those points, the per cent of crime exceeds that expected under the conditions in the proportions of 22:16.5 and 24:18 (suicides), and 21:16.5 and 29:18 (murders).

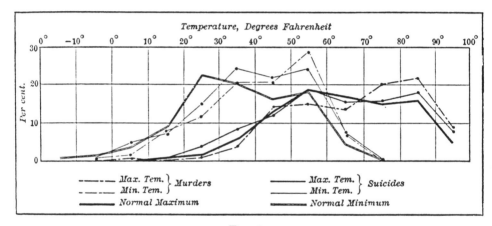

FIG. 3.

The same general relation exists between the maximum curves, where it is shown that for temperature between 80 and 100 degrees the actual crime is about thirty-three per cent in excess of the expected. These facts have their bearing upon the already noted statement that the summer months show a preponderance of homicide.

BAROMETER.—Figure 4, disassociated from the others, shows but little. Naturally, we should not look for very marked effects from variations of an inch or less in the barometric readings, when in the course of a journey from the sea level to Denver a

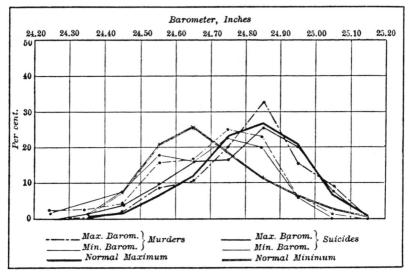

Fɪɢ. 4.

change of six inches is brought about, and in going from the same point to the summit of Pike's Peak one of nearly twelve inches without producing any marked emotional abnormalities, but we must take into consideration the fact that sudden barometric variations generally accompany or more frequently precede other important meteorological changes. In the latter case, though they might be the primary cause of factors considered in this study, they themselves would fail to show upon the tables.

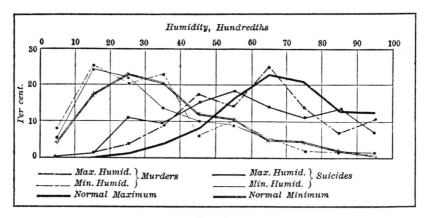

Fɪɢ. 5.

HUMIDITY.—Figure 5 indicates in a very decisive manner that states of low relative humidity, as shown by both maximum and minimum readings, are conducive to excesses in both the classes of crimes studied. For instance, for maximum humidities between ten and twenty the proportion of actual crime to that expected is 1 : 0.1; between twenty and thirty (suicide), 11 : 1; between thirty and forty, 9.5 : 4.5; between forty and fifty, 15 : 8. The maximum curves show somewhat the same general relation though not with quite so marked divergences. To one who has experienced the general low humidities of our Colorado altitudes (Denver is one mile above the sea level) this result is not surprising. There is no doubt that a nervous tension much in excess of that common in the lower altitudes exists, due in part, perhaps, to the deficiency in barometric pressure and a consequent effect upon the respiratory processes, but probably, as shown by these curves, more largely to the dryness of the atmosphere, as indicated by low humidity. I hope at some future time to verify or disprove this supposition by a comparative study made at some lower altitude.

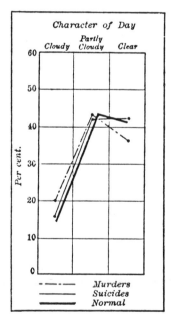

Fɪɢ. 6.

CHARACTER OF THE DAY.—Figure 6 shows the relation between the expectancy of crime, based upon the actual per cents of cloudy, partly cloudy, and clear days (records of nineteen years), and its actual occurrence. By the United States Weather Bureau days are characterized as "cloudy" when for 0.8 or more of the possible hours of sunshine the sun is obscured; "partly cloudy" when from 0.4 to 0.7 inclusive is obscured; and "clear" when 0.3 or less. The disagreements are very slight, although a slight excess of murders is shown for cloudy days.

SUMMARY.—Figure 1 shows at a glance no generally prevailing meteorological conditions to which can be ascribed, with any degree of certainty, the monthly variations of crime. Figure 2 shows that high velocities of wind seem to increase to a marked extent the tendency to crime. For the highest velocities increasing the probability twenty times (two thousand per cent). Figure 3 shows that high temperatures seem to have the same effect, that of between 90 and 100 degrees increasing the probability one hundred percent. Figure 4 fails to show that barometric changes are accomplished by any marked excesses in crime. Figure 5 shows that low conditions of relative humidity are attended with very marked excesses, those below thirty increasing the probability of suicides eleven times (eleven hundred per cent). Figure 6 fails to show that the character of the day has any considerable effect.

Considering briefly, in conclusion, the results of the foregoing study, and comparing them with a somewhat similar one for children (see "The Child and the Weather," _Pedagogical Seminary_, April 1898), we may safely conclude that the tendency to homicide varies with those meteorological conditions which bring about an emotional state necessitating a considerable discharge of motor stimulus. The same conditions which bring about irritability and unruliness on the part of the child accompany suicidal tendencies.

This supposition is upheld by the fact that suicide is less common in the colder climates, where the metabolic processes are slow, and in the torrid zone, where the heat produces a general depletion of energy for motor discharge, than in the temperate regions, where the climate is exhilarating. The study, from the social standpoint, too, leads us to the same conclusion. The excess of crime in the social whirlpool of our great cities is convincing, and especially the careful study made by Morselli of the prevalence of suicide in the different countries of Europe, interpreted in the light of what we know of their social conditions.

Yet, in considering the facts disclosed by the present paper, we must not dogmatically assert that each is of the importance that the figures indicate. In fact, it seems evident from a careful study of the sheets, which show all the conditions together for the same day—a thing impossible with the charts illustrating this paper— that the various conditions for the day mutually react and interact upon one another, certain combinations seemingly resulting in a re-enforcement of the tendency to crime, while certain others inhibit it. Space forbids any full discussion of this phase of the problem in the present paper, but it very probably will be made the subject of some future study.

Author's Note.—The above paper was written more than a year ago. Since that time the work of comparing the prevalence of crime with the meteorological conditions has been carried on upon a much larger scale in the city of New York. An immensely greater number of data have served to corroborate the earlier conclusions arrived at in this Denver study, only in minor points —and those directly traceable to the very different climates— proving at all in opposition to them. —New York, July 1899.

THE MENTAL EFFECTS
OF THE WEATHER

BY

EDWIN G. DEXTER

SCIENCE

NEW SERIES VOL. 10, NO. 241 (AUGUST 11, 1899), PP. 176-180

The influence of the weather upon mental states has been a matter of comment since the days of the ancients, though but little scientific work has been done to determine, either qualitatively or quantitatively, just what the effect is. The weather maxims of wiseacres have been based very largely upon the peculiar activities of various members of the animal kingdom under definite meteorological conditions—usually those immediately preceding a storm—but, aside from these literary curiosities, material bearing even indirectly upon the subject is extremely limited. The effect of climate upon racial traits has been much more fully treated, both by the anthropologist and the criminologist, and the literature of the subject is quite extended. We are most of us, however, convinced that, whatever racial differences may be ascribed to the varying climates of different parts of our planet, we as individuals are influenced in our conduct to a marked degree by varying meteorological conditions. Literature is full of allusions to such influences, and not a few of the world's great thinkers have left on record observations of such effects upon themselves.

The study which forms the basis of this paper is an attempt to throw some light upon the problem by comparing the occurrences of certain misdemeanors and other data of conduct, under definite weather conditions, with the prevalence of those conditions. The method of its prosecution was as follows: At the New York City station of the United States Weather Bureau the mean barometer, temperature and humidity, the total movement of the wind, the character of the day and the precipitation for each one of the 3,650 days of the years 1888 to 1897 inclusive were copied upon specially prepared blanks. From these records were then computed, by a process of tabulation, the exact percentage of days which were characterized as fair, partly cloudy, as rainy or clear, or as having come within a definite temperature group of 5 to 10 degrees, ten to 15 degrees, 15 to 20 degrees – and, in a similar manner, within arbitrarily determined groups for barometer, humidity, and wind. In this way the normal prevalence of any definite meteorological condition was determined as a basis for comparison with the occurrence of the data studied.

The latter were taken from various records available in New York City and consisted for the most part of misdemeanors under the observation of the police force of the city, the teachers in the public schools, and the warden of the penitentiary, although the death record kept by the Board of Health was also considered. The total number of data considered exceeded 400,000, made up of cases of assault and battery, suicide, and arrests for insanity by the police, recorded misdemeanors committed in the penitentiary and public schools, records of errors made by clerks in several of the larger national banks and records of strength tests made in the gymnasium of Columbia University. The classes of data varied in number from 1,000 to more than 100,000, and were for the years included within the period for which the weather conditions had been tabulated. By a somewhat elaborate process of computation the exact percentage of each class of data occurring under each of the definite meteorological groups was determined; for example, the percentage of fair or cloudy days, of days when the temperature was between 15 and 20 degrees, etc., for all the fifty or more conditions studied.

We have already stated that from the meteorological data, the normal prevalence of these conditions had been determined. It may be readily seen, however, that the normal prevalence of a condition equals the expected occurrences of each of the classes of data for that condition – for instance, if 30 per cent of the days for the ten years were fair we should expect 30 per cent of the assaults, suicides, etc., to have occurred upon fair days *if the character of the day had no influence.* If, however, 35 per cent did actually occur we should infer that the effect of fair days was to increase the number of assaults, as, indeed, this study has shown to be the case.

The conclusions of the paper are based entirely upon this comparison of occurrence of data under a given meteorological condition, with the prevalence of that condition. Both were reduced to percentages. When the occurrence for a given condition was found to exceed the expectancy the exact *excess* was computed. More than one hundred and fifty curves were constructed showing these relations (see "Conduct and the Weather," Monograph Supplement No. 10 to *The Psychological Review*), a few of which are shown in this paper.

Moderately high temperatures were found to be accompanied by excess in all the misdemeanors considered; low temperatures by deficiencies. The temperature group 80 to 85 degrees

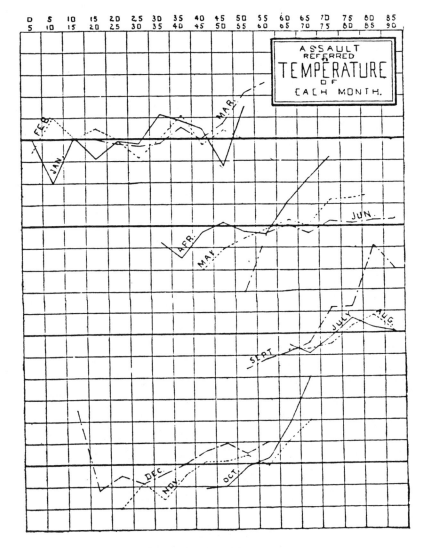

Fig. 1.

showing an excess of 68 per cent for assaults by males and 100 per cent for those by females. The next higher group, however, shows a drop to 33 per cent excess for the former and a deficiency of 33 per cent for the latter. This sudden falling-off for conditions of intense heat is shown for nearly all classes of data, and is undoubtedly due to the fact that under such temperature there is little energy available for offensive conduct. Death, suicide and the recorded errors in banks alone remain excessive under such conditions.

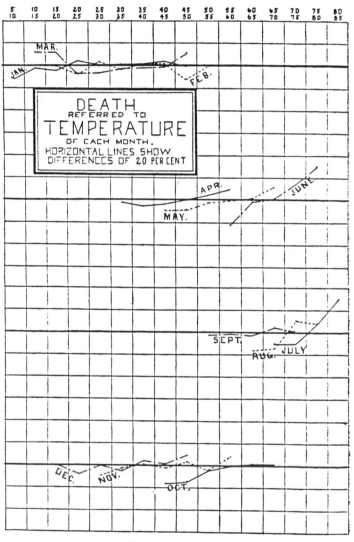

Fig. 2.

Figures 1 and 2 give a comparison of the occurrence of assault and death (male) referred to the temperature conditions for each month of the year. It may be seen from them that during the winter months the temperature produces but little effect, there being but slight excesses or deficiencies for any of the groups. Excesses and deficiencies read vertically. The horizontal lines show differences of 20 per cent, read from the heavier base lines.

When, however, we come to the spring, the higher temperature for the months are accompanied by a very marked increase in the number of assaults (April, 70 to 75 degrees, an excess of 64 percent) and one less marked for death. During the heated summer time the highest temperatures do not show the greatest excesses for assaults, but the increase in the death rate is parallel with that of heat. During the unusually hot days in September and October we have about the same relation between the curves that was shown for the spring months – *i.e.*, a great excess in assaults and only a moderate one in deaths. These relations are fairly conclusive, as they are based upon 36,000 assaults and 100,000 deaths.

Generalizations based upon the study of the barometrical conditions show that nearly all the data studied were excessive during the low readings of the instrument. There are many reasons for concluding, however, that the actual density of the atmosphere is not the influencing factor here, but the barometrical conditions as accompaniments of other meteorological states which are themselves the effective ones—for instance, storms.

The study of humidity, in its effect upon the data of conduct give some interesting results, since it demonstrated, beyond a doubt, that conditions of low humidity are those most productive of misdemeanor behavior. When we consider that the muggy, sticky days on which we feel it our natural prerogative to be "out of sorts" are of the opposite character this is quite surprising. The deficiency of disorders on such days is, however, undoubtedly due to the fact that although they are emotionally depressing they are also physically weakening, and however "ugly" a man might feel, if energy were lacking, to be offensively active the police court is none the wiser, and the fact is lost to our study. A tabulation of profanity or even a record of the ducking stool of colonial days might give different results. In Denver, Colorado (see also *Conduct and the Weather*), where the humidity is normally very low, the number of misdemeanors reached an excess of more than

600 per cent for reading between 15 and 25, which is a condition never experienced at the low altitudes.

The study of the seeming effects of the wind discloses the fact that misdemeanors of the classes studied show marked deficiencies during calm (50 per cent) with the greatest excesses during moderately high winds and moderate deficiencies again for great wind velocities. Death and suicide alone are excessive on calm days.

The state of conduct on days of different character – that is, fair, partly cloudy, cloudy, rainy and clear – presents, I believe, a genuine surprise (see Figure 3). This figure is to be interpreted in the same manner as the others. From it we see that misdemeanors are less frequent upon cloudy and rainy days (latter under "Precipitation" marked " + .01" inches) than upon those which we are accustomed to consider more agreeable. In fact, of all the classes of data studied, that for errors in banks is the only one showing an opposite result. Reference to the curves shows that for assault by males (Assault M) the greatest excess occurred upon days characterized by the Weather Bureau as partly cloudy. Such days have from 4/10 to 7/10 of the hours from sunrise to sunset obscured, fair days having more than that amount of sunshine and cloudy days less.

Perhaps the most surprising curve is that for suicides, showing as it does that those who are weary of life choose the fair day, upon which there is no precipitation as the time for ending an unhappy existence. This, together with the fact that the months of May and June show the fullest record of suicides of any of the year, is directly contradictory to what seems to be the accepted opinion upon such matters. Perhaps fiction is largely responsible for the prevailing idea, and fiction would certainly lose much of its thunder if the proverbial gloomy weather could not be brought in for tragic effect. The prevailing climate may, however, influence these results, as the study for Denver (see "Suicides" Denver upon the figure), where cloudy days are something of a rarity, their effect seems to have been more disastrous upon the suicide. There an excess of 32 per cent is indicated for such days. The social conditions there are, however, somewhat peculiar, as the population contains a large number of people who have gone to the region in search of health, which the sunshine was depended upon to restore, and the discouragement of even a brief deprivation of its presence was too great to be borne. Even the death rate is

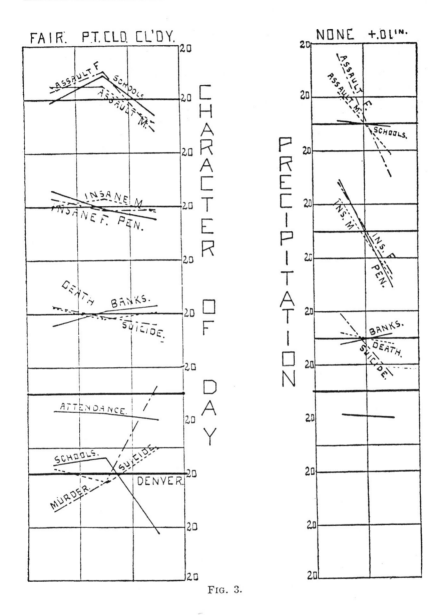

FIG. 3.

shown by the curves to be slightly higher during bright weather, although the difference for days of varying character is not great.

Perhaps the most interesting general conclusion to be drawn from the study is that during those meteorological states which are physically exhilarating, excesses in deportment, in the ordinarily accepted sense of the word, prevail to an abnormal extent, while death and irregularities in mental processes (errors in banks) are below expectancy. During such weather conditions, without doubt the quality of the emotional state is more positive than under the reverse conditions, but the results seem to show that in the long run an excess of energy is a more dangerous thing, at least from the standpoint of the police court, than the worst sort of a temper with no energy.

SUGGESTIONS FOR FURTHER READING AND INQUIRY:

COSMICOLOGICAL INFLUENCES

"Has the Moon Any Influence on Plants and Animals?" *Saturday Magazine*, vol. 20 (1842), p. 101.

The earliest article in the English language periodical literature of the nineteenth century treating upon cosmicological influences on flora and fauna, including people.

"Climate, Phrenologically Considered." *American Phrenological Journal and Life Illustrated*, vol. 41 (865), pp. 142–143.

A discussion from the phrenological perspective of the effect of cold, temperate, and tropical climates on the mental development, character, and temperamental predispositions of the indigenous peoples of these three climactic zones.

"Influence of Climate Upon National Character." J. W. Draper. *Harper's New Monthly Magazine*, vol. 31 (1865), pp. 390–396.

An interesting discussion synopsized from the work by John William Draper, M.D., titled *Thoughts on the Future Civil Policy of America*.

"Effect of the Weather on Morals." *Tit~Bits*, vol. 2 (1882), p. 140.

A short but interesting synopsis of the effect of barometric pressure on moral behavior.

"On Sunspots and Crime." *Harper's New Monthly Magazine*, vol. 67 (1883), p. 967.

A lengthy and sarcastic editorial comment highly critical of the notion that electrical disturbances, especially in the form of sunspots, are a cause of moral disorders and crime.

"The Effect of Weather on Crime and the Death Rate in India." S. A. Hill. *Nature*, vol. 29, (1884), pp. 338-340.
A fine synopsis of research into the connection between temperature, barometric pressure, relative humidity, and wind velocity on rates of mortality and crime on the Indian subcontinent.

"The Moral Influence of Climate." Felix L. Oswald. *Popular Science Monthly*, vol. 22 (1888), p. 37.
An examination, with a global perspective, of the relationship between climate and moral behavior.

"Influence of Climate on Veracity." Charles Dudley Warner. *Harper's New Monthly Magazine*, vol. 83 (1891), pp. 320-321.
Editorial commentary on the popular notion that a predisposition toward prevarication is associated with a warm, humid, and debilitating climate, and that cold climes are a tonic or stimulant for truthfulness.

"The Influence of Climate on the Human Race." *Public Opinion*, vol. 12 (1891), p. 109.
The history of the thesis that morality and criminality are greatly influenced by climate is explored. Translated from the French of Louis Proal in *Revue Scientifique*.

"Weather and the Mind." *Popular Science Monthly*, vol. 45 (1894), p. 572.
Synopsis of an article by T. D. Crothers in *Science* regarding the effect that weather has on human behavior.

"M. Lacassagne of Paris." *Public Opinion*, vol. 21 (1896), p. 463.
Synopsis of Lacassagne and Dr. Bertillion's statistical researches demonstrating that crimes are far more prevalent in summer than in winter.

"Mental Effects of the Weather." Henry Helm Clayton. *Science*, vol. 10 (1899), p. 378.
An addendum to the article in *Science* (vol. 10, 1899, pp. 176-180) of the same title by Edwin G. Dexter.